S0-AIV-497

Erasmus

ℬ

Erasmus

A Critical Biography

LÉON-E. HALKIN

Translated by John Tonkin

BLACKWELL
Oxford UK & Cambridge USA

Copyright © Librairie Arthème Fayard, 1987
Copyright © English translation Basil Blackwell Ltd, 1993

First published 1987

English edition first published 1993

Reprinted 1994

First published in paperback 1994

Blackwell Publishers
108 Cowley Road, Oxford OX4 1JF
UK

238 Main Street
Cambridge, Massachusetts 02142
USA

British Library Cataloguing in Publication Data
A CIP catalogue record for this book is available from
the British Library

Library of Congress Cataloging-in-Publication Data
Halkin, Léon-E. (Léon-Ernest), 1906–
  [Erasme parmi nous. English]
  Erasmus: a critical biography/Leon-E. Halkin; translated by
John Tonkin.
    p. cm.
  Translation of: Erasme parmi nous.
  Includes bibliographical references and index.
  ISBN 0–631–16929–6—0–631–19388 X (pbk.)
  1. Erasmus, Desiderius, d. 1536 – Biography. 2. Authors, Latin
(Medieval and modern) – Netherlands – Biography. 3. Humanists –
Netherlands – Biography. 4. Scholars – Netherlands – Biography.
I. Title.
PA8518.H3313   1994
199'.492 – dc20
  [B]   92–20943
                                                                    CIP

Typeset in 10 on 12pt Baskerville
by Graphicraft Typesetters Ltd., Hong Kong
Printed in Great Britain by T.J. Press Ltd., Padstow, Cornwall

This book is printed on acid-free paper

Contents

Foreword to the English Translation of Léon-E. Halkin's *Érasme parmi nous*

Léon-E. Halkin is one of Europe's leading historians, an authority on the Renaissance, Reformation and Counter-Reformation. Here he offers us something other than an introduction to the life and works of Erasmus: he is convinced that Erasmus gains from being thought of as being still *parmi nous*, as living on 'amongst us' as a vital encouragement towards oecumenism and civilized tolerance. He aims to show (often by means of the actual words of Erasmus, closely rendered) what Erasmus had to say on basic problems of philosophy, ethics and theology within the cancered body of Christ's Church.* Professor Halkin is persuaded that what Erasmus had to say is not without lessons for us today – providing, that is, that we fully grasp his meaning in his original contexts.

But Erasmus, as we know, wrote so much; and all that he wrote is in Latin! No wonder, then, that he is more written about than read. His thoughts now need skilled midwives if they are to be born afresh for a wider public.

In his own day his mastery of an elegant subtle form of Christian Latin was the basis of his strength and of his wide appeal. He was as readily readable in Geneva as in Rome; in London as in Paris; in Wittenberg as in Louvain, Coïmbra or Alcalá de Henares. He was known to be a Batavian, a native of Rotterdam, but was perceived to be a citizen of a wider Europe, the sinews of which ran across borders and were rooted in the languages and cultures of Jerusalem, Rome and

---

* Of course Léon-E. Halkin's close French translations have not been re-translated into English and most of the versions in this edition are from the Toronto *Collected Works of Erasmus* (see Translator's Preface).

Greece. He was, as a poorish, illegitimate orphan, pitch-forked into a monastic life for which he had no vocation. But somebody had taught him well. Eventually he was courted as a sage and scholar by great kings – Henry VIII of England and Francis I of France among them – and by a brace of Popes. And, rarity indeed, he was sometimes listened to by them.

In our own times his attractiveness still lies for many in his being a European, not a sectarian or a national figure. Since he belongs nowhere, he belongs everywhere. All Renaissance scholarship is polyglot: Erasmian scholarship is particularly so, including all the major languages of Europe. One of the strengths of this present book is that its author has mastered that polyglot scholarship and has digested much of it for us. Erasmus's writings have many facets: some are more clearly glimpsed by scholars writing in one tradition than in another.

Erasmus was a troublesome priest in a Western Church which quarrelled with him, over him and around him. That Western Church, already in a state of schism with the Eastern Church, was in his lifetime shattered apart into rival Churches all claiming catholicity, one at least exclusively so. And that one concluded at Trent that Erasmus deserved a prominent place on her *Index Expurgatorius.* Yet all those shattered Western Churches were indebted to some extent to what Erasmus edited, thought, satirized or advocated. And many outside the Church gladly acknowledged their debt to him: Voltaire for one.

To lead us through the maze of Erasmus's writings and of Erasmian scholarship sound guides are welcome indeed. Léon-E. Halkin is just such a guide. His long life has been devoted to scholarship. He is listened to with respect and (since he opposed Nazism in his native Belgium when it took great bravery to do so) with veneration. His books span an extraordinary sixty years, the first, on a Prince-Bishop of Liège, appearing in that city in 1930. The book presented here was first published, in French, in 1987. And it is not his last.

To those who are attached to England or to her language, culture and history, Erasmus has a special appeal, since England was a home from home for him. He reminds us of what seems a more happy age. Erasmus's admiration for Henry VIII and his friendship for Sir Thomas More were blazed throughout Europe and formed at a time when neither King nor Lord Chancellor had blood on their hands. It seemed then (not least in England) that most of what was wrong in Church and State could be put right by laughter, dialogue and reasoned persuasion among civilized men. Much of what Erasmus stood for did eventually find a lasting home in England and her Church, but not until both had been torn by strife and splattered with blood. (You can still find a Church or two with Erasmus's *Paraphrases* chained to the lectern, as they had once been in hundreds throughout the land.)

Erasmus could criticize so trenchantly the errors and superstitions which flourished around him since his own religious faith was based on Christ, not on an excluding ecclesiology or complex and confessional dogma. His concept of Christ was deeply influenced by sources most honoured in Renaissance Europe: by Platonic idealism, by Aristotelian ethics, by early, especially Greek, patristics and by what he knew of the Eastern Churches. He was not going over old ground, but throwing what was for many an absolutely fresh light on to almost everything he touched. He pleaded for a more charitable (and hence, for him, a more Christ-like) understanding of schism, heresy and error; he wanted, in charity, to free men and women who, ensnared in harsh matrimony or anguished celibacy, were confronted, when they cried out for help and understanding, by condemnation and legalism.

Erasmus admired marriage, but pleaded for the right to divorce; he could venerate a monk such as Saint Bernard, yet plead that monks with no lasting sense of vocation should be free to return to the world they had wrongly vowed to leave; he could laugh at Mariolatry, yet deeply venerate that Mother of Christ whose virginal grace and beauty were hailed by Gabriel in Scripture. He remained a priest of the Church, but would condemn outright, in all respects, not even the Anabaptists (whom virtually all others condemned) when they peacefully sought a hearing for their teachings. The Spirit, as he knew, bloweth where He listeth.

Erasmus was sometimes dismissed as a temporizer or a trimmer. Such is often the lot of subtle minds who see shades of grey where coarser minds see black or white. He was a master of *nuance*, dialogue, humour, apologetics and repartee. He was eirenic where others were vengeful or belligerent. His religion was centred upon Christ, who, once fully incarnate as Man and fully revealed as God at the Transfiguration, is now eternally triumphant with the Holy Ghost and the Father. In an age of increasing intolerance and cruelty, he warned that the wheat might be plucked out with the chaff. He was not prepared to die, nor to cause others to die, for the mere accessories of true religion. And for him such accessories included logomachias about whether the powers of popes truly derive from the Apostles; whether the College of Cardinals is of the essence of the Church; whether faith alone saves (and in what sense) or whether the Mass should be defined in strict literalness as a sacrifice. For many those allegedly marginal matters were the very anchors to which they clung: for Erasmus they were as nothing compared to the charity of Christian men and women rising again to that

New Life which is ever restored to them by a truly pious partaking of the Holy Communion.

Erasmus, as Léon-E. Halkin rightly insists, was an innovator. His portrait is drawn here largely from his own works. This study has something of the quality of a synthesis; something, too, of the quality of an anthology. It is not the only portrait of Erasmus that may be drawn, but it is an attractive and coherent one. and, if Léon-E. Halkin is correct, it is a portrait of an original thinker who is present 'among us' as never before, as the representative of a Humanism most surely needed.

M. A. Screech
All Souls College,
Oxford

Translator's Preface

One of the roles which translators habitually adopt is to justify the importance of the work translated and commend it to the prospective reader. Although I would happily have assumed such a role, I am most grateful to Professor Michael Screech for having made such comment from me unnecessary. His eloquent Foreword to this work, based on his personal knowledge of the author and his own scholarly expertise in Erasmian studies, so tellingly introduces the author and his subject as to leave the translator with largely routine tasks to discharge.

Two matters of translating policy require a brief explanation. On the spelling of sixteenth-century names I have adopted the policy of the editorial board of the University of Toronto Press's *Collected Works of Erasmus* – namely, to use vernacular versions of all names except for those of prominent humanists who are better known by their humanistic nicknames.

The author's extensive use of citations from Erasmian writings raised a more complex problem. Since it was clearly inappropriate to translate Halkin's French renditions of Erasmian Latin into English, an obvious solution was to rely wherever possible on the English versions of the Toronto edition of the *Collected Works of Erasmus*, and I am grateful to the University of Toronto Press for providing blanket permission to use these versions. Since, however, this magnificent edition was far from complete at the time this translation was ready for publication (including, for example, only nine of the projected twenty-two volumes of Erasmus's correspondence), other solutions were required for much of the Erasmian material. My thanks are due especially to Craig Thompson for generous permission to use substantial extracts from his lively translation of the *Colloquies*, soon to be re-issued in the Toronto edition, and to Cambridge University Press, for permission to use Margaret Mann Phillips's translation of the *Adages*. Other cases where good modern versions have been borrowed are noted in the Acknowledgements.

There remained, however, extensive materials not adequately covered by such translations, especially the correspondence after 1523, and these have been translated directly from the Latin originals, some by myself, but most by Bruce McClintock, a postgraduate student at the University of Western Australia, whose expert assistance is gratefully acknowledged. A related problem was that a large number of these citations were not precisely documented in the French version; happily most of these were eventually tracked down through a systematic search of the Latin originals, together with some guidance from Professor Halkin and his assistants. If these problems occasioned frustrations and delays, their positive by-product was a far closer knowledge of the Erasmian sources.

Professor Halkin himself was vitally interested in the English translation of his work and, notwithstanding his advanced years and less than robust health, made important contributions. The bibliography was updated to some extent and modified for English readers, while certain errors of detail in the French text were corrected and some paragraphs were rewritten to clarify the author's views since the publication of the French version in 1987. I thank him and his associates most sincerely for their interest and assistance. I acknowledge also the generous help of Brian Willis of the University of Western Australia who was invariably available to offer advice when the historian-translator was regularly forced to confront his limitations as a French linguist.

Though a translator necessarily adopts a neutral role of letting the author speak, a historian who assumes such a time-consuming task usually has particular reasons for doing so. In my case it was a quest for greater breadth and balance after three decades' concentration on Luther and Calvin, and I trace that quest to the long-term influence of Roland Bainton and Gordon Rupp, each of whom conveyed to me in person and through his writings a breadth of historical sympathy which transcended the divisions of the past. I acknowledge also, from more recent times, my debt to Bruce Mansfield for his persuasive advocacy of Erasmian studies over many years and for particular advice about Erasmian sources, and to Geoffrey Dickens, for fifteen years of animated discussion about the world of the Reformation, in which the figure of Erasmus was never far from the centre stage.

Translation can be a tedious chore, but it can also be a rich learning experience. I am happy to say that in this instance the latter has been the case.

John Tonkin
University of Western Australia

Author's Preface

All that I am you will find in my books.
Erasmus to Érard de la Marck

I have carried this book around within me for a long time, pondering over it with passion and returning to it quite effortlessly. No study has held my attention more or been dearer to me.

My aim has been to understand Erasmus through Erasmus, to explain him by himself. This biography is neither an apology nor an indictment, but a book written in good faith, broadly open to the history of ideas and the history of mentalities. It is neither an Erasmian encyclopedia, nor a collection of monographs, but an attempt at a synthesis, an overall vision and the outline of a portrait. It is through his work that we can perceive Erasmus's intellectual and spiritual journey; and it is through reading his letters that we learn of his successes, his struggles, his ambitions and his setbacks. For this reason I have quoted him very freely in what amounts to an Erasmian anthology.

Why is Erasmus so little read? Doubtless because he wrote in Latin in forbidding folio volumes. Four hundred and fifty years after his death, he remains more famous than well known, despite a growing number of translations. Moreover, he is misunderstood because the great subjects which he chose are foreign to what makes for fashionable success and cannot interest the sheeplike masses whose minds are closed to the critical spirit. Erasmus was not a popularizer, but a pioneer.

Erasmus was a humanist, a pacifist, a defender of critical Christianity. Now humanism presupposes a certain knowledge of Graeco-Latin literature from which our contemporaries sadly continue to distance themselves. Pacifism is inseparable from the struggle against nationalism, yet nationalism has never been as powerful as today. Finally, critical Christianity demands a real familiarity with the Gospel, a familiarity that remains exceptional, even among believers. In Erasmus, only the artist has triumphed over indifference to his general ideas: *The Praise of Folly* and the *Colloquies* have never lost their audience among the well-read and have attracted to Erasmus readers who are daily more convinced of the topicality of his subjects.

I may add that, despite the huge volume of studies devoted to him for three-quarters of a century, many points about Erasmus's life remain obscure. Without pretending to make everything clear, I have tried to put forward coherent explanations.

All of the questions posed and discussed in this biography are open questions and my answers never presume to be the best or the only ones possible. Erasmus is an inexhaustible subject and it is essential that a dialogue should be engaged between him and his readers. Whether he surprises or charms us, he always has something to say to us and much to teach us.

The title of this book declares its intention: *Érasme parmi nous*, because his thought is at this point so remote, yet at the same time equally present.

Liège, 1 May 1987

Acknowledgements

The translator and publishers would like to thank the following for permission to reproduce extracts (from works cited in the notes):

Augsburg Fortress Publishers, Minneapolis, for lines from *Luther's Works*, vol. 48, ed. Gottfried G. Krodel, copyright © 1963 Fortress Press, and from *Luther's Works*, vol. 31, ed. Harold Grimm, copyright © 1957 Fortress Press; Cambridge University Press, for lines from M. M. Phillips, *The Adages of Erasmus*; HarperCollins Publishers, New York, for lines from J. C. Olin (ed.), *Christian Humanism and the Reformation*; Hodder and Stoughton, for lines from R. E. DeMolen (ed.), *Erasmus (Documents in Modern History)*; Phaidon Press, Ltd, for lines from J. Huizinga, *Erasmus and the Age of the Reformation*; Stanford University Press, for lines from P. O. Kristeller, *Eight Philosophers of the Renaissance*; Professor Craig R. Thompson, for lines from *The Colloquies of Erasmus* (University of Chicago Press, 1965); University of Toronto Press, for lines from the *Collected Works of Erasmus*; Yale University Press, for lines from *The Complete Works of Thomas More*, vol. 8, part 1.

1

Childhood and Youth

The origins of Erasmus remain shrouded in mystery.[1] He was born out of wedlock at Rotterdam on 28 October, perhaps in 1466 or 1467, but more probably in 1469. His parents, Gerard and Margaret, were of the Dutch lower middle class, and he had an elder brother named Pieter. From his father, a skilled copyist of manuscripts in Italy, he acquired his taste for humanism.[2] This is the extent of our knowledge of Erasmus's family; and even this is probable rather than certain. A more detailed and precise chronology is beyond our reach, as the statements about his birth are vague and contradictory. He showed no interest in his own age[3] and the writing published under the title *Compendium Vitae*[4] is not at all clear as to his origins.[5]

Erasmus's first name was Desiderius, and here too we may note some uncertainty. In 1496 he called himself in turn *Herasmus Rotterdammensis* and *Desyderius Herasmus*.[6] Gradually, however, the written form stabilized and we read in the frontispiece of his works *Desiderius Erasmus Roterodamus*, though later the first name frequently disappeared from the headings of his letters.

Erasmus was a Dutchman from Rotterdam. The man who was to proclaim himself a 'citizen of the world' was not an orphan. This future champion of the Renaissance was born at the close of the Middle Ages, in a little town geared more to commerce than to literature. While still very young, he left Rotterdam, never to return. He seems to have forgotten his birthplace and preferred to ignore the language of his parents, though its accents were to return to his lips at the hour of his death.[7]

Of the youth of Erasmus we know only what little he said of it in his recollections as an adult,[8] and none of his feelings as a young boy for his father and mother. His early childhood eludes us completely. We have no knowledge of his first words or his first steps, no confidence, direct or indirect, no allusion, no record at all! We possess no portrait of Erasmus as a youth or as a student, but then, why should anyone paint a portrait of a poor young man?

No intimate journal of Erasmus survives and all the indications are that this was one literary genre that he did not exploit. It was through his correspondence and his poetry that he expressed himself, but his first efforts are lost. We have no account of his dreams. We do not know if he liked the games of his time. He revealed no nostalgia for his childhood: it was enough for him to be adult. Doubtless he had his complexes and his secrets, but we shall never know what they were.

In 1473 or 1474 at Gouda he went to school for the first time; he was four years old, he tells us. What could he have learned at this age? We know nothing of this, or of the outcome of his brief experience as a young chorister at the Cathedral of Utrecht. At the age of nine, Erasmus was sent by his father to the school of the chapter-house of St Lebwin at Deventer. His mother followed him to this town, where he remained for five years, from 1478 to 1483. At school Erasmus discovered a new world, the world of studies, which became the world of his whole life. He spoke of his teachers generally with detachment, sometimes even with disdain. His disappointment was not that of the lazy rebel against scholarly labours; it revealed the bewilderment of an over-talented child whose hunger for knowledge remained unsatisfied. The future prince of humanists was shaped intellectually by the scholarly books of the Middle Ages and the philosophy of medieval scholasticism.

Erasmus was to observe that the school at Deventer was 'barbarous'. It was from older fellow-students, who had had the good fortune of attending the lessons of Jan Sinthem, one of the Brethren of the Common Life, that he received his first experience of a more enlightened style of teaching, more broadly open to the classical authors. Sinthem appears to have been Erasmus's teacher on occasion, and to have predicted a brilliant future for him.

If the structure and the curricula of the schools were rigid, some teachers were nevertheless already humanists. At the school of St Lebwin, Erasmus profited from the teaching of Alexander Hegius, who inspired him with an enthusiasm for Graeco-Latin literature. Another opportunity for the young Erasmus was a meeting with Rodolphus Agricola, the German humanist poet; and many years later he was to recall this encounter with enthusiasm.

Despite mediocre textbooks and some not very gifted instructors, Erasmus was a very good pupil. He read voraciously and accorded Horace the highest place of honour. At the age of fourteen, when most students are still grappling with recalcitrant prose, Erasmus was speaking Latin as a living language. Poetry attracted him. He composed poems inspired, he said, by 'barbarian muses'. Of these attempts only the *Carmen Bucolicum* remains, a Virgilian eclogue of no great originality.

Erasmus's spiritual formation is more difficult to define. The orthodoxy of his masters is beyond dispute. At Deventer religion was inhaled as much as learned. Like all the children of his age, setting and time, Erasmus was raised 'amidst the sound of hymns and canticles'. His education was a Christian one and he described himself as 'a child disposed towards piety'.

He was thirteen when his mother died of the plague. When the epidemic reached the students, the school was closed. Erasmus returned to his father, who died in turn, struck down by the same disease. Now an orphan, Erasmus was obliged all too early to exchange the innocence of childhood for the harsh realities of the adult world. He took pains to keep in touch with his elders, but too many memories linked him to his parents for him not to have been shaken to the deepest roots by his tragic loss. These memories, joyful as well as painful, Erasmus kept secret, for he was one of those who seek rather to forget than to remember their early years. The distressing complexes which illegitimacy, loneliness of heart and poverty bring with them dwelt in full measure within this helpless adolescent.

The first ray of sunlight into this darkness came from his studies, despite the inadequacies of the syllabus. Erasmus would have liked to prepare himself for the University, but the tutors who taught him and his brother planned to make monks of them – if necessary, in spite of their wishes. Erasmus was placed with the Brethren of the Common Life at s'Hertogenbosch, and spent almost three years in this famous house. 'Wasted years,' he wrote with obvious exaggeration and excessive severity. Indeed, the quality of that training is revealed in the increasing taste he showed for poetry. Here he stored up intellectual provisions for a whole lifetime.

Erasmus also owed to his masters at s'Hertogenbosch contact with the 'modern devotion',[9] the spiritual ideal lived and taught in the Netherlands from the beginning of the fourteenth century by Gerard Groote and his disciples, the Brethren and Sisters of the Common Life, as well as by the canons and canonesses regular of Windesheim. The followers of the modern devotion emphasized personal piety, and the common condition of the devout Christian remained their sufficient frame of reference. The spirit of Gerard Groote was not that of a philosopher, and scarcely that of a theologian. He wanted to train men and women, priests and laity, for practical Christian living. His reforming outlook set begging in opposition to work, and he did not flinch from the hostility he inspired among the mendicant orders. Moreover, he protested against the usage that reserved the term 'religious' to convents; for him, the authentically religious person was the one who lived piously, in chastity, humility, poverty and, above all, charity.

The classic features of the modern devotion included distrust of all that glitters, and even of knowledge that does not lead towards God; return to the sources of Christianity, attraction for meditation, voluntary asceticism, exercises of inward and structured piety; in short, conformity to the divine model, the suffering Christ. None of these traits was new, but the harmonious wholeness of this spiritual teaching made of it something progressive and powerful. Thomas À Kempis (d. 1471) was the most celebrated representative of the modern devotion. He wrote a great deal, but *The Imitation of Christ* alone was enough to ensure his fame.

Was Erasmus – the most gifted and the most ungrateful of the pupils of the Brethren of the Common Life – attracted to the *Imitation?* Though he never cited Thomas À Kempis, the spirituality he taught throughout his life was inspired by the same impulses and rooted in the same tradition. A wide-ranging kinship of ideas and expressions clearly establishes this profound influence. Whether it was a matter of advocating the examination of conscience, meditation on death or heartfelt piety, Thomas A'Kempis and Erasmus spoke the same language, though with no trace, in Erasmus's case, of the anti-intellectualism of some of the leading exponents of the modern devotion.

Erasmus's contemporaries were not all blind to this spiritual link. Though some denounced him as an enemy of true piety, it is significant that a little Erasmian work, the *Sermon on the Infant Jesus*, was placed with the *Imitation* in many Spanish editions of this classic of the modern devotion. Today the great majority of Renaissance historians take the view that Erasmus did read the *Imitation*. His Christian humanism would have taken on another hue had he not been subject to its influence.[10]

When Erasmus left the school at s'Hertogenbosch, he was still undoubtedly thinking of studying at University, but his tutors insisted on pushing the two brothers towards the religious life. The quarrel was a painful one. Erasmus resisted valiantly, while Pieter remained silent. The tutors increased their pressure and the elder brother entered the monastery at Sion. Erasmus, who showed evidence of a strong spirit in a frail body, planned to leave for Italy as Gerard his father and Agricola his model had done before him. Only poverty held him prisoner in the Netherlands.

2

A Humanist in the Monastery

Erasmus was obliged to yield in the end to the pressures of those around him and in 1486 or 1487 he entered the monastery of the canons regular at Steyn, near Gouda. This monastery was not a part of the congregation of Windesheim, but its spiritual milieu was essentially the same.[1]

The young orphan had still much to learn, and though no newcomer to sorrow, he was still unaware of how vulnerable innocence is. 'I was just a sick and solitary child,' he wrote, 'ignorant of the things of the world, passing from school to school'.[2] Erasmus remained for five or six years at Steyn, and in fact he was less ill at ease there than he anticipated. At the monastery he found a fine library and made some very close friends.[3] To the joys of friendship were added the pleasure of learning and writing, for reading the good authors gave him a taste for style.

Somehow or other Erasmus's life took shape. He sang the office, assisted at the Mass, and availed himself of the sacraments. With his fellow-monks he fasted, interrupted his sleep for Matins and cultivated a life of abstinence. What remains uncertain is the fervour of the young Erasmus in the cloister, at least during the first two years. His letters and poems at this time of his life were inspired by the writers of classical antiquity and reveal a general absence of spiritual effusiveness. In the end the religious preoccupations manifested themselves; they were to assert themselves more and more, especially under the influence of the Church Fathers whose works he discovered in the monastery library.

If the library offered Erasmus Christian authors, it also provided, remarkably enough, classical ones. Before his entry to Steyn, his former fellow-pupil Cornelis of Woerden had already painted for him a glowing picture of the resources of that library. When Erasmus discovered the classical authors, some had still not been accorded the honour of an edition worthy of them, so he read them in manuscript or in incunabula.

He recopied them and learned them by heart. Some months later, he expounded Terence to his colleague at night-time, by candlelight. He sent a copy of the same Terence to another friend and, showing himself to be already a philologer, he amended its text. Erasmus read the great authors with profit and delight, *cum fructu et voluptate.*

Despite his later claim that Steyn had been closed to all culture, it was clearly in the monastery that Erasmus found the books of the masters. The ancients first of all: Virgil, Horace, Ovid, Juvenal, Terence, Cicero and Quintilian, among others; following that, the moderns: Filelfo, Poggio, Aeneas Sylvius and, above all, Valla, to whom he paid tribute as the restorer of literature. All these books enchanted him, and led him to the discovery of chaste style and the wonder of poetry. Stimulated by these models, he became full of enthusiasm for the literary aesthetic of the ancients and devoted himself to Latin literature.

Erasmus loved to write, for writing was no effort to him. 'The more I write, the more I wish to write,' he said to his friend Cornelis Gerard. 'To send and receive letters', he adds eloquently, 'is the sole means of uniting absent friends. One can find no more pleasant or familiar kind of intercourse, among those who are separated, than an exchange of letters in which the correspondents draw a picture of themselves for each other.'[4]

Did Erasmus write too well for his age? One might believe so, reading the oldest of his letters to have been preserved, addressed from Steyn to his old tutor Peter Winkel. In it the young Erasmus expressed himself like an experienced student of the faculty of Arts. He cited Ovid in a business letter and his correspondent reproached him for a style that was too affected.

The days of the young monk passed slowly and were unrelentingly repetitive. This enervating monotony taught him that one is often alone in the midst of a community. Cut off from familial affection, Erasmus had a need for confidences, secrets, interchange, in a word, for friendship: a need that showed itself at this time in prose or in verse with a controlled passion. 'Life without a friend I think no life, but rather death; or, at least, a friendless life, if life it may be called, is first of all unhappy and, secondly fit for beasts and not for men. And I am, if I may sing my own praises, so constituted that I think nothing in this life to be preferable to friendship; nothing that should be sought for more eagerly or preserved with greater care'.[5]

This thirst for friendship was directed towards several young monks in whom Erasmus found tastes similar to his own. He sent them excited letters, full of tears and laments. If they are very literary in character, they remain for all that no less sincere and touching. The letters to

Servatius Rogerus breathe an ardent and exalted affection, while plainly limited with regard to feeling.

I should write to you more often if I were quite sure in advance that you were not more apt to be wearied by reading my letters than I in writing them. But your entire well-being is so dear to me that I would far rather be tortured by your silence than cause you to become weary of my self-indulgence. However, since friends are wont to find it more distressing than anything else if they cannot meet, which you and I have only the rarest opportunities to do, I could not avoid bidding this letter go to you in my place. And I wish we might at long last enjoy such a stroke of fortune that we might now cease having recourse to letters and be able to meet as often as we wished. As things are, since we are denied this by fate (I cannot mention the fact without tears), am I to be entirely deprived of your company? And if we cannot be together in person, which would of course be the most pleasant thing possible, why should we not come together, if not as often as might be, at least sometimes, by exchanging letters? As often as you look upon these and read them over you can believe that you see and hear your friend face to face...

Considering that my affection for you is and always has been so deep, dearest Servatius, that I value you more than my very eyes and life and, in a word, myself, what is it that makes you so hard-hearted that you not only refuse to love him who loves you so well but do not even regard him with esteem? Are you of so inhuman a disposition as to love those who hate you and hate those who love you? Never was anyone so uncivilised or criminally-minded or obstinate as not to entertain some kindly feeling towards friends at least: is it that you and you alone cannot be moved by remonstrances or swayed by entreaties or melted even by the tears of a loving friend? Are you so savage as to be incapable of pity? I have tried upon you all my appeals and prayers and tears, but you close up your heart and implacably repel me with a harshness like that of the hardest rocks, all the more so the more I continue to plead with you, so that I could with justice apply to you the complaint that we find in Virgil: 'Nor wept o'erbourne, nor pitied love's distress.'

What am I to call it, dear Servatius – harshness or obstinacy or pride or arrogance? Can your nature be like that of a young girl so that my torments yield you pleasure, and your comrade's pain gives you happiness, his tears, laughter? How well might I reproach you in the words that appear in Terence! 'O that I had an equal share and just division of love with you, so that you might either feel this pain as I do, or I might care not what you have done: ... For you are ever on my lips and in my heart: you are my one hope, the half of my soul, the consolation of my life. When you are away nothing is pleasant to me, and when you are with me nothing is unpleasant. If I see you happy I forget my own grief, while if anything grievous happens to you I swear I suffer keener pain than you do yourself.

If serpents and lions and dogs love those who love them, will you, Servatius, scorn one who is dying for love of you? Can that which moves the affections of wild beasts fail to move yours, who are a human being and young withal? Indeed, you would have some reason to excuse yourself, if what I were asking of you were something arduous or difficult or wrong. But you yourself are surely aware what it is that I beg of you, inasmuch as it was not for the sake of reward or out of a desire for any favour that I have wooed you both unhappily and relentlessly. What is it then? Why, that you love him who loves you. What is easier, more pleasant, or more suited to a generous heart, than this? I would repeat: only love me, and it is enough for me . . . I had reposed in you alone all my hope, all my life, all the consolation of my heart, reserving nothing of me to myself; and, alack for me, you on your part withdraw yourself so cruelly and avoid me so determinedly – especially considering that you were not unaware of my despondency which, if it has no one to 'recline and repose on' overwhelms me with such bitter tears that I cannot face the prospect of living. I call God and the genial light of Heaven to witness that each time I seem to see you in my heart suddenly tears burst forth from my eyes . . . Farewell, thou one hope of my life.[6]

In the tender avowals of his first letters, Erasmus, an adolescent and an orphan, poured out his heart in painful agitation. He was not ashamed of his tears. He was living through the anxious experience of a particular friendship, of the kind that develops in resident communities, at the very time when the need to love was being awakened. Servatius Rogerus inspired in Erasmus these tumultuous thoughts akin to love. In this experience Erasmus, who was eager for affection, played and lost, wasting himself for a passion without hope. These accents are not deceptive. Despite an obvious bombast, Erasmus loved and suffered. This ardent friendship – entirely platonic though it was – revealed a delicate temperament, craving for tenderness, ill suited to the rigidity of the rule.

We have no reply from Servatius Rogerus. Was he touched or irritated? How did he put up with this intrusive friendship, this persistent tenderness? On the other hand, with the passing days and months, we see the tone of Erasmus's letters changing profoundly. 'Strive towards manhood,' he says to his friend, and he concerned himself henceforth above all with Servatius's intellectual progress. 'You must not suppose that I am so dull-witted and stupid as to be unable to make out what is your own and what is borrowed from others. Rather, write down as well as you can, and I would rather you do it spontaneously too, whatever comes into your head.'[7]

The expression of a bruised sensibility gave way to brotherly solicitude and sincere comradeship. Subtly the sentimental importunate beggar was transformed into a master of thought. Servatius Rogerus was not the only one to benefit from Erasmus's solicitude. The letters to Cornelis Gerard and Willem Hermans are in the same vein. Erasmus became a stimulating example and a valuable mentor to his friends. This evolution indicates that his problems of feeling were resolved, whether by a burst of inward pride, by an effort of sublimation, or simply by an interest in other problems. The sentimental interlude of Steyn was over.

Some historians have wanted to see in the letters to Servatius Rogerus and in the poems which accompany them simple exercises in style. The form is undoubtedly conventional, full of reminiscences of Virgil, Horace and Ovid, yet it is no less the case that these are genuinely felt emotions, of an affective life which is understandable in relation to Erasmus's age and situation. When Horace or Ovid speak through the mouth of the young monk, we recognize them in passing. We feel, however, that Erasmus is more than an echo: he loves and he suffers.[8] He was not spared the pettiness and meanness to which the monastic life gives rise, but succeeded, with some difficulty, in maintaining a perilous balance between the demands of his heart and those of the rule.

With his friends, Erasmus found diversion and consolation in the Latin authors. He wrote only in Latin; he forced himself even to speak only in Latin. Gradually, the concern for ancient letters prevailed over his sentimental anxieties and Christian inspiration forced its way through in his correspondence as well as in his poetry. The influence of his confidant Cornelis Gerard was decisive here. The Fathers of the Church were cited in the correspondence between the two friends. In it Erasmus transcribed the letters of St Jerome and seemed to want to devote his writings to religious subjects, sometimes mimicking the Christian poets of Antiquity. Yet he remained faithful to the elegance of pagan models and he offered his friend a fulsome eulogy of Lorenzo Valla.

The richness of Erasmus's literary production at this time was impressive. He wrote more and more, and of better and better quality. Doubtless inspired by the civil wars which were then laying waste Holland, he penned a *Discourse on Peace and Discord*. This statement was the first witness to his unceasing struggle for peace. At the conclusion of it he composed a poem which recalls the *Dies Irae*. He dedicated a heroic song to the Resurrection of Christ and the paschal mystery. His major poetic creation was an ode of more than 400 verses in honour of the Virgin Mary. This poem evokes Olympus, the Styx, Rhadamanthus and the Sybil, but also, and above all, Christ and the Virgin: we can recognize in it the diverse influences assimilated by the young Erasmus, the disciple at one and the same time of Virgil and Horace, of Prudentius and of Fortunatus, perhaps even of Spagnuoli, the Christian Virgil.[9] Erasmus boldly linked together the love of literature and biblical inspiration, according to the eloquent precept: 'May the Muse adorn your style and may the Bible give you the meaning of what you write.'[10] Our hero practised his scales in a versification which masked, better than prose, the weakness of a thought still searching for itself. Erasmus was thus an active member of the friendly little group of poets in Gouda, with Cornelis Gerard and Willem Hermans. In collaboration with Cornelis, he wrote the poem *Apology against the Barbarians* which anticipates the dialogue of the *Antibarbari*. Later, with a Parisian editor, he was to publish the verse of Willem Hermans.

It was to this period of his life that the first edition of the little treatise *On Contempt of the World* goes back, a veritable eulogy of the monastic life, set in an ideal convent rather than in real life. In it Erasmus showed his attraction for St Jerome, the patron of monks, an attraction which would mark his life both in and out of the cloister. Monastic piety was familiar to Erasmus. When he spoke of the 'garden of delights', it had to do not with an Epicurean paradise, but with the monastery as the Middle Ages dreamed of it. Likewise, the 'pleasure of the solitary life' denoted, under his pen, and according to monastic terminology, the pure pleasure which the soul experiences in tasting the divine presence.[11]

Though beguiled by his charm and his personality, Erasmus's companions did not misjudge him. Cornelis Gerard called him 'poet, orator, divine' and added, with the boldness of youth, 'the most knowledgeable man in the world'. For his part, Erasmus became aware of his own importance, but his literary ambitions were not such as to reassure his superiors. Nevertheless his reputation extended beyond the monastery walls. When he was ordained – we do not know with what feelings – by David of Burgundy at Utrecht, on 25 April 1492, the year of Christopher Columbus, we can guess that his bishop singled him out and that it was he who recommended the young humanist to the bishop of Cambrai, who was in need of a secretary.

So Erasmus, who had become a priest *ad aeternum*, did not stay in the monastery. Later he was to invoke the deplorable state of his health to justify his departure from Steyn. This argument has a certain weight, for the monotonous length of the ceremonies, the inadequate diet and the bodily mortifications were so many ordeals for the frail Erasmus; but there were more deep-seated reasons for his departure. At Steyn he was cramped, and stifled for air; he did not feel at home in a house where there was no real love of literature.

St Jerome was able to help Erasmus temporarily to endure the monastery, but he could not prevent him leaving after it became possible to do so without scandal. A monk with a vocation which was dubious if not lacking – something which would mark his entire life –

Erasmus had believed that he had found at Steyn the time and security necessary for study. He proved to his cost that the monks' pious spare time was not the studious leisure of the humanists. Weakness of body and independence of spirit pushed him towards a profession which would not be interrupted by the bell and the offices, nor threatened by the silent opposition of his unlettered colleagues.

Another disappointment was that monastic piety no longer satisfied this authentic Christian, doubtless because he did not find there the biblical and patristic resources for which he asked in his prayers. It is reasonable to suppose that his struggle for inward piety began here. Nothing can show that Erasmus had been a bad monk, but he was not a happy monk. He left the monastery with the authorization of his superiors, who expected him to return. He was in no respect an unfrocked priest. Over the years, he wore the habit of a canon regular, but 'the habit does not make the monk.' He would never separate himself from his Book of Hours and he would maintain a nostalgia for Gregorian chant.[12] Prayer and the Mass would continue to shape the rhythm of his spiritual life. Despite all his criticism of Steyn, Erasmus owed it much – above all, his theological formation and the basis of his classical culture.

One of the pathways of Erasmus's youth was now closed off for ever. Despite the friends whom he kept at Steyn, he never returned to the life of the cloister. Thenceforth he followed his true destiny: to write, to write again, to write always! In short, at Steyn Erasmus's vocation was already confirmed – a vocation not as a monk, but as a Christian humanist. He had chosen his pathway, he would not change it or ever renounce it; to it he would dedicate his powers and his life, without being discouraged by the obstacles he encountered, without letting himself be distressed by the vanities of the world. To reach his goal he would make any sacrifice. Honours would not turn his head, trials would not lay him low. He would be neither a flatterer nor a functionary, less still a parasite. This was the price of the glory to which he aspired.

3

The Hard Apprenticeship
of Freedom

Erasmus was about twenty-four years old when he left Steyn [1] to become secretary in the household of the bishop of Cambrai, Hendrik of Bergen, a patron of great ambition, but limited means. In so doing, he exchanged freedom for obedience, but also security for penury.

A new life began, with new illusions. Did he suspect that this life would sometimes be hard? He was as happy as a spoilt child. The young monk, passionately devoted to good Latin, now became a free priest, whose priestly consciousness remained firmly loyal to the Church. Set free from his monastic obligations, he found his balance again; he retained his taste for friendship, though he gave up its too ardent expressions. Enthusiasm for study delivered him from himself. He wanted to forget his unhappy childhood and his lost vocation. After the long monastic winter, the springtime of his life in the world seemed brimming with promise. He hoped to follow Hendrik of Bergen to Italy, the promised land of humanism, but this agreeable plan was postponed. Instead, he accompanied his patron on his travels [2] to the Netherlands, and rendered him there the services expected of a good secretary.

In attaching himself to Hendrik of Bergen, Erasmus drew nearer to the halls of power, for his patron came from an illustrious line. He was a member of the Regency Council of the Archduke Philip the Fair, son of the Emperor Maximilian and Mary of Burgundy. Through his mother, Philip was master of the Netherlands, and by his marriage to Joanna the Mad, he was destined to become King of Spain. His premature death was to open up to his son Charles the doors to royal and imperial power.

In following his bishop around, Erasmus also drew nearer to France. French was the language of the Brussels court and of all the nobility of the age, and it was not without difficulty that Erasmus learned it. Hendrik of Bergen was not the ideal patron, but being in his company showed Erasmus something of the pettiness of court life. He had no liking for the courtiers who had more fine manners than genuine sensibility. Their most trivial conversations revealed ruthless rivalries and a desire to attract the unceasing attention of the prince. Erasmus had too much native discrimination to behave like an upstart and he avoided this fashionable drudgery as much as he could.

He gained the friendship of Jacob Anthoniszoon, the bishop's vicar-general, and wrote a preface for the latter's treatise *Of the Superiority of Imperial Power*.[3] Yet this book scarcely represented the ideas of the young humanist, and in the preface there appeared only a measured eulogy of the Empire 'which takes up arms on behalf of all' and 'preserves the peace of Christendom'.

Humanism – the literary and moral expression of the Renaissance – was inconceivable without the study of literature. It clamoured for a return to the sources, direct contact with the texts, the personal experience of knowledge, and cared not a fig for verbal wrangling, subtle distinctions and quintessential abstractions. Humanism sought the study of 'the languages', that is to say, Latin and Greek in the best authors – the ancients – and in the best texts of those authors. These were the *humaniores litterae*, centred on literature. 'Many men', Erasmus was to say, 'are capable of judging correctly without having studied logic. Without the knowledge of language, no one can understand what he hears or reads.' Already a perfect Latinist, Erasmus soon turned his attention to the study of Greek.

The arts in the Renaissance attracted disciples, not copyists, and Renaissance Latin was not classical Latin resuscitated. For the humanists, it was a matter of adapting the language without falsifying it to a new framework, a new situation. The mental universe of the humanists was not that of Aristotle and Cicero, Plato and Augustine: it was the contemporary world of Francis I and Leo X, of Michelangelo and Christopher Columbus. Renaissance Latin served as a vehicle for modern and innovative thought. From England to Poland, humanism spread through Europe without regard to frontiers.

The renewed contact with ancient pagan wisdom could not but arouse the suspicion of certain men of learning for whom literature was perceived as a menace to a rigid Catholicism. But if Erasmus felt any tension between literature and religious preoccupations, this tension was quickly and harmoniously resolved in an increasingly conscious accord, which we call Christian humanism. Erasmus was a Christian humanist like Thomas More and Guillaume Budé, Juan Luis Vivès and Philip Melanchthon, all distant heirs of Petrarch.[4] Like them, he wanted to reconcile Christianity and Antiquity without confusing them, to regenerate mankind by baptizing his culture and purifying his religion. Christian humanism held out to him an ideal of serenity and harmony which did not cut him off from his roots, but rather raised him in his entirety towards God. It represented a spirit of optimism, moderation and adaptation; a will to be 'man in perfection'. It was a method of a total religious philosophy, appealing to all the gifts of man, all his experience, all his virtues, all his potentialities.

At Steyn Erasmus had already cultivated the best authors. He had already experienced the hostility of the 'barbarians' who, in their rejection of ancient culture, confused ignorance with piety. He had nevertheless discovered unexpected allies, St Jerome and St Augustine, for whom the ancient writers were so precious that they deserved to be placed alongside the Bible. From this period Erasmus began to sketch out one of his major works.

About 1493–4 Erasmus, who often stayed at Brussels, went off to the monastery of his order at Grenoble, where the great mystic Ruysbroeck had lived. In the library there he found a version of St Augustine's treatise *On Christian Doctrine*.[5] Day and night he studied it: he was to use it against the 'barbarians' in his apologetic work on behalf of literature. The 'barbarians' whom Erasmus fought represented uncultivated and warped learning. Scholastic education had replaced the ancient authors with commentaries, glosses and compendiums, too often teaching a programme of study which was elementary and superficial, in which the argument from authority took an undue place.

This work, which Erasmus had sketched out at Steyn before his twentieth year, he was to take up again many times, and though some fragments of it were lost in the course of his travels, he completed it successfully with the publication of the *Antibarbari* in 1520.

If was from Halsteren, near Bergen-op-Zoom in Hendrik of Bergen's country house, that he described his current project to his friend Cornelis Gerard:

If you ask me what I am up to, I have in hand at present a work on literature which I have been threatening for a very long time to write and have been attending to during my retreat in the country, though I do not very well know how it is going. I intend, at any rate, to finish this work in two books. The first book will be almost entirely concerned with refuting the absurdities perpetrated by the barbarians, while in the second I am going to depict you talking about the glory of letters with some scholarly friends of your own sort. So, since the credit will be shared among us, it is proper that the toil of preparation should be shared between us also. Accordingly, please be sure to send me, and be kind enough to share with me for our friendship's sake, anything you have read (what have you not read?) which you may think relevant to this subject – that is to say, any arguments for or against the study of letters.[6]

From this collaboration emerged the eloquent manifesto of humanism and the vigourous denunciation of its ignorant opponents.[7] Citing St Augustine, Erasmus made an ardent plea to justify the agreement of ancient wisdom with Christianity.[8]

In the course of his work Erasmus, who now considered himself a Brabantine, became acquainted with Jacob Batt, secretary of the village of Bergen-op-Zoom and director of the village school.[9] The invaluable character of this friendship showed itself in Erasmus's letters to his friend, such as this delightful expression of anxiety about his friend's health:

> Thereupon I was torn between two emotions: at first glance I began to be a little annoyed with you for sending such a short note, since my appetite for my dear Batt is such that I would wish you to write not letters but books. Subsequently, as I read on with flying eye, as they say, and discovered that you had caught a most persistent fever, I trembled all over and began to concentrate on the letter and reread it, with rather more attention. When I found that my letter had made you better I was at once relieved of my anguish, and I read the rest in a more cheerful frame of mind.[10]

For his book Erasmus chose the dialogue form, much favoured during the Renaissance and developed by him to perfection. He introduced Batt into the dialogue of the *Antibarbari*, as the author's spokesman, and it is he who cites with approval the advice of an unknown philosopher: 'Live as if you are to die tomorrow, study as if you were to live for ever.' Erasmus had made this precept his own. He wanted to die with his pen in his hand: 'Death will take over, but I would rather it took me studying than idling.'[11] And he added, as a good disciple of Socrates:[12] 'When I have learned everything, I shall know only that I know nothing.' He said that he knew nothing, but this was not for want of having sought much and studied much. He had earned the right to scoff at the lazy, who declare that, since the knowledge of God comes from heaven, they will deal with it when they get to heaven.[13]

The 'barbarians' continued to haunt Erasmus's consciousness, preventing him from being entirely happy because 'everything is full of bitterness.' 'Nothing is fit for me', he confided to Willem Hermans, 'but to weep and wail; and through these distresses my brain has already so lost its edge and my heart has so wasted away that I have come to take no joy at all in my former studies. I find no pleasure in the poets' Pierian charm, and the Muses, who were once my only love, repel me now.'[14]

Erasmus's malaise, aggravated by his patron's parsimony, was not to last much longer. Jacob Batt helped him to recover his balance with a taste for literature, and advised him to continue his studies at the University of Paris. With the consent of his bishop and the promise of a subsidy, Erasmus left the Netherlands, and was enrolled at the Sorbonne from 1495 to study theology for his doctorate.[15]

Hendrik of Bergen recommended him to his protégé Jan Standonck of Malines, who ran the Collège de Montaigu, an educational institution reserved for the less well-to-do students, ruling it with an iron hand. So Erasmus rediscovered with no joy at all the self-denial of the cloister and the rigours of discipline. The memory of Lenten fasts and of rotten eggs was to haunt him all his life, though he spent only a year at Montaigu.[16] During that year he sometimes preached on saints' festivals and interpreted the sacred texts to his fellow-students.[17]

The Sorbonne – queen of the medieval Universities – was still the most famous in the world. Erasmus, who had been ardently longing to resume his studies, was happy with his lot, although he condemned the importance given to scholastic method in the teaching. He scoffed at the rigid structures, the Palaestra, and the cap of the Sorbonne, he turned up his nose at the word games of his masters, but he persisted because he was ambitious for the doctorate, even in the act of resisting it. The doctorate, he reasoned, would put him on a level footing with the theologians of every land. He already felt himself the equal of his fellow-students, despite the differences due to wealth and age. Every day he encountered other young men who nurtured other dreams. Like them, he chattered in Latin and French and read at random. The constraints of the University seemed to him intolerable encroachments; external constraints were always to exasperate this studious man who knew how to discipline himself. With him, one senses at the same time the patience of the poor man and the impatience of the ambitious man – ambitious for knowledge, that is to say. Enthusiasm for study delivered him from himself; he gradually matured, while his unhappy childhood and the problem of his vocation receded.

Erasmus was untiring in his search for intellectual direction and for books to increase his knowledge. He was also looking for patrons and benefactors to provide a living. He kept company with the leading spirits of the capital, the Italian poet Fausto Andrelini and the scholar Robert Gaguin, among others. Gaguin[18] was then one of the masters in Paris most in demand. Dean of the Faculty of Law and general of the Trinitarians, he was devoted to the cause of the restoration of learning and piety. Erasmus, who was unfailingly anxious to please those whom he admired, drew nearer to the great man whose zeal and learning beguiled him.

A poet, statesman, theologian and historian, Gaguin had published (with Pierre La Dru at Paris) his great work *On the origin and the great deeds of the French* in 1495. He concluded the last book of the volume with a letter from Erasmus – then almost unknown outside the Sorbonne – a letter commonplace enough in its unfolding of history, a letter of somewhat bombastic panegyric, which argued more for the competence of its author than for his literary talent. This letter was the first of Erasmus's writings to be published, and it was in Paris – *adamata Lutetia* – that 'his temerity began to expose him to the world.'

Emboldened by this first success, Erasmus submitted the manuscript of his *Antibarbari* to Gaguin, and received in return a friendly critique:

> You have undertaken, Erasmus, to conduct a war against a contemptible sort of man, who unceasingly denigrates the humanities: a war not so much difficult as distasteful for no one can by any warlike devices overcome those whose ignorance only makes them more stubborn in defeat. . . . Now although I myself simply hold the impudence of these people in contempt, nevertheless I do not disapprove of the campaign you have launched against them. They should be assailed with every kind of weapon; you have accummulated these with discretion and can shoot them skilfully and brandish them most fiercely. . . . You outline your scheme most succinctly, clearly classify the divisions of your subject matter, and conduct the argument with great skill. Your arrangement is well-planned, you adorn your theme attractively, and you have something of Carneades' vigour in controversy. Please do not take one observation amiss from a friend: your preface is too long-drawn-out and it may be that fault will be found with the leading role given to Batt on the ground that his monologue is somewhat too protracted, for a speech that goes on too long is boring, but when the discussion is relieved by a change of speaker the hearer is both refreshed and entertained. I should not like you to take only my advice on this point. Look at those who make use of dialogue: they seldom employ continuous speeches, but often use brief clauses and phrases. Among the Greeks the celebrated Plato will serve as a leading instance; among the Latin writers, Cicero and some others of later date.[19]

If Gaguin provided Erasmus with moral support, financial backing came through Jacob Batt, who introduced him to Anna Van Veere, the mother of his pupil Adolphe. For a time she was to become Erasmus's patron and while the plague was raging in Paris, they were all to be found at the Chateau of Tournehem, between Calais and St Omer. Erasmus wrote 'in bad French' for the young woman who knew no Latin.[20] He regathered his strength while beginning one of his most significant works, *The Handbook of the Christian Soldier.*[21]

Erasmus returned to the Collège de Montaigu, but unable to bear the regime of the house any longer, he fell sick and returned to

Bergen-op-zoom, where the bishop received him with goodwill. Like all students of meagre means, Erasmus had to look for a patron – several patrons if possible – to continue his works of learning without dying of hunger. By 1496, he was back again in Paris, determined this time to live alone, and from day to day, but he came up against the barrier of money and was unable to get around it. The minimum for survival – as determined by his sponsors – soon became irksome to him, but he would not go back to Montaigu. Paris, despite the stench of its streets,[22] beguiled the young Hollander, doubtless because the freedom that he enjoyed at this time was subtly transforming his life.

4

Paris: The Attractions and Burdens of a Tutorship

While he was pursuing his theological studies in Paris, Erasmus was also teaching Latin, settled in a tutorship, that humble anteroom of a literary career. Little by little, the young teacher assembled the pedagogical weapons that he needed to teach elegant Latin. The task was not an easy one, for though he had a small personal library,[1] he did not have at his disposal any of those working tools familiar to us: dictionaries, encyclopedias, critical editions and reference works of various kinds. When we come across him again in Paris, Erasmus is still a medieval man, formed by medieval methods in philosophy, theology, and even in the liberal arts.[2]

Erasmus's genius was first of all to have renewed the learning of Latin by his bold initiatives. He compiled some introductory notebooks, the *Colloquies*, to inculcate in his pupils the secrets of graceful conversation, a treatise *On the Writing of Letters*, aimed at polishing the style of beginners and finally a treatise *Foundations of the Abundant Style*, to enrich their vocabulary. From these trial pieces, which circulated for a long time in manuscript form, many books were to appear much later, to guarantee their author's reputation with both students and teachers. Moreover, Erasmus wrote freely to his friends, as he tells us himself when recalling his memories of Paris. "I gave my pen daily practice in writing letters to my acquaintance, throwing off any kind of nonsense to one or two dear friends and rattling on in the way one man talks to another in the intimacy of a glass of wine between friends and cronies.'[3]

Maintaining a lively inclination towards piety,[4] Erasmus published his first book in Paris – it was a little booklet – with a touching poem entitled *The Room Where Jesus was Born*.[5] The preface, addressed to his fellow-pupil, the Scotsman Hector Boece, illustrates the author's affectation. He blushed to be called a poet while publishing his verses and he was more flattered than angered when he replied to the admirer who asked for more:

You keep writing again and again, threatening and abusing me, in fact declaring open war upon me if I do not send you a copy of my poems. Please consider how unfair it is of you to insist upon having something which I do not even own myself. I swear to you most solemnly that for a long time now I have not been engaged in the pursuit of poetry and if I wrote trivial verse as a boy, I left it in my native land. I did not even venture to import my barbarous Muses, with their uncouth foreign accent, into this famous University of Paris, for I was aware that it contained a great many persons who were exquisitely gifted in every branch of letters. Yet you believe none of these things and think I am being poetical even in asserting this! Confound it, who has put it into your head that Erasmus was a poet? This expression, by which you keep describing me in your letters from time to time, is in bad odour nowadays through the foolish ignorance of many of its practitioners, although it once implied reverence and honour. So please be good enough to refrain from using it to address me in future.[6]

A little later Erasmus praised the Christian inspiration of poetry. In a letter to Hendrik of Bergen, he rebuked those who have nothing but an aversion for piety and 'in choosing models . . . prefer to set before themselves Catullus, Tibullus, Propertius, and Ovid, rather than St Ambrose or Paulinus of Nola or Prudentius or Iuvencus'.[7] To the prior of Steyn, Nicholaas Werner, who invited him to return to the monastery, he confirmed his stern determination. 'I have no desire to be diverted from religious studies by any monetary inducement. I did not come to Paris to teach, or to make piles of money, but to learn; and indeed my intention, God willing, is to seek my doctorate in theology.'[8] It is likely that Erasmus wanted to placate the prior and bring about further delays, but the sincerity of his remarks is not in doubt.

Erasmus's extended and ponderous theological studies clearly could not make him turn his back on humanism, with its return to the sources and its disdain of scholasticism. The young student merrily poked fun at the Sorbonne, 'the holy of holies of Scotist theology'. His humour was displayed when he confided to a friend:

If only you could see your Erasmus sitting agape among those glorified Scotists, while 'Gryllard' lectures from a lofty throne. If you could but observe his furrowed brow, his uncomprehending look and worried expression, you would say it was another man. They say the secrets of this branch of learning cannot be grasped by a person who has anything at all to do with the Muses or the Graces; for this, you must unlearn any literary lore you have put your hands on, and vomit up any draught you have drunk from Helicon. So I am trying with might and main to say nothing in good Latin, or elegantly, or wittily; and I seem to be making progress; so there is some hope that, eventually, they will acknowledge me.[9]

There is a cruel irony in this last phrase: the teachers whom Erasmus caricatured would never recognize him as one of them. They and he were separated by an incompatibility of thought and temperament which would only become clear with the passage of years. Criticism of false doctors and bad theologians is a commonplace to be found in all ages. In Erasmus's case it was accompanied by the praise of good, sincere doctors of the Gospel. At heart he was taunting the second-rate masters out of a love of the pure doctrine to which he wanted to consecrate his life.

We are not well informed about Erasmus's university activities. They were neither regular nor punctual, but interrupted by frequent absences and long journeys. and every year Erasmus was ill, especially during Lent. 'A sickness has quite worn me out, and my body and my coffers are both in a sadly depleted state; meat must mend the former, money the latter.' His health remained fragile. Moreover, this teacher, despite himself, wrote books which scarcely prepared him for examinations, but assured his future fame. At the very most we can assume that he obtained his bachelor's degree in theology.[10]

What Erasmus objected to in the scholastic philosophy in which Christianity had become bogged down, and particularly in the decadent scholasticism which was taught to him, was its arid rationalism, its rigid systematization, its authoritarian moralism, its sterile logic and its pretentious verbiage. More fundamentally, he deplored the intrusion of this philosophy into theology. He had little appreciation for the four theological giants of the Latin Middle Ages: Gratian, Lombard, Thomas Aquinas and Duns Scotus. He set Jesus in opposition to Aristotle[11] and made fun of St Thomas, denouncing him for his overdone Aristotelianism.[12] He preferred the pagan Socrates to the Christian Scotus, for Socrates was, he said, 'the most saintly of the philosophers', who brought philosophy down from heaven to earth. 'Holy Socrates, pray for us,' one of the guests dared to say in the Colloquy, *The Religious Banquet.*[13] Plato himself comes only second in Erasmus's estimation, after his master Socrates.[14] Thus Erasmus was not antagonistic to philosophy, and even less to the art of reasoning. On occasion he paid homage to scholasticism for having preserved part of Greek thought,[15] but he would never forgive it for having cluttered up theology, eclipsed the Fathers and obscured piety.[16]

A pedagogue and a humanist, Erasmus believed the classical languages and ancient literature to be the essence of culture. Grammar, which embraced the knowledge of the languages, poetry and history of Antiquity, should be the basis of all knowledge, not excluding the sacred sciences to which it forms the essential introduction.[17] This was what some theologians would never allow. With his pupils, Englishmen like Thomas Grey and Robert Fisher, or Germans like the brothers Northoff, Erasmus applied this method. In this manner he taught them variety and precision of language, logical progression of ideas and elegance of style. He explained his programme to Christian Northoff, who had just left him, in this way:

Since, Christian, my excellent friend, I had no doubt whatsoever that your passion for letters was extraordinarily keen, I thought you needed no exhortation, but only some guidance and, as it were, signposting of the road you had entered upon. This, I thought, was my duty: to point out to you, as a person closely linked to me in many ways and highly congenial, the paths I myself have followed from boyhood onwards. If you attend to them with the degree of care I shall now devote to explaining them, I shall not regret having given the advice, nor will you be sorry that you took it.

Your first endeavour should be to choose the most learned teacher you can find, for it is impossible that one who is himself no scholar should make a scholar of anyone else. As soon as you find him, make every effort to see that he acquires the feelings of a father towards you, and you in turn those of a son towards him. Not only ought we to be prompted to this by the very principles of honour, since we are no less indebted to those from whom we have acquired life itself, but your friendship with him is of such importance as an aid to learning that it will be of no avail to you to have a literary tutor at all unless you have, by the same token, a friend. Secondly, you should give him attention and be regular in your work for him, for the talents of students are sometimes ruined by violent effort, whereas regularity in work has lasting effect just because of its temperance and produces by daily practice a greater result than you would suppose. As in all things, so in literature, nothing is worse than excess; accordingly you should from time to time abate the strenuousness of your studies and relieve them with recreation – but recreation of a civilised kind, worthy of the vocation of letters and not too far separated from it in nature. Indeed, a constant element of enjoyment must be mingled with our studies so that we think of learning as a game rather than a form of drudgery, for no activity can be continued for long if it does not to some extent afford pleasure to the participant. . . .

What matters at the outset is not how much knowledge you acquire, but how sound it is. But I shall now explain a method by which you can learn more easily as well as more accurately; for a craftsman usually obeys certain rules of his trade that make it possible for him to produce a given quantity of work, not only more accurately and quickly, but also more easily. Divide your day into tasks, as it were; this is reported to have been the practice of those universally celebrated writers, Pliny and Pope Pius. First of all, and this is the essential thing, listen to your teacher's explanations not only attentively but eagerly. Do not be satisfied simply to follow his discourse with an alert mind; try now and then to anticipate the direction of his thought. Remember everything he says and even write down his most important utterances, for writing is the most faithful custodian of words. On the other hand avoid trusting it too much, like that absurd man of wealth in Seneca who had come to believe that he had preserved in his own memory everything that any of his servants remembered. Do not be guilty of possessing a library of learned books while lacking learning yourself. In order that what you have heard may not vanish from your mind, go over it again, privately at home or in discussion with others. And do not be satisfied with these measures alone: remember to devote a part of your time to silent thought, which St Augustine records as the most important of all aids to intellect and memory. In addition, the contests of minds in what we may call their wrestling ring are especially effective for exhibiting, stimulating and enlarging the sinews of the human understanding. And do not be ashamed to ask questions if you are in doubt, or to be put right whenever you are wrong. Avoid working at night and studying at unsuitable times and seasons; these things quench the light of the mind and are very bad for the health. Aurora is the Muses' friend: daybreak is an excellent time for study. After lunch, take some recreation, or go for a walk, or enjoy gay conversation; reflect that even such opportunities as these can afford opportunity for studying. As to food, eat only what suffices for health, and not as much as you long to eat. Take a short walk before supper, and again after it. Just before you go to sleep you should read something of exquisite quality, worth remembering; let sleep overtake you while you are musing upon it and when you awaken try to recall it to mind. Always keep fixed in your heart Pliny's dictum that all the time which one fails to devote to study is wasted, and reflect that youth is the most fleeting thing on earth, and that when once it has fled away it never returns.

But now I'm beginning to offer advice, though I promised only to point the way. It is for you, my sweetest Christian, to follow this method – or a better one, if you can discover it.[18]

For Thomas Grey he invoked his personal experience to recall that study is a strength and consolation. 'It is to literature that I attribute the fact that I am now alive and well: literature, which has taught me never to give way in the face of fortune's buffeting.'[19] As in his early youth, Erasmus found the sweetest comforts in friendship. His letters and his exchanges with his pupils breathe a shared affection and, in their company, he took long walks in the vineyards around Paris or shared simple and cheerful meals. Thirty years later he recalled a charming memory of Stephen Gardiner, the future Bishop of Winchester, a better cook than his teacher: 'He gave evidence of as much intelligence in the preparation of salads as for the study of literature.'[20]

Worth noting also is his reflection on friendship, confided to Thomas Grey in 1497:

A lasting affection, based on virtue, can indeed no more come to an end than virtue itself, whereas, if greed be friendship's foundation, then when the money runs out so will the friendship, and when pleasure lures men to love, they cease to love when satiety supervenes. Finally, those who seek each other's friendship from some childish freak of mind desert their friends as wilfully as they joined them. But our comradeship, which arose from far finer causes than these, rests upon bases also far stronger: for we were brought together not by considerations of advantage or pleasure, or any youthful whim, but by an honourable love of letters and for the studies in which we shared.[21]

What a distance had been travelled since the passionate declarations of the letters to Servatius Rogerus ten years earlier!

There was no place for women in Erasmus's life. Having reported to Robert Fisher the sour conversation of their landlady and her daughter, he concluded: 'It is when I think about these characteristics of womankind that I feel happy to have hit upon my own kind of life. If this was by chance, I am lucky; if I chose it deliberately, I am wise.'[22]

Exchanging college quarters for a family lodging house immersed Erasmus in the picturesque drama of popular life. He gave Christian Northoff a graphic account of a violent dispute between the servant and her mistress:

'I was extremely busy.' 'Indeed, and what was the business?' I was watching a play, a very enjoyable one. 'A comedy,' say you, 'or a tragedy?' Call it which you like, but no one played a part in character, there was only one act, the chorus had no flutes, the type of play was neither Roman nor Greek but down-to-earth miming, all done on the ground, without dancing, viewed from the dining room, most exciting crisis, bloodcurdling final scene. 'Confound you, what is this play you are inventing?' you'll say. Well Christian, I will tell you the story.

The spectacle we saw today was that of a battle royal between a housewife and her maidservant. The trumpet had sounded repeatedly before the engagement. Resounding insults were exchanged by both sides. At this stage the contest was indecisive, and nobody carried the day. It all went on in the garden, while we looked on in some amusement from the dining-room. Now for the denouement: the girl left the battle and came upstairs in order to make the beds in my room. In the course of conversation with her, I complimented her on her courage in giving her mistress as good as she got in insults and abuse, but said that I had wished her hands might have proved as formidable as her tongue, for the mistress, a stoutly built female who might well have been an athlete so far as appearance went, kept on boxing the girl's head with her fists. 'Why', said I, 'have you no nails at all, to endure such treatment without any response?' She answered with a smile that, for herself, it was not spirit she lacked so much as strength. 'Do you', I said to her, 'think that the outcome of a battle depends on strength alone? In every case, the most important factor is planning.' When she asked what plan I had in mind, I said: 'When she next attacks you, at once pull off her headpiece' (for the women of Paris are extraordinarily vain about a sort of black headdress, of false hair), 'this done, go for her hair.'

I then imagined that she took my suggestion in the same jesting spirit in which it was offered but, just before supper, up rushed mine host, all out of breath (he was a herald in King Charles' service, commonly nicknamed Gentil Gerson) 'Come, my masters,' said he, 'you will see a gory spectacle.' We ran forward and found the lady of the household and the girl at grips upon the ground. We had difficulty in separating them. The evidence showed clearly how bloody the fight had been. On one side the woman's headpiece, on the other side the girl's veil, lay on the earth in shreds. So cruel had been the massacre that the ground was covered with piles of hair. When we sat down to supper, Madame told us with much indignation how violently the girl had behaved. 'When I set about correcting her,' she said, 'giving her a beating, I mean, she at once pulled my headpiece off my head.' I recognized that I had not sung my tale to deaf ears. 'Then,' she went on, 'when she had pulled it off, the witch brandished it before my eyes.' That had not formed part of my advice. 'After that,' she continued, 'she pulled out all this hair you see here.' She called Heaven and earth to witness that she had never come across a girl who possessed so much naughtiness in so small a person. We proceeded to urge the vicissitudes of human life, the uncertain outcome of war, and negotiated to establish peaceful understanding between them for the future. In the meantime I was privately congratulating myself that the mistress had no inkling that my advice to the girl had prompted the affair, else I too would have been made aware that she was the owner of a tongue![23]

Thus, if Erasmus, either through affectation or modesty, declared that he spoke French badly, there is no doubt that he understood it very well!

Life in Paris was only a stage in Erasmus's intellectual formation. He dreamed all the time of seeing Italy. Hendrik of Bergen wanted to take this much-hoped-for journey with his secretary, but the project was again abandoned.[24] Erasmus's ill health returned. He invoked St Geneviève, the patroness of the city: 'Turn your eyes towards me and deliver my body from the fever. Send me back to my dear studies without which life will be bitter to me.' Then he described his experience: 'Lately I fell into a quartan fever, but have recovered health and strength, not by a physician's help, though I had recourse to one, but by the aid of St Geneviève alone, the famous virgin, whose bones, preserved by the canons regular, daily radiate miracles and are revered.'[25]

What follows in this letter respectfully describes the procession of the saint, whose reliquary was transported with great pomp from its sanctuary in Notre-Dame. It seems likely that Erasmus had piously joined in this city pilgrimage.[26]

The year 1497 unfolded without any further unforeseen developments. Between two courses at the Sorbonne, Erasmus continued to give lessons to his pupils, and this assured him of a meagre livelihood. Meanwhile his pupils came and went. Not all of them were agreeable and enthusiastic. Some were called back to the countryside under orders from their families, as happened in the case of Christian Northoff, who went back to his father, a Lübeck merchant. Erasmus wrote to him, on behalf of his brother who was living in Paris, a careful letter praising the teacher and his methods.

> What could I have got that was more desirable, or serviceable, than a tutor at once learned and amiable? And my tutor is the most learned, and the most amiable, on earth; I found him after a long and painful search: the celebrated Erasmus! And what is more, I have him entirely to myself; I own him with sole title, enjoying his undivided attention continually by day and night. As a result I have at command, within the four walls of my room, the mount of Helicon itself. If this be not to live as one of the Muses' band, what is? Our whole existence is seasoned with literature, be it play or earnest business or leisure. Our talk is of letters at the noonday meal; our suppers are made exquisite by literary seasoning. In our walks we prattle of letters and even our frivolous diversions are no strangers to them; we talk of letters till we fall asleep, our dreams are dreams of letters, and literature awakens us to begin the new day. It seems to me that I am not studying but playing; nevertheless I now perceive I am studying indeed.[27]

Erasmus's pedagogical method clearly shows itself in this playful piece. With such a teacher, 'our whole existence is seasoned with literature.'

Erasmus's spiritual preoccupations were shown here more profoundly than behind the high walls of Steyn or Montaigu. 'I have long since lost interest in the world,' he confided to a Carmelite friend, 'and find no merit in my own hopes. I only ask to be given leisure to live a life entirely devoted to God alone, in lamentation for the sins of my rash youth, absorption in holy writ, and either reading or writing something continually. This I cannot do in a retreat, or under a monastic regime.'[28] Erasmus combined this programme for moral renewal with a decided interest in the milieu of the pre-Reformation, whose leaders were aiming to restore the Church and correct abuses.

The years unfolded with courses to be taken and lessons to be given. Out of a love of Greek, Erasmus took lessons with Georgius Hermonymus of Sparta, who had a rather mediocre knowledge of ancient Greek.[29] The pupil's progress was a measure of the teacher's incompetence. Erasmus prepared for his doctorate with no great sense of urgency and planned improved manuals for the use of his pupils. To bring together examples with his advice, he asked for his letters back from his friends and had already drafted a preface for a treatise *On the Art of Writing Letters,* which was to see the light of day a quarter of a century later. 'I am giving myself entirely to my books,' he wrote, 'I am bringing together scattered texts, and composing others, I allow myself no leisure but what my health permits me.'

Like all students bored by courses, Erasmus and his friend Fausto Andrelini exchanged short notes under the noses of their teachers.

FAUSTO TO ERASMUS: I want my dinner to be quite a simple one. I ask for nothing but flies and ants. Farewell.

ERASMUS TO FAUSTO: Confound it, what are these riddles you set me? Do you think I am an Oedipus, or the owner of a Sphinx? Still, I imagine that your 'flies' are fowls, your 'ants', rabbits. But shall we put off joking to another time? We have to buy our supper now; so you should stop talking in riddles. Farewell.

FAUSTO TO ERASMUS: I can see clearly now that you are an Oedipus. I want nothing but fowls – small ones will do. Not a word about rabbits, please! Farewell, you first-rate solver of puzzles.

ERASMUS TO FAUSTO: My most witty Fausto, how at one and the same time you have made me blush and that theologian rage! For he was in the same lecture hall as ourselves. But I do not believe that it serves any purpose to stir up a nest of hornets. Farewell.

FAUSTO TO ERASMUS: Everyone knows that Fausto is capable of dying boldly for his friend Erasmus. As for those prattlers, let us take no more notice of them than an Indian elephant does of a gnat. Farewell. Yours, whatever envious tongues may say.[30]

Erasmus was perhaps thinking about his treatise *On the Art of Writing Letters* when he carefully and lovingly stored away these models of laconic and epigrammatic style.

Disappointed in the Sorbonne, Erasmus wanted to leave Paris and present his doctorate of theology at the famous University of Bologna.

> I had previously made up my mind to withdraw to Italy this year, and to study theology for a few months at Bologna, taking my doctorate there, and to visit Rome in the jubilee year . . . But I am afraid I cannot

complete this course in the way I desire. I fear especially that this health of mine may be unable to stand a journey of such length in a hot climate, and lastly I reflect that neither the journey into Italy, nor supporting oneself while there, is anything but very expensive. Even to acquire the degree itself one requires a substantial amount of money; and of this the Bishop of Cambrai is a very poor provider.[31]

The days passed in fact without the arrival of the subsidy for which he had hoped against hope. 'Goodbye to the title of theologian, to fame, and to profitless dignity!'[32]

An enthusiastic letter from his colleague at Steyn, Willem Hermans, shows that Erasmus's optimism survived his disappointments. My friend Erasmus . . . has been here to visit us perhaps (though Heaven forbid) for the last time; since he means to go to Bologna after Easter (what a long and difficult journey!) and is now making financial arrangements for it. If all goes well, he will return in triumph with his degree.[33]

Erasmus's poverty and poor health were to keep him in Paris, but a new pupil, William Blount, the future Lord Mountjoy, entered his life and brought him the comfort of his keen friendship. 'He loves me, and treats me well,' said Erasmus. However, bitterness gave way this time to optimism. Erasmus the teacher knew the risks of his job. His enemies spread abroad calumnies about him. From Steyn, Willem Hermans himself sent his friend a reproachful letter, now lost, and Erasmus replied with a liveliness full of emotion.

You tell me there is much talk of me there, and that it is anything but pleasant to hear. Well, what I can do, dear Willem, is to keep myself blameless, as I am doing; what I cannot control are the things men say about me. I am much more concerned about what you think of me, for, upon my soul, I value your opinion above all others. Now, what was the meaning of the letter in which you appear to censure my way of living? Do you really wish to learn (for it is proper that you should know every detail of my affairs) how your Erasmus conducts his life in this place? He is alive, or rather I think he may be; but alive on the most wretched terms, exhausted by grief of every kind: endlessly intrigued against, cheated of friends' support, and tempest-tost upon waves of disaster. Nevertheless he lives in perfect blamelessness. I know that I shall hardly be able to convince you of the truth of all this. You still think of me as the Erasmus of old: of my personal freedom, and of such lustre as my reputation retains; but if I had a chance to speak with you in person it would be the simplest thing on earth to persuade you of its truth. Therefore, if you wish to form a true picture of your friend, you must imagine him, not indulging in frivolity or feasting or love-affairs, but distraught with grief: tearful and loathing himself; with neither a mind to live nor a chance to die; in short, utterly wretched, not through his own fault it is true but through Fate's cruelty: still (for what difference does that make?) utterly wretched, and yet full of love, devotion and warm enthusiasm for you![34]

On the contrary, it mattered a great deal that Erasmus should be cleared of every serious reproach! He could not leave for Italy without money for the journey and he would not have money if he could not convince a patron of his perfect integrity. Freedom was indispensable to Erasmus. Without it, he could not live, but he was aware of its limits and dangers. To the same friend at Steyn he confided: 'On me, certainly, experience has imposed too much familiarity with this kind of freedom – and on you, just as certainly, too little![35]

At this difficult time, Erasmus thought that he had found a more generous and secure patron in Anna Van Veere, Lady of Tournehem.[36] At the beginning of 1499, he addressed to his patron's young son Adolphe, a pupil of his friend Batt, a long letter designed to encourage him in his studies. The last lines of the letter are simple, direct and personal:

> And at this moment when you are beginning to imbibe Christ along with your early lessons, I am sending you a few prayers: prayers that I wrote at your mother's request and on Batt's urging, but wrote for you, and so I have somewhat adapted their language to suit your age. If you use these carefully, you will at one stroke improve your own style and come to despise, not only as most ignorant but also as very superstitious, those 'soldier's prayers' which men of the sort who frequent courts generally find attractive.[37]

The whole of Erasmus is expressed in these lines: literature joined with piety and devotion to friendship.

5

England: A Second Homeland

Negotiations with Anna van Verre came to nothing, but in the end fortune smiled on Erasmus at the moment when he no longer thought it possible. Mountjoy invited him to accompany him to England. For eight months, from May 1499 to January 1500, he was to live an exciting life, find unforgettable friends, complete his education and formulate precisely his joint programme of biblical theology and humanist culture.

In London, Erasmus became close friends with a young lawyer and philologist, Thomas More, the future author of *Utopia*, later to become Chancellor of England and a martyr.[1] There is an unverified tradition that Erasmus and More met each other at an official banquet without having been presented to each other. After a moment of conversation with his companion, Erasmus cried out: 'This man can only be Thomas More,' and for his part, More had replied: 'If it is not the Devil, this man can only be Erasmus.' This trenchant dialogue is as good as any possible snapshot.

Erasmus was eight years older than More. Between these two men of exceptional intellectual ability what bold ideas found expression, what passionate discussions took place on inexhaustible subjects: God and man, the universe and Christianity, peace and war! A great friendship began, which was to be interrupted only by death. Erasmus said of Thomas More: 'Nature has produced nothing more tender, sweeter or happier than the character of Thomas More.'[2]

Erasmus spent the next two months in Oxford, where he was a guest of Richard Charnock at St Mary's College. There he met John Colet, the renowned theologian, and was present at his lectures on the Epistles of St Paul. A happy man, Erasmus was received without question as a humanist who was under no compulsion to know the country's language. He loved England with a romantic passion and spent many bright hours, such as he had never known in Paris. In London, he didn't see the fog. The sun, rarer and more timid than in Paris, seemed more sparkling and precious. Nobody reminded him of his humble origins. He was no longer the starving student of the old Sorbonne. He was possessed of an exultant feeling of beauty, of joy – in a word, of life. He joined enthusiastically in horse-riding and participated in the worldly, as well as the intellectual, life of high London society. His ignorance of English was no handicap, for he was friends only with the humanists, and Latin was enough for him.

His love for England, where during several sojourns he spent more than five years between 1499 and 1517, shone out in his exchanges with Fausto Andrelini, whose taste for banter was well known to him:

> There are in England nymphs of divine appearance, both engaging and agreeable, whom you would certainly prefer to your Muses; and there is, besides, one custom which can never be commended too highly. When you arrive anywhere, you are received with kisses on all sides, and when you take your leave they speed you on your way with kisses. The kisses are renewed when you come back. When guests come to your house, their arrival is pledged with kisses; and when they leave, kisses are shared once again. If you should happen to meet, then kisses are given profusely. In a word, wherever you turn, the world is full of kisses.[3]

This letter, the first written from England, and possibly in imitation of Catullus, is the only example of an almost playful gaiety, and is an exceptional expression from a generally reserved man. Doubtless some would see in the evocation of this social function the vague yearning for pleasures that he had not known, but of which he dreamed. Erasmus, who had quickly readapted to the most austere form of real life, was to publish this amusing letter in one of his collections, which seems to show that he judged it to be no danger to his reputation. Courteous, friendly and eloquent, he could have become, in this fickle and sensitive atmosphere, a man of the world, perhaps even a dandy, but he was too hungry for knowledge to lose long hours in the salons, with pretty nymphs. But there was no doubt that the sunny side of his nature was developed and strengthened in a climate of confidence, joy, culture and comfort. This character trait was to remain very marked through the rest of his life.

The most gratifying event of his first English season was undoubtedly his meetings with the children of Henry VII. Thomas More came to Mountjoy's home at Greenwich. He took Erasmus off for a walk to Eltham, to the palace where the royal princes, the future King Henry VIII and his sisters, were being brought up. During the meal, the young prince sent Erasmus a note, which is sadly lost. The reply came some days later: a letter and a poem, both in Latin.[4] Erasmus was to preserve for a long time a great admiration for a prince who showed himself so advanced and so welcoming from his tenth year.

The culture of the English humanists who received Erasmus as an equal or a master, in London, Oxford, and later in Cambridge, seemed to him exceptionally enviable. He expressed enthusiastic praise of it to Robert Fisher, his old pupil, who had become the king's agent in Italy:

> But you ask, 'how does our England please you?' If you trust me at all, dear Robert, I should wish you to trust me when I say that I have never found a place I like so much. I find here a climate at once agreeable and extremely healthy, and such a quantity of intellectual refinement and scholarship, not of the usual pedantic and trivial kind either, but profound and learned and truly classical, in both Latin and Greek, that I have little longing left for Italy, except for the sake of visiting it. When I listen to Colet it seems to me that I am listening to Plato himself. Who could fail to be astonished at the universal scope of Grocyn's accomplishment? Could anything be more clever or profound or sophisticated than Linacre's mind? Did Nature ever create anything kinder, sweeter, or more harmonious than the character of Thomas More? But why need I rehearse the list further? It is marvellous to see what an extensive and rich crop of ancient learning is springing up here in England; and therefore ought you all the more to hurry home.[5]

His admiration for John Colet was particularly accentuated and the correspondence exchanged by the two men shows the depth of their friendship. Colet exercised a decisive influence on the spiritual evolution of Erasmus.[6] Thanks to him, Erasmus discovered the Platonism of Marsilio Ficino. He came to appreciate modern theology and exegesis, a far cry from the wearisome reasonings of the Sorbonne.

Erasmus presented himself to Colet in a relaxed and confident manner and not without a degree of complacency:

> The person you are to confront is of slender means, or rather, none; knows nothing of ambition, but has a great disposition towards affection; enjoys but little experience of letters, but admits to a consuming passion for them; is scrupulous in respecting others' moral excellence, having none himself; yields pride of place to all in scholarship, to none in loyalty; is straightforward, frank, outspoken, incapable alike of pretence or concealment; in character humble but sincere; no great talker; in fact, one from whom you should not look for anything, except a friendly attitude. If you, Colet, can love a man of this sort, if you consider him worthy of your friendship, then pray stamp Erasmus as the most securely yours of all your possessions.[7]

This is how Erasmus saw himself, and it is thus that we can imagine him.

Colet, for his part, expressed the admiration which he had felt for Erasmus after reading his letter to Gaguin, the praises he had heard in Paris, and Charnock's recommendations. He concluded:

> So far, therefore, as letters and knowledge and integrity of character may go to recommend anyone to a person who rather desires and longs for these things than can boast of them himself, so far are you, Erasmus, most highly recommended to me on the strength of these virtues which exist in you ... I hope you may like our country as much as I think you are capable of benefiting her by your scholarship; while for my part I regard you, and shall continue to regard you, as a person whom I consider to be eminently virtuous as well as eminently learned.[8]

Erasmus was offered a teaching post, but refused it and declared emphatically to Colet: 'I have not come to these shores to teach literature, in verse or prose. Literature ceased to have charms for me as soon as it ceased to be necessary to me.'[9] With Colet and other friends on whom he could rely, Erasmus expounded freely on one passage or another of Scripture. From these exchanges, sometimes lively, but always cordial, there remains for us the *Disputatiuncula de tedio, pauore, tristicia Jesu, instante crucis hora.*[10] In it we hear Erasmus and Colet taking opposite sides in a friendly fashion on the subject of the reason for Christ's suffering. While Colet accorded the primary role to the metaphysical anguish of the redemption, with Jesus taking on himself the sin which the Jews have committed, Erasmus remained faithful to tradition: it was the human nature of Jesus that experienced the horror and terrified him when he cried out: 'Father, let this cup pass from me,' at the same time adding, 'Let your will be done, not mine!' Taking the logic of the Incarnation to its extreme, Erasmus underlined its realism.[11] He added – certainly with Colet on this point – that Christ thought more of the love of men than of their admiration. He remained faithful to this conclusion, and was to develop it and later to write: 'Compulsion cannot be joined with sincerity and Christ accepts only the voluntary gift of our souls.'[12]

In between two periods of work the friends continued their debates and sometimes exchanged less orthodox remarks in the course of fraternal revels. Erasmus was to describe mockingly one of these little colloquies. 'Colet asserted that the sin by which Cain first angered God was that, as though he lacked faith in the Creator's goodwill and placed too much trust in his own efforts, he was the first to plough the earth, whereas Abel pastured his sheep, in contentment with things that grew of themselves.'[13] Erasmus did not contradict this classic explanation, but he told this chapter in the experience of Cain in his own way.

'This Cain', said I, 'was not merely a hard worker but greedy and avaricious as well. Now, he had often heard his parents say that in the paradise they had been forced to leave bountiful crops grew of their own accord, with ears of generous size and enormous seeds and stalks so tall that they matched an alder tree of today, and not a tare or thorn or thistle growing among them. He laid this well to heart and, as he observed that the soil he was working at the time grudged him even a mean and meagre crop, he added a dash of cunning to his hard work. Approaching the angel who stood watch over the gate of the garden, and laying siege to him with artful tricks, he managed, by making extravagant promises, to persuade the angel secretly to make him a gift of just a very few seeds from its more abundant harvests. He claimed that God had ceased to pay heed or attention to the matter for some time past, and that, even if he were to find out, it would be easy for the angel to escape punishment as it was an affair of no consequence so long as hands were not laid upon the actual fruit, to which alone God's prohibition under penalty had applied.

'Now, then', he said, 'you ought not to show an excess of zeal in your capacity as gatekeeper. What if your overconscientiousness is positively unwelcome to the Lord, and he wishes you to be deceived and is likely to be more gratified when mankind displays brains and hard work [than] idleness and sloth? Do you get any satisfaction from your present post? God has turned you from an angel into an executioner so that you might cruelly keep us poor, lost creatures out of our fatherland. He has chained you to the door, sword and all, a function that we have begun lately to assign to dogs. It is true that we are most unhappy, but it seems to me that you yourself are in considerably worse case; for, while we are deprived of the garden for tasting too-sweet fruit, you for your part have to miss both Heaven and garden alike, in order to keep us out, and are more wretched than we, inasmuch as we at least can wander hither and yon wherever we choose . . . Cain won his wicked case – a thoroughly bad man, but a consummate orator.[14]

And so Erasmus joked, to entertain himself and his friends, with no concern for dispelling myths.

Another form of diversion was poetry. Erasmus was a harsh judge of the poem which he had just dedicated to the English royal children,[15] but he was to continue to write verse to the end of his life. For him, there was no contradiction between theology and poetry,[16] between lyricism and spirituality. However, here too Erasmus had a perceptive assessment of himself, for it was not his poetry, but his prose, that was to make of him one of the great Latin writers.[17]

The first stay in England was a great success for Erasmus, the fireworks which crowned his thirtieth year. The generosity of his English hosts allowed him to face the future with confidence. Armed with some savings, he left London at the beginning of 1500 for Paris to oversee the printing of his first important work, the *Adages*. A regulation of which neither More nor Mountjoy was aware strictly limited the amount of gold and silver coin that could be taken out of the country, whether it was English or foreign. And so at Dover zealous customs officials confiscated almost all the traveller's resources.

Overcome and deeply affected by this humiliation, Erasmus saw his hopes disappear. A precarious life and thankless work awaited him anew. Once again he was going to have to beg support from the rich. Moreover, on the way to Paris, he escaped only with difficulty from the greed of those who were hiring out horses. He was to talk for a long time about this disastrous return, even if, after getting over the first shock, he came to look upon his misadventures with more humour than bitterness.

In the midst of these problems, his friend Batt was quick to inform Mountjoy:

> The return of my friend Erasmus is something I looked for and longed for ardently, not because I envied you his company, but because my affection for him was boundless. At the same time, I could not fail to be most distressed by the news he gave me of that dreadful misfortune he had suffered, a misfortune I foresaw long ago. Of course I always was apprehensive on his behalf.
>
> ... What a wonderful thing is philosophy, which he has always preached as well as practised! It was my duty to alleviate his distress with comforting words; but instead he smiled and checked my tears and told me to be cheerful. He said that he had no regrets at having gone to England. He had not lost that sum of money without receiving great rewards in its place, because in England he had made such friends as he preferred to the wealth of Croesus.
>
> We spent two nights together. He spoke with passionate enthusiasm, and great eloquence, of the graciousness of prior Richard, of the erudition of Colet, and of the sweetness of More, with the result that if I were free I should myself like to visit men as scholarly and affable as these.[18]

Erasmus happily returned to England. In 1505 he enrolled in the Faculty of Theology at Cambridge to prepare himself for his doctorate. At the same time he perfected his Greek, applying himself at the same time to pagan literature and to the Bible. In collaboration with Thomas More, he translated the dialogues of Lucian into Latin and put into his preface a portrait of the author which equally matched each of the translators:

> How graciously he expresses himself! How fertile is his imagination! What charm in his joking! What bite in his criticism! He irritates in his

allusions, he confuses the serious with the trivial and the trivial with the serious. He speaks the truth while having fun and has fun while speaking the truth. He describes so well the behaviour of men, their passions, their efforts, that one seems to be not reading but seeing in reality what he paints in words. No satire, no comedy equals his dialogues.[19]

Erasmus also translated Euripides; he dedicated the *Hecuba* and the *Iphigenia* to William Warham, Primate of England and Archbishop of Canterbury, who protected and assisted him with all his powers. 'He is my only patron,' said Erasmus, 'and I owe him everything.' Under Colet's watchful eye he applied himself to the critical study of the Vulgate, a thankless task which was only to see the light of day ten years later. Eventually he made the acquaintance of an Italian resident in England, Andrea Ammonio, who was to become his most intimate confidant.

At this time Erasmus received a dispensation from Rome which enabled him to obtain a benefice despite his illegitimate birth.[20] The doctorate seemed to him to be within his grasp. He no longer faced the difficulties he had faced on the Continent. England seemed to open the way towards ecclesiastical benefices and University honours. His personal charm served him well. But then the old plan of a trip to Italy rose up again and Erasmus could not resist it. Leaving England, he was in Paris in June 1506 and wrote to his friend Thomas Linacre, the king's doctor, that his heart was torn between France and England.

France pleases me so much, now that I have returned to it, that I am not sure which country holds the greater charm for me – England, which has made me so many good friends or France, which is sweet to me for old acquaintance's sake, and because she it was who gave me my freedom, and lastly because of the pronounced favour and encouragement she has accorded me. As a result I am luxuriating in a kind of double pleasure: it gives me equal joy to remember my stay in England, especially since I hope I may repeat it soon, and to revisit my friends in France.[21]

Erasmus was in Italy during the second half of 1506, as we shall see later. He stayed there for three years, after which he returned to England, in 1509, for a stay of some years, interrupted with brief return visits to the Continent. He left Rome as suddenly as he had left London, three years earlier. He felt the call of England again. A young king, Henry VIII, a friend of learning and letters, had just ascended the throne. He seemed to Erasmus destined by Providence to become the great patron who would finally bring him security and stability. It was not the king who invited him, though Erasmus said so later, but his friend Mountjoy, who was in favour in court and overflowing with enthusiasm.

Oh, Erasmus, if you could only see how happily excited everyone is here, and how all are congratulating themselves on their prince's greatness, and how they pray above all for his long life, you would be bound to weep for joy! Heaven smiles, earth rejoices; all is milk and honey and nectar. Tight-fistedness is well and truly banished. Generosity scatters wealth with unstinting hand. Our king's heart is set not upon gold or jewels or mines of ore, but upon virtue, reputation, and eternal renown. Here is a mere sample: a few days ago, when he said that he longed to be a more accomplished scholar, I remarked, 'We do not expect this of you; what we expect is that you should foster and encourage those who are scholars.' 'Of course,' he replied, 'for without them we could scarcely exist.' What better remark could be made by any king? . . . The reason why I have decided to place these few scraps of compliment to his divine highness at the very beginning of my letter is just so that I may lose no time in abolishing any vestiges of depression left in your mind. . . . So look after your health and come back to us as soon as you can.[22]

Erasmus received this unexpected request during the month of June 1509. How could he resist it? No one at this time could foresee the bloody future of Henry VIII. This warm, tempting invitation was accompanied by a substantial letter of credit. A month later, in July, Erasmus was in London, after travelled rapidly through Bologna, Chur, Constance, Strasbourg and Antwerp. The Italian interlude was over: Erasmus would never return beyond the Alps. While crossing the Alps, in rhythm with his horse, Erasmus had begun *The Praise of Folly*. He was to conclude it very quickly while staying at More's house. More, who had now remarried, remained his favourite friend, but he was not the only one.

'Friendship', said Erasmus, 'is to be preferred to everything in the world; it is no less necessary than water, air or fire.'[23] Love, which is self-giving by definition, does not impoverish the one who gives. There was only one limit to the expression of friendship for Erasmus, that which he laid down for himself to protect his daily work from useless conversation and babbling. For him, the heart did not hinder the spirit: he was always to maintain a genuine veneration for friendship, and total loyalty for his intimate friends.

Though rich in friends, Erasmus was often without funds. The money promised by Henry VIII was handed out to him parsimoniously, while the *Folly* earned him renown, but no fortune. He looked like a humble beggar. He liked neither the climate nor the beer of Cambridge, and wrote about his situation to John Colet:

But I ask you, what could be more shameless or abject than I, who have long been a-begging publicly in England? I have received so much from the archbishop that it would be unspeakably selfish to take anything more from him, even if he were to offer it . . . Now I am appearing too immodest even to our friend Linacre; though he knew I was leaving London furnished with barely six nobles, and he well knows my health and also that winter is coming on, yet he solicitously advises me to spare the archbishop and Lord Mountjoy and rather to accustom myself to bear poverty bravely. What friendly advice! Yet it is for this reason most of all that I hate my luck, in that it will not allow me to be modest.[24]

Erasmus was miserable, and realized it. He suffered from this unjust fate. Some days later, he confided to Ammonio: 'I will return to you about the first of January – so at least we shall feel the cold less by keeping each other warm. For I would rather summer than winter here.'[25] At the request of John Colet, who had been called to run St Paul's school, Erasmus wrote a *Sermon on the Infant Jesus*, which is a prayer put into the mouths of pious students.

If Erasmus aspired to material independence, if he suffered privations in London, he was no less the devout and faithful Christian that he remained throughout his life. This aspect of his personality seems to have escaped some of his biographers, blinded by his anticlerical violence and his merciless critique of superstition. He spoke of it in this way: 'Dear Andrea, I have taken a solemn vow for the happy outcome of the Church's affairs. I see you approve my piety already! I am to pay a visit to Our Lady of Walsingham, and I will there hang up a votive offering of a Greek poem. Look for it if you ever visit the place.'[26] In the votive offering presented by Erasmus after his pilgrimage, he depicted himself as a poor poet who had only his verse to offer to Our Lady. His piety expressed itself ingenuously. The only grace for which he asked was a pure heart pleasing to God.

Later, in the dialogue *The Pilgrimage*, Ogygius recounts how he offered a Greek poem to Our Lady of Walsingham.[27] This was a transposition of Erasmus's experience; but if Ogygius defines Erasmus's thought, he also conveys his disenchantment. Erasmus's critique was born of his disappointment, but it was a different disappointment from that of his pilgrimage to St Thomas of Canterbury.[28] He accompanied John Colet there and stressed his friend's indignant impatience in the presence of the indecent relics which the guardian of the sanctuary exhibited without batting an eyelid. In his *Colloquies*, Erasmus was to deplore the sumptuousness of the shrine of St Thomas and condemn the commercialization of his cult.[29]

Erasmus often criticized the errors of popular devotion. A striking example of this was the cult of relics and favoured places which had become the centre of pilgrimages. He did not like these too-well-orchestrated displays, with their great gatherings of people and exhibitions of suspect relics. Their boisterous crowds were repugnant to this pious and solitary Christian, who went neither to Compostella nor to Jerusalem nor to Loreto.

In Erasmus's time, pilgrimages were many and intrusive. There was no church without its miraculous statue or notable relic. There was always a saint waiting for the believer at the turn in the road, and not just on the famous roads of the major pilgrimages. It was impossible to travel without seeing churches overrun with pilgrims. The 'Golden Legend' had accentuated the glory of the healing saints and miracle workers at the expense of history. The Renaissance era was still saturated with these pilgrimages on the cheap, and Erasmus – a pilgrim on occasions, but with a totally different spirit – was scandalized and bothered by them. He accepted the religious value of pilgrimages as well as of devotions in general, but he could not but denounce their abuses and deviations. In this, Erasmus showed himself to be at once revolutionary and traditional – revolutionary in fighting against the best-established conformism, and traditional because his reservations were those of the better minds, from St Jerome to Thomas À Kempis.[30] This apparent contradiction was entirely Erasmian. Thus one cannot say that Erasmus wanted to desacralize the pilgrimage: he desired only a return to its primitive function and a purification of its methods.

In summary, for the individualist Erasmus, the pilgrimage had all the faults of the gregarious spirit, and even of tourism, of which it constituted the original form. Now, our humanist did not enter a country to visit it, but to meet its men of learning, to read manuscripts there. Being in crowds affronted his delicacy and threatened his fragile nature. Yet he was not one of those aristocratic believers who, to practise an enlightened religion, parted from the common way. If he preferred other manifestations of piety, more intimate and personal, he nevertheless yielded to this one with simplicity and without malice. Erasmus knew how difficult it was to be only God's pilgrim. He wanted to be, and felt himself to be, in the Church; his ambition was to be a Christian among others, if not like the others. Pilgrimage, despite all his justified criticism of it, remained for him a brotherly gesture and a proof of the childlike spirit without which there was no true philosophy of Christ.

The plague, which was rife in London, drove Erasmus to Cambridge where he mainly lived from 1511 to 1514. At the University, of which his friend John Fisher was Chancellor, Erasmus lived at Queens' College and he gave public lessons in Greek. In quick succession he published two pedagogical works whose success was to be immediate and long-lasting: the *On the Method of Study*[31] and *Foundations of the abundant style.*[32]

On the Method of Study put forward the idea of reducing the teaching of grammar to the basic essentials and introducing the young to the art of conversation: 'For since young children can pronounce any language, however barbarous, within months, is there any reason why the same thing should not occur in Greek or Latin? But there is no scope for this in a large crowd of boys and it requires the private company of a teacher.'[33] These pedagogical ideas of Erasmus found warm approval with John Colet. *Foundations of the abundant style*, whose title indicates its purpose well, was dedicated to Colet, and brought forth from Thomas More a telling word: 'Erasmus has delivered us his *Abundant Style*. What remains for him, if not extreme destitution?'

Through his books, Erasmus became the teacher of the teachers and the champion of precise language for the sake of elegant and effective discourse. A shrewd letter from the Parisian printer Josse Bade shows the success of Erasmus's books and the meagre nature of their author's revenue.

> As to the rest, let me briefly tell you the price I have personally settled upon. We agreed on fifteen florins for the *Adagia*, if I remember correctly. You have received ten, and I am to pay you five more, and three for the original text. I shall gladly agree to pay another fifteen florins for the revision of the letters of St Jerome, and as much again for what you have just sent me. You will protest loudly at the smallness of the price. I admit that I could offer no recompense to match your ability, application, scholarship, and toil; but the most glorious rewards will be accorded in the first place by Heaven, and then by your own virtuous character. As you have eminently well served secular literature, both Greek and Latin, so you will in this way serve sacred literature also, and help your humble friend Bade, who has a large family and no income save the fruits of his daily toil. Come, then Erasmus, my cherished refuge; send me your agreement . . .[34]

In 1513 and 1514 Erasmus prepared a new edition of the *Adages*, a St Jerome, a Seneca, a Cato and, above all, he worked tirelessly on one of his greatest works, the Greek and Latin edition of the New Testament. His correspondence with European men of learning was considerable, but the couriers were often unreliable. They lost the letters, drank the wine they were transporting, or disappeared without leaving a trace.

Erasmus could not allow himself the luxury of rejecting thankless, but profitable, tasks. He received £20 for drafting the epitaph for Margaret, Countess of Richmond, in Westminster Abbey. He found himself to have become, besides, an 'Anglophile Hollander.'[35] To the great Hebraist Johann Reuchlin he confided: 'In these days, England has its own Italy and (unless I am quite wrong) something more distinguished than Italy.'[36] Meanwhile, to an intimate he revealed his worries:

I have been living a snail's life for several months now, Ammonio; enclosed and bottled up at home, I brood over my studies. Everything is very deserted here, most people being away for fear of the plague; though even when all of them are present, it is a lonely place for me. Expenses are impossibly high, and not a penny to be made. Imagine that I have just sworn this to you by all that is holy. I have been here for less than five months so far, but in this period I have spent about sixty nobles. I have received just one from certain hearers of my lectures, and I took that under strong protests and with unwillingness. I have determined in these winter months to leave no stone unturned and in fact to 'cast my sheet anchor' as they say. If this is successful, I shall then find myself some retreat; but if it fails, I have made up my mind to fly away from here, I do not know where. If nothing else, at least I shall die elsewhere.[37]

At last, thanks to the liberality of the Archbishop and Primate, William Warham, Erasmus was named Curate of Aldington, in Kent. He breathed again. Incapable of filling his charge, since he did not know the language of his parishioners and, besides, was not keen to renounce his vocation of learning, the new curate had himself replaced by a priest-in-charge, with whom he divided the revenues of the benefice.[38]

After a stay in Basel and a brief journey to the Frankfurt fair, Erasmus returned to England for some weeks during the month of May 1515. From London he wrote many letters declaring his enthusiasm for his English friends and patrons. He did not forget his printer in Basel, Johann Froben, and the Hebraists, the brothers Amerbach: all of them were working on Erasmus's edition of St Jerome. Finally, he nostalgically recalled his stay in Rome.

Erasmus's life was illuminated by his friendship with Thomas More. A complete intimacy grew between the twice married layman and the discharged monk, thanks to their intellectual and spiritual affinities. It was More who defended *The Praise of Folly* against the Louvain theologian Martin Dorp. When *Utopia*[39] appeared – the legendary story of Wisdom which exists Nowhere – it was Erasmus, assisted by the obliging Pieter Gillis, who found him an editor at Louvain in 1516. *Utopia*, a humanist and anti-scholastic work like *The Praise of Folly*, is at once Morean and Erasmian. Like Erasmus, More unites a spiritual irreverence for men with a deep respect for faith and, if Folly is everywhere, one should rather look for Wisdom at a distance, even in some fortunate island.

The correspondence of the two friends was built on a friendly exchange of information and services. More intervened whenever it was appropriate to obtain pensions or subsidies for Erasmus. He was pre-occupied with his manuscripts, his books, his health, and even with his horses; and his attentive solicitude allowed him to penetrate to the heart of his friend's personality. He wrote to Dorp in 1515:

In fact nothing gives [Erasmus] more pleasure than to praise absent friends to friends present, and since his learning and his delightful disposition have endeared him to so many people in various parts of the world, he is constantly trying to make all of these share with each other the same special attachment which binds them to him. Thus he never stops mentioning each of his friends one by one to the rest or describing the gifts for which each one merits love.[40]

Erasmus, for his part, assured More of his true place in literary history. He was to preface the Basel edition of *Utopia*. More confided to Erasmus in 1516: 'We are "together, you and I, a crowd"; that is my feeling, and I think I could live happily with you in any wilderness.'[41] Meanwhile, the opportunities for the two friends to live together, in solitude or in the world, became more rare. If More's household, since his remarriage in 1511, remained an occasional sanctuary, it could no longer be a permanent home for Erasmus. In 1517, while a guest at Louvain of his friend Desmarais, Rector of the University, Erasmus explained his perplexities to More.

I have not yet made up my mind where to settle. I do not care for Spain, to which I am again invited by the Cardinal of Toledo. In Germany I do not care for the stoves, nor for the roads beset with robbers. Here there is a lot of mutual recrimination and no advantage to be enjoyed, and I could not stay here very long, however much I might want to. In England I am afraid of riots and terrified of becoming a servant.[42]

In the spring of 1517, Erasmus stayed in England for the last time. There he received from Ammonio the pontifical absolution from the censures that he had incurred by having abandoned the monastery and the habit. His return ended with a dramatic and perilous disembarkation on the French coast near Boulogne. He was never to go back to England, but he maintained many contacts with his friends and protectors. Sadly, Ammonio died in 1517 and Colet in 1519. As for More, he had accepted, with heroic loyalty, a position in the service of Henry VIII. Erasmus was not pleased with this, feeling sorry for his friend for having to accept a political role as time-consuming as it was prestigious. He wrote to him: 'As for your being haled to court, I have one consolation, that you will serve under an excellent king, but certainly you are lost to literature and to us.'[43]

In 1517 also, Erasmus and Pieter Gillis had themselves painted at Antwerp for their friend More, by Quentin Metsys.[44] Pieter Gillis was one of those second-rank people whom friendship had made a part of history. He divided his time between the administration of the city of Antwerp and literature. For his friends he was a host at once modest and generous. Thomas More dedicated the *Utopia* to him and Erasmus the *Parables*.

The bad health of Erasmus and Gillis slowed down the work of painting. With humour – perhaps England's most precious gift to Erasmus – the latter described the situation to More:

> Pieter Gillis and I are being painted on the same panel, which we shall soon send you as a present. But it so happened, very inconveniently, that on my return I found Pieter seriously ill, even dangerously, from some sickness I know not what . . . I myself was in capital health, but somehow the physician took it into his head to tell me to take some pills to purge my bile, and the advice he foolishly gave me I was fool enough to take. My portrait has already started; but after taking the medicine, when I went back to the painter, he said it was not the same face, and so the painter was put off for several days, until I look more cheerful.[45]

To this More replied: 'The panel which is to record for me the likeness of you and our dear friend Pieter I await with indescribable impatience and curse the ill-health that so long keeps my hopes unfulfilled.'[46]

Finally, Erasmus was able to send the double portrait. 'I send you the pictures,' he declared to More, 'so that you may still have our company after a fashion, if some chance removes us from the scene. Pieter contributed one half and I the other – not that either of us would not have gladly paid the whole, but we wanted it to be a present from us both.'[47] More acknowledged his receipt of the panels: 'You would hardly believe, my most lovable Erasmus, how my affection for you, which I was convinced would admit of no addition, has been increased by this desire of yours to bind me still closer to you.'[48]

More's enthusiasm was displayed in the text that he dedicated to the famous diptych:

> . . . Erasmus and Pieter Gillis were portrayed together by that excellent artist Quentin, in such a fashion that behind Erasmus, who is beginning his Paraphrase on the Epistle to the Romans, his books were painted each with its title, while Pieter held a letter addressed to him in More's hand, which was actually imitated by the painter. The picture speaks:
>
> > *Castor and Pollux were great friends of old:*
> > *Erasmus such and Gillis you behold.*

Far from them, More laments with love so dear
As scarce a man unto himself could bear.[49]

The double portrait – More called it *tabula duplex* – was divided at an unknown date, with the portrait of Pieter Gillis preserved at Longford Castle, while that of Erasmus can be admired at Hampton Court.

The painter represented Erasmus in three-quarter face, at his work table with his pen in hand. The facial expression is serious and serene, the nose straight and rather long. The model seems to be in good health, but he is not really smiling. Erasmus has 'the look of a reader of Utopia. The eyes are seeking, a little over the horizon, a happy image for which the mouth is about to smile, and which the beautiful fine, firm hand awaits to record with confidence.'[50] This admirable portrait is the oldest one of which we know. Thanks to it, we at last see Erasmus in his prime, on the threshold of the sad conflicts which were to poison his existence.

Erasmus spoke of More with a full heart:

He takes a particular pleasure in contemplating the shapes, character, and behaviour of different living creatures. Thus there is hardly any kind of bird of which he does not keep one in his household, and the same with any animal that as a rule is rarely seen, such as monkey, fox, ferret, weasel and the like. Besides these, if he sees anything outlandish or otherwise remarkable, he buys it greedily, and has his house stocked with such things from all sources, so that everywhere you may see something to attract the eyes of the visitor; and when he sees other people pleased, his own pleasure begins anew. . . . In his younger days he was not averse from affairs with young women, but always without dishonour, enjoying such things when they came his way without going out to seek them, and attracted by the mingling of minds rather than bodies. . . . And all the time he applied his whole mind to the pursuit of piety, with vigils and fasts and prayer and similar exercises preparing himself for the priesthood. In this indeed he showed not a little more sense than those who plunge headlong into so exacting a vocation without first making trial of themselves. Nor did anything stand in the way of his devoting himself to this kind of life, except that he could not shake off the desire to get married. And so he chose to be a God-fearing husband rather than an immoral priest.

However he chose for his wife an unmarried girl who was still very young, of good family and quite inexperienced as yet, having always lived in the country with her parents and her sisters, which gave him the more opportunity to mould her character to match his own. He arranged for her education and made her skilled in music of every kind, and had (it is clear) almost succeeded in making her a person with whom he would gladly have shared his whole life, had not an early death removed her from the scene, after she had borne him several children. Of these there survive three daughters, Margaret, Alice and Cecily, and one son, John. Nor did he endure to remain a widower for very long, though the advice of his friends urged a different course. A few months after his wife's death, he married a widow, more to have someone to look after his household than for his own pleasure, for she was neither beautiful nor in her first youth, as he used to remark in jest, but a capable and watchful housewife, though they lived on as close and affectionate terms as if she had been a girl of the most winning appearance. Few husbands secure as much obedience from their wives by severity and giving them orders as he did by his kindness and his merry humour. He could make her do anything: did he not already cause a woman already past the prime of life, of a far from elastic disposition, and devoted to her household affairs, to learn to play the zither, the lute, the monochord, and the recorder, and in this department to produce a set piece of work every day to please her exacting husband?[51]

Erasmus and More were to meet again for a last time at Bruges in 1521. Their friendship was to transcend all separations.[52] Though Erasmus may have suffered from the English climate, once the colourful memories of his first stay had faded, though he may have fallen into the hands of 'butchers' (doctors) and 'harpies' (pharmacists) and his death had been foretold twice there, he loved England.[53] It would remain his 'second homeland', the country of the great friendships of his mature years. Nowhere else was he to find this sweet euphoria.

6

Paris and Louvain: From the First *Adages* to the *Panegyric*

Returning from his first journey to England at the beginning of 1500, Erasmus lived for most of the time in Paris, where he rediscovered his friends and his editors. From the vast array of his reading he drew out material for several books, not by stringing together the texts of his favourite authors, but by building up well-chosen collections of extracts with commentary. And so in 1500 the *Adages* was brought to birth, not a very accessible work to the modern reader, but one read and re-read a hundred times by Renaissance schoolboys, who discovered in it ancient culture represented by proverbs and quotations, both given in full and set in the context of the history of thought, language and institutions.[1]

The volume had the appearance of a little dictionary of some hundreds of expressions sanctioned by good usage, with brief explanations. In it Erasmus created his self-portrait as Hercules, the collector of adages, and he skilfully recalled that in Antiquity, 'adages were seized upon as if they were oracles.'[2] The dedicatory letter to Mountjoy explained the author's purpose in evocative terms:

> So I put aside my nightly labours over a more serious work and strolled through divers gardens of the classics, occupied in this lighter kind of study, and so plucked, and as it were arranged in garlands, like flowerets of every hue, all the most ancient and famous of the adages. . . . Now it is surely common knowledge that, as far as prose style is concerned, its resources and its pleasures alike consist of epigrams, metaphors, figures, paradigms, examples, similes, images, and such turns of speech; and while these devices always add considerably to the distinction of one's style, they confer an exceptional amount of elegance and grace when they have come to form part of the accepted idiom and the daily coin of language, inasmuch as everyone gives a ready ear to what he recognizes; but especially is this true when there is the additional recommendation, so to speak, of antiquity. Proverbs improve with age exactly as wines do. . . .

If at this point you look for a single instance, among the multitudes that you will meet with everywhere, here in front of your very eyes is one that I have for better or worse commented upon: 'Let us laugh sardonically', to be found in Cicero's letters. Into what devious explanations, what mazes of error does it not send its commentators? If, again, as Christians we feel more drawn to an instance taken from a Christian writer, then I should not hesitate to put forward Jerome to represent this numerous class, for his scholarship is so profound and so various that, compared with him, the others appear able neither to swim, as the saying goes, nor to read and write. And, furthermore, his power of expression is so great, he writes with such authority and incisiveness, and possesses such a rich and varied equipment of metaphor and illusion, that in comparison with him one would pronounce other theologians to be mere Seriphian frogs. Now, you will find in Jerome's books a greater number of adages than in the comedies of Menander, and extremely witty ones too, such as these: 'The ox taken to the wrestling ring', 'A camel has danced', 'A hard wedge for a hard knot', 'To drive out a nail with a nail', 'The weary ox more heavily doth tread', and 'The cover suits the dish'. Again, his allegorical sobriquets ('The Christian Epicurus', 'The Aristarchus of our generation') have a very strong natural resemblance to adages. . . .

But – not to extend the list too far – the whole point of this verbose review was to show that the amount of attention paid by authors to proverbs is in proportion to the distinction of their literary style, so that we puny critics should not believe that we have the right to despise the genre. . . . It is just this metaphorical style of expression that has always been the special distinguishing mark, not of professional stylists, but of philosophers and prophets and divines. And this was easily the favourite among many objects that the sages of ancient days strove to attain. We, today, alas, are as far behind them in wisdom as we have outrun them in garrulity.[3]

Here then was a book of readings for a Christian humanist, with a preface by Fausto Andrelini. In Erasmus's thought the *Adages* – it was the fame of his book that brought the word into modern usage – amounted to a summation of ancient wisdom, an anthology of good authors, the weapon of Minerva, the herbarium of classical culture. The prodigious success of the work and its widespread use by scholars proved that Erasmus had perceived things correctly and had chosen his pathway well. From now on his reputation was established. Within the astonishing intellectual enterprise of the Renaissance, and the general movement for a return to the sources to provide a firm anchor for modern culture, no one knew better than he the institutions and the literature of Antiquity. The *Adages* contributed powerfully to the spreading of the classical spirit and through this their author reinforced the international character of culture.

If Erasmus was fast becoming famous as a man of letters, he received few of the rights of an author. Publishers did not always buy his works from him. Some of them did not even ask his authorization to print the manuscripts that he had imprudently entrusted to his pupils or to friends of meagre scruples. In the best cases, he received a number of copies which he could sell for his own profit. Moreover, publishers presented him with gifts if his books sold quickly and well, which often happened in the case of such a fashionable author; besides, those to whom the books were dedicated showed their gratitude to the author who was making their names famous and who praised their generosity. Some, unfortunately, would not give a cent.

While he was composing scholarly books, Erasmus was also preparing critical editions of Latin authors and Latin translations of Greek authors. He was to publish, among others, Euripides, Demosthenes, Lucian and Plutarch, Cicero, Horace, Ovid, Titus Livy, Plautus, Terence and Seneca.

His native Dutch was reduced to the level of a purely utilitarian language. Erasmus wanted to speak only Latin because for him Latin was a living language! All his letters, all his works, were in beautiful Latin. He knew all the tricks of writing. His style was lively, full of imagery, often racy, sometimes vivid. As a narrator he was full of verve, but the essay with its digressions and repetitions remained his preferred sphere, his chosen field.

The place occupied by Erasmus in literary history was due in good measure to his talent as a letter-writer. He wrote letters – like Cicero or like Voltaire – with a certain agreeable style, knowing that he would not just be read by his correspondents, but by other readers, and so addressing himself to the world and to posterity. He himself was to publish some of his own letters, the most typical, the best finished, the most lively. His mastery of Latin compelled recognition from the reader throughout this rich, spiritual, graceful, if not always spontaneous, correspondence. The letters to his friends represent a particularly beguiling blend of affection and mischief. A good example is his reply to a somewhat sermonizing letter from his friend Jacob Batt, director of the school at Bergen-op-Zoom and a good friend of Anna Van Veere, his patron at the time:

> Have you revived only to slay me with an abusive letter? The news came that you had already taken to your bed, and that the doctor was already preparing to operate and you were waiting for the knife. Meantime I was mourning for you, and sadly rehearsing your epitaph. Then, of all things, up you sprang and challenged me to a duel of invective! And yet, dear Batt, I should far rather be writing a war of invectives, even the fiercest, with you, than playing the part even of a devoted friend if it involved the

duty of writing your epitaph. Come on, then: let us gird on our swords, since you are the first to issue the call to arms. What desperate rashness! Do you venture, puny creature that you are, to insult and provoke a hero with such a fortune at his command? And if you have conceived a contempt for my wealth, surely you are at least afraid of the pen of an Erasmus? You know the weapons that poets were wont to use: if I should loose one of these against you in a rage, all would be over for you, and those encircling moats and ramparts and those walls of yours, however well built, would not avail to protect you. But this, so far, is only the skirmishing; and unless you voluntarily sue for peace I shall decide the issue with you in a pitched battle.[4]

Erasmus wanted above all to perfect his Greek.

My readings in Greek all but crush my spirit [he confided to Batt], but I have no spare time and no means to purchase books or employ the services of a tutor. And with all this commotion to endure I have hardly enough to live on. . . .

If there is a chance, I shall set out for Italy in the autumn with the intention of obtaining a doctor's degree; and it is for you, in whom my hope resides, to see that liberty and leisure come my way. I have turned my entire attention to Greek. The first thing I shall do, as soon as the money arrives, is to buy some Greek authors; after that, I shall buy clothes.[5]

Why was Erasmus so relentless in his determination to master Greek? Clearly, it was to understand the Holy Scriptures better, as Greek was one of the sacred languages of the Bible, and also because Greek was the language *par excellence*, the language of science, philosophy and poetry. The study of ancient Greek was essential for a good knowledge of Latin. Without Greek, Latin remained crippled, and learning blind. Erasmus preferred Greek literature to Latin. He was even to publish a Greek grammar – that of the Byzantine humanist, Theodore of Gaza. Hebrew was to give him more trouble than Greek and Latin combined. He studied it quite late, became discouraged and abandoned it. He was to consult the specialists, like Reuchlin or the Amerbach brothers, when he ran into difficulties. But he never ceased to commend the study of the three languages for the development of the ideal theologian.

Erasmus was neither a polyglot nor a linguist, though he had made ingenious comparisons between the two languages. He remained a philologist and a humanist. He proudly ignored modern literatures, did not know Machiavelli and did not read Luther's German writings. As for Rabelais, who claimed to be his disciple, there is no evidence that Erasmus read *Pantagruel.* When Gaguin published his *History of the French*, Erasmus had praised him for having chosen to write in Latin. In his eyes, modern literatures were only particular, limited literatures without a future. Only Hebrew, Greek and Latin deserved to be regarded as the mother tongues of the West. In this domain of languages, he did not share the aspirations of the Renaissance. He did not foresee the prodigious blossoming of modern languages or understand their literary worth. He still dreamed of a universal language: Latin! The man who seemed in so many ways a breath of fresh air showed himself in this to be reactionary and, in a way, anti-modern.[6]

Erasmus loved reading, with his pen in hand. He spoke of his reading with enthusiasm and regarded books as his best companions:

> Perhaps you wonder what I am up to. My friends are my occupation; and in their company, which I enjoy enormously, I refresh my spirits. 'What friends are you boasting of to me, you frivolous fellow?' you ask. 'Would anybody wish to see, or listen to, anyone so insignificant as yourself?' For my part I am ready to acknowledge that successful men have troops of friends; yet even poor men do not lack them; indeed the latter possess friends that are considerably more pleasant in character, as well as firmer. With such friends, then, I closet myself in some secluded nook and in their company, avoiding the fickle mob, I either indulge in some delightful musings, or else listen to their whispers, speaking to them as freely as to myself. Can anything be more agreeable than this? They, on their side, never hide their secrets, and observe perfect loyalty in the keeping of secrets entrusted to them. They never blab abroad such remarks as we commonly voice freely among close friends. When you call for them they are at once at your disposal, yet never thrust themselves upon you uninvited. They speak when they are bidden to, and otherwise keep silence. Their conversation is what you will, as much as you will, and for as long as you will. They never flatter or feign or dissemble. They are frank in telling you your faults, but never complain of them to anyone. What they say is either for pleasure or for profit; in prosperity they curb one's vanity, while in adversity they offer consolation. They do not alter as one's fortune changes. They go with you into every perilous situation, and stay by you until the very end of life, while their relations are perfectly amicable. From time to time I exchange them, taking up first one and then the other, in fairness to all.
>
> These then, my dear X, are the friends with whom I am burying myself at present. Tell me, what wealth, what royal sceptre, would I take, in exchange for leisure such as this? But in case my metaphor escapes you, you must understand that, in all I have hitherto said about my good friends, I was speaking of my books; it is their friendship that has made me perfectly happy, my only misfortune being that I have not had you to share this happiness with me.[7]

Unfortunately, books were expensive, and he had to eat every day. At the age of thirty, Erasmus was a scrawny student, lacking both financial support and self-confidence. He was full of plans, and his mind was bubbling over with ideas. Though he wrote without stopping, he hardly ever managed to get his work published. His poverty and isolation drove him to despair. How could he overcome the wall of resistance surrounding him? He had to pursue his research and win the doctorate, but the doctorate was more costly than books. Erasmus tried to get his friend Jacob Batt to understand the precariousness of his situation, sharing with him his distress and his ambitions.

Now, even if the business should turn out exactly according to my wishes, and I do not so much hope for this as refuse to despair of it, still I must scrape together from each and every source a small sum of money to clothe myself and to buy the complete works of Jerome, on whom I am preparing a commentary, and a Plato, and to get together some Greek books, and also to pay for the services of a Greek tutor. Although I think you are quite aware how much all these things mean to my reputation, indeed my survival, yet I ask you to trust me when I state them as facts, out of personal experience. My mind is burning with indescribable eagerness to bring all my small literary works to their conclusion, and at the same moment to acquire a certain limited competence in the use of Greek, and thereby go on to devote myself entirely to sacred literature, the discussion of which has long been an ardently sought goal in my mind. Heaven be thanked, I am well enough, and hope to continue so, and thus I must this year stretch all my sinews to ensure not only that the present objects of my labours see the light but that by editing works of divinity I am able to bid my multitudes of hostile critics go hang, as they deserve. For a long time past, whenever I promised great achievements I have been held back, either by my own listlessness or by some unlucky mischance or by the state of my health. . . .

But there: I have been seriously slighting our friendship for some time by making such elaborate requests to you, when simply to remind you would have been more than enough. I shall not, therefore, pray you to hold me in affection, for this you do with the greatest possible warmth; or to promote my well-being, for this you consider before your own; or to grant me your loyalty and devotion in attending to my affairs, for in these respects you outdo even me; but the one thing it is really important for me to persuade you to do is a very little thing: that you should not suppose that the written accounts of my affairs which I send to you are but verbal embroidery or artistic fictions, designed for the furtherance of my own interests. And if in moments of leisure I have ever indulged in jesting or improvisation, there is a time and a place for such things, dear Batt; but my present situation affords me no opportunity whatsoever for the exercise of wit, and I have no reason for telling anything contrary to the truth. So may Heaven vouchsafe that we may both grow old in happiness and mutual love, and that even among posterity the memory of our unalloyed affection may endure through long ages. I have not set down in this letter a single jot that disagrees with the feelings of my heart. What secret indeed is there, that I could not safely, or should not freely, share with you, who are my very soul?[8]

Without waiting for Batt's reply, he returned to the charge, begging his confidant, not without some ponderousness, to plead his cause with Anna Van Veere.

Please explain to her how much greater is the glory she can acquire from me, by my literary works, than from the other theologians in her patronage. They merely deliver humdrum sermons; I am writing books that may last for ever. Their uneducated nonsense finds an audience in perhaps a couple of churches; my books will be read all over the world, in the Latin west and in the Greek east and by every nation.[9]

Batt was to do his best, but this appeal, like so many others, went unheard.

Erasmus threw himself again into the study of St Jerome, whom he preferred to St Augustine. He prepared the edition of this Church Father, whose exegetical knowledge and eloquence he had long valued.

I am trying to encompass a difficult achievement, one, if I may so put it, worthy of Phaeton, namely to restore, as well as I can, the works of Jerome, which have been partly corrupted by those half-taught critics, partly blotted out or cut down or mutilated, or at least filled with mistakes and monstrosities, through ignorance of classical antiquity and of Greek. And I intend not only to restore them, but to elucidate them in a commentary, so that every reader in his study may come to recognize that the great Jerome, the only scholar in the Church universal who had a perfect command of all learning both sacred and heathen, as they call it, can be read by anyone, but only understood by accomplished scholars.[10]

Just the same, he did not forget the doctorate and Italy. 'If my doctorate is deferred, I fear that my courage may fail before my life ends.'[11]

The plague which periodically devastated Europe during the sixteenth century drove Erasmus out of Paris in the autumn. He took refuge in Orleans where a significant incident was to occur. A man, of whom we know nothing, was accused of heresy by the auxiliary bishop of Thérouanne. Erasmus was moved by the distress of the suspect's daughter, and, with Batt's help, obtained the unfortunate man's liberation. It was also at Orleans that Erasmus encountered Jacob de Voecht, a young jurist originally from Antwerp. This new friend was to be his guardian angel, and that of other poor students, during this remarkable stay.

Time was insufficient for Erasmus to do everything. Nevertheless, he did not hesitate to help his friends, indeed to recommend them to possible providers of funds, while not hesitating to bewail his lot when he was forgotten in the handouts. His solicitude for the young who surrounded him or crossed his path was limitless and he rarely went without the pleasure of giving his advice, always to the point and often appreciated. He was scarcely able to handle his health well, and his plans for a journey continued to haunt him. 'I have some faint prospect of a visit to Italy, and my heart hankers after it not a little.'[12]

Returning to Paris, Erasmus sent his patron a surprising letter:

> My works, your foster-children, raise their hand to you in supplication, calling upon you both in the name of your own fortune, which you so creditably despise in prosperity and have so bravely borne in adversity, and in that of their own fortunes, which are ever foes to them and against which they cannot stand, save with your help; and for the love of that splendid queen, ancient Theology, whom the divinely inspired psalmist, as he is translated by Jerome, describes as sitting on the right hand of the king eternal, not in dirt or in rags, as she is now seen to be in the lecture halls of the sophists, but in a vesture of gold, wrought about with divers colours; whom to save from squalor and neglect is the earnest endeavour of all the poor fruits of my nightly toil.
>
> And to this very end there are two things I have long perceived to be most necessary: first, that I should visit Italy, in order that from the fame of that country some measure of authority may accrue to my small scholarship; and second, that I should be able to style myself a doctor. Now both of these ambitions are trivial enough; for, as Horace says, men do not all at once 'alter their souls, who cross the main'; and I should not be made one jot more learned for the shadow of a mighty name; yet one has to follow the present-day fashion, since nowadays not only the vulgar but even the most highly reputed scholars are unable to regard anyone as a learned man unless he is styled magister noster – though Christ, the prince of theologians, forbids this. In antiquity, on the other hand, no man was reputed to be learned merely because he had purchased a doctorate, but those who in their published books showed clear proof of sound doctrine were alone entitled to the appellation of doctors.[13]

This letter, combining high-flown language with realism, was not honoured with a reply.

The new century did not begin under happy auspices. In 1501, however, Erasmus published Cicero's *De Officiis* in Paris, and dedicated it to Jacob de Voecht. Like his other editions of ancient authors, this publication helped him to struggle along, getting himself known among scholars, extending his renown as a respected intellectual. If his material life was indifferent, his intellectual life was intense! He left

Paris again for the provinces, always needy, always hard working. 'Erasmus', he said, 'feeds himself on his substance and dresses himself with his pens.' Ill and short of money, he led a wretched existence. Anna Van Veere remarried and forgot her client. The Prior of Steyn extended his leave by a year so that he could finish his studies, but without the slightest subsidy! Holland bored him. France no longer seemed so hospitable, though he continued to appreciate its printers. The Bishop of Cambrai, his patron, who had long before stopped assisting him financially, abandoned him and behaved, Erasmus said, 'like an anti-patron'. One pleasant interlude on his difficult path was his stay with Batt at Tournehem in July 1501. All his cares were forgotten, friendship blossomed, a friendship prematurely cut short by Batt's death in the following year.

Was Erasmus going to renounce his grand projects in theological study? In no way, and he made a new friend who encouraged him in his vocation. Jean Vitrier, a Franciscan of St Omer, introduced him to Origen. An irreproachable monk who was nevertheless controversial, Vitrier had everything to engage Erasmus, as he accorded little importance to ceremonies and accentuated personal piety. 'He loved what he preached,' said Erasmus of him, thus emphasizing the direct and sincere character of this effective preaching.[14]

If there had been anything in Erasmus's life resembling a conversion, it would have been at this point in his story that it might have taken place. Still, it was not a question of passing from indifference to faith, but of the transformation of conventional piety to a demanding fervour. In the presence of Vitrier's heroic virtue, Erasmus felt himself very humble, and he ardently took up again the preparation of his *Handbook of the Christian Soldier*.

Erasmus again tried to break through his patron's silence by writing to the provost of Utrecht, Nicholas of Burgundy, a close relative of Anna Van Veere.

My affection for you is such that any letter is bound to seem excessively short when it is measured against my enthusiasm; yet I am so busy that even the shortest letter must appear unduly long. The ancients used to describe poets and men of eloquence allegorically as swans – with good reason, in my opinion, for the pure white plumage of the latter answers to the formers' purity of inner being, while both tribes are sacred to Apollo; both take particular delight in clear streams and well-watered meads; both are tuneful. Yet nowadays each of them seems to have fallen silent, especially in our own country, and not to have a voice even at death's approach. The reason for this I conjecture to be that of which naturalists inform us: that no swan will sing unless the west wind blows – and can we wonder that all the swans are silent today, when so many rough breezes blow from north and south, but never a one from the balmy west? I, at least, was so completely deprived of voice, as well as cash, when that British blizzard blew, that no wolf-who-saw-you-first could equal its performance. But it is only in early springtime that the soft westerlies blow. Wherefore if you, my most gracious Provost, should be like spring for the Lady of Veere, my patroness, and from her the west wind should blow upon me, then I in turn shall be such a singing swan to both of you that even later ages will hear the tune. There is no need for me to explain the riddle: for of course I am writing this to an Oedipus.[15]

What a masterly blend of erudition with shrewdness and of subtlety with irony.

From 1502 to 1504, Erasmus lived most of the time at Louvain. Adrian of Utrecht, professor at the University, and future Pope, suggested that he should give public classes, an honour which Erasmus declined in order not to provoke ill will among his colleagues at Steyn.[16] He pursued his studies unhurriedly, continuing his search for a generous and understanding patron who would guarantee him the studious leisure necessary for the organization of his work and the realization of his grand projects: renewing literature, shaking the dust from theology, and promoting universal peace.

After the death of Hendrik Van Bergen in 1502, Erasmus found a new protector, Nicholas Ruistre, Bishop of Arras and Chancellor of the University of Louvain. Ruistre was part of the Council of Philip the Handsome and belonged to the national party which opposed the Habsburg political programme of the Emperor Maximilian. Ruistre charged Erasmus with the daunting honour of welcoming Maximilian's son to Brussels. It was on 6 January 1504 that the young humanist read to Philip the Handsome a speech in Latin, composed for the occasion, before the Brabant Estates. It was in this way that Erasmus, still little known and still wearing the garb of a canon regular, made his entry into the world of international politics. His *Panegyric for Archduke Philip of Austria* was to assure the recognition of his worth and the beginning of his fame in the Netherlands.[17] This speech, handsomely paid for by the one addressed, a little revised, considerably enlarged and dedicated to Ruistre, was to be published some weeks later by Dirk Maartens, at whose place Erasmus met Pieter Gillis, another very dear friend. In his preface, Erasmus made clear that he had written less of a eulogy than an admonition. 'There is certainly no other method of correcting princes so effective as giving them an example of a good prince for a model, on the pretext of pronouncing a panegyric.'[18]

The *Panegyric* nevertheless deserved its name, because the eulogy of the Archduke occupies an important place in it. Nevertheless, the author denied that he was a flatterer. This somewhat reluctant courtier was not afraid to say to his prince: 'We prefer you as a man of peace rather than as a conqueror.'[19] He thus expressed his deepest thoughts while supporting the political ideas of his patrons of the moment. Like them, he recommended the maintenance of peace with England and, above all, with France.[20] He then rose above the topical, painting a solemn picture of the evil outcomes of all wars. In contrasting vein, he glorified the inestimable advantages of peace and concluded that an unjust peace is better than the most just of wars. He made an exception of defensive wars and indirectly established their legitimacy. Finally he developed his religious conception of peace: 'The Christian world is one country.'[21]

7

An Introduction to the Devout Life: *The Handbook of the Christian Soldier*

Despite his declared pacifism, at the beginning of 1504 Erasmus did not hesitate to give a martial title to his first work of spirituality, the *Handbook of the Christian Soldier*, printed by Dirk Maartens at Antwerp.[1] Yet the *miles christianus* evoked in this long-planned work has nothing of the military man about him, still less of the crusader; he is a soldier for Christ. Written in the form of an open letter to a lay friend in court circles, this book was at once a 'method of piety' and a treatise on spiritual combat, all in the tradition of Christian asceticism. Very systematically, Erasmus set forth precepts for living as a Christian in the world, for recognizing and averting spiritual perils. We are a long way here from *The Imitation of Christ*, which was directed at clerics and religious.[2]

This evangelical breviary, in which were to be found more than 500 biblical citations and many formulas inspired by Origen, Augustine, or even Plato and Pico della Mirandola, had no other purpose than to introduce its reader to the essentials of Christianity. Its aim was to raise the man of the world above himself without drawing him out of the world. It recommended to him the renewal of piety by a return to the Bible and going beyond 'Judaic observances'. Everything for Christ and by Christ: there is no other religion and this absolute rule also governs the practice of literature.[3]

> Do not think of 'Christ' [says the *Handbook*] as an empty word, but that it stands for charity, simplicity, patience, purity, in brief, all that he taught. . . . Therefore 'let your eye be single, and your whole body will be filled with light.' Let it look towards Christ alone as the sole and highest good, so that you love nothing, admire nothing, hope for nothing save Christ or because of Christ. . . . It is from this point of view that you must measure the usefulness or lack of usefulness of all neutral matters.

You love the study of letters. Good, if it is for the sake of Christ. If you love it only in order to have knowledge, then you come to a standstill at a point from which you should have gone on. But if you are interested in letters so that with their help you may more clearly discern Christ, hidden from our view in the mysteries of the Scriptures, and then, having discerned him, may love him, and by knowing and loving him, may communicate this knowledge and delight in it, then gird yourself for the study of letters. Yet do not allow it to go beyond what you think will be profitable for your virtuous intent. If you have confidence in yourself and hope for an immense reward in Christ, continue on your way like a bold merchant, ranging afar in the realm of pagan letters, and convert the riches of Egypt into the adornment of the Lord's temple. . . . It is better to know less and love more than to know more and not love.[4]

The two arms of spiritual combat are prayer and knowledge. 'The one makes prayerful entreaty; the other suggests what should be prayed for.' Prayer must be heartfelt. Its power does not rest in verbosity. There is no need to be eloquent in order to be heard. 'It is not a loud noise coming from the lips but the ardent desire of the mind that like some piercing sound strikes the ears of God.'[5] The author carefully distinguishes between interior and exterior piety. The piety that is satisfied with listening to or reciting formulas is not true piety, any more than religion which prefers observances to charity is true religion. Without vigilance, mechanical piety can feed on foolishness, which is pardonable, on bigotry, which is worse, or even on a loathsome hypocrisy. In short, authentic piety spreads through the whole of life, it is life. Prayer is a state of the soul, a desire more than a process. Is one who does not pray daily still a Christian?

Erasmus appealed to the Scriptures, and especially to St Paul, who wanted to preach only Christ crucified, 'a scandal for the Jews, and folly to the Greeks', yet without condemning good works.

Without [good works] you will not be a pious Christian, but they do not make you pious. They will lead to piety if you use them to this extent, but if you begin to derive pleasure from them, they extinguish piety once and for all. The Apostle makes little of the works of Abraham, which everyone will admit were extraordinary, and you have confidence in yours? God is opposed to sacrificial victims and sabbaths and new moons for his people, although he was the author of all these things. Will you be so bold as to compare your petty observances with the precepts of divine law? . . . When he mentions observances and sacred rites and multiplied prayers, does he not single out with his finger, as it were, those who measure religion by the number of psalms or prayers recited? . . . Do not tell me now that charity consists in being an assiduous churchgoer, prostrating yourself before the statues of the saints, lighting candles, and repeating a certain number of prayers. God has no need of this.[6]

Erasmus did not conclude that it was necessary to reject all the practices of piety.

What, then, will the Christian do? Shall he neglect the precepts of the Church? Shall he despise the honourable traditions of his ancestors? On the contrary, if he is weak, he will preserve them as necessary to him, but if he is strong and mature, he will observe them all the more lest through his superior knowledge he offend his weak brother and bring about the spiritual ruin of one for whom Christ died. It is right not to omit these observances but it is necessary to perform those others. Corporal works should not be condemned, but those that are invisible are preferred. Visible worship is not condemned, but God is appeased only by invisible piety.[7]

Piety worthy of its name does not despise popular piety, but surpasses and fulfils it. It represents a persistent struggle against the insidious deviations and massive abuses which eclipse the evangelical message by the introduction of superstition, and sometimes even by the mentality of magic. Erasmus, whose sincere devotion to St Geneviève is well known, did not condemn pilgrimages any more than the invocation of the saints, but he criticized confessors who imposed on their penitents lengthy expeditions to Rome, Jerusalem or Compostella. He made fun of pilgrims who ran all over the world to invoke a 'specialized' saint or to venerate relics subject to guarantees, without being sufficiently preoccupied with hearing the word of God, imitating the virtue of his disciples and reading their works. Even the relics of Christ, supposing them to be authentic, had less importance than his word. Ill-considered vows, like commercialized pilgrimages, distracted piety from its true character. Purification of the soul was not obtainable without repentance. Costly pilgrimages, ostentatious almsgiving, letters of indulgence, would not be enough.

Erasmus harshly criticized selfish prayers and bargains concluded with the saints.

Is it any great feat to visit Jerusalem bodily when within you there is Sodom, Egypt and Babylon? . . . One person greets Christopher each day, but only if he sees his image. To what end? Evidently because he is convinced that thus he will be preserved from a violent death that day. Another worships a certain Rocco, but why? Because he thinks that this saint will ward off the plague from his body. Another mumbles special little prayers to Barbara or George to avoid falling into the hands of the enemy. You gaze with awe at what is purported to be the tunic or shroud of Christ, and you read the oracles of Christ apathetically? You think it an immense privilege to have a tiny particle of the cross in your home.

> But that is nothing compared to carrying about in your heart the mystery of the cross.[8]

By contrast, Erasmus defined the true meaning of devotion to the saints: the imitation of their virtues. 'Would you like to win the favour of Peter and Paul? Imitate the faith of the one and the charity of the other, and you will accomplish more than if you were to dash off to Rome ten times.'[9] For Mary also, the devotion most acceptable to her is the imitation of her humility. Erasmus emphasized that the greatness of the Virgin's destiny lay in her choice; there would have been no advantage in having given to Jesus her own flesh if she had not also conceived his spirit from the Holy Spirit.

The *Handbook* affirmed, moreover, that the death of the soul was more to be feared than that of the body. Erasmus cited Socrates, who taught in the *Phaedo* that philosophy is nothing but meditation on death. In passing, he denounced the illusion of the dying one who believed himself to be saved because he would be buried in the Franciscan cowl: 'Likeness of habit will be of no profit to you when you are dead if your morals were unlike his in life.'[10]

Erasmus went much further by entreating the Christian to examine his conscience without being fooled by himself.

> You pray to God that you may not suffer a premature death rather than pray that he grant you a better frame of mind so that wherever death overtakes you it will not find you unprepared. You give no thought to amending your life, yet you ask God that you may not die. What is the object of your prayer? Obviously that you may go on sinning as long as possible. You pray for riches, but you do not know how to use them. Are you not praying for your own undoing? You pray for good health and you abuse it. Is not your piety really impiety?[11]

As for hell, it was nothing else, Erasmus said, than 'the perpetual anxiety of mind that accompanies the habit of sinning' and sin 'carries with it a concomitant factor which should make us stand in horror of it.'[12]

If a Christian who prays is a committed Christian, piety consists in the last analysis of the practice of the three theological virtues. No concession can be made to superstition.[13] No way of life has exclusive rights to piety. The monks themselves do not hold the monopoly of it, for they are doomed to pharisaism if they forget the Gospel to apply themselves exclusively to observances. It is vain to believe that 'Christianity does not exist outside the monk's cowl.'[14] The monastic state is only one kind of life open to Christians. It is good or evil according to the physical and moral disposition of each of its followers.[15] The religious life is not the last word in sanctity, but charity demands that the good faith of those who are attached sincerely and simply to the traditional practices of piety should not be condemned.

> I do not disapprove in any way of the external ceremonies of Christians and the devotions of the simple-minded, especially those that have been approved by the authority of the church, for they are often signs or supports of piety. Since they are almost a necessity for infants in Christ until they grow up and arrive at complete manhood, they should not be scorned by those who have achieved manhood, lest the weak suffer hurt from bad example.[16]

The book abounded in recommendations and rules of conduct. First of all, concerning the means of reading the Scriptures. Erasmus was not afraid to affirm that the biblical account of Creation had no more interest than the myth of Prometheus, unless one discovered in it the spiritual meaning. Also notable were the encouragements dispensed to his disciple:

> When the eyes of the heart are so obscured that you cannot perceive the bright light of truth, when you cannot hear the divine voice with the ears of the soul, when you are bereft of all feeling, do you think that the soul is alive? You see your brother treated unjustly, but your feelings are not disturbed as long as your own fortunes are not endangered. Why is the soul insensitive in these circumstances? Obviously because it is dead. Why is it dead? Because its life is not present, which is God. For where God is, there is love. 'God is love.' . . . Christ called the Pharisees whitened sepulchres. Why? Because they carried a dead soul around with them.[17]

After this emphasis on vigilance of spirit, Erasmus suggested how to pass from the visible to the invisible:

> Therefore, my brother, do not progress slowly by dint of reluctant effort, but by moderate exercise arrive at quick and vigorous adulthood in Christ. Embrace, zealously, this rule, not to be willing to crawl along the ground with unclean animals, but supported on those wings whose growth Plato thinks are induced in our minds by the heat of love and shoot out anew, raise yourself as on the steps of Jacob's ladder from the body to the spirit, from the visible to the invisible, from the letter to the mystery, from sensible things to intelligible things, from composite things to simple things. In this way the Lord will draw nigh in his turn to the one who draws nigh to him, and if you will attempt to the limit of your powers to rise out of your moral darkness and the tumult of the senses, he will obligingly come forth to meet you from his inaccessible light and that unimagined silence . . .[18]

Clearly, it was necessary to choose for the spirit and against the world. Erasmus denounced the hypocrisy of these soulless devotions in order to make the liberty of the children of God more secure. Such is the deep meaning of the *Handbook of the Christian Soldier*, a true manifesto of interior Christianity and Catholic reformism.[19]

When Erasmus declared that it was necessary 'rather to know less and to love more', he was expressing a deep conviction and uniting himself resolutely with the mystical tradition so well expounded by the scholar Pico della Mirandola. 'My poor Angelo,' the latter had written to Politian,

> what fools we are. In our mortal condition we are more capable of loving God than of explaining him or knowing him. In loving, we toil less, we gain more and we honour God more. But in spite of all that, we prefer to search for him tirelessly by speculation, without ever finding him, instead of taking possession of him through love, even though it would be fruitless to find him without loving him.[20]

At once austere and fervent, the *Handbook* was not an immediate success, but it gradually earned recognition as a breviary for the committed layman. It remained one of the most famous books of its day, patiently taken up again and developed by its author, published more than fifty times in less than a century. It could be said to be 'an introduction to the devout life for the use of humanists'[21] and 'the fortress of the philosophy of Christ.'[22]

Despite its pledge of orthodoxy, Erasmus was not understood or accepted as he would have wished to be. Too many well-known theologians, jealous of their prerogatives, disdained the exegesis of the Fathers. Erasmus felt himself ill at ease with them, scared of their ignorance or their knowledge, or both: they knew all the methods of casuistry, held forth interminably on the articles of faith, but seemed to ignore the fact that charity was the alpha and omega of Christianity. It was thanks to their unqualified and unremitting opposition that the *Handbook* was put on the Index after Erasmus's death.

The *Adages* and the *Handbook* put Erasmus in the first rank of philologists and theologians. The disgruntled souls were disturbed by the boldness of his thought; they gave him a hard time, but they could no longer ignore him. His sense of vocation as a Christian humanist coincided with the growth of his reputation. He promised Colet that he would devote his life to theological research. He was to keep his word, as we shall see, and was to expose the results of his research in works sometimes serious, sometimes mischievous, always animated by the same spirit and the same fervour. His book showed vividly what a master of the spiritual life Erasmus was and how committed he was to the service of a demanding Christianity.[23]

Erasmus forged ahead. In the Norbertine Abbey library of Parc, near Louvain, he discovered a manuscript of Lorenzo Valla, not a work of pure literature, but an exegetical treatise. He became enthusiastic about this writing, and it was to determine the direction of his own exegetical work. In 1505 he published his *Valla's Annotations on the New Testament*, with a stirring preface:

> Nor do I assume that theology, the very queen of all disciplines, will think it beneath her dignity if her handmaiden, grammar, offers her help and the required service. For even if grammar is somewhat lower in dignity than other disciplines, there is no other more necessary. She busies herself with very small questions, without which no one progresses to the large. She argues about trifles which lead to serious matters. If they answer that theology is too important to be limited by grammatical rules and that this whole affair of exegeting depends on the Holy Spirit, then this is indeed a new honor for the theologian that he alone is allowed to speak like a barbarian. [Then he added] Shall we now attribute our errors to the Holy Spirit?[24]

In expressing himself in this way, Erasmus was standing up for a humanist solution to the biblical question. He pleaded for philology and proclaimed the necessity of what we would today call a scientific exegesis. This standpoint was to justify his subsequent critique of the Vulgate, corrected by appeal to the Greek text of the New Testament. The Vulgate, the Latin text uniformly accepted, was regarded as untouchable in the eyes of certain theologians.

Erasmus's critical efforts came up against his ignorance of Hebrew. To be sure, he counted Hebrew among the three sacred languages indispensable to the formation of the ideal theologian, but he had to give up his pursuit of an apprenticeship that was too difficult.[25] 'I began to take up Hebrew as well,' he declared to John Colet, 'but stopped because I was put off by the strangeness of the language and at the same time the shortness of life and the limitations of human nature will not allow man to master too many things at once.'[26] Eleven years later, writing to Johann Reuchlin, Erasmus showed himself more modest: 'To Hebrew I make no claim, for I barely set my lips to it.'[27] Meanwhile, he was absorbed by his edition of the works of St Jerome, which demanded a constant recourse to Hebrew, in which Reuchlin was to provide him with valuable assistance. Help also came from the brothers Amerbach of Basel, as Erasmus was to acknowledge gladly.

Erasmus's knowledge of Greek was far from superficial, but it was not enough for him. He wanted to go to Italy for love of Greek, for it was in Italy that the best Hellenists could then be found.

8

Italy and the Return to the Sources

Like all Northern humanists, Erasmus was drawn towards Italy. In England he had discovered Florentine Platonism and developed a taste for good literature. The English humanists had shown him their source: Italy. In the sixteenth century Italy was still – and was to remain for along time – a mosaic of states and the combat zone for international greed. For Erasmus it was at one and the same time the fatherland of ancient literature, the heart of the Roman Church and the home of the new humanist movement. He was fully aware of this triple inheritance of pagan Rome, Christian Rome and the Italian Renaissance. It was the land of Cicero and of St Ambrose, of Valla and Pico della Mirandola. It was also the land of Bramante, of Botticelli, and of Raphael, but Erasmus never referred to them, though he called Petrarch 'the prince of the new eloquence'.

To see the land of Petrarch and Valla for its sheer visual pleasure, to admire the ancient and modern masterpieces, was surely for a man of good taste a good enough reason for visiting Italy. To kneel before the tombs of St Peter and St Paul could only bring pleasure to the Christian and the exegete. To greet at last the disciples of the great Florentine Platonists was to reawaken his enthusiasm for a new philosophy. All this was true, doubtless, but there were subtle nuances. In 1518, Erasmus was to write to Mark Lauwerijns: 'To Italy alone I have journeyed of my own free will, partly to pay at least one visit to her holy places, partly to profit from the libraries of that part of the world, and make the acquaintance of its men of learning.'[1]

The truth is that there remain too few letters from Erasmus in Italy to enable us to present a satisfying picture of his activities. In fact, nothing in the fragmentary accounts of his travels leaves any echo of a visit to the Roman basilicas. And nothing, or almost nothing, gives us information about Erasmus's taste in the realm of art or philosophy. He was not a man of the world who devoted his leisure hours to visiting monuments or curiosities, still less to the life of the salon, but an impatient scholar as well as a clear observer of the society of his time. If he was a great traveller, he was in no way a tourist! Of course he could not fail to take note in Florence of Michelangelo's David, or in Rome of the ruined Colisseum or St Peter's in the process of construction. Like most of the first humanists, he made few archaeological observations.

The Erasmus who burned to know Italy was a philologist. He came to study classical Greek in the country where it was already best known, thanks to the learned Greeks who had fled from the Turkish occupation. 'I came to Italy mainly in order to learn Greek,'[2] he was to say. It was the librarians, exegetes and philosophers who were to receive the longest and most productive visits from him.

At last, in 1506, the journey, so long hoped for and indefinitely delayed, was decided on in London at a few days notice. Erasmus agreed to accompany Giovanni and Bernardo Boerio, the two sons of Henry VII's doctor to Italy, to chaperone them while they were pursuing their studies.

Erasmus's Italian journey lasted for nearly three years. He crossed the most beautiful provinces in the peninsula and experienced all their seasonal changes. The time seemed propitious to him: the French had left Naples; peace was being maintained, despite some serious snags. In August Erasmus reached the promised land. He complained not of weariness of the journeys, but of the coarseness of the governor and of the Boerio children's bodyguard. For a diversion he composed a poem on old age: he was only forty years old, but his hair was greying. He described himself, meditating on the fragility of this life, noting down his verse as he went along, the paper pressed upon the pommel of his saddle. At night, in the inn, he made a neat copy of the days work. He entitled his work *Carmen de senectute*.

> *How quickly my days have been speeding*
> *Since I played with nuts as a lad,*
> *Wrangled with sophists and rhetors*
> *And read all the poets to be had,*
> *Painted tenuous fancies,*
> *Sucked every book like a bee,*
> *To know the Greek and the Latin,*
> *Encompassed the land and the sea.*[3]

The first stop was Turin, whose inhabitants Erasmus praised for their cheerful nature. With a speed which would be the envy of candidates of our own time, he acquired the theological doctor's gown in theology on 4 September.[4] One would like to know the feelings of the new 'Master' on the evening of that day which marked the end of a long process of suffering for him, but unfortunately he left no record of them. Once he had won the battle for the doctorate, he said no more about it. His discretion was not only the result of modesty. More proud of his genius than of his titles, Erasmus soon forgot this official certificate of competence, at once useless and necessary, too long awaited, too soon gained. His correspondents – popes, emperors, friends – sometimes gave him his title, but his enemies affected to disregard it, make fun of it or mention it with bitterness. For Erasmus, the page was turned, the doctorate was over and done with, the matter was filed away.

From Turin the new doctor left for Bologna, passing through Milan and Pavia. In Milan, he saw the Last Supper of Leonardo da Vinci, observing that the painter had unaccountably made the Apostle John look younger. Near Pavia, he stopped at the celebrated Charterhouse, then in all its youthful splendour. His ideal of evangelical simplicity was offended by the abundance of white marble and he pitied the monks who were constantly disturbed by visitors. But at Pavia he was enchanted to meet Paolo Ricci, the Jewish physician and Professor of Philosophy at the University of that city.

With the help of Louis XII, the Pope was planning to spread the war across the whole country, and the city of Bologna was preparing to undergo a siege. Erasmus prudently crossed the Appenines and established his headquarters in Florence for some weeks. Almost nothing remains for us of his stay in the city of Machiavelli and Savonarola, of Botticelli and Michelangelo; no cry of enthusiasm for the work of the greatest artists of his time! Not even a word on Florentine Platonism! It was philology alone that guided his steps. In order not to remain inactive, he translated some dialogues of Lucian into Latin. Returning to Bologna, he was present at the triumphal entry of Julius II – a spectacle that left him with a feeling of horror and sadness, which found clear expression in a number of his writings.

It was Julius II who confirmed Erasmus in a resolute pacifism. 'Pope Julius', he remarked ironically, 'is waging war, conquering, leading triumphal processions; in fact, playing Julius [Caesar] to the hilt.' All this military activity Erasmus condemned as a Christian, but also as a man of learning, a researcher, whom the war irritated and disturbed, since the University was closed and its teachers scattered. 'Studies are remarkably dormant in Italy, whereas wars are hotly pursued', he deplored, and he added that he was thinking of returning. He fled the plague as he fled war, and avoided war like the plague.[5]

Soon after the death of Julius II (21 February 1513) Erasmus was to write a daring dialogue about him. Julius, accompanied by his spirit and a great crowd of soldiers, presents himself at the gates of Heaven.

St Peter opens a little grilled window and interrogates the warrior pope who, without any discomfort, gives an account of the way in which he has exercised his temporal and spiritual power. Towards the end of the dialogue St Peter freely gives his verdict on the merits of the sovereign pontiff and finally Julius has to retrace his steps, pouring out protestations and threats.[6] This dialogue, printed by Maartens, was not acknowledged by Erasmus, but can safely be attributed to him.

When the danger abated, Erasmus took courage. He was to spend a little more than a year in Bologna, where his friend, the Hellenist Paolo Bombace, helped him in the education of the Boerio boys. He perfected himself in the practice of Greek and carried on with his great works, the *Antibarbari* and the recasting of the *Adages*. In his spare moments he practised writing exercises and printed a *Declamation in Two Parts*, the first against the monastic life, the second in favour of this vocation. Finally he began a correspondence with the great Venetian printer Aldo Manuzio, and entrusted to him the new edition of his translations of Euripides.

Erasmus was invited to Venice by Aldo Manuzio, but he declined at first, citing the unfavourable season and his precarious health. Meanwhile, the climate of Bologna scarcely suited him, especially since the plague had made an appearance in the city. He took refuge in the countryside and waited for the epidemic to end.

A curious incident made this humanist reflect on the limitations of Latin in everyday life. His religious habit was confused by the crowd with the white scarf of the doctors attending plague victims. Unable to explain himself or to be understood, Erasmus escaped being beaten only by flight. It was doubtless then that he adopted secular garb. This incident must have led Erasmus to learn some words of Italian, without great success. It was natural that he should have forgotten the small talk of daily conversation, since he no longer had need of it. In 1529, one of his friends was to tell him of the Italian translation of the *Handbook of the Christian Soldier*. Erasmus thanked him, adding that he would willingly learn Italian through reading this book. In 1535, he was to write very bluntly: 'I do not know Italian.'

Erasmus arrived in Venice in the first days of April 1508, at the latest. There he met neither Titian nor Giorgione, but a group of scholars, among whom were Joannes Lascaris and his French pupil Germain de Brie. His literary activity was as vast as it was varied and lasted for nearly eight months. He was received as a distinguished guest by the printer Aldo Manuzio, in his house near the Rialto. Girolamo Aleandro, the great Hellenist, the future minister of Érard de la Marck and apostolic nuncio, was a regular visitor in what was undoubtedly the most illustrious printery of the age. Erasmus lived with him in a great friendship, which was to give way later to a falling out approaching hatred. With Aleandro and the Greek Arsenius Erasmus perfected his Greek, thus fulfilling one of the hopes of his journey to Italy.

While he was staying with Aldo Manuzio, Erasmus published a new edition of his *Adages*, now greatly enlarged.[7] The first pages were printed as the author reviewed the following ones and discussed them with his friends, whose generous help he appreciated. Each adage allowed him to explain his personal thoughts in agreeable digressions: these were 'essays' before such things existed. This edition, universally well regarded, made Erasmus the most famous interpreter of classical civilization and the mentor of Europe. The book abounded in terse formulations on life and death, optimism and pessimism: 'Man is a wolf for man', 'Man is only a bubble', and so on. Quoted proverbs were often followed with a particularly short commentary, which did not detract from their charm or piquancy. One example, chosen from a hundred, exemplifies this laconic presentation. The adage is entitled: 'If you cannot play the role of a cow, content yourself with the role of the donkey.' And the whole commentary is: 'If you cannot do what you want to, do what you can. If fortune has not fulfilled you, take a good part of what is yours. If you cannot gain what you desire, occupy yourself with what is within your reach.'

Erasmus spoke, read and wrote unceasingly. He studied the Greek authors – Pindar, Plutarch, among others. He prepared many works at the same time. His health gave him some anxiety and once again he complained about his food. He continued to observe everything with a critical eye, but his mixed feelings could not hide or diminish what his work owed to his visit to Venice. Later he would say that Venice was 'the most magnificent of cities'.

Once the *Adages* were printed, bound and put on sale, Erasmus was finished with Venice. He was in Padua before the winter of the year 1508. There he again saw Germain de Brie and, as the Boerio children had rejoined their family, he found a new teaching role there, and a new income. His pupil was a man of some importance, Alexander Stuart, aged eighteen, the natural son of James IV of Scotland and already Archbishop of St Andrew's. The young prelate was taking courses in the University and benefited from special lessons with Erasmus.

Erasmus probably spent only some weeks at Padua but, perhaps for that reason, maintained tender memories of it. The weather there was better than elsewhere. The philologists that he knew there received nothing but praise: Marcus Musurus, Scipione Carteromachus and Raphael Regius.

He confided his thoughts to Aldo Manuzio, the 'defender of good literature':

Germain has delayed me here with his magical spells, though I was already booted and spurred. Please urge Francesco to hurry his copying of my modest treatise, for I shall meanwhile see if I can oblige someone by offering it to him, and thus obtain some reward, so that my activity of these last months does not go for nought. Andrea has shown considerable foresight in paying everything in écus; but I am sure he will do his duty in this business.[8]

Meanwhile the war once again closed the Universities, threatened the traveller and obliged him to make new plans. From 19 December 1508 Erasmus was ready to leave. Some days later, he was in Ferrara with Alexander and his company. A young Englishman, Richard Pace, offered him hospitality, and it was there that Erasmus met a new group of humanists including Daniel Scevola.

The League of Cambrai then brought together the Pope, the Emperor and the kings of France and Spain in opposition to Venice. As the Duke of Ferrara had joined the League, Erasmus left the city, which had been transformed into a fortress. By January 1509 he was in Siena, where he was to spend some months looking after his health. There he acquired an Aulus Gellius and allotted part of his time to publishing the *Declamation on death.* He was undoubtedly present with his pupil, a student at the University, at the Carnival celebrations, but he drew no lasting pleasure from them. During his stay in Siena, Erasmus learned that his Hungarian friend, Jacob Piso, had discovered a manuscript collection of his correspondence in a Roman library. Once he had gained possession of it – how he did so is not clear – Erasmus burned it. This at least is what he said twelve years later, but one could well ask whether this unforeseen success of his correspondence was not to play a role in his later decision to publish some of his letters.

At the end of February 1509, Erasmus saw Rome for the first time. He received an enthusiastic welcome from men of letters and ecclesiastical dignitaries – Cardinals Giovanni de' Medici (the future Leo X), Raphael Riario, Dominic Grimani, Giles of Viterbo and Jean-Étienne de Ferreriis, the humanists Filippo Beroaldo the younger and Girolamo Donato.

A second stay in Rome followed a quick journey to Siena. Erasmus had brought back from there his pupil Stuart, for whom he had developed a deep sympathy, and to whom he showed the Eternal City. He heard an extraordinary sermon, on Good Friday, in the Pope's chapel, in which the sacred orator began with a eulogy of Julius II, said some words on the Passion, then gave a long discourse on ancient mythology and Roman history. For a Christian humanist who considered Antiquity as indispensable for the formation of – but only preliminary to – the Christian message, this sermon was as astounding as it was inadequate![9]

It is understandable that at the end of his life Erasmus devoted all his attention to a treatise on his conception of preaching.

Erasmus was more appreciative of the charm of walks, interspersed with knowledgeable discussion, and of the pleasant atmosphere of the Campo dei Fiori. The Romans' taste for spectacles of violence brought no pleasure to this peaceable and refined man, but he appreciated a good actor's performance.

> We laughed at a spectacle of this sort in Julius II's palace, where I had been dragged by some friends to the bull fights: for I myself have never enjoyed those bloody games and remnants of ancient paganism. There, in the intervals which fell between the death of one bull and the bringing out of the next into the contest, a masked man leapt into the middle with his left hand covered with a cloak, bearing a sword in his right hand, and he imitated all the movements which those attacking a bull usually make; gradually approaching the flank, he waited: then he would flee, as if he were seen by a bull. Meanwhile, as if a bull were boldly following [on his heels] he threw down his cloak: for this object usually delays the cloak attack; then, as if the bull had turned aside, he went back timidly to pick up the cloak. Sometimes his sword also failed him, as if through fear. Meanwhile he would throw himself under the stone arch which is in the middle of the space, because it is usually the last refuge from an enraged bull. Finally he would leap over a dead bull, sitting on a horse as if scoffing at a defeated victim. The drollness of this man seized me more strongly than the rest of the show.[10]

Another unpleasant surprise was the pomp of Rome. Erasmus objected to the Pope's monarchical style, the trappings of Papal sovereignty, the patrimony of St Peter,[11] the splendour of ceremonies, the luxury of the vestments, the worldliness of the sermons. He was scandalized by the troops of employees, servants, guards and parasites who surrounded the prelates. More deeply, he could not support the institutions which regarded themselves as ends and forgot their serving roles. The *enfant terrible* of the Roman Church, he did not keep his disappointments to himself, but spoke and wrote about them. If he had lived in our day, it would be said that he was for ever holding press conferences.

The rivalry between Rome and Venice also occupied his thoughts and awakened his anxiety. He presented two discourses on conflict to Cardinal Riario, one choosing war and the other peace.[12] But one cannot doubt Erasmus's aversion for Julius II and his politics.

Erasmus took his work as a tutor seriously. He took Alexander Stuart with him to visit Naples and the den of the Cumaean Sybil. It was the last act of this responsibility, and a very pleasant one. They returned to

Rome in July and the pupil left his master to return to Scotland, not without having left him a token of his gratitude: a ring whose carved stone represented a bearded God. Erasmus recognized in it the God Terminus and made it his emblem, with the motto *Concedo nulli*, 'I yield to no one', a fitting motto for death.[13]

At the moment when he decided to leave Rome, Erasmus paid a visit to Cardinal Grimani, the ambassador of the most serene Republic, at the Venetian palace. The account he gave of it much later to his friend Guido Steuco preserved all the freshness of recollection engraved on the memory.

When I was in Rome, I was invited by him again and again to talk – and unless I am mistaken, this was through Pietro Bembo – although I then shrank from the splendour of great men; finally I visited his palace, more through politeness than from desire. No man's face appeared either in the court or in the entrance hall. For it was afternoon. I left my horse with my servant and went up alone. I come to the first room, I see no one: to the second and third, the same: I found no door closed. Wondering to myself at the emptiness, I come to the end: there I found someone, a Greekling doctor (I think) with a shaved head, the guardian of an open door. I ask what the Cardinal is doing. He says that he is talking inside with some noblemen. When I say nothing more, he asks what I want. I say, 'I would greet him if convenient. Because he is not free now, I shall another time.' While going to leave I look a little while at the view through a window; the Greek came back to me, asking me if I wanted anything announced to the Cardinal. I say, 'There is no need to interrupt his conversation, but I shall return shortly.' Finally, at his request, I give my name. When he heard it, he hurried inside, without my notice, and came out quickly, ordering me not to go away, and I am immediately summoned. The cardinal – and such a cardinal! – is not receiving me when I come as an insignificant person of the lowest type, but as a colleague. A seat was put in place, we talked for more than two hours, nor was my hand allowed to move to my cap in the meantime . . .

He started to exhort me not to leave Rome, the nourisher of clever people. He invited me to the companionship of his house and the fellowship of all fortunes, adding that the Roman climate, being moist and warm, was suited to my poor body, and especially that part of the city in which he had his palace, built once by a pope who had chosen the site as being the most healthful of all.

After many discussions held on either side, he summoned his nephew (already an archbishop then), a young man endowed with a divine talent. When I was about to rise, he forbade it, saying, 'It is fitting for a pupil to stand before his teacher.' Then he showed me his library 'of many languages'. If I should happen to have known this man at another time, I should never leave the City; so far above my deserts I found his favour. But I had already decided to leave, and events had proceeded to the extent that it was hardly right to stay there. When I had said that I was summoned by the King of England, he stopped insisting; but he prayed repeatedly that I should not suspect that what he promised did not come from his heart, and that I should not judge him by the habits of common courtiers ... But since he did not wish to delay me longer ... he asked me with his last words to visit him once again before I left the City. I (unhappily) did not return, lest, defeated by the man's eloquence, I should change my plan. My mind was never so bad to me.[14]

Thus it was that in July 1509 Erasmus's stay in Rome came to an end and his journey to Italy concluded with a last crossing of the peninsula, apparently alone, without a pupil. He left Italy because England called him. He fled the oppressive atmosphere of the Roman summer and hastened towards his second homeland. A new king, a friend of learning and letters, had just mounted the throne: Henry VIII seemed to him destined by Providence to become the great patron who would at last bring him security and stability.

In 1506, Erasmus had crossed the Alps meditating on old age. In 1509 he crossed them with a very different disposition: *The Praise of Folly*, also roughed out on horseback, expressed the extraordinary youth of his spirit. Three years spent in Italy had allowed Erasmus to acquire an opinion of the Italians. Here, as elsewhere, friends rubbed shoulders with rivals and enthusiasm battled against disappointment, with disappointment usually gaining the upper hand. Erasmus praised the simplicity of life and the gentleness of the Italian people, but he deplored its vanity which made it consider all foreigners to be barbarians. Basically, he felt himself and knew himself to be superior to so many boastful and proud Italians, for whom it was enough to be born in the land of Cicero to believe themselves to be humanists.

The promised land, full of delights and fancies, had not fulfilled all its promises. However, with the years, Erasmus came to perceive lasting values and forget ephemeral vexations.

A deep regret for Rome is inescapable [he would say], when I think of its great store of great advantages available together. First of all the bright light, the noble setting of the most famous city in the world, the delightful freedom, the many richly furnished libraries, the sweet society of all those great scholars, all the literary conversations, all the monuments of antiquity, and not least so many leading lights of the world gathered together in one place.[15]

This compliment was reserved for the laity. Christian Rome disappointed Erasmus as it would Luther. Both reacted against the sight of a triumphant papacy and an anaemic Church, Luther with anger,

Erasmus with irony. On essentials, their agreement remained, and Erasmus could write to Pierre Barbier: 'Would that Luther's accusations against the Roman Curia, tyranny, greed and dissolute morals were false!'[16]

This disenchantment nourished Erasmus's anti-clerical vigour and extended sometimes to Italians in general and Romans in particular. Soon the *Folly*, and later the *Ciceronian*, were to translate these complex sentiments in stylized form. Erasmus had perhaps lost his first illusions about Churchmen: but he did not become on that account either a cynic or an unbeliever.

9

A Religious Pamphlet: *The Praise of Folly*

While crossing the Alps on the way back from Italy, Erasmus sketched out a new work quite different from anything he had written before. He finished it in a few days in London at the home of his favourite friend, Thomas More, to whom he dedicated *The Praise of Folly*.[1]

During my recent journey back from Italy to England, not wishing to waste all the time I was obliged to be on horseback on idle gossip and small talk, I preferred to spend some of it thinking over some topic connected with our common interests or else enjoying the recollection of the friends, as learned as they are delightful, whom I had left there in England. You were amongst the first of these to spring to mind, my dear More. I have always enjoyed my memories of you when we have been parted from each other as much as your company when we were together, and I swear that nothing has brought me more pleasure in life than companionship like yours. And so since I felt that there must be something I could do about this and the time was hardly suitable for serious meditation, I decided to amuse myself with praise of folly. What sort of a goddess Athene put that notion into your head, you may well ask. In the first place, it was your own family name of More, which is as near to the Greek word for folly, *moria*, as you are far from it in fact, and everyone agrees that you couldn't be farther removed. Then I had an idea that no one would think so well of this jeu d'esprit of mine as you, because you always take such delight in jokes of this kind, that is, if I don't flatter myself, jokes which aren't lacking in learning and wit. In fact you like to play the part of Democritus in the mortal life we all share. Your intelligence is too penetrating and original for you not to hold opinions very different from those of the ordinary man, but your manners are so friendly and pleasant that you have the rare gift of getting on well with all men at any time, and enjoying it.

I am sure that you will gladly accept this little declamation of mine as a memento of your friend and will also undertake to defend it. It is dedicated to you, so henceforth it is yours, not mine. There may well be plenty of critical folk rushing in to slander it, some saying that my bit of nonsense is too frivolous for a theologian and others that it has a sarcastic bias which ill becomes Christian decorum. They will clamour that I'm reviving Old Comedy or Lucian, carping and complaining about everything. . . . Nothing is so trivial as treating serious subjects in a trivial manner; and similarly, nothing is more entertaining than treating trivialities in such a way as to make clear you are doing anything but trifle with them. The world will pass its own judgement on me, but unless my self-love entirely deceives me, my praise of folly has not been altogether foolish.

Now for the charge of biting sarcasm.[2] My answer is that the intelligent have always enjoyed freedom to exercise their wit on the common life of man, and with impunity, provided that they kept their liberty within reasonable limits. This makes me marvel all the more at the sensitivity of present-day ears which can bear to hear practically nothing but honorific titles. Moreover you can find a good many people whose religious sense is so distorted that they find the most serious blasphemies against Christ more bearable than the slightest joke on pope or prince, especially if it touches their daily bread. And to criticize men's lives without mentioning any names – I ask you, does this look like sarcasm, or rather warning and advice? Again, on how many charges am I not my own self-critic? Furthermore, if every type of man is included, it is clear that all the vices are censured, not any individual. And so anyone who protests that he is injured betrays his own guilty conscience, or at any rate his apprehensions. St Jerome amused himself in this way with far more freedom and sarcasm, sometimes even mentioning names. I have not only refrained from naming anyone but have also moderated my style so that the sensible reader will easily understand that my intention was to give pleasure, not pain. Nowhere have I stirred up the cesspool of crime as Juvenal did; the ridiculous rather than the squalid was what I set out to survey. Finally, if anyone is still unappeased by all that I have said, he should at least remember that there is merit in being attacked by Folly, for when I made her the narrator I had to maintain her character in appropriate style. But why do I say all this to you, an advocate without peer for giving your best service to causes even when they are not the best? Farewell, learned More; be a stout champion to your namesake Folly.[3]

This introduction, perhaps a little long, suggests the tone of the book. It was at once a letter and an apology. In each line, Erasmus let himself go and soon pulled himself up. If he sensed negative reactions from certain readers, he trusted in Thomas More's friendship, wrapping himself in this friendship with a delicacy which did not preclude sincerity. His confidence could not have been better placed and More, in letters as brilliant as they were impassioned, was to defend his friend's ideas against proud or aggressive theologians.

The Praise of Folly, printed in Paris in 1511, is without doubt Erasmus's major work and one of the great books of the Renaissance, a book which has never grown old. Whatever the author says in his preface, it is a satirical declamation written with a fast, prickly, sometimes cruel, pen. It is also a lyrical declamation praising the wise foolishness of an authentic Christianity. The only person in this strange composition is Folly, everywhere and always present, thanks to the stupidities of her innumerable disciples. The distinctive feature of Folly is not to know her limits. She accompanies men from morning to night and from night to morning. Her bells sound in every head, and when they are no longer heard, death is not far away.

In this way the best-known and the most arcane of Erasmus's books presents Folly and the world, her theatre. Folly presents herself, from the very outset:

> I've a fancy to play the sophist before you, and I don't mean by that one of the tribe today who cram tiresome trivialities into the heads of school-boys and teach them more than feminine obstinacy in disputation – no, I shall follow the ancients who chose the name sophist in preference to the damaging title of wise men. Their concern was to provide eulogies in praise of gods and heroes, so it's a eulogy you are going to hear now, though not one of Hercules or Solon. It's in praise of myself, namely, Folly. . . . For I am as you see me, the true bestower of good things, called *stultitia* in Latin, *mōria* in Greek.
>
> But is there any need to tell you even as much as that, as if I didn't make it perfectly clear who I am from the look on my face, as they say? Anyone who argued that I was Minerva or Wisdom could easily be convinced of his mistake simply by the sight of me, even if I never spoke a word, though speech is the least deceptive mirror of the mind. I've no use for cosmetics, my face doesn't pretend to be anything different from my innermost feelings. I am myself wherever I am, and no one can pretend I'm not – especially those who lay special claim to be called the personification of wisdom, even though they strut about like apes in purple and asses in lion-skins. However hard they try to keep up the illusion, their ears stick up and betray the Midas in them.[4]

If Folly is responsible for human errors, she none the less helps man to live, for she is the hidden mainspring of his spontaneity and receptiveness. It is the 'honey of Folly' that makes possible social life, perceptible happiness and daily joys. That said, no one escapes the characteristics of Folly. Popes and bishops, philosophers and sages, princes and soldiers, merchants and magistrates, writers and swords-men, women and monks, all are foolish, faithful customers of Vanity Fair.

The popes first of all! The very principle of a temporal power descended on the successor of St Peter shocked Erasmus, especially when this successor was called Julius II. In the *Folly* there are biting allusions to the decrepit pontiff who made war in the name of Christ. The way in which the popes defended the patrimony of St Peter had nothing to do with the Gospel.

Then the supreme pontiffs, who are the vicars of Christ: if they made an attempt to imitate his life of poverty and toil, his teaching, cross, and contempt for life, and thought about their name of 'pope', which means 'father', or their title of 'Supreme Holiness', what creatures on earth would be so cast down? Or who would want to spend all his resources on the purchase of their position, which once bought has to be protected by the sword, by poison, by violence of every kind? Think of all the advantages they would lose if they ever showed a sign of wisdom! Wisdom, did I say? Rather a grain of the salt Christ spoke of would suffice to rid them of all their wealth and honours, their sovereignty and triumphs, their many offices, dispensations, taxes and indulgences, all their horses and mules, their retinue, and their countless pleasures . . . In place of all this it would bring vigils, fasts, tears, prayers, sermons, study, sighs and a thousand unpleasant hardships of that kind. Nor must we overlook what this will lead to. Countless scribes, copyists, clerks, lawyers, advocates, secretaries, muleteers, grooms, bankers, and pimps (and I nearly added something rather more suggestive, but was afraid of being too blunt for your ears) – in short, an enormous crowd of people now a burden on the Roman see (I'm sorry, I meant 'now an honour to') would be left to starve. A monstrous abominable crime! And even more execrable, the supreme princes of the church, the true lights of the world, would be reduced to taking up scrip and staff.

But as things are today, any work that has to be done they can leave to Peter and Paul, who have plenty of time on their hands, while claiming all the pomp and pleasure for themselves. Consequently, and again, thanks to me, practically no class of man lives so comfortably with fewer cares; for they believe they do quite enough for Christ if they play their part as overseer by means of every kind of ritual, near theatrical ceremonial or display, benedictions and anathemas, and all their titles of 'your Beatitude', 'Reverence' and 'Holiness'. For them it's out of date and outmoded to perform miracles; teaching the people is too like hard work, interpreting the Scriptures is for schoolmen, and praying is waste of time; to shed tears is weak and womanish, to be needy is degrading; to suffer defeat is a disgrace and hardly fitting for one who scarcely permits the greatest of kings to kiss his sacred feet; and finally, death is an unattractive prospect, and dying on a cross would be an ignominious end. . . .

This [the threat of excommunication] the holy fathers in Christ, who are in fact the vicars of Christ, launch against none so savagely as those who at the devil's prompting seek to nibble away and reduce the patrimony of Peter. Lands, cities, taxes, imposts, and sovereignties are all called Peter's patrimony, despite the words of the Gospel 'We have forsaken all and followed thee.' Fired with zeal for Christ they will fight to preserve them with fire and sword, and Christian blood flows freely while they believe they are the defenders, in the manner of the apostles, of the church, the bride of Christ, through having boldly routed those whom they call her foes. As if indeed the deadliest enemies of the Church were not these impious pontiffs who allow Christ to be forgotten through their silence, fetter him with their mercenary laws, misrepresent him with their forced interpretations of his teaching, and slay him with their noxious way of life![5]

Are the kings and princes any better than the popes?

I've long been wanting to say something about kings and their courtiers, who cultivate me quite openly, with the candour one expects from those of gentle birth. Indeed, nothing would be so dismal and as much to be shunned as the life they lead if they had even a grain of good sense. No one would think power worth gaining, at the cost even or perjury or parricide, if he seriously considered the burden that has to be shouldered by the man who wants to exercise true sovereignty. Once he is at the helm of government he has to devote himself to public instead of his personal affairs, and must think only of the well-being of his people. He can't deviate by so much as a hair's breadth from the laws he has promulgated and set up himself, and he has to guarantee personally the integrity of every magistrate and official. Every eye is trained on him alone and he can either be a beneficial star, should his character be blameless, and the greatest salvation to mankind, or a fatal comet leaving a trail of disaster in his wake.[6]

What does Folly think of philosophers and theologians?

The philosophers, cloaked and bearded to command respect . . . insist that they alone have wisdom and all other mortals are but fleeting shadows. Theirs is certainly a pleasant form of madness, which sets them building countless universes and measuring the sun, moon, stars, and planets by rule of thumb or a bit of string, and producing reasons for thunderbolts, winds, eclipses and other inexplicable phenomena. They never pause for a moment, as if they were private secretaries to Nature, architect of the universe, or had come to us straight from the council of the gods. Meanwhile Nature has a fine laugh at them and their conjectures, for their total lack of certainty is obvious enough from the endless contention amongst themselves on every single point. They know nothing at all, yet they claim to know everything. Though ignorant even of themselves and sometimes not able to see the ditch or stone lying in their path, either because most of them are half-blind or because their minds are far away, they still boast that they can see ideas, universals, separate forms, prime matters, quiddities, ecceities, things which are all so insubstantial that I doubt if even Lynceus could perceive them.

Then there are the theologians, a remarkably supercilious and touchy lot. I might perhaps do better to pass over them in silence without stirring the mud of Camarina or grasping that noxious plant, lest they marshal their forces for an attack with innumerable conclusions and force me to eat my words. If I refuse they'll denounce me as a heretic on the spot, for this is the bolt they always loose on anyone to whom they take a dislike. Now there are none so unwilling to recognize my good services to them, and yet they're under obligation to me on several important counts, notably for their happiness in their self-love, which enables them to dwell in a sort of third heaven, looking down from aloft, almost with pity, on all the rest of mankind as so many cattle crawling on the face of the earth. They are fortified meanwhile with an army of schoolmen's definitions, conclusions, and corollaries and propositions both explicit and implicit. They boast of so many bolt holes that the meshes of Vulcan's net couldn't stop them from slipping out by means of the distinctions they draw, with which they can easily cut any knot (a double axe from Tenedos wouldn't do better), for they abound in newly coined expressions and strange sounding words.

In addition, they interpret hidden mysteries to suit themselves: how the world was created and designed; through what channels the stain of sin filtered down to posterity; by what means, in what measure, and how long Christ was formed in the Virgin's womb; how, in the Eucharist, accidents can subsist without a domicile. . . . Then add those maxims of theirs, which are so paradoxical that in comparison the pronouncements of the Stoics, which were actually known as paradoxes, seem positively commonplace and banal; for example, that it is a lesser crime to butcher a thousand men than to cobble a poor man's shoe on a single occasion on the Lord's day, and better to let the whole world perish down to the last crumb and stitch, as they say, than to tell a single tiny insignificant lie. These subtle refinements of subtleties are made still more subtle by all the different lines of scholastic argument, so that you'd extricate yourself faster from a labyrinth than from the tortuous obscurities of realists, nominalists, Thomists, Albertists, Ockhamists, and Scotists – and I've not mentioned all the sects, only the main ones.

Such is the erudition and complexity they all display that I fancy the apostles themselves would need the help of another Holy Spirit if they were obliged to join issue on these topics with our new breed of theologian. . . .

I was recently present myself (as I often am) at a theological debate where someone asked what authority there was in the Scriptures for ordering heretics to be burnt instead of refuted in argument. A grim old man, whose arrogance made it clear he was a theologian, answered in some irritation that the apostle Paul had laid down this rule saying, 'A man who is a heretic, after the first and second admonition, reject [*devita*]', and he went on thundering out this quotation again and again while most of those present wondered what had happened to the man. At last he explained that the heretic was to be removed from life [*de vita*]. Some laughed, though there were plenty of others who found this fabrication sound theology.[7]

With the added irony, this satire on philosophers and theologians recalls *The Imitation of Christ*, that admirable book which Erasmus never quotes, though he was sometimes inspired by it. 'What good', said Thomas À Kempis to his reader, 'are these sublime discussions on the Trinity, if you displease him through lack of humility?' 'I would rather experience contrition than know its definition.' 'What do genus and species matter? How many men are lost in the world because of their vain knowledge?' 'What is the value of knowledge without the fear of God?' 'A humble peasant who serves God is certainly happier than a proud philosopher who, neglecting his salvation, observes the movement of the stars.' 'Moderate in yourself an over-eager desire to know for you will only draw from it a great misbehaviour and a great illusion.' 'What is the purpose of subtle disputes on hidden and obscure things?' etc. In both cases, in the *Folly*, as well as in the *Imitation*, false knowledge and impious curiosity are rejected with scorn, if not with horror.

Folly then takes for her target the mendicant religious.

The happiness of these people is most nearly approached by those who are popularly called 'religious' or 'monks'. Both names are false, since most of them are a long way removed from religion, and wherever you go these so-called solitaries are the people you're likely to meet. I don't believe any life would be more wretched than theirs if I didn't come to their aid in many ways. The whole tribe is so universally loathed that even a chance meeting is thought to be ill-omened – and yet they are gloriously self-satisfied. In the first place they believe it's the highest form of piety to be so uneducated that they can't even read. Then when they bray like donkeys in church, repeating by rote the psalms they haven't understood, they imagine they are charming the ears of their heavenly audience with infinite delight. Many of them too make a good living out of their squalor and beggary, bellowing for bread from door to door, and indeed making a nuisance of themselves in every inn, carriage and boat, to the great loss of all other beggars. This is the way in which these smooth individuals, in all their filth and ignorance, their boorish and shameless behaviour, claim to bring back the apostles into our midst![8]

Folly then launches an attack on bad preachers:

Is there a comedian or cheapjack you'd rather watch than them when they hold forth in their sermons? It's quite absurd but highly enjoyable to see them observe the traditional rules of rhetoric. Heavens, how they gesticulate and make proper changes of voice, how they drone on and fling themselves about, rapidly putting on different expressions and confounding everything with their outcry! This is a style of oratory which is handed down in person from brother to brother like a secret ritual. I'm not one of the initiated but I'll make a guess at what it's like.

They start with an invocation, something they've borrowed from the poets. Then if they're going to preach about charity their exordium is all about the Nile, a river in Egypt, or if they intend to recount the mystery of the cross they'll happily begin with Bel, the Babylonian dragon. If fasting is to be their subject they make a start with the twelve signs of the Zodiac, and if they would expound the faith they open with a discussion on squaring the circle. . . . I myself have heard one notable fool – I'm sorry, I meant to say scholar – who set out to reveal the mystery of the Trinity to a large congregation. In order to display the exceptional quality of his learning and to satisfy the ears of the theologians he made a novel beginning, starting with the alphabet, syllable and sentence, and going on to the agreement of noun with verb, adjective with noun and substantive. There was general astonishment amongst his listeners, some of whom whispered to each other the quotation from Horace, 'What's the point of all this stink?' Finally he reached the conclusion that a symbol of the Trinity was clearly expressed in the rudiments of grammar, and no mathematician could trace a figure so plain in the sand. And that great theologian had sweated eight whole months over this discourse, so today he is blinder than a mole, all his keeness of sight doubtless gone to reinforce the sharp edge of his intellect. But the man has no regrets for his lost sight; he even thinks it was a small price to pay for his hour of glory. . . .

But they've heard from someone that the opening words of a speech should be restrained and quietly spoken. As a result they start their introduction so softly they can scarcely hear their own voices – as if it really did any good to say what is intelligible to none. They've also heard that emotions should be stirred by frequent use of exclamations, so they speak in a low drone for a while and then suddenly lift their voices in a wild shout, though it's quite unnecessary. You'd swear the man needed a dose of hellebore, as if it didn't matter where you raise your voice. Moreover, as they've heard that a sermon should warm up as it goes along, they deliver the various sections of the beginning anyhow, and then suddenly let out their voices full blast, though the point may be of no importance, and finally end so abruptly that you might think them out of breath. . . . In fact their entire performance might have been learned from the cheapjacks in the market squares.[9]

Folly treats writers scarcely any better:

Of the same kidney are those who court immortal fame by writing books. They all owe a great deal to me, especially with any who blot their pages with unadulterated rubbish. But people who use their erudition to write for a learned minority and are anxious to have either Perseus or Laelius pass judgement don't seem to me favoured by fortune, but rather to be pitied for their continuous self-torture. They add, change, remove, lay aside, take up, rephrase, show to their friends, keep for nine years, and are never satisfied. And their futile reward, a word of praise from a handful of people, they win at such a cost – so many late nights, such loss of sleep, sweetest of all things, and so much sweat and anguish. Then their health deteriorates, their looks are destroyed, they suffer partial or total blindness, poverty, ill will, denial of pleasure, premature old age, and early death, and any other such disasters there may be. Yet the wise man believes he is compensated for everything if he wins the approval of one or another purblind scholar.[10]

After the writers, the swordsmen. Folly inspires all evils, and first of all war, the most appalling manifestation of man's inhumanity. War and warriors are evoked in harsh phrases, contemptuous of the soldiers of the time, the mercenaries of all armies, slaves condemned to an infamous servitude:

What is more foolish than to embark on a struggle of this kind for some reason or other when it does more harm than good to either side? For those who fall in battle, like the men of Megara, are of no account. When the mail-clad ranks confront each other and the trumpets blare out their harsh note, what use, I ask you, are those wise men who are worn out with their studies and can scarcely draw breath now their blood is thin and cold? The need is for stout and sturdy fellows with all the daring possible and the minimum of brain. Of course some may prefer a soldier like Demosthenes who took Archilochus' advice and had scarcely glimpsed the enemy before he threw away his shield and fled, as cowardly in battle as he was skilled in speech-making. People say that judgement matters most in war, and so it does for a general, I agree, but it's a soldier's judgement, not a philosopher's. Otherwise it's the spongers, pimps, robbers, murderers, peasants, morons, debtors, and that sort of scum of the earth who provide the glories of war, not the philosophers and their midnight oil.[11]

Piety contaminated by superstition does not escape the mockery of Folly.

Closely related to them are the people who've adopted the foolish but pleasurable belief that if they see some carving or painting of that towering Polyphemus, Christopher, they're sure not to die that day, or if any one addresses a statue of Barbara in the set formula he'll return unhurt from battle, or a man will soon become rich if he approaches Erasmus on the proper days with the proper bits of candle and the proper scraps of prayer. They've already got a second Hippolytus, but in George they've found another Hercules too. They piously deck out his horse with trappings and amulets and practically worship it. Its favours are sought with some new small offering. . . . Now what am I to say about those who enjoy deluding themselves with imaginary pardons for their sins? They measure the length of their time in Purgatory as if by water-clock, counting centuries, years, months, days, and hours as thought there were a mathematical table to calculate them accurately.[12]

Indulgences, whatever a poorly understood publicity campaign might have led us to believe, do not remit sins. They are not an assurance of eternal life.

Folly reproaches pilgrims for abandoning wives and children, without good reason, for vain journeys. She points the finger at 'those who lay down such precise instructions in their lifetime for the funeral ceremonies they want that they even list in detail the number of candles, black cloaks, singers, and hired mourners they wish to be there, as if it were possible for some awareness of this spectacle to return to them or the dead would be ashamed if their corpses didn't have a splendid burial.'[13]

If we ask how this satire was able to shock so many honest Christians, from the sixteenth century until our own day, we must blame the provocative form of the work. Malice and irreverence disconcert simple souls who are content with themselves and their lot and persuaded that one cannot set about Churchmen without doing damage to the Church. Many have only noticed those things which affected their egos. It is true that among those whom Folly praises, there are just as many ecclesiastics and laity, if not more. Irony censures the 'right-thinking' people in the Church as it does in the secular world. It spares no one, and denounces the pride of theologians and monks, the bellicosity of popes and princes, the presumptuousness of the learned, the vanity of philosophers and the stupidity of the devout.

The conservative theologians who read the *Folly* were scandalized. They publicly questioned Erasmus and his orthodoxy. Erasmus replied that Folly only attacked abuses and errors. His speech can be understood by enlightened Christians and for them his book is in no way harmful or blasphemous.

Now, if the first and longer part of the *Folly* is satiric, the second is developed altogether differently. After condemning the world without appeal, Folly brings about a genuine conversion. She abandons herself to Divine wisdom, to be rapt in God. Listen to her peroration:

To sum up (or I shall be pursuing the infinite), it is quite clear that the Christian religion has a kinship with folly in some form, though it has none at all with wisdom. If you want proofs of this ... in the first place, Christians come very near to agreeing with the Platonists that the soul is stifled and bound down by the fetters of the body, which by its gross matter prevents the soul from being able to contemplate and enjoy things as they truly are. Next, Plato defines philosophy as a preparation for death because it leads the mind from visible and bodily things, just as death does. And so long as the mind makes proper use of the organs of the body it is called sane and healthy, but once it begins to break its bonds and tries to win freedom, as if it were planning an escape from prison, men call it insane. If this happens through disease or some organic defect, by general consent it is called insanity. Even so, we see this type of person foretelling the future, showing a knowledge of languages and literature they had never previously learned, and giving clear indication of something divine. Undoubtedly this happens because the mind is beginning to free itself from contamination by the body and exercise its true natural power. I think this also explains why those who are struggling at the hour of death often have a somewhat similar experience, so that they speak wonders as if inspired.

Again, if this happens through pious fervour it may not be quite the same kind of insanity, but is so like it that most people make no distinction, especially as the number of folk who differ in their whole way of life from the general run of mankind is very small. And so we have a situation which I think is not unlike the one in the myth of Plato, where those who were chained in a cave marvelled at shadows, whereas the man who had escaped and then returned to the cavern told them that he had seen real things, and they were much mistaken in their belief that nothing existed but their wretched shadows. This man who has gained understanding pities his companions and deplores their insanity, which confines them to such an illusion, but they in their turn laugh at him as if he were crazy and turn him out. . . .

I quote this only as one example; in fact the pious man throughout his whole life withdraws from the things of the body and is drawn to what is eternal, invisible and spiritual. Consequently there is total disagreement between the two parties on every point, and each thinks the other mad; though in my view the epithet is more properly applied to the pious, not the common man.

This will be clearer if I do as I promised, and show briefly how the supreme reward for man is no other than a kind of madness. First consider how Plato imagined something of this sort when he wrote that the madness of lovers is the highest form of happiness. For anyone who loves intensely lives not in himself but in the object of his love, and the further he can move out of himself into his love, the happier he is. Now, when the soul is planning to leave the body and ceases to make proper use of its organs, it is thought to be mad, and doubtless with good reason. This, surely, is what is meant by the popular expressions 'he is beside himself', 'he has come to', and 'he is himself again.' Moreover, the more perfect the love, the greater the madness – and the happier. What, then, will life in heaven be like, to which all pious minds so eagerly aspire? The spirit will be the stronger and will conquer and absorb the body, and this it will do the more easily partly because it is, as it were, in its own kingdom, partly for having previously in life purged and weakened the body in preparation for this transformation. Then the spirit will itself be absorbed by the supreme Mind, which is more powerful than its infinite parts. And so when the whole man will be outside himself, and happy for no reason except that he is so outside himself, he will enjoy some ineffable share in the supreme good which draws everything into itself. Although this perfect happiness can only be experienced when the soul has recovered its former body and been granted immortality, since the life of the pious is no more than a contemplation and foreshadowing of that other life, at times they are able to feel some foretaste and savour of the reward to come. It is only the tiniest drop in comparison with the fount of eternal bliss, yet it far exceeds all pleasures of the body, even if all mortal delights were rolled into one, so much does the spiritual surpass the physical, the invisible the visible. This is surely what the prophet promises: 'Eye has not seen nor heard, nor have there entered into the heart of man the things which God has prepared for those that love him.' And this is the part of Folly which is not taken away by the transformation of life but is made perfect.[14]

Thus the *Folly* concludes, satire transforming itself until it becomes raised to mystery. The folly of the Cross is the purest and highest of follies; it reckons neither prayers nor merits, neither sacrifices nor tests, it is enough for it to love! The Christianity exalted in this book is a mystical Christianity, far removed from the moralism to which some have wanted to reduce Erasmus's religion. Does not the wise fool who does good to his enemies live in defiance of common sense? . . . Dare it be said that Erasmus has not explained all his thought? He leaves us the task of concluding that Jesus Christ himself is the fool *par excellence*, rejected by the world. He is totally lacking in egoism and human prudence, for he loves all men, even those who betray and persecute him.

To the detestable folly of the fashionable, who believe themselves wise and practise the religion of egoism, is opposed holy folly – that of God's fools. What is similar in the different fools is their absence of common sense. The fools of the world do evil without moderation. God's fools do good without calculation. The first part of the book, because it is the most extended and most emphasized, is often the only part cited. The second nevertheless represents its ardent conclusion. It has generally been badly understood by unbelievers and has had little success with believers, who are disconcerted by its unexpected development.

Meditation on death appears to be folly to the worldly. For the Christians it is a spiritual training which draws them from the world to bring them towards the invisible. This is why *The Praise of Folly* should not be assimilated to 'the substitution of the theme of Folly for that of death'. The Folly presented by Erasmus has not forgotten the teaching of Plato.[15]

This pamphlet, which is unlike any other, is no respecter of persons and spares no one, but contains nothing evil or unorthodox. The problem of the *Folly* is essentially a catholic one, and all the great themes of Erasmian thought are present there: humanism, pacifism and Christian commitment. Whereas the wisdom of the world is made up of deceptive security, material satisfaction and intellectual vanity, the wisdom of God is folly, the folly of the redemption, the folly of Calvary, mysterious intimacy with the invisible: the universe retains its inspiration, the Master is there!

It would be vain to see an autobiographical preoccupation in this book, though one can find in it the trace of some memories and the imprint of profound convictions. The *Folly* transmits and transcends the experience of the author, as Christian and theologian, as traveller and humanist. Erasmus gives himself entirely in this breviary of nonconformism and reformism, feigning protection by the choice of an unexpected orator: it is not he, but Folly, who speaks! To be sure, this literary artifice deceives no one, but despite the lightness of tone, the fiction reveals Erasmus to the reader, not only the artist, but also the pamphleteer, with his disillusionments and his hopes, his doubts and his certainties. Erasmus skilfully renews the ancient theme of the clear-sighted fool. He piles up paradoxes and provocative formulas. He allows his gifts to unfold in a euphoric exhilaration which he was never to recover again. The imagination which he shows in the parody is controlled throughout by reason and taste.

The Praise of Folly is indeed a religious pamphlet, but would it be too much to affirm that Erasmus became a pamphleteer out of love rather than malice? If he ridicules the weakness of a devout piety, it is to make that piety worthy of its object. If he condemns war, it is because he loves peace. If he denounces vices, it is in order to exalt virtues. His irony is a tonic because it sweeps away illusions and challenges what it stigmatizes. One senses in him a deceived love which never admits that its cause is lost. His critique is constructive because his lucidity is caring. When he shows in Julius II the warrior Pope, he allows his horror of the man to be shown, but he respects the pontifical function. In effect he continually compares St Peter to his merciless successor in order to recall to the latter the duties of his charge, strange duties according to the calculations and the wisdom of the world. Jesus did not advocate to his Apostles any other conquest than that of souls, any other weapons except those of prayer and sacrifice. Julius II's folly, in the Pauline sense of the term, is what we call the will to power.

Erasmus was not the minstrel of spiritual comfort. When he taunted the spokesmen of the Church, priests, monks, theologians, he reproached them for having forgotten the Gospel and betrayed the Church. It was because he loved the Church, the mystical body of Christ, that he wanted it to be without compromise, a stranger to the covetousness of the world, entirely consecrated to the timely or troublesome preaching of the Gospel. The shepherds were sleeping, unfortunately, while the people of the living God crept along in the dust or wallowed in mud.

For Erasmus, preaching was never far from imprecation. His words sometimes recall, by their vigour and their vitality, those of the leading lights among the medieval preachers.[16] To the sombre picture of his precursors he added a deliberately paradoxical and provocative note. Paradoxes and provocations arise from a pedagogy which is very Erasmian and no less biblical. Erasmus accentuated the trait in order to be more clearly understood; he raised his voice to awaken the sleepers, he magnified his reproaches to get reaction and reflection from his readers. His grievances were born of a harsh analysis of the role of the Church in the Catholic world. The obstacles that he perceived in the way of the Gospel were scandalous and menacing realities: war, Machiavellianism, greed, immorality. Add to these the worldliness of the prelates, the ignorance of the priests, the rigid systematization of theology and canon law, the superstition of popular piety, and finally, the politicization of the Church and general intolerance.

No one could deny the existence of these abuses, even if Erasmus generalized their manifestations and exaggerated their extent. The opinion of his time would accommodate them too often. Erasmus himself saw them and suffered from them. He condemned those responsible and proposed remedies, without jeopardizing the authority of the Church. He was able to appear a free-lancer, but he was in no way a rebel. That is why his teaching foreshadows the Catholic reform of the end of the century, without being merged with it.

It would be a mistake to see the *Folly* as only a diversion, a profane work without religious dimension. It never betrays the sniggering of the sceptic. Erasmus laughs in order not to cry; if he ridicules men, he never ridicules God. Despite his mocking, this is not a scathing attack on religion, but he unmasks those who identify their own glory with that of God.

For Erasmus true wisdom is folly, Christianity is folly. Mystical ecstasy is the highest of follies. St Paul, author of the first praise of folly, said and said again: 'The language of the Cross is folly to those who are lost, but to those who are saved, it is the power of God.' 'What is foolish to the world, God has chosen to confound the wise.' 'If someone among you thinks to be wise in this manner, let him become foolish in order to become wise, for the wisdom of this world is Folly in the eyes of God.'[17] Erasmus is no more radical than St Paul in his letter to the Corinthians. His *Praise of Folly* is first of all an act of accusation, then a catharsis, finally an overwhelming affirmation of faith. Erasmus transcends satire after revelling in it.

The triumph of the *Folly* was rapid[18] and lasting. Its author became an important person in the eyes of his readers and doubtless in his own. The book was read in all settings, appreciated by those who often saw in it only the brilliant essay of a new Lucian, or a second Petronius, rejected by others who confused anti-clericalism and irreligion; it was even to be put on the Index. The remarkable destiny of the book illustrates the cosmopolitanism of its author. In effect, the *Folly* was conceived on the way back from Italy, completed in England, published in France and widely translated into other languages.

The reputation of the *Folly* was due in part to the superficial pleasure it gave readers in too much of a hurry to understand its final lesson well, but sensitive to mockery and paradox. As for Erasmus, he had to recognize that a critical spirit could easily be taken for an evil spirit. Besides, the anger of the scandalized theologians increased tenfold the renown of a work whose form masked its serious purpose so effectively. The worldly success of the book rested on a huge misunderstanding. It is a difficult text: to skim through it is to falsify it; to touch lightly is to spoil its charm. It must be grasped in its totality to gauge all its significance and rediscover in it wisdom alongside folly.

Erasmus at last had readers capable of appreciating the shape and depth of his work. His friend More was one such person.[19] Moreover, England showed itself to be more capable than other countries of understanding the profundity concealed within Erasmus's humour. In Spain also, Erasmus's folly remained contagious and invigorating. If St Ignatius did not support the bold irreverence of Erasmus, it was not the same for Cervantes. There can be no doubt that Don Quixote is a fool. Books on chivalry caused him, delightfully, to lose his head. Sancho is no less a fool, with a different folly, since his role is to demystify the 'point of honour', to ridicule formalism, to incarnate finally this astonishing person of the wise and garrulous fool who swiftly reels off his rosary of adages. If it is true that Erasmus conferred an original depth on the traditional conception of the fool who possesses a superior penetration to common sense, Cervantes must be considered as one of his heirs, by reason of the honour and love with which he paints Don Quixote and Sancho Panza. Thus he has enabled us – like those other heirs of Erasmus, Shakespeare and Rabelais – to have a better perception of the harmony of universal folly as the unexpected image of eternal wisdom.

Thus Erasmus owes a prodigious renown to a work which, in appearance, takes up neither philosophy nor theology. The secret of his genius is to have put in this inimitable masterpiece all his knowledge and all his skill, all his criticism and all his faith. Erasmus's interpreters have rarely looked for traces of his theology in the *Folly*. These traces are nevertheless numerous, visible and eloquent.

Today, *The Praise of Folly* is read with less prejudice than by eighteenth- and nineteenth-century readers. Nevertheless, there was no sudden rediscovery of the religious sense of this unique book. The second part of the book is clearly Pauline. Everything depends on the importance accorded to that part which makes us listen to Folly turned theologian.[20] Everything also depends, and at the same time, on a positive interpretation of the first part, which does not contradict the second, but prepares for it. The discourse of Folly is sometimes difficult to follow, and between foolish wisdom and wise folly the distinction is not always clear. I would not dare to assert that this debate is over.

Beyond the critique of Christianity, the *Folly* is the manifesto of a critical Christianity: a religion inspired by the philosophy of Christ and the teachings of the Church. A spiritual life freed from fear and panic and reassuring formulas. The *Folly* repeats, but with humour, what Erasmus had suggested from 1504, in the *Handbook of the Christian Soldier*. Yes, the men most to be pitied are those who despise works of brotherly charity and misunderstand authentic religion. In short, the pious folly of those who abandon themselves to God in mystical delirium, to the great scandal of the world, is that folly which death does not come to destroy, but to fulfil.[21]

In his defence of the misunderstood *Folly*, Erasmus refined his thought. His book, he said, ought to make Christians rejoice, because it reacted against insidious deviations which obscured the teaching of the Gospel.[22] A paradoxical invitation to wisdom, the *Folly* willed the conversion of the heart in the freedom of love. Such is the profound significance of this religious pamphlet. With this title it deserves to remain the most famous of Erasmus's books.

10

From the *Foundations of the Abundant Style* to *The Education of the Christian Prince*

With *The Praise of Folly*, Erasmus had become fully aware of his talent and had gained a certain notoriety. The time of his tutorship was over, but he remained without permanent means of support, in relative dependence on his patrons and without money. To achieve real success, he had to rely on the trump card of his pen, put to work in the task of criticism. He worked keenly, sometimes angrily, to conquer his public – the public which read Latin – and it was on them that his hopes rested.

He was in England again before the end of 1511, and was to remain there, as we have seen, nearly three years, not wasting his time. On 24 August 1511, from Queens' College, Erasmus recounted to Colet his recent experiences and touched on the miracles of medicine.

> There is a physician here, a fellow-countryman of mine, who relies on the fifth essence to promise amazing feats: he makes old men young and brings the dead to life. This gives me hope that I may grow young again, if only I can get a taste of this fifth essence. If this comes my way, I shall not be altogether sorry I came. . . . When I begin to lecture, I shall report how it goes, to give you even more occasion for laughter.[1]

Between two courses of Greek given to Cambridge students, he prepared books intended for the learning of Latin. Among these books, the *Foundations of the Abundant Style*, printed in Paris by Josse Bade in 1511, was to have an astonishing success: more than fifty editions during the author's lifetime.

Peace in the Netherlands was once more threatened in 1512. Always attentive to the political problems of the day, especially when they concerned his homeland, Erasmus wrote from London to Pieter Gillis: 'I cannot tell you how grieved I am to see our fellow-countrymen gradually slipping into the present conflict, when they have already been harassed by so many wars or, to put it more correctly, robberies. Ah, those tongue-less theologians, those mute bishops, who look on at such dire disasters and say nothing!'[2]

Though he was living in England, Erasmus retained no less privileged relations with the learned men on the Continent. The great French humanist Jacques Lefèvre d'Étaples, whom he had met some years before in Paris, expressed his warm admiration for him: 'Who can fail to respect, admire and love our Erasmus? . . . Long may you prosper for the benefit of all of us and this world of ours; and pray keep a warm corner for one that feels so warmly towards you.'[3]

Erasmus abominated war, and emphasized this forcefully to Antoon van Bergen, the brother of his old protector the bishop of Cambrai:

> I often wonder what it is that drives the whole human race, not merely Christians, to such a pitch of frenzy that they will undergo such effort, expense and danger for the sake of mutual destruction. Indeed, what do we do but wage war, all our lives long? Not all dumb animals engage in combat, only wild beasts, and even they do not war among themselves, but only with animals of other species. Furthermore they fight with the weapons nature has given them, not as we do with the machines invented by a devilish science. Again they do not fight on any kind of pretext, but only for food or in defence of their young, whereas our human wars are generally caused by ambition, lust, or some such disease of the mind. Finally they do not muster serried ranks of troops by the thousand, as we do, for the purpose of mutual slaughter. For us, who boast of naming ourselves 'Christians' after Christ who preached and practised naught but gentleness, who are members of one body, one flesh, quickened by the same spirit, nurtured upon the same sacraments, joined in union to a single head, called to the same eternal life, hoping for that supreme communion whereby, even as Christ is one with the Father, so we too may be one with him – how can anything in this world be so important as to impel us to war, a thing so deadly and so grim that even when it is waged with perfect justification no man who is truly good approves it? . . . If we would find something to call glorious, it is far more glorious to found states than to destroy them; but, as things now stand, it is the common people who build and keep up the cities, whereas the folly of princes brings about their ruin.[4]

This moving plea did not pass without notice, and was soon translated and published in German. Eventually it was to be developed in the edition of the *Adages* which appeared in 1515.

Meanwhile, Erasmus was doing his best to break the last ties which linked him to Steyn. The new prior was the Servatius Rogerus to whom he had earlier made his ardent declarations. We have no letter from

Rogerus, but the insistence with which the return of the former monk had been sought is very clear in Erasmus's reply to these 'marching orders'. In this summer of 1514 Erasmus was settled in Ham, near Calais, with Mountjoy, in a studious retreat, the only kind which suited him. To return to Steyn was out of the question.

> You know, indeed, that it was my guardians' obduracy and the relentless insistence of other people that drove me, rather than persuaded me, to adopt that kind of life. Afterwards I was kept there by the scolding tongue of Cornelis of Woerden, together with a kind of boyish diffidence, although I was clearly conscious how ill-adapted I was to the life; for not everything suits everyone. Through some peculiarity of my constitution I have always found it hard to endure fasting. Once I was awakened I could never go to sleep again for several hours. My mind was attracted solely to literature, which is not practised in your community. In fact I feel certain that, had I entered upon some free kind of life, I could have been accounted good as well as happy.[5]

There is pathos in the retrospective tenderness of this letter. Erasmus's emotion is as visible here as his determination. He was no longer the unknown monk of 1492: he would not return to Steyn. He left the friend of his youth with no illusions, and ended his letter with the words: 'Farewell, once my sweetest companion and now my revered Father.'[6]

After putting his affairs in order, Erasmus decided to leave for Basel. He was to remain there for some months close to the printer Johann Froben who was to be for him a second Aldo and much more. For it was with Froben that he was to publish his great works and his huge patrology.

As was his custom, he moved about on horseback. Between Roulers and Gand, a sudden shying of his mount obliged him to make an awkward movement to maintain his balance. The pain distressed him and left him exhausted. He made a promise then to St Paul to complete his commentary on the Epistle to the Romans if, by the Apostle's intervention, he should recover his health.[7]

Erasmus had regathered his strength and resumed his travels, preceded by his new fame. He was feted spontaneously at Strasbourg, by Jacob Wimpfeling, Sebastian Brant, author of *The Ship of Fools*, and the printer Matthias Schürer. His triumphal progress culminated in Basel on 15 August 1514. Everywhere Erasmus was received with respect and affection. At Basel he met Ulrich Zwingli, while the German humanist Willibald Pirckheimer embarked upon a friendly correspondence with Erasmus which was to forge a deep bond between the two men. Erasmus busied himself with the publication of his latest works. 'Now I am

avoiding every engagement that might take me away from my books,'
he confided in Wimpfeling, on 21 September 1514.[8]

The third edition of the *Adages*[9] came off the press in 1515 with a preface describing the daily work accomplished over more than fifteen years.

In the first edition, published in Paris [1500], which was among the most hastily prepared, the subject put the young author on a false scent. I was thinking that this would involve a small amount of work, but the actual experience showed me that no other literary genre demanded more of the writer. I had no Greek manuscripts, in the absence of which wanting to write about proverbs amounted to wanting to fly without wings, as Plautus said. Following this, I prepared a second edition in Venice [1508]. By then I was no longer unaware of the extent and difficulty of the subject; nevertheless all the work was finished in about eight months, and that immense labour for which a Hercules would not have sufficed, had been brought to fruition by this puny little man. I take as my witness men who could refute me if I was lying: Aldo Manuzio, in whose workshop the work had been edited by my hand and printed with his characters, Joannes Lascaris, then spokesman of the King of France, Marcus Musurus, Giambattista Egnazio, Girolamo Aleandro and many other witnesses to the trouble which I took over this work....

Later, I inherited a very rich library, and had some spare time at my disposal, thanks to the wonderful and unbelievable generosity of a man, or rather of a hero worthy of eternal respect, William Warham, Archbishop of Canterbury, Primate of all England, and deservedly of the whole universe, if men were to be judged by their virtues.... Helped and encouraged by his benevolence, I went back to the drawing board with the commentaries on the proverbs and, reviewing the work from head to toe, as it were, I first corrected the typographical errors, which were not too many. Moreover, in a good number of places I had, in my haste, omitted the translation of Greek words: I added it now at the request of many readers. The passages which seemed to me a little short I boosted by the citation of lesser-known authors. I mentioned, here and there, authors of whom I had not previously thought, or whom I had not had the time to enlist. Finally, there were points on which I was no longer in agreement with myself – why hide it? – and I adjusted myself honestly to the proverb approved by the most worthy men, which says that the second movement is worth more than the first. I downgraded, if I dare to say so, from the rank of proverbs statements which – without having merited it – appeared to have been retained by sluggish or pretentious compilers. By way of compensation, I added a number of new adages to the annals, so that with these additions and some others, the size of the volume grew by more than a quarter.[10]

This edition was more severe than the preceding ones on ecclesiastical institutions and on ecclesiastics themselves. It aroused an unprecedented response. The present took on a more important role and the author made of it a kind of journal before such things existed. He inserted into his learned commentaries the lessons of his religious philosophy, his politics of tolerance and his universalism. He made use of the digression with subtle skill, excelling and taking pleasure in it. As was his custom, he alternated irony and fervour, and on occasion he excused his digressions with a disarming smile: 'What a hunter of proverbs, have I become a preacher?' Once again, Erasmus asserts his position as champion of the two classical civilizations and teacher of the Christian elite.

One of the most famous adages developed in this edition represented the *Sileni*:

> It seems that the Sileni were small images divided in half and so constructed that they could be opened out and displayed; when closed, they represented some ridiculous, ugly flute-player, but when opened they suddenly revealed the figure of a god, so that the amusing deception would show off the art of the carver. The subject of these statuettes is taken from that ridiculous old Silenus, the schoolmaster of Bacchus, whom the poets call the jester of the gods (they have their buffoons like the princes of our time). Thus . . . in the Symposium of Plato, Alcibiades starts his speech in praise of Socrates by drawing a comparison between him and the Sileni, because he looked quite different to the eye of an intent observer from what he had seemed at first appearance. Anyone who took him at his face value, as they say, would not have offered a farthing for him. He had a yokel's face, with a bovine look about it, and a snub nose always running; you would have thought him some stupid, thick-headed clown. He took no care of his appearance, and his language was plain, unvarnished, and unpretentious, as befits a man who was always talking about charioteers, workmen, fullers and blacksmiths. For it was usually from these that he took the terms with which he pressed his arguments home. His wealth was small and his wife was such as the lowest collier would refuse to put up with. . . .
>
> But once you have opened out this Silenus, absurd as it is, you find a god rather than a man, a great, lofty, and truly philosophic soul, despising all those things for which other mortals jostle and steer, sweat and dispute and struggle – one who rose above all insults, over whom fortune had no power, and who feared nothing, so that he treated lightly even death, which all men fear; drinking the hemlock with as cheerful a face as he wore when drinking wine, and joking with his friend Phaedo even as he lay dying. 'You had better sacrifice a cock to Aesculapius to liberate yourself from your vow,' he said, 'since when I have drunk this medicine I shall feel the benefit of true health' – leaving the body, from which arise all the many maladies of the soul. So it was not unjust that in a time when philosophers abounded, this jester alone should have been declared by

the oracle to be wise, and to know more – he who said he knew nothing – than those who prided themselves on knowing everything.

But is not Christ the most extraordinary Silenus of all? If it is permissible to speak of him in this way – and I cannot see why all who rejoice in the name of Christians should not do their best to imitate it. If you look on the face only of this Silenus image, what could be lower or more contemptible, measured by popular standards? Obscure and poverty-stricken parents, a humble home; poor himself, he has a few poor men for disciples, chosen not from kings' palaces, not from the learned seats of the Pharisees or the schools of the Philosophers, but from the customs-house and the fisherman's nets. Then think of his life, how far removed from any pleasure, the life in which he came through hunger and weariness, accusation and mockery to the cross. . . . But if one may attain a closer look at this Silenus image, that is, if he deigns to show himself to the purified eyes of the soul, what unspeakable riches you will find there: in such service to mankind, there is a pearl of great price, in such humility, what grandeur! in such poverty, what riches! in such weakness, what immeasurable strength! in such shame, what glory! in such labours, what utter peace! And lastly, in that bitter death, there is the source of everlasting life.[11]

Erasmus could have stopped there with the spectacle of the suffering Christ. But he wanted to go further, as in *The Praise of Folly*, and utilize the dialectical force of contrasts. That is why the second part of the adage shows us the 'upside-down Sileni'. They have a brilliant exterior, but if opened, their faults break out into view. Princes are revealed as tyrants and prelates as sensualists.[12] The *Silenus* adage, despite its religious intentions, or rather because of them, caused scandal. Though it had treated the theme of the primacy of the spiritual eloquently, it was the only adage of which Rome demanded not merely correction, but total suppression.

The *Dulce bellum inexpertis*[13] provided a marvellous opening for the fourth chiliade of the *Adages*. War is a monstrosity which its victims cannot support. It is a folly for which any praise is unthinkable. Finally, when it is waged by Christians, it is a defiance of God. Arguments for war are without value, if not without force. Erasmus describes the atrocities of war and the crimes of belligerents with indignation and anger. 'War engenders war.' Mourning, destruction, misery, demoralization, tyranny, disability, sickness and death are the inevitable companions of every war, even of victorious ones. Against the lawyers and theologians who had betrayed law and religion to justify war, Erasmus shows that the remedy is always worse than the disease. Peace is without price, as the blindness of Christians is without bounds.

No one is astonished, no one is horrified. There are those who applaud this thing, greet it with cheers and call it holy when it is worse than hellish, and urge on the princes already crazed with fury, adding as they say 'oil to the flames'. One, from the sacred pulpit, promises pardon for all the sins committed by those who fight under the banner of his prince. Another cries: 'Your invincible highness, only remain in your present favourable state of mind towards religion and God will fight on your side.' Another promises certain victory, perverting the words of the prophets by applying them to wickedness, quoting such things as: 'Thou shalt not be afraid of any terror by night, nor for the arrow that flieth by day, nor for the demon of the noon', and 'A thousand shall fall beside thee, and ten thousand at thy right hand', and, 'Thou shalt go upon the asp and the basilisk, the lion and the dragon shalt thou tread under thy feet.' In short, the whole of this mystical psalm was twisted to apply to profane things, to this or that prince. There was no lack of prophets like these on both sides, and no lack of people to applaud such prophets. We heard warlike sermons of this sort from monks, theologians, bishops. All go to war, the decrepit, the priest, the monk, and we mix up Christ with a thing so diabolical! Two armies march against each other carrying the standard of the Cross, which in itself might teach them how Christians should conquer. Under that heavenly banner, symbolising the perfect and ineffable union of all Christians, there is a rush to butcher each other, and we make Christ the witness and authority for so criminal a thing![14]

By their servility, the kings' theologians cover the imperatives of charity with a mantle of silence or a disguise of falsehood. Scandalized to the depths of his soul, Erasmus firmly formulated the duties of ecclesiastical advisers in this area:

> One is suspected of heresy if one earnestly tries to dissuade men from war; but those who water down the Gospel teaching with interpretations like these, and offer princes the opportunity to flatter their own desires, they are orthodox, and great doctors of divinity. A doctor who is truly Christian never approves of war; perhaps sometimes he may think it permissible, but with reluctance and sorrow.[15]

This last quotation leads us to the delicate question of the just war. Erasmus comes to this point without enthusiasm and with reserve. He accepts with difficulty the scholastic theories on the subject. He speaks ironically of theologians who declare every war legitimate, provided that it is declared by a prince, even if this prince is a child or has lost his reason. He adds: 'Who does not think his own cause just?' and concludes: 'He who is responsible for war is ungodly.'[16]

Erasmus's political thought has never had the appearance of a time-less theory. This is why he never developed the Thomist theory of the just war. For psychological and moral reasons, without saying so, he departed from St Thomas. For him kings, even legitimate ones, cannot legitimize war. For him it sufficed to reflect on the concrete data along with the great principles, to repeat his praise of peace and condemnation of war without flagging. His political morality is a morality of situation. Opposed in his character to all kinds of subversion or disorder, he teaches that war and peace are too important to be left in the hands of one man. All men must share responsibility for the decision.

Would a crusade be a just war? Erasmus doubts it, and hopes for a different policy towards the Turks, in the case of legitimate defence.

To me it does not even seem recommendable that we should now be preparing war against the Turks. The Christian religion is in a bad way, if its safety depends on this sort of defence.... What is taken by the sword is lost by the sword. Are you anxious to win Turks for Christ? Let us not display our wealth, our armies, our strength. Let them see in us not only the name, but the unmistakeable marks of a Christian: a blameless life, the wish to do good even to our enemies, a tolerance which will withstand all injuries, contempt of money, heedlessness of glory, life held lightly; let them hear that heavenly doctrine which is in accordance with this kind of life. These are the best arms with which to defeat the Turks....

We are getting ready to annihilate all Asia and Africa with the sword, though most of the population there are either Christians or half-Christians. Why do we not rather acknowledge them, give them encouragement and gently try to reform them? If we have designs for political expansion, if we are hankering after their wealth, why do we cover up such a worldly thing with the name of Christ? While we attack them with human means alone, why do we bring the entire part of the world which remains to us into certain peril? What a small corner of the world is left to us. What a multitude of barbarians we are challenging, few as we are! Someone will say: 'If God be for us, who can be against us?' And he will have the right to say it, if he trusts solely in God....

If we wish to conquer for Christ, let us gird on the sword of the word of the Gospel. Let us put on the helmet of salvation and take the shield of faith, and the rest of the truly Apostolic panoply. Then it will come about that when we are conquered, we are conquerors all the more. Even supposing the outcome of the war was favourable to us, who ever saw anyone made truly Christian by the sword, by slaughter, fire and pillage? There would be less harm in being frankly Jew or Turk than a Christian hypocrite.... I am not saying that I would absolutely condemn an expedition against the Turks, if they attacked us first, and so long as we conducted the war which we claim to wage in the name of Christ, with Christian minds and with Christ's own weapons. Let them feel they are being invited to be saved, not attacked for booty.[17]

Returning to this difficult problem, Erasmus made some concessions. He acknowledged, with difficulty, a defensive war, far removed from a crusade, but he associated it with so many moral conditions that he made it almost impossible. Sometimes, even, peace should be bought: one could never pay too much.

This was an adage of extraordinary length and richness. Reissued in a separate volume, it was to have lasting success, and, above all, it was to serve as a sketch for an even more famous work, *The Complaint of Peace*, which we shall meet again on our way.

Other additional adages in the edition of 1515 served as testing ground for Erasmus for the exposition of his political and ethical thought. There he condensed his observations, reflections and experience. The *Silenus Alcibiades*, mentioned above, in some places recalled the famous dialogue, *Julius Excluded from Heaven*, while the famous adage, *To be born king or fool*,[18] foreshadows *The Education of the Christian Prince*. *The Beetle searches for the Eagle*[19] draws the portrait of the tyrant: the eagle, cruel, hateful, treacherous, whom the poor beetle put in check by a trick. *Happy the man who owes nothing*[20] expressed the money problems that had weighed so heavily in Erasmus's life: it is difficult to gain money and easy to lose it. The adage entitled *You have obtained Sparta*[21] recalls to the prince that his absolute duty is to administer his state well, without seeking to enlarge it at the expense of his neighbours. In passing, he had a dig at Charles VIII, Louis XII, and even Charles the Bold and Philip the Good, all victims of their ambition.

In March 1515 Erasmus left Basel and returned to the Netherlands for several months, staying successively with Pieter Gillis in Antwerp, Jean le Sauvage in Gand and Lord Mountjoy at Tournai.

Of the men whom Erasmus praised at this time the foremost was Leo X, to whom he wrote from London: 'As soon as the world perceived that Leo had been put at the helm of affairs, at once that age of worse than iron turned into an age of gold. . . . Julius was a very great man – the fact that he embroiled almost the whole world in war shows that, I grant you; but to have restored peace to the world proves Leo greater still.'[22]

Erasmus wrote this on 21 May, before Francis I's victory over the Swiss. He would then have needed a strong optimism to believe in the peaceful intentions of the victor of Marignano and the possibilities of papal action. In this letter Erasmus, faithful to his ideal of justice, unhesitatingly paid homage to his friend the Hebraist Johann Reuchlin, who was threatened with accusations of heresy by narrow-minded theologians.

Jean Le Sauvage, chancellor of Burgundy, also received Erasmus's approval for his policies of peace. Like Leo X, he valued and protected Erasmus, without demanding too much of him. The latter was to refuse the patronage of Duke Ernest of Bavaria, despite the friendly insistence of Urbanus Regius,[23] because the prince wanted to attach him permanently to the University of Ingolstadt. Erasmus saw his vocation as an independent writer in danger of vanishing: there was no question of renouncing it. It was through his books that he presented to his contemporaries the fruit of his socio-political observations and his meditation on Christian learning.

Meanwhile, *The Praise of Folly* continued on its way, from success to success, from critique to critique. To Martin Dorp, who regretted that Erasmus had not written a praise of Wisdom, he replied with moderation, describing his spiritual journey.

Nor was the end I had in view in my *Folly* different in any way from the purpose of my other works, though the means differed. In the *Enchiridion* I laid down quite simply the pattern of a Christian life. In my book on the education of a prince I openly expound the subjects in which a prince should be brought up. In my *Panegyricus*, though under cover of praising a prince, I pursue indirectly the same subject that I pursued openly in the earlier work. And the *Folly* is concerned in a playful spirit with the same subject as the *Enchiridion* . My purpose was guidance and not satire; to help, not to hurt; to show men how to become better and not to stand in their way.[24]

Erasmus pressed home his advantage in a caricature of the scholastic theologians.

What can Christ have in common with Aristotle? What have these quibbling sophistries to do with the mysteries of eternal wisdom? What is the purpose of these labyrinthine *quaestiones*, of which so many are pointless, so many really harmful, if for no other reason, as a source of strife and contention? But, you will say, there are things we must enquire into; on some points we must even have a decision. I do not dissent. But on the other hand there are a great many better let go than pursued (and it is part of knowledge to recognise that certain things are not for our knowing), a great many things on which to doubt is a more healthy state than to lay down the law. Finally, if laws must be laid down, let it be done reverently and not in arrogance, and in accordance with the Scripture, not with the so-called reasoning thought up by ordinary men. As it is, there is no end of these petty arguments; yet even in them what disagreements arise between parties and factions! And every day one pronouncement gives rise to another. In short, things have come to such a pass that the sum of the matter depends not so much upon what Christ laid down as upon the definitions of professors and the power of bishops, capable or otherwise; and in all this everything is now so much involved that there is no hope even of recalling the world to the old true Christianity.

All this, and a great deal else, is perceived and regretted by men of great piety and at the same time of great learning, and they regard as the principal cause of it all this bold irreverent tribe of modern theologians.[25]

Erasmus finally commends the ancient works of literature. 'A knowledge of these is so important for our understanding of Scripture that it really seems to me monstrous impudence for one who knows none of them to expect to be called a theologian.'[26] Dorp allowed himself to be persuaded, but the coterie of 'new' theologians maintained his criticisms and kept their distance. None of them wanted to understand the religious intention of the book.

If Erasmus's books absorbed the main part of his life, he did not meanwhile neglect his correspondence. The multiple relations forged by chance on journeys, friends faithful but distant, beggars, occasional admirers, the great ones of the world; there were so many correspondents, so many letters to write or dictate, to keep or to correct. The letters were read by persons other than the correspondent, some were surreptitiously reproduced – indeed, printed by less scrupulous messengers. Why not publish himself some of these letters? In August, back in Basel, Erasmus modestly put in place the first stone of his most considerable work: the edition of his correspondence.[27]

There were only four letters in this first edition, but they were important letters and carefully chosen for a publicity operation in the grand style. Three were addressed from London, where Erasmus had made a brief journey in May: the famous letter to Leo X, whose praise by Erasmus, sincere as it was, perhaps prepared the way for the forthcoming appearance of the *New Testament*. The two others had been sent to two influential cardinals, who had received Erasmus in friendly fashion in Rome some years before: Raphael Riario and Domenico Grimani. The first expressed an unreserved admiration for the Pope, England and the achievement of peace, the other contained in addition more intimate references. Erasmus called to mind his projects and his works, not without some condescension. He talked about himself, he gave of himself a little. It was to Riario that he confided: 'if deprived of [freedom] . . . I should think life not worth living.'[28]

The fourth and last letter had been sent by Erasmus to Dorp, from Antwerp, some weeks earlier. It was a veritable apology of Erasmian thought, as it has come to be seen. The collection represented a kind of synthesis of Erasmus's position in the spring of that year. His concern to publish some of his letters added from then on to his multiple literary preoccupations.

So that these letters might serve better the interests of their author, Erasmus had 'enriched' the text and on occasion modified the date. He did not hide this, nor was he embarrassed by it. Many examples are to be found in other editions of his correspondence. Similarly, modifications brought by others to his letters only shocked Erasmus if they altered the meaning of the phrase or introduced faults in Latin. Johann Witz, schoolmaster at Sélestat, sent Erasmus a poem in honour of the circle of humanists in Basel, Erasmus's friends and collaborators. He responded in a warm and delicate letter.

> To be a schoolmaster is an office second in importance to a king. Do you think it a mean task to take your fellow-citizens in their earliest years, to instil into them from the beginning sound learning and Christ himself, and to return them to your country as so many honourable upright men? Fools may think this a humble office; in reality it is very splendid. . . . No one does more for it than the man who shapes its unformed young people, provided he himself is learned and honourable – and you are both, so equally that I do not know in which of them you surpass yourself.[29]

In his *Lucubrationes*, the same year, Erasmus published his first commentary on a Psalm (the psalm *Beatus vir*), which he dedicated to his friend Beatus Rhenanus, with a constant play on words on the name of the addressee.[30]

When Charles of Austria inaugurated his reign in the Netherlands, in the same year, 1515, Erasmus was a writer respected at the court at Brussels. Similar political views and a great regard united the humanist to Jean Le Sauvage, friend and protégé of the illustrious family of Croy-Chièvres. Jean Le Sauvage had just obtained the post of chancellor of Burgundy. It was doubtless thanks to his influence, and despite Erasmus's indifference to every political responsibility, that he was named a counsellor and received the promise of an annual pension. He replied in 1516 with his *Education of the Christian Prince* a copy of which he offered to the future Charles V,[31] who probably did not read it.

Charles, soon to be king of Spain and Emperor, was not a model of the Christian, peaceful prince. But in 1516 Erasmus could still hope that the Archduke would listen to his advice. He was young and popular, as his father had been in 1504. Erasmus greeted him with the title of 'prince of the Burgundians'. There was no appeal there to revenge: the inhabitants of the Netherlands continued to be called Burgundians,[32] though their country was often given the name of lower Germany. The deeper perspective of the *Education* is, it is true, more imperial than Burgundian or Spanish. It was to the grandson of the Emperor that Erasmus offered this book, which described the ideal education for the ideal prince. Erasmus pitied princes who were ill prepared for their task by flatterers, and kings who let themselves be persuaded that they were always right. The formation of the personality should put the prince on guard against the cult of the person.

In the preface, Erasmus pointed out to Charles the way of peace.

> But you, noble prince Charles, are more blessed than Alexander, and will, we hope, surpass him equally in wisdom too. He for his part had seized an immense empire, but not without bloodshed, nor was it destined to endure. You were born to a splendid empire and destined to inherit one still greater, so that, while he had to expend great efforts on invasion, you will have perhaps to work to ensure that you can voluntarily hand over part of your dominions rather than seize more. You owe it to Heaven that your empire came to you without the shedding of blood, and no one suffered for it; your wisdom must now ensure that you preserve it without bloodshed and at peace.[33]

In this breviary for a prince faithful to the doctrine of Christ there was no theory of conquest, no appeal to the lessons of history to justify annexations, not even a reflection on national defence. The ideal monarchy would doubtless be a truly elective monarchy, but Erasmus would be quite content with a monarchy tempered by appropriate institutions.[34] He refuted and denied Machiavellianism and so-called 'realist' politics in the name of the Gospel.[35] He stood up against the omnipotence of reasons of State and took pains to describe the model of a prince sincerely in love with peace. This prince should submit himself to the laws of Christ for, if the blood of Christ had been shed for the small as well as for the great, the laws of Christ were obligatory for the great as well as for the small. The king, an 'image of God', should display exemplary virtue. Erasmus never went beyond this argument aimed at convinced Christians. He repeated it insistently and granted no part to the civic teaching of Antiquity, which he certainly knew, but which he dismissed as no longer valid, and pagan. He even went so far as to reproach Xenophon for having given many bad examples to kings. 'When you hear of Achilles, Xerxes, Cyrus, Darius or Julius, do not be overwhelmed at all by the enormous prestige of their names; you are hearing about great raging bandits.'[36]

The last chapter of *The Education of the Christian Prince* is entirely devoted to the subject of war. Having recalled that it is more difficult to construct than to destroy, Erasmus suggests recourse to arbiters in case of conflict and condemns every war that is not entirely defensive.

> I have no doubt, most illustrious prince, that you are of one mind with me, by your birth and by your upbringing at the hands of the best and most upright of men. For the rest, I pray that Christ, perfect and supreme, will continue to favour your noble enterprises. He left a kingdom unstained by blood and he would have it remain unstained. He rejoices to be called

the Prince of Peace; may he do the same for you, that your goodness and wisdom may at last give us relief from these insane wars.[37]

As a theorist of Christian peace and a scholar devoted to his books, Erasmus was not to stay long at the court in Brussels. It was Basel that drew him more and more and for many reasons. He was soon to make it the centre, and not just one of the anchorage points, of his activities.

11

The *New Testament*

In 1516 Erasmus stayed briefly in Basel because two important works were appearing at that time from the Froben press: the works of St Jerome, in many volumes, dedicated to the generous Warham, and also that work of his most forgotten today by the general public, but in his own time undoubtedly the most influential, the Greek and Latin *New Testament*.[1] It was a large volume of a thousand or so pages, a genuine pioneering work, to which Erasmus had devoted long years gathering together manuscripts, comparing versions and on occasion correcting the Vulgate. In publishing a new Latin translation, he did not intend to dethrone the Vulgate in the official usage of the Church, but merely to put forward a correct text for the studious reader. The dedication to Leo X was followed by a number of methodological introductions.

The philological exegesis was part of Erasmus's strategy to reawaken Christian philosophy by restoring a Christianity which was at the same time critical and pious. If believers were to read and meditate on Jesus' words, it was desirable to provide a careful foundation course for them by giving an exact, attractive and lively translation which did not alter the message, but made it more accessible. Erasmus believed in the contagious quality of the Good News. The Gospels and Epistles revealed the mind of God in its depth and diversity, and it was a matter of urgency to free the sacred text from the dross of a thousand years.

Erasmus had collected the most ancient manuscripts, not without making some mistakes about dates, which he tended to take back too far.[2] Then, according to the custom of the times, he had chosen a basic text which he corrected and annotated as he went along. Around Erasmus his collaborators, among whom the foremost were Capito and Oecolampadius, formed a team united for action and in action; and Erasmus's high praise for their work showed the extent of his pleasure and gratitude: 'They all know Latin and Greek and most of them even know Hebrew. One excels in history, another in theology. This one is a specialist in mathematics, this one in law, this other again in ancient literature. . . . And what enthusiasm, what gaiety, what perfect concord! One could swear that all these men shared the same spirit.'[3]

The volume caused a sensation. His Latin text, despite its weaknesses, was to be republished more than 200 times and to serve as the basis for all the great translations of the New Testament into modern languages to the end of the Ancien Régime. The Greek text was only joined to it as a reference text. The critical observations and textual corrections were numerous. For example, the famous introduction to John, *In principio erat verbum,* was modified by Erasmus into *In principio erat sermo.* The variant was legitimate – and Thomas More defended it – but *verbum* was too deeply entrenched in the memory to disappear, and in later editions, Erasmus was to put it back.[4] He omitted the Johannine comma (I John 5: 7–8) on the three witnesses. Accused of Arianism for having suppressed a Trinitarian formula, he promised to reproduce it if anyone showed him an ancient manuscript which gave it.[5] He accepted an isolated reading, but posterity was to prove him right. Erasmus moreover rejected the attribution of the Epistle to the Hebrews to St Paul. He indicated that if the Church instructed him with certainty that this epistle was Pauline, he would accept its decision,[6] but it was impossible to contradict him on this point.

In his philological work proper, Erasmus thus showed the reliability of his method and the prudence of his conclusions. The prefaces and notes, completed later by the *Paraphrases,*[7] put forward a personal interpretation of the sacred book. Thus, starting from the verse 'Do not resist one who is evil' (Matt. 5: 39), Erasmus defined the code of non-violence: 'Christ absolutely forbids resistance to evil . . . or to respond to war with war.' Never again was he so radical.[8]

Commenting on the parable of the Sower (Matt. 13: 24–30) he constructed a justification for religious toleration. The commentary on Christ's words 'My yoke is easy' (Matt. 11: 30) ends with a very Erasmian development against the burden of ceremonies. One of the longest notes illuminated the famous passage from the First Epistle to the Corinthians (I Cor 7: 39) and suggested the possibility of divorce in the case of adultery. Another note criticized the proliferation of obligatory holidays, and pointed out the social advantages of diminishing their number. Finally, Erasmus's devotion to Mary was offended by certain inadequate interpretations of the Gospel text. In the *Magnificat, respexit humilitatem* was deftly modified to *respexit ad humiliatem* for, Erasmus said, it was not a question here of the virtue of humility but of the lowliness of the Lord's servant.

On occasion, Erasmus showed the superiority of the Holy Scriptures over relics. Even the relics of Christ were less precious than his word.[9]

A ship would not be large enough to transport all the alleged fragments of the Cross of Jesus! He also ridiculed the absurd objects which were shown to pilgrims under the name of relics: milk from the Virgin, a shoe of St Joseph, a comb of St Anne, a cowl of St Francis, and many others. 'These relics', he said, 'were shown for the profits that were hoped for from them.'[10] Money soiled everything that it touched and piety was compromised by the spirit of greed of those who exploited it.

Erasmus wanted to weigh up the significance of the sacred text, without increasing or minimizing it. He even tried hard to control his reasonable doubts. His exegesis was critical, but not radical, it never denied inspiration, and had the immense merit of integrating harmoniously with the inward life of the Christian. If the reader allowed himself to be guided by the Holy Spirit, Scripture would be illuminated by Scripture.[11] For Erasmus, anyone who studied the Gospel without seeking to apply its teaching to himself was neither a true Christian nor a true theologian.

In the *Paraclesis*, which appeared as a preface to the *New Testament*, he introduced an idea which he was to develop enthusiastically all his life, the philosophy of Christ. He called it a rebirth because it was nothing but the restoration of a nature that had been created good.

Why have we steadfastly preferred to learn the wisdom of Christ from the writings of men than from Christ himself? And he, since he promised to be with us for all days, even unto the consummation of the world, stands forth especially in this literature, in which He lives for us even at this time, breathes and speaks. I should say almost more effectively than when He dwelt among men. . . . I disagree very much with those who are unwilling that Holy Scripture, translated into the vulgar tongue, be read by the uneducated, as if Christ taught such intricate doctrines that they could scarcely be understood by very few theologians, or as if the strength of the Christian religion consisted in men's ignorance of it.[12]

Thus Erasmus wanted all the faithful to be able to read the Scriptures. Modern languages, whose potential he had clearly underestimated, interested him in this respect. He explained his concession in terms which it is difficult to know whether to describe as generous or reserved. 'No tongue can be called barbarian, from the standpoint of charity, if it serves to preach Christ to men.' In this writing Erasmus brings theology and spirituality into a profound unity. His critical spirit resurfaces when he declares: 'God is not offended by solecisms, but he finds no attraction in them.' Or again: 'There are very few learned men, but no one is prevented from being a Christian, from having faith, I would even dare to say, from being a theologian.'[13]

Given that the Gospel was too often forgotten, Erasmus protested unceasingly against all its failures. He denounced the introduction of the worldly spirit and of politics into the Church, the shameless drive of prelates towards honours and money, the hypocritical pharisaism of some religious, the dulling of piety by puerile or reassuring devotions, the decadence of preaching, the abandonment of the missionary ideal. He denounced a moralizing, juridical, military and bureaucratic conception of the Church, the excessive importance accorded to observances of detail and, finally, an external triumphalist religion.

He condemned the abuses rather than the institutions; formalism, not piety; mechanical devotions, not the sacraments and the liturgy. His theology of the heart looked towards conversion in the freedom of love. This conviction lay behind his cry: 'I prefer a sincere Muslim to a hypocritical Christian!'[14]

Erasmus was not afraid to attack the errors of a decadent monasticism.[15] Monks who pronounced vows of chastity, poverty and obedience claimed to have been placed by this fact in a 'state of perfection' which was for them like an eighth sacrament. Erasmus who knew the religious life, could only laugh at this spiritual pretentiousness. The Rule was not above the Gospel. He ridiculed monks who were satisfied to the point of ostentation and trusted even in their own humility, in order to define the ideal better for his readers. The day when the religious exchanged their baptismal name was not a lucky day. Erasmus reminded his readers that baptism could not be actually devalued in this way while so many monks abandoned themselves to desires directly opposed to their vows: luxury, greed, authoritarianism.

For monks withdrawn into themselves in a closed world, the temptation was great to absolutize the Rule, to lose the meaning of Christianity little by little and to set up a Church within the Church. To absolutize the Rule was almost as harmful as cheating with it in order to water it down. In both cases the founders are betrayed by their successors. Besides, Erasmus could not approve of the manipulators of souls who, without discernment, recruited novices too young and inexperienced. The Christian, whether he be lay or cleric, who respected the divine promises of his baptism, had nothing for which to envy the religious who obeyed vows instituted by men. To be pious it was neither necessary nor sufficient to be a monk.

Affirmations as radical as these can be explained only by the lamentable state of the Church at the time of the Renaissance. How many regular clergy, especially in the mendicant orders, had forgotten the moral imperatives of their holy founders? How many secular preachers were incapable of preaching the Gospel without lapsing into prattling or ranting. Numerous bishops and the popes themselves were living in wealth and ease. And the laity, by their very ignorance, were often inclined to the most degrading superstition.

The Praise of Folly had already vigorously expounded what the crying abuses of the Church owed to the decadence of the Papacy and the negligence of the episcopate. Within the Faculties of Theology, nevertheless, it was not so much *The Praise of Folly* as the edition of the *New Testament* which had caused a scandal. The philological critiques disturbed the theologians who saw there a process of undermining aimed at shaking the foundations of the faith. Erasmus was to be accused of recklessness, error and heterodoxy.

One note on the *New Testament* had corrected the translation by Jacques Lefèvre d'Étaples of a passage from the Epistle to the Hebrews (2: 7). From a debate among philologists a theological conflict was to arise which degenerated into a confrontation over the meaning of the Incarnation. Lefèvre seized his pen to defend his version and dismissed Erasmus as 'impious'. For an exegete already suspect, there could be no worse insult! Erasmus defended himself energetically, taking the view that allowing himself to be so described without reacting would itself be 'grossly impious.'[16] Despite his explanations, he was to be publicly accused of irreligion by a Dominican of Louvain: and we might well wonder about the part played by envy in this persistent denigration.

John Eck, a well-known theologian, reproached Erasmus for having written that the Apostles had learned Greek, not by reading Demosthenes, but by talking with uneducated men; he would rather, he said, invoke the gift of tongues to the advantage of the apostles. Erasmus replied to him: 'I do not deny the gift of tongues, but yet it does not follow that the apostles could not learn their Greek from ordinary people.'[17] For him the message was more important than the words which expressed it.

On the other hand, other Church men recognized the author's talents and praised his merits. 'The name of Erasmus shall never perish,' wrote John Colet in his enthusiasm.[18] As for Erasmus, he defended himself with humour against his detractors.

> They think it beneath them [he observed] to descend to these small and schoolmasterly questions; for so they are wont to refer to those who have had a good literary education, regarding it as a great insult to call a man a schoolmaster, as though it would be to the credit of a theologian to be innocent of schooling. Knowledge of grammar by itself is not the making of a theologian, but much less is he made by ignorance of grammar.[19]

It was in the name of the Gospel that Erasmus commended a thoroughly inward spirituality. If, generally speaking, his religion avoided recommending fasting and abstinence for Christians living within the world, if it wished to ignore the austerity of the cloister, it was not on that account any easier.[20] Obedience to the Beatitudes was added to respect for the Decalogue. 'True perfection', he said, 'does not reside in the kind of life, in clothing, or food, but in the vigour of the soul.'[21]

Erasmus was questioned, but he was read. In France and in Spain, admirers would have welcomed him freely, but they invited him in vain, as he did not want to allow himself to be distracted from his great works.

Despite his celebrity, Erasmus still experienced difficult times. He had to sell his two horses to buy clothes as winter approached. Then he wrote from Antwerp to Thomas More from whom he had just received the manuscript of *Utopia*: 'The risk now is that in my smart new clothes I shall starve to death.'[22] Doubtless he exaggerated, to attract friends and benefactors. Despite his privations, his independent spirit did not weaken and humour quickly took the upper hand again. When he heard that the Catholic King wanted to give him a bishopric in Sicily, he exclaimed: 'I was unwilling . . . to exchange my liberty for any bishopric however distinguished.'[23]

A little drawing of Holbein's in the margin of *The Praise of Folly* – one dares not say a portrait – represented Erasmus in 1516 at his work table. On seeing this drawing, he joked: 'If Erasmus had such a fine appearance, he could certainly take a wife!'[24]

As his first edition of letters had met with public favour, he planned to put together without any further delay a second volume of correspondence: *Letters of some famous men to Erasmus*. The collection appeared in October 1516 from the press of Dirk Maartens and not from Froben like the previous one.[25]

Pieter Gillis declared in the preface that it was he who had chosen the best letters from his friend's huge correspondence. Of the twenty letters of the edition, eleven were addressed to Erasmus, seven were from his hand and the last two, which did not belong to his correspondence, celebrated the genius of the exegete. The volume as a whole skilfully highlighted the importance and orthodoxy of the recent edition of the *New Testament*. England was well represented in this volume with six letters, among them one each from Warham, Colet and More. From France there was a letter from Lefèvre and one from Budé, as well as two replies by Erasmus to the same Budé. It is surprising that no letter, apart from the preface, referred to the Netherlands.

Erasmus confided to Budé his hopes and fears. Charles of Spain was a great king, but the Netherlands did not look favourably on scholars.

There is a move in circles near the prince to cover me with gold. But somehow it happens that in my opinion nowhere is good literature held of less account than here; the reason, our quite uneducated rulers. But I have great hopes of Jean Le Sauvage, the chancellor of Burgundy, who is himself not only a very great man and a very wise man but a very learned one, and what is more, a devoted supporter of all men who have distinguished learning to recommend them. If the gods in their goodness will but allow this great man a long life, my hope is that in our country too men will come forward, the fruits of whose genius will bring honour and glory to the reign of a prince who has every other blessing.[26]

A little quarrel, which was not to be the last, cast a passing shadow over the friendship between Budé and Erasmus. Budé reproached Erasmus for wasting time over trifles, and Erasmus replied with humour that he was not a dabbler at all and was irritated at the confusion between versatility and dilettantism. Budé placated him and made honourable amends. This incident showed that the two scholars shared a common susceptibility and aggressiveness.[27]

Writing to Leo X, Erasmus recalled that the New Testament had seen the light of day under his patronage and had earned his favour.

The New Testament published simultaneously in Greek and Latin, revised by me together with my notes, appeared some time ago under patronage of your most auspicious name. Whether this work wins universal approval I do not know; so far at any rate I find it approved by the most approved and leading theologians, and in particular by that incomparable prelate, Christopher, bishop of Basel, who authorized the publication of the book. For by this labour of mine the ancient and commonly accepted text is not pulled up by the roots; here and there I correct it where it is corrupt, in some places I explain its obscurities, and this I do not out of my own fancies nor, as they say, with unwashed hands, but partly on the evidence of very ancient copies and partly in accordance with the views of men whose learning and sanctity alike have been approved by the Church – Jerome, Hilary, Ambrose, Augustine, Chysostom, Cyril. Meanwhile I am always ready either modestly to defend my view where I am right, or gladly to correct it if, being only human, I have made an unwitting mistake.[28]

Returning to Brussels, Erasmus confided in Andrea Ammonio that he felt more and more distant from the Faculty of Theology at Louvain. Some of the most peevish of their professors wanted to refer Erasmus's books to the examination of experts even more touchy. This suggestion had no sequel, but the opposition was not defused.[29] During this period of his life Erasmus was very close to Pieter Gillis. It was the time of the double portrait sent to More, their common friend. As always, affection led Erasmus to offer advice:

Good health, believe me, is mainly in your own hands. Most of our ailments take their rise in the mind, and you will find your work less laborious if you arrange your studies on some rational plan. Your library, your letters, and all your notes should be arranged in definite places; and do not be carried away first into one author and then another, but take in hand one good book at a time and do not abandon it until you have finished it, making notes as you go along of the things that seem worth remembering. Lay down for yourself some definite course of life, deciding what you wish to do at what time of the day. Do not pile one task on another until the earlier one is finished; thus you will make the day seem longer, which is now almost entirely wasted. And since you complain of your memory, I think you may find it useful to set up a kind of journal for each year (it does not take much trouble), and enter in it briefly day by day anything that happens which you would not wish to forget.[. . .]

But above all I urge you in the conduct of business to follow judgement rather than impulse. If there is anything you do not like, look at once to see if you can put it right or if the wrong can be made less; and you will see this more clearly in tranquillity than if you are upset. If anything can be done, do it; if not, what pray is the use of indignation or laments, except to make things twice as bad with only yourself to thank? I beg you in the name of our friendship, consider your life and health more important than anything. If you can maintain your position in life without harming them, by all means do so; but if not, it is false economy to keep one's possessions intact and lose one's health and peace of mind. Above all, if you have too little concern for yourself, mind you do not prove the undoing of someone else as well; for I shall not regard myself as safe and sound unless you are so too, whom I reckon (as I hope for the love of God) the better part of me. Do not spend too much time on things of no account. Youth speeds by, health can break like glass; they must not be squandered. Some things one ought to look down on, and raise one's spirit to the big things. Seneca and Plato – make them your familiar friends; if you converse with them often, they will not let your spirit lie down. A truly great spirit should overlook some wrongs done to it, and to some men's calumnies have neither ears to hear nor tongue to reply. Make the experiment sometimes: discover how much more compliance and intelligent courtesy can do than a spirit headstrong and wayward.[30]

12

The Age of Gold

The success of the *New Testament* left Erasmus in a state of euphoria. He believed that a new age of gold was approaching. His enthusiasm prompted him to write to the theologian Wolfgang Capito: 'We may shortly behold the rise of a new kind of golden age.'

> The enlightened study of literature [he confided in Afinius] blossoms so wonderfully everywhere. This we owe principally to the generosity and goodness of princes, who have begun to concern themselves with the rewards and honours due to outstanding minds, especially since, as though some divine power had altered their intents, they have begun to concentrate all their policy on anchoring peace in the world with everlasting chains?[1]

This theme was spelled out in a letter to Leo X:

> This age of ours . . . has good hopes of becoming an age of gold, if such a thing there ever were. For in this age, under your most auspicious leadership and through your saintly wisdom, I foresee that three of its greatest blessings will be restored to the human race: that true Christian piety which in so many ways is now decayed, the study of the humanities in part neglected hitherto and in part corrupted, and that public and perpetual harmony of the Christian world which is the fountain and the parent of religion and learning.[2]

For Erasmus, the age of gold was the favoured moment, the most blest of all possible times.[3]

His personal situation had improved since the pope had released him from the penalties relating to his absence from the cloister, and this had enabled him to receive a prebend from Courtrai.[4] He had been reconciled with Dorp, who had taken it on himself to placate the theologians of Louvain. It was at Louvain that Erasmus finished the year, after many long weeks at Antwerp with Pieter Gillis. Though he regarded himself as old at fifty years, he was well and was savouring his successes. He now stood at the centre of the great ferment of ideas leading to the spread of culture, theology and peace.

Erasmus's pacifism led him to reject nationalism, but this did not prejudice his patriotism. King Charles of Spain was 'his prince', though this had not prevented the humanist from speaking of France as his country. It is true that he said it in Latin. *Gallia nostra* accorded the French world the generous borders of northern Gaul, the Rhine, according to Caesar. This expansive geography justified in his eyes regarding himself as German and French at one and the same time.[5]

Undoubtedly, Erasmus loved France, which had welcomed him in his youth. He admired its people and its scholars, its capital and its king.[6] The man who has given us so few descriptions waxed eloquent when he evoked the Seine at Paris, or when he celebrated the wine of Burgundy. Even if he showed a strange perception of the French language when he called it 'a barbarous and abnormal language which is written differently from the way it is pronounced and which has strident sounds and accents which have almost nothing human about them,'[7] he certainly had a practical knowledge of daily speech and he was undoubtedly reliving his own experience when he declared that one could learn French in a year, provided that one shared the life of the French.

To his *famulus*, the young Franconian Daniel Stibarus, staying in Paris, Erasmus was to write from Basel, many years later, proposing to him a much more rapid method:

> To learn French you should wisely betake yourself to the school of talkativeness, the barber's shop, where you may now and then observe Pythagorean 'reserve'. For what can you be there other than a listener? Yet one French girl may help you in the language not less than thirty men. The most sure way to progress is to learn the inflexion of the nouns and verbs first, then go to books written in good French; but after you have employed a master, or (if you prefer) a mistress.[8]

From the beginning of his reign Francis I had desired, alongside the old Sorbonne, a new institution with a freer spirit and programme, a royal college of higher learning, a place truly worthy of that cultural revolution that we call the Renaissance. Guillaume Budé, leader of men of letters in Paris, wanted to attach Erasmus to the future Collège de Paris.

> The king [he wrote] had it in mind to attract picked men to his kingdom with generous offers, and to set up in France what I may call a nursery-bed of scholars ... If you could be induced to leave your present abode

and devote yourself to learning here as you have been accustomed to do where you are now, he himself would undertake to confer on you a benefice worth a thousand francs or more ... What a distinction! How it will redound to the high standing of scholars as a whole, if learning like yours recommends you to the greatest and most illustrious of monarchs and he seeks you out and summons you to a land afar off! The monarch in question is not merely French, which is already a great thing in itself; he is Francis, a name introduced by him for the first time into our royal house and, we may fairly conjecture, full of promise of great things. True, he knows nothing of literature, a normal quality of our kings by a tradition which I myself do not much approve; but he has a natural sense of style, is clever, seemly, of gentle and easy access and freely approachable, generously endowed by nature with rare gifts of body and mind ... Besides which he has the wherewithal to be generous.[9]

Budé thought that Erasmus would appreciate the honour which was thus being offered him. His arguments were direct and a little heavy. Erasmus, a reflective as well as a passionate man, was both moved and disconcerted. He would not and could not decide in a few days. He suggested first that the Swiss humanist Glareanus should be chosen in his place, and then wrote to Francis I. His thanks were almost excessively eloquent, but he neither accepted nor refused. He temporized and profited from the occasion to advise the Most Christian King not to seek to enlarge his territory, but to make his subjects happier. With Budé he was scarcely more explicit.

I am deeply obliged to all of you, and above all to your most generous and excellent king; but for the moment I can give no definite answer, until I have taken advice from the chancellor of Burgundy, who is now absent ... as soon as I know what he thinks, I will give you my opinion without reserve. All I will say for the moment is this, that I have always been fond of France for many reasons, but now it has no greater claim on my affection than its possession of Budé.[10]

Budé was hardly satisfied with this response, Francis I even less! Being attached to an institution, however brilliant, had never attracted Erasmus. It was no less true that, despite his titles and connections, he feared Paris just as he feared Louvain, for their Faculties of Theology, which were often hostile to his thought and his writings. If he had been an unquestioning supporter of French policy, he could have seized the occasion to be installed in Paris and to defy the Sorbonne. But this was not the case.

Erasmus's procrastinations had a more important cause. In the same year – 1517 – he had to prepare for the foundation of the Trilingual

College at Louvain. His friend the humanist Jérôme de Busleiden had richly endowed the future institution. By a coincidence which is explained by the intellectual preoccupations of the age, Busleiden also had wanted to create a centre of higher teaching in conformity with the ideal of the Renaissance. To set up this College alongside the University of the Netherlands, no one was better prepared than Erasmus who knew all the famous philologists. He himself did not teach, but he recruited the best masters of Latin, Greek and Hebrew. That task suited him admirably. It was less pleasing to his opponents at the Faculty of Theology, who saw disciples of Erasmus put in place over against them, partisans of the renovation of theology through the study of the three sacred languages. In fact, Erasmus succeeded in achieving in Louvain what Budé had asked him to do in Paris. The Trilingual College was to serve as a model for the College of France.[11] Erasmus dedicated himself to his task until he settled at Basel in 1521. Throughout his life, he continued to interest himself in the work of Busleiden, which had become his own work.

Meanwhile, by his vacillation, Erasmus had tried Budé's patience. The College of France was to come into being without Erasmus. The defeat of Francis I by Charles V, after the election of the emperor and in the Habsburg–Valois War which was its fatal consequence, was to succeed in separating the Dutch humanist from the French humanist, as their countries were separated.[12]

The Complaint of Peace, published in Basel at the end of 1517, like *The Praise of Folly*, employs a bold personification.[13] Peace, like Folly, described men's battles with each other, whether they were scholars, religious or Christians. But while Folly claimed victory and rejoiced in the number of her faithful, Peace claimed defeats, showed her wounds, deplored her loneliness and mobilized in her favour all the healthy forces, that is to say, the moral forces: reason, humanity, brotherly love.

The epoch was well chosen to rally the friends of peace. The policy of the government in Brussels, under the influence of Jean Le Sauvage, was a policy of friendly co-operation with France, a peaceful policy therefore, doubtless dictated more by the national interest than by the impulses of the Gospel, but a policy of which a friend of peace could legitimately hope for a happy outcome, especially when, like Erasmus, he was in no way seduced by the notion of Empire. The work was not a propaganda piece and, if his intentions coincided with those of the chancellor of Burgundy who was their inspiration, one could not doubt Erasmus's sincerity, seasoned and convinced pacifist that he was.

From the preface, Erasmus declared that peace with France, always desirable, was more than ever necessary. Despite the threat of conflict, he still wanted to believe in the good will of Francis I. He had written to him on 21 February of that year: 'You, once you had shown by a war against the Swiss that you lacked neither spirit nor resources for a war, chose none the less to devote all your energies to quelling the tumults of war in perpetuity, that the leading princes of Christendom might henceforward be united in perpetual peace among themselves.'[14] Erasmus's optimism seemed justified, as the Treaty of Cambrai of 11 March 1517 for the moment brought France and the Netherlands closer together and proclaimed a general reconciliation.

Though Erasmus knew how precarious peace remained, it was in a relatively favourable climate that the *Complaint* was set. War was a scourge condemned by Christian morality; it was always fratricide and must be outlawed. Peace, betrayed and denied by all, did not know where to seek refuge; Christians themselves rejected her. Besides, the faith was odiously exploited even among the ranks of soldiers and on their banners. There was a kind of sacrilege there. 'They carry the cross as their standard . . . so that what alone could lead man away from war has become its symbol.' So Peace laments. The disciples of Christ have forgotten the teaching of their master, whereas 'whoever brings tidings of Christ brings tidings of peace [and] whoever preaches war preaches one who is the very opposite of Christ.' Peace exhorts Christians that they 'should surely either cease to pride themselves on the name of Christian or put into practice the teaching of Christ through concord.'[15]

Peace addressed herself to the princes because the institution of monarchy was then the general rule. Among the occasions for war were dynastic marriages.[16] Among the causes, envy. 'Today, if a neighbouring kingdom is rather more prosperous throughout, it seems almost a just cause for starting a war. For if we are willing to admit the truth, what has stirred so many in the past and still stirs them today to take up arms against the kingdom of France except the knowledge that it is the most prosperous of all powers?'[17] Erasmus then has Peace say, 'In times past the Rhine separated the French from the Germans, but the Rhine does not divide Christian from Christian.'[18]

If the princes were the mischief-makers in wars, their troops were scarcely any better. The soldiers whom Erasmus knew and despised were mercenaries who could not be compared to the citizen soldiers of our time. Mercenaries were the terror of the countryside and the dregs of the earth, killers in time of war, assassins in time of peace, savages and plunderers at all times. Soldier priests horrified Erasmus almost as much as mercenaries, for he refused to see in every combattant anything other than a man endowed with a responsible conscience. To kill by obedience is to participate in a crime. How can the combattants, whoever they are, recite the *Our Father* without shame?

'Our Father'? What impudence, to dare to call on God as Father, when you are making for your brother's throat! 'Hallowed be thy name.' How could the name of God be less hallowed than by your violence towards each other? 'Thy kingdom come.' Is this how you pray, when you are planning so much bloodshed to get a kingdom for yourself? 'Thy will be done, on earth as it is in heaven.' But God's will is for peace, and you are preparing for war. Do you ask for daily bread from our common Father when you burn your brother's crops and would prefer them to be lost to you rather than to benefit him? And then, how can you say 'Forgive us the debts we owe, as we forgive those who are indebted to us', you who are hurrying to murder your kin? You pray to be spared the danger of being put to the test, but you risk danger to yourself so that you can endanger your brother. Do you beg to be delivered from the evil one while you are plotting the worst of evils against your brother at his prompting?[19]

Finally, Peace addresses a solemn and emotive appeal to all the powerful ones in the world and to each Christian:

I call on you, princes, on whose assent especially the affairs of the world depend, who bear amongst men the image of Christ the Prince: heed the voice of your King, who summons you to peace. Consider that the whole world is exhausted by a long period of misfortune and demands it of you. If any grievance is still outstanding, it must be endured on a proper concession to the general happiness of all. The matter is too serious to be delayed for frivolous reasons. I call on you, priests, dedicated to God to express in all your endeavours what you know is most pleasing to God, and to cut out what is most hateful to him. I call on you, theologians, to preach the gospel of peace and to make your message ring unceasingly in the ears of the people. I call on you, bishops, and you others who are high in the offices of the church, to see that your authority prevails and peace is held firm in bonds which will last for all time. I call on you, nobles and magistrates, to ensure that your will supports the wisdom of kings and the piety of pontiffs. I call on you all alike who are counted Christians to work together with united hearts. Here you must show how the combined will of the people can prevail against the tyranny of the powerful; here must be the focal point of all endeavour. Eternal concord should unite those whom nature has made one in many things and whom Christ has unified in more, and all should join in a united effort to bring about what concerns the happiness of one and all.[20]

In all his writings on war, Erasmus always came to similar or convergent conclusions. According to him, to assure peace, it was necessary to reconcile the kings and remove from them the outrageous and sole right to decide about war. It was also necessary to make men conscious of their deep solidarity and to stabilise frontiers. Finally – and here is the original aspect of his thought – arbitration must be provided for. It is true that he did not make his wish very clear. He had put forward an idea which would only slowly work itself out. On the other hand, he was sufficiently realistic to admit the possibility of a defensive war. He was to make no other concession.

In 1517 still, Erasmus took one more step against the principle of universal monarchy. In the important preface to his edition of Suetonius, he spoke out against the prestige of the conquerors of former times and the ambition of future ones. Of the Empire he said that 'scarcely anything remains except the shadow of a mighty name.' To want to resurrect the Empire would be to thrust the people into the most frightful wars. 'The true and only monarch of the world is Christ; and if our princes would agree together to obey His commands, we should truly have one prince and everything would flourish under Him . . . I do not think the mind of one mortal man capable of such extensive rule.'[21]

Did the kings listen to Erasmus's voice, the voice of Peace? Did they understand his message? Because of the success of his books, Erasmus was able to hope: the royal houses of France and Spain were for the moment reconciled. He was tempted to have faith in the agreement of princes as well as in progress in good literature and the renovation of theology. His hope was to be passing, his disappointment lasting.

When Charles left for Spain, at the end of the year, his policy changed. It was no longer that of the Netherlands: it became a dynastic and anti-French policy. Some months later the death of the chancellor Jean Le Sauvage lessened the chances of a lasting peace, while Luther was shaking the religious unity of the West. The European sky was full of disturbances. The age of gold faded like a dream!

Erasmus did not evade the most burning theological problems. He replied vigourously to Wolfgang Capito on the subject of faith and the Church. He recalled that 'whatever human speech can utter is mere stammering.'

> It is kind of Baer [he added] to suggest that I should declare continually that I submit what I write to the judgement of the church. So indeed I do, but to give and take many sureties argues lack of confidence. I suppose no man of good will ever writes in any other spirit than dependence on the judgement of the church; but sometimes it is none too clear where the church is to be found. I shall take care never knowingly to write anything that Christ would disown. Those thorny niceties of which you are thinking – I do not believe the Christian faith depends on them. Not that I undertake to secure that there is never anything with which someone somewhere could find fault; no such success has yet fallen to the lot of anyone, either ancients or moderns.[22]

He could not have been clearer or more direct.

In April 1517 Erasmus made a rapid trip to London – his last! – to receive there from the hands of Ammonio absolution from the penalties that he might have incurred, dispensation from the canonical habit and the right to obtain ecclesiastical benefices. On returning to Louvain in August Erasmus, who was longing for a stable home, found lodging with his friend Desmarais. Meanwhile the importance of his library obliged him to move for four years to the college of Lys which was run by another friend of his, Jean de Nève. He appreciated the large room in which he lived, the fine table, the large garden and, above all, the company of his friends. He was happy and worked enthusiastically on the revision of his *New Testament.* To those who reproached him for publishing too much, he replied with Horace that he wrote a lot because he slept badly. He was included in the number of the professors of theology, which allowed him to declare mischievously that he had become one of 'Our Masters', though he was always amused by this title, which he found not very evangelical.

It was also in Louvain that Erasmus applied himself to the composition of his *Paraphrases* of the books of the New Testament, with the exception of the Apocalypse, in which he found little inspiration. The *Paraphrases* were essentially devotional books, intended to make the Gospels, the Acts of the Apostles and the Epistles better known. All of them emphasized the central place of Christ in spirituality. They characteristically celebrated the mystery of Jesus freely undergoing his passion for the salvation of the world.[23] They were printed at various times, the first, the *Paraphrase on the Epistle to the Romans,* being published by Dirk Maartens in 1517.

In the course of his difficult career, we have seen many a time how Erasmus looked to many protectors for the financial security which his work deserved. Hendrik of Bergen, Lord Mountjoy, William Warham and Jean Le Sauvage figure in this way among the number of the patrons of Erasmus, who showed them intermittent gratitude and a fidelity sometimes tinged with ill humour. In any case, any too strict allegiance to a court or an institution repulsed him. His dilatory responses on the subject of the Collège de France bear witness to this.

The story of Erasmus's dealings with the prince-bishop of Liège, Érard de la Marck, is another example of these difficult relations, full of hesitations and misunderstandings.[24] Érard de la Marck was a powerful and impressive prince. He was Erasmus's bishop, and Erasmus, who was living in Louvain, tried his hand with him in 1517. He addressed a respectful message to the prelate and announced that he was sending him his *Paraphrase on the Epistle of Paul to the Romans* which had just appeared.

To these overtures Érard replied with his fine pen.

> I owe you therefore undying thanks for writing to me and for the favourable opinion of me which you express in the same letter. I rejoice in praise from you, whom all men praise. Hitherto you have been unknown to me personally, but your name and fame have been most familiar for the past ten years, both for your high standing as a scholar and for the open and friendly manner of which they tell me. If you would pay me the honour of a visit, I shall consider that you have done me a welcome service. If however you are unwilling to come here, I shall arrange to call upon you myself for the pleasure of your society and conversation... Your sincere friend.[25]

Erasmus was touched, but he avoided acting in haste. There were no pressures on him except work. He replied carefully and tactfully, for he knew that the etiquette of court was not to be treated lightly. He was a past master at prevarication and procrastination.

> Greeting, right reverend Prelate and illustrious Prince. Allow me to reply briefly and without formal prologue to your Highness' most kind letter. You say that you have long known me by reputation and desire to see me face to face.... There is nothing in me worth seeing: and if there were, it is all expressed in my published work. That is the best part of me, and what remains would be dear at a farthing.
>
> All the same, on such a kind invitation I would gladly have come running to your Highness. I am deterred first by this more than wintry weather and secondly by my state of health, weak in itself and so much exhausted by the labours on which I am now engaged that I can hardly keep it up, even if I bury myself at home. Such is the effort with which I toil at the renewal of my New Testament that I myself have grown old at my task, and while I rescue the text from age and decay, I have incurred a double ration of them for myself. For I am resolved either, now that I have started, to work on till I die at my task or to make it worthy the attention of Leo the Tenth and of posterity. I have got so far that, though I am still battling on the high seas, the harbour is beginning to appear little by little, and if Christ sends a fair wind, I shall make the land before Lent. Then, at a kinder season and in leisure of mind, I shall hasten to visit your Lordship, outstripping the swallows and the storks. But if you do not favour even a short delay, I will throw over everything and come.[26]

This attitude was at first sight surprising. Erasmus was making himself popular, he seemed even to have wanted to raise the bidding. He was very little concerned about the disappointment he was inflicting on the one who counted on his visit. Once again he thought only of his work and it was to preserve that that he expected subsidies from his patrons, but keeping full liberty of his movements. Only the peaceable rhythm of his daily work maintained his serenity. We should make no mistake about Erasmus, a priest of fragile health, who did not feel himself made either for the austerities of the cloister or for pastoral charges; a writer without fortune who wanted to be neither professor nor official, even less a courtier. What did he want? Simply to live by his pen. Such a programme is never easy, at any time or in any country, for independence always remains precarious for one who is neither born with riches nor acquires them. His books were only going to bring him real financial security some years later.

For his part, Érard did not realize what this hesitation meant. He wanted a clear reply and did not understand a man who was so unlike him. Erasmus was not to come to see him before Lent of 1518. He was to avoid coming again at the time of his 'prospecting' visit to Basel. To go there, he did not pass through Liège where the prince-bishop was waiting for him. On the return, he hoped to make a visit to him, but a serious illness obliged him to shorten his journey and he returned to Louvain, more dead than alive.[27] It was apparently only a postponement, but the prince-bishop did not like the procedure. Erasmus always hoped for financial support. To make Érard aware of his work, and at the same time to honour him, he published his letter of invitation in a new edition of selected letters.[28] Nothing came of it. The prince doubtless judged that his patronage was worth all the gifts. The humanist appreciated the patronage and came to expect the gifts.

The two men finally did meet some months later in Brussels, that city which Erasmus loved and which, to hear him talk, was populated by *Galli*.[29] He referred to their conversation enthusiastically and often praised the prince-bishop as a friend of good letters. Finally, he dedicated to him his fine *Paraphrase on the Two Epistles of Paul to the Corinthians*, printed in Louvain by Dirk Maartens.

This paraphrase was one of the finest Erasmian commentaries on the theme of mystical 'foolishness' according to St Paul. But it was Pieter Gillis who took it on himself to bring the volume to Liège together with a letter full of extravagant praises. Érard must have appreciated the gesture and the letter which praised him as a prestigious patron, a model for bishops and a peaceful prince.

A little later Erasmus offered the prince the second edition of the *New Testament*, in two volumes printed on parchment and lavishly decorated. Érard de la Marck certainly replied to these gestures of courtesy and respect, but his letter no longer exists. Doubtless it repeated his invitation, but it was not accompanied by any largesse, to the great disappointment of the humanist. No word came from Liège. Erasmus then decided not to make up his mind. He let things go, counting on luck to obtain what he hoped for without doing what he did not want to do. He added the prince-bishop to the list of failed patrons, alongside other ecclesiastics equally rich and parsimonious.

Erasmus entrusted to Pieter Gillis the task of presenting to the public a new edition of his correspondence which represented a pithy summary of his activities. The volume appeared towards the end of April from Dirk Maartens under the title *Aliquot epistolae sanequam elegantes.*[30] These elegant letters were models offered to students. The year 1517 was moreover that of Erasmus's greatest epistolary activity. There remain for us more than 250 letters, but Erasmus must have written and received many more. Serious, sometimes severe, rarely polemical, they have an unexpected point here and there, the effect of Erasmus's irony. Because for him clarity was the prime quality of a letter, he did not hesitate to say to Budé: '[Your reader] has to work almost harder in reading than you did in writing.'[31] Afterwards he was to be surprised at Budé's ill humour.

A Cambridge friend, John Watson, praised Erasmus for the quality of his publications, and expressed particular appreciation for the *New Testament.* Erasmus replied to him that he had tried hard to make the Christian philosophy loved by his readers.[32]

Sadly, the news from England was bad at times. Andrea Ammonio who had officially granted Erasmus his long-awaited dispensations at Westminster in April, was carried off in August by an acute fever. It was a testimony to the disappearance of youth, and Erasmus's grief, as well as More's, was profound. The two friends mutually comforted each other and the double portrait offered to More by Erasmus and Pieter Gillis was to be a source of happiness for each of them.

The theologian and Hebraist Wolfgang Capito of Basel, who was very attached to Erasmus, showed his appreciation for Erasmus's advice in spirited fashion: 'I am grateful for your letter. It is a most elegant piece and, to indicate all its virtues in a single word, purest Erasmus. You not so much commend your Fabricius, my dear Erasmus, as rouse and inspire him wonderfully to model his work on the picture you draw of him.'[33]

At the end of 1517, Erasmus contemplated the future with a reasonable optimism. He wanted to believe in a durable peace, in the unqualified triumph of good literature and the restoration of theology. There was no blindness there. The Habsburg-Valois wars were still to come and Luther appeared no more to be feared for the unity of the Church than Henry VIII.

The age of gold proved to be fragile and vulnerable. Nevertheless Erasmus pursued his task with unqualified hope.

13

From Louvain to Antwerp via Basel and Cologne

The years 1518 and 1519 were as lively for Erasmus as they were industrious. He moved around at will, but was generally based in the Netherlands and most often in Louvain.[1] Everywhere he went he received his friends and was unsparing in offering them his advice. Was it to escape suspicion that he moved around so much? This could be so, though he had many other motives for moving around: to follow or rejoin his patrons, to see his friends again, to study his precious manuscripts.

His journeys did not worry him and hardly interrupted his work at all. He worked while travelling, and he travelled while working. On horseback, he managed to make notes as well as could be expected. In carriages, he re-read his authors. Blessed with an exceptional talent for concentration, he was able to remain impervious to distractions and unexpected circumstances. Though he may have appeared indifferent to the charms of nature and events on the way, he was nevertheless a sharp and penetrating observer. Very little of what he had taken in came out in his letters. The essentials were to reappear in that mirror of life, the *Colloquies*.

The professors of the Brabantine University, especially Jean Desmarez, Jean de Nève and Maarten Dorp, made Erasmus very welcome. The books he had on hand and the organization of the Trilingual College devoured his time and energies.[2] He dreamed of returning to poetry when he had the leisure, but that leisure was to elude him for ever.

In March, his *Praise of Marriage*[3] came off the Maartens press, a spirited statement, the first edition of which went back to Erasmus's years in Paris. The marriage which he praised was clearly Christian marriage. His feminism did not extend to the point of putting in doubt St Paul's doctrine on the submission of woman to her husband, but he praised 'pure and chaste marriage, a very holy form of life'.[4] It is far from certain that he would have intended to set Christian marriage in opposition to monastic celibacy, when the latter was not accompanied by a sacrament. We know what Erasmus thought of the supposed perfection of the religious. He was interested in ecclesiastical celibacy almost as much as in marriage because, in his time, celibacy and marriage were conceived as correlative terms, if not exactly opposed. He intended to show that virtue was also possible within marriage, a fact sometimes underestimated by some theologians, while the vow of chastity, despite the pious halo which surrounded it, too often accommodated itself to serious transgressions.

Having exalted marriage in general, Erasmus did not shrink from taking up the subject of the marriage of priests.

> In my view it would not be ill-advised for the interests and morals of mankind if the right of wedlock were also to be conceded to priests and monks, if circumstances required it, especially in view of the fact that there is such a great throng of priests everywhere, so few of whom live a chaste life. How much better it would be to turn concubines into wives, so that women they now keep dishonourably and with troubled conscience might be retained openly and with honourable reputation; then they could beget children whom they could love as truly legitimate offspring and educate conscientiously, to whom they would not be a source of shame, and by whom they might be honoured in turn. And indeed, I think the representatives of the bishops would have seen to this long ago, were it not that concubines are a greater source of revenue than wives.[5]

The end of this passage emphasized a double scandal, that of the fornicating priests and that of the officials and bishops who took advantage of the priests' fornication. Of that, there was no possible doubt – though abuses could not be measured with statistical precision – so numerous were the witnesses on the subject of ecclesiastical immorality: too many priests then led a scarcely secret conjugal life. The existence of a tax collected by the ecclesiastical judges, as a penalty for the concubines, showed the extent of the evil. Erasmus was not the first to have denounced this tax, and he condemned it more severely than the immorality which it sanctioned. The offended reaction of the theologians and monks was predictable. It was to be so much more severe because Erasmus, in the very same month, appeared to approve of Luther's views on the matter of indulgences. 'The Roman Curia', he wrote, 'has abandoned any sense of shame. What could be more shameless than these constant indulgences?'[6]

Personal worries about his friends distracted him for the time being from the problems of Christendom. He wrote affectionately to Pieter Gillis in April:

In the name of our friendship, than which none could be closer, and for the sake of your own well-being, which is as dear to me as my own, do all you can, my dear Pieter, to speed your recovery. On my return, let me find you cheerful and in good heart, for only then shall I feel that I have returned safely. Live carefully until your friend Adrian gets back, in whom I must say I have much confidence; it is a great thing to have such a friend as one's physician. Meanwhile, do not lower yourself with too much physic. Above all, avoid all strong emotion, excessive joy, unrestrained laughter, too much walking, excessive study, anger especially. My dear Pieter, life is what matters most. Maybe my good advice is tedious; I only hope it may be as successful as it is heartfelt. I think nothing of my own danger, if I may but have the good fortune to see you recovered, by which I mean really vigorous and strong again. Farewell, with your beloved wife and your dear little ones.[7]

In another context he listed the names of his patrons with a complacency which could not conceal his disquiet. At heart, this great traveller was by nature a homebody. 'Home for me is where I have my library and a few pieces of furniture', he was to confide in this same friend.

In May 1518, Erasmus returned to Basel for some months. He was ill there, but did not interrupt his work. Froben printed the revised edition of *The Handbook of the Christian Soldier* in July or August. The volume opened with a long letter to a German monk, Paul Volz, in which Erasmus clarified and justified his aim. There we again find his criticisms and exhortations. He recalled the joke of an earlier friend 'that holiness of life is more noticeable in the book than in its author', but made clear that he had no regrets about the work 'if it encourages so many people to the pursuit of true piety.'[8]

To the criticism that the *Handbook* ignored scholasticism, the author replied that he had wanted to write a short and practical book so that the philosophy of Christ might bring to the faithful peace within.

It need not equip men for the wrestling-schools of the Sorbonne if it equips them for the tranquillity proper for the Christian . . . Why deal with the questions that everyone deals with? . . . Of makers of summaries there is no end; one cannot count them – mixing this thing and that over and over again, and like the men who sell drugs making old out of new, new out of old, one out of many and many out of one all the time?[9]

The great mass of Christian people was disturbed by the unworthy lives of the clergy and the arguments of the doctors. It was necessary to react vigorously against the spirit of the world which had invaded the Church and to return to Christ as the rock from which the living water flowed forth. Around this unshakable centre, there were three circles. The first was constituted by the ecclesiastical hierarchy; the second by the kings and princes; the third by the whole Christian people. Each Christian, whatever his situation, must develop and deepen his faith and his knowledge of essential truths according to the possibilities open to him.

Some criticized the *Handbook* for not having given enough weight to ceremonies. Erasmus did not condemn them, but in his eyes it was 'Judaistic' to believe oneself justified by ceremonies, while daring to offend gravely against one's neighbour. Too often monks seemed to believe that ceremonies led to perfection and that they were themselves perfect. The piety which Erasmus advocated for his readers was 'a piety illuminated by pious doctrine': *pia doctrina et docta pietas.*[10] The antithetical structure of the phrase expressed its double requirement and explained well what the philosophy of Christ really was. Nothing was more opposed to true piety than 'the mask of piety', a piety without sincerity, without depth and without resources: the Christian should reflect on Holy Scripture with a pious spirit.

In order to clarify the ideal to be put forward for priests, Erasmus observed that lust was not the greatest of evils.

> One offence we exaggerate in tragic fashion as the last degree of horror – to handle the Lord's body with the same hands that have touched the body of a whore . . . A priest may be a gambler, a warrior or a swordsman, quite illiterate, wholly immersed in secular business, devoted to carrying out criminal orders from criminal princes: they do not protest so loudly against him, although as he handles the holy mysteries he is entirely profane. A priest may be a scandalmonger who with poisoned tongue and contrived scurrilities attacks the reputation of a man who has done nothing to deserve it and has in fact done him a service: why do we not greet this with cries of 'Outrage! How dare you with that hellish poison on your tongue, with your mouth with which you butcher an innocent man, both consecrate and eat the body of him who died for the ungodly too?' But this is an evil of which we think so little that men who profess religion in its purest form almost get credit for it.[11]

All these words were familiar to Erasmus and we have already met them from his pen. What was new was the yet unpublished presentation of Erasmian ideas and the insistence with which the author defended his work and his ideas. The new edition of the *Handbook* was to be well received by those who earnestly desired that the Church be put right. With others, it was to arouse polite indifference or a deep suspicion.

In August and September Erasmus published a new volume of letters, modestly entitled *Supplement to Selected Letters*, with a fine frontispiece by Holbein.[12] These letters, especially the most recent ones, were of great interest and of a refreshing variety, like his letter in April to Pieter Gillis. In others the polemicist or the pacifist were to be revealed again.

He was keen to republish his letter to Ernest of Bavaria because it developed the theme of *The Complaint of Peace* and criticized conquerors.

In this *Supplement,* Erasmus succeeded in grouping together very beautiful examples of his epistolary skills: it was an anthology and not a manual. In it the polemicist appears to be sure, but so also do the humanist, the poet, the pacifist and the man. Some letters were only letters of personal courtesy or recommendations in favour of one or other of his pupils. Sometimes Erasmus drew himself to the attention of the great. Most often his letters expressed a straightforward and cordial friendship. Moreover, this collection of letters is the one in which the stylistic preoccupations of the author can best be discerned. Teachers were to enjoy reading and explaining to their pupils these model letters, where they found a pure language and elevated sentiments. Through its charm and lack of affectation, the *Supplement* was also to please numerous readers far away from the school benches.

On 4 September 1518 Erasmus left Basel to return to Louvain, beckoned by the foundation of the Trilingual College. This journey was very testing for the humanist; he dragged himself along there with suffering.[13] He had undoubtedly contracted the plague in the course of his journey, but he was not resigned to it. 'If it was indeed plague,' he was to say, 'I drove the plague away at the cost of great effort and discomfort and determination.' He arrived in Louvain half dead and found shelter with the printer Dirk Maartens. He gave a long account of his tribulations to Beatus Rhenanus, but his piety remained unchanged. When he was ill in Cologne or in Louvain, he went out only to attend Mass. 'When I was a young man,' he added, 'I remember how I used to tremble even at the mere name of death. In this at least I have profited as I grew older: I fear death very little, nor do I measure a man's felicity by length of days. I have passed my fiftieth year; and seeing how few out of so many reach it, I cannot fairly complain that my life has been too short.'[14]

For a long time Erasmus had thought of himself as old, though he still had eighteen years to live! It is true that meditation on death had occupied his thoughts throughout his life and that, as the years passed, he had become more detached, if not more serene. Little by little the frightening vision of his parents, who had been victims of the plague while their son was scarcely out of childhood, had faded. Erasmus's Christian education had inculcated in him the sense of death as a difficult passage towards a joyful eternity. Despite his sufferings and his fears, his faith had not vacillated: 'In Christ alone was all my hope, and all I asked of him was that he should give me what he might think best for me.' Erasmus was happily among those disconcerting old men who survive their illnesses and reach a great age without giving up.

Having regained his health, Erasmus revised his edition of the *New Testament*. He added to it a new methodological introduction which appeared separately from Dirk Maartens in November 1518 under the title: *Method of a True Theology*.[15] This was to be republished and enlarged several times. In this work there was no exposition of the truths to be believed, still less any apologetics! The author knew that, like him, his readers accepted without question that the books of the New Testament contained the saving message of Christ and the exemplary history of the beginnings of the Church. As its title indicated, it amounted to an introduction to theological method, and here Erasmus's exegesis received its definitive formulation.

The first part described the spiritual disposition which would protect the true theologian from the attacks of rationalism. The second recommended the study of the three sacred languages and the good utilization of the liberal arts. The third provided an initiation into doctrine and into the mystery of Christ. The fourth and the fifth specified the role of exegesis. Finally, the last part affirmed that method was no less authentically theological for not being indebted to scholasticism. 'Perhaps you may find in the books of Plato and Seneca things which may not be inconsistent with the precepts of Christ; you may find in the life of Socrates things which often agree with the life of Christ. But you may find this circle and harmony of all things agreeing amongst themselves in Christ alone.'[16]

Erasmus did not hesitate to repeat his praise for the theology of the Church Fathers, the 'old' theology, which he opposed to scholastic theology and which he defined as an initiation into the mysteries and a nourishment of the pious soul. It is easy to appreciate the anger of the influential theologians, whose monopoly of teaching was under threat from a 'grammarian' who made light of their too human curiosity. They came up with useless or absurd 'questions' which claimed to unravel or demonstrate the mysteries of faith. They knew the secret of the procession of the divine persons, they described the virginal conception and the resurrection of the body. If they could, they would have explained the Gospel to Jesus himself!

Erasmus praised St John Chrysostom whose view it had been that one could teach the hypostatic union, but not be able to explain it. 'It is true', he said 'that we can only speak of God with inadequate words.'[17] Human words cannot explain the fullness of the Word.

Another example of Erasmus's impudence was that in the notes of this second edition of the *New Testament*, he returned to the question of ecclesiastical celibacy as a burden too heavy for many. 'Perhaps it will be judged to be better', he wrote, 'that a law of public marriage be made for those who are not completely continent, so that they might worship purely and in holiness, rather than gratify lust in unhappiness and shame.'[18]

The growing success of Erasmus's books stimulated the keenness of the printers and aroused their eagerness. From now on, manuscripts were always to find a publisher and sometimes several.

In November 1518, a first edition of the *Colloquies* appeared, with Froben in Basel.[19] It was a printing, unauthorized by the author, of a little pedagogical work composed twenty years earlier, when he had been studying in Paris. The publisher, in a brief preface, recommended the book to all those desirous of learning to speak Latin in a short time. Beatus Rhenanus, a friend of Erasmus and of Froben, explained the story of the book in this way:

> So, by the service of Lambert Hollonius, a learned young man of Liège, when I received the formulas of the *Familiar Colloquies* which Erasmus wrote as a jest twenty years ago or more, while he was staying in Paris, on account of Augustine Caminade (unless I am mistaken), who was teaching some Zealand boys, I took care to have them printed straightway by Froben, to please you especially, and so that other learned people also might have this treasure, which till then was guarded by certain rascals, not unlike that golden fleece by the wakeful dragon, and sold again and again for a great deal by that Caminade. . . . Although the copy had been corrupted in many places, several of which I have corrected, I have left some to the author, who thought that this book was completely lost.[20]

Erasmus received the little volume with surprise. He was shaking when he began it and angry as he finished. To print a book without the author's approval was not unusual at that time: still what was necessary was that the work had to live up to its promises. Did Froben and Rhenanus seriously expect that Erasmus would appreciate their initiative? The author's disappointment was as plain as his displeasure at the presence of the great errors in the text attributed to him. To be sure, he had not forgotten these dialogues devised long before for the benefit of pupils. These were formulas of familiar conversation: how to greet one's friends, how to ask after their health, what to say during meals; finally, how to translate the same idea by several equivalent expressions.

The time necessary for learning did not discourage Erasmus. When Froben promised his readers that his manual would rapidly teach them to speak Latin, nothing could be more foreign to the thought of the author, who believed that time had little regard for anything accomplished without it. Erasmus's vexation grew when the volume was reproduced, with its errors, in Paris, Antwerp, Vienna, Leipzig and Cracow. The success was such that Erasmus was as flattered as he was angered by it. What could he do, but respond to Beatus Rhenanus and correct the text? Erasmus did not resolve to do this with good grace: he was no longer the poor student in Paris and it cost him to let himself be led by indiscreet friends.

In March 1519 he published, with Maartens in Louvain, a corrected edition of the *Colloquies*, at the same time declaring that he was not the author. This disavowal was strange and rather clumsy, and no one was deceived by it. Success was transformed into triumph and the editions, both official and clandestine, continued to multiply.[21] As the number of colloquies grew and their content developed under the author's pen, the book was to increase tenfold in fifteen years.

Meanwhile, Erasmus was always complaining about having too little time. Half amused, half angry, he confided to a teacher and humanist among his friends, Jan Becker of Borssele:

> After such severe illness I must make some provision for re-establishing my health. Here, so far have I been from giving myself any indulgence that I have not even had leisure to be ill; and this Lent would nearly have been the death of me, had I not gone to Antwerp for a change of climate and of food. Moreover, while I was obliged to play the courtier at Mechelen, and to pay my respects to my patrons the bishop of Liège, the bishop of Utrecht, and the other magnates, your Adolph amongst them, I wasted several days. Finally, I am assailed by so many letters from all directions that in answering them a large part is wasted of the time that might have been spent on study.[22]

But he did not hesitate to show his library to the young cardinal-archbishop of Toledo, Guillaume de Croy, who called himself his disciple.

At about the same time, the court called on Erasmus to direct the studies of the young Prince Ferdinand, brother and future successor of Charles V. Erasmus declined this honour, which did not fit in with his aspirations and suggested his friend Juan Luis Vivès, the great Spanish humanist resident in the Netherlands.

The Louvain theologians' offensive against Erasmus got under way in 1519. When the *Dialogue* of Jacques Masson, known as Latomus, appeared, Erasmus took up the defence of the three languages, and through this, of the 'true theology'. His *Apology*, published in Antwerp in March, did not quote Latomus, but supported the Trilingual College by refuting his objections. Philology was necessary for the theologian, Erasmus recalled, but theology went beyond philology because it was inseparable from piety and pastoral work.[23] The scholastic theologians held interminable discussions on those matters which they themselves declared to be inexpressible.

In May he replied to Jan Briaert who, in turn, had criticized *The Praise of Marriage*, and reproached him for having belittled virginity. A new *Apology*, cautious and even self-conscious, appeared in Basel.[24]

In August, Erasmus made a brief journey to Brabant, re-reading Cicero on the way. After a brief visit to Antwerp, he attended a religious service with his friend Pieter Gillis. The preacher, who had recognized him in his audience and wanted to give him a lesson, had no hesitation in insulting him:

> I myself heard a Carmelite I know, a man with powerful lungs and the title and violet bonnet of a doctor of divinity: when he knew I was there (for I was standing opposite him), he proceeded to lay to my charge two out of the three sins against the Holy Spirit. I was guilty of presumption, because I wrote new books to do down all the old ones and actually had not hesitated to emend the Lord's prayer and the song of Mary; and of attacking received truth . . . Pieter Gillis, a very faithful friend, was standing beside me, and he was so angry I thought he would explode; I could not refrain from laughing.[25]

Erasmus was not too worried by this colleague's aggressiveness, which was due to ignorance and envy. He also knew that spitefulness is most effective when it is not totally unwarranted, but linked to small, unverifiable facts. All that had to be done was to signal their presence clearly. Sometimes half-truths were more prejudicial to the truth than were lies.

Erasmus's *Farrago nova epistolarum*[26] appeared in 1519. This large collection of more than 300 letters was, as the title modestly suggests, astonishingly diverse. The letters from the author's correspondents were also as varied as they were picturesque. The Italian Ambrogio Leoni, whom Erasmus had known in Venice, gave a spirited account on the theme of the mobility of Erasmus, who was everywhere and nowhere.

> Hitherto, dearest Erasmus, I have regarded as fabulous the ancient accounts of Pythagoras and Proteus, one of them returning often to this life-giving air and each time dying afresh, the other changing himself into various shapes whenever he pleased; for you know there was not much difference in the behaviour of the two. But now I no longer smile at such tales as trumpery or fables; I believe them to be history, for I know that we are blessed with both of them in your sole person. In such a short space of time you have often died and returned to life, and no less often changed your shape for something new and different. First I heard, actually from Aldus, that you had died in France and a few years later come to life again in Germany. Then it was reported that your loss was mourned in Germany and soon afterwards you reappeared in Italy.

Lastly I was given to understand that you had met your end in England and have now retraced your steps from Avernus and appeared in France, whence you have written to me and to fellow-countrymen of mine and made us all feel much better. So I thought I must be seeing a second Pythagoras. Besides that, you not only changed from an Italian into a Frenchman and from a Frenchman into a German (like the change from a calf into a bird and from a bird into a kind of breadcorn, for which they wrongly read semen in the text of Pliny) but you have turned from a poet into a theologian and effected a transmigration from theologian to Cynic philosopher, and then finally exchanged the Cynic for an orator – marvellous metamorphoses, which we thought the property of Proteus and no one else. For I have seen numberless books of yours in print, in which you have rung the changes on the different personalities or characters of which I speak and have won praise and admiration from a large circles of readers, who moreover all speak constantly of you and of what you say, not as though you were one individual who produced these important opinions, but as if they had three or four different authors.[27]

Erasmus replied in the same tone:

You must not think any of this is due to my own inconstancy; in all the changes and chances of my fate I have always been the same Erasmus who never changes. Nor have I ever been different from what I am now; but the plot of the play took charge, and at different times I have had different parts to play. Yet it is really not until you know all the scenes in which I have had to play my part that you could accuse me of being a Pythagoras or a Proteus. The number of times, after all that has happened, that those men have buried me, the number of times I have survived my own decease! The enemies of human letters kill me off nearly every year and report me dead and buried. How often have I made my way to Basel through the thick of robbery and plague! The monsters I have had to contend with, the labours I have had to get through! You might well think your old friend Erasmus, who used to be made of glass, was now pure adamant. What would you? So runs my destiny.[28]

Erasmus was aware, despite his ordeals, that he had put together a durable achievement. 'Even now, the monument which will recall my name to posterity has been raised.'

Though the letters presented by Erasmus were spread out from 1499 to 1519, a quarter of them belonged to the last two years and in this edition polemic figured excessively: clichés, insinuations, injurious words. When, at the last minute, Erasmus sent two supplementary letters to the printer, they were the most scathing ones in the volume. The first was addressed to the Englishman Edward Lee, the ruthless detractor of the

New Testament, the second to the Inquisitor Jacob Hochstraten, whom Erasmus regarded as a personal enemy. To read them is saddening. How, for example, can one justify the threat expressed in covert words, of an intervention of his German friends against Lee?[29] Moreover, the correspondence exchanged in 1519 between Erasmus and Luther reappeared, perhaps unwisely, in the *Farrago*.

This time, there were other bold and imprudent moves, in the political arena. Erasmus was not content with taunting the warlike Pope Julius II; he let it be understood that he, Erasmus, was no stranger to the pamphlet *Julius Exclusus*. Of King Francis I, who had invited him to Paris and promised him a substantial pension, he wrote with more malice than courtesy: 'I replied to him without really replying.' Charles of Spain, his sovereign, was no longer safe from his epigrams. Erasmus deplored his dull-wittedness. 'Prince Charles', he wrote, 'is called to reign over nine or ten kingdoms. A marvellous fate! I hope that he may be as favourable to our country as to its prince.'

These taunts which spared no ruler were partly to be explained by the author's detachment from nationality. While the nations competed for Erasmus, he gave himself to all and belonged to none. 'For those devoted to studies', he declared, 'it is quite unimportant to belong to one country or another. Every man who has been initiated into the worship of the Muses is my compatriot.' Among his 'compatriots' across frontiers, Erasmus gave pride of place to the Germans Ulrich von Hutten and Philip Melanchthon, the Spaniards Juan Luis Vivès and Francisco Vergara, the Frenchmen Germain de Brie and Nicolas Bérault, the Italians Alciat and Bembo, the Bohemian Jan Slechta and certainly the Englishman Thomas More, the lifelong friend whom he praised to Hutten and with whom he entered into a correspondence full of affectionate enthusiasm.

In publishing his letter of November 1519 to Jan Slechta, an educated nobleman attached to the Utraquist Church in Bohemia, Erasmus tried to publicize the essence of his conception of faith:

> . . . the whole of the Christian philosophy lies in this, our understanding that all our hope is placed in God, who freely gives us all things through Jesus his son, that we were redeemed through his death and engrafted through baptism with his body, that we might be dead to the desires of the world and live by his teaching and example, not merely harbouring no evil but deserving well of all men; so that, if adversity befall, we may bear it bravely in hope of the future reward which beyond question awaits all good men at Christ's coming, and that we may ever advance from one virtue to another, yet in such a way that we claim nothing for ourselves, but ascribe any good we do to God. These above all are the things that must be implanted in the hearts of men.[30]

The tone was more familiar in a letter to Nicolas Bérault which complained of not having obtained a quick reply:

> Such is the pressure, my dear Bérault, of the mass of work by which I am overwhelmed. If you calculate how much time has to be given to religious duties, how much to sleep (of which I need a good deal, and drop off again about dawn), how much to nursing my health, and how much to writing and revising my books, you will easily discover how little remains which I can devote to answering all my correspondents.[31]

That said, Erasmus published his letter in his collected correspondence, which was some comfort to Bérault.

The impact of the *Farrago* on public opinion must have been considerable. In this time of scarce information, an edition of some hundreds of letters dealing with the present was an event. In the mind of their author, the volume was intended to leave a portrait of him as a writer dedicated to literature and theology. Erasmus hoped that in his work readers would discern the witness of the faithful Christian and the word of the open theologian, and see these not as opposed, but united. Had he succeeded in his plan? This is doubtful, and the years ahead were shaping to be difficult.

A little-known episode in Erasmus's ecumenical relations belongs in this period. In 1519 he met the Bohemian Hussites, those Christians separated from Rome and internally divided.[32] Erasmus's ideas were well known to their leaders, who superintended the translation into their language of two of his works: *The Handbook of the Christian Soldier* and *The Praise of Folly*. They believed that they found in them several ideas like their own and they liked the author's independent judgement. Erasmus was never lacking in a clear and critical perspective on the Church to which he belonged, and was thus well placed in their eyes to appreciate a particularly explosive religious situation.

The Bohemian brethren sent an embassy to Erasmus in the hope of gaining his moral authority in service of their struggle. Mikuláš Klaudyán and Laurentius Voticius presented themselves to Erasmus, who was then at Antwerp. They sent him an apology for their faith, printed in Latin some years before. Erasmus accepted the volume and asked for time in order to read it. When the brothers visited him a second time, they were to be disappointed. Erasmus could not give his approval, though he did not condemn them. His attitude can be understood when we realize that the text given to him went beyond many of his most advanced positions. In fact, it expressed a clear hostility to the Roman Church and its rites, which were seen as expressions of idolatry.

However, Erasmus did approve of some minor claims, while declaring his personal preference for communion in two kinds. He also took the Hussites' part over the question of holy days, which had increased, while the forced idleness resulting from this reduced the poorest people to starvation. In the final analysis, Erasmus appealed to the goodwill of all to re-establish unity by reciprocal concessions. He could go no further and his efforts were to be in vain.

14

Polemics in Louvain and Relaxation at Anderlecht

The death of the Emperor Maximilian in 1519 opened the way to the bloody rivalry between his grandson Charles, king of Spain, and Francis I, king of France. With the election of Charles V, the Holy Roman Empire, which appeared to have declined into a purely Germanic institution, regained a measure of its original prestige. Charles in fact appeared to his own peoples and his neighbours as a universal monarch, the arbiter of the world. It is true that the rebirth of the idea of Empire was to prove illusory. Charles entered into the future backwards. He appeared to be master of the world, but he was not. Considered as a whole, the sixteenth century was not to be an imperial century, but a Spanish century, under Charles V's son Philip II with his Atlantic dominions.

The myth of Empire, under Charles V, was revealed in the new Emperor's motto: 'Still further!' The meaning of the imperial emblem, with its famous pillars, was clarified by the motto which accompanied it. Apart from its obvious meaning, namely that his territory extended further than that of the Romans, whose limits had been fixed by the Pillars of Hercules, the motto also recalled that the discovery of the New World coincided, within a few years, with the advent of the king of Spain to the Empire.

Charles V believed the Holy Roman Empire to be a necessary, providential and sacred institution. Was he not the Emperor of Christendom? It was no longer the memory of Charles the Bold that possessed him, but rather that much more prestigious memory of the other Charles, Charlemagne.

Such pretentions could not but exasperate other sovereigns. Henry VIII met Francis I on the field of the Cloth of Gold in June 1520, then Charles V at Calais a month later. On 14 July, the treaty of Calais established an alliance between the king of England and the Emperor against Francis I. Henry VIII's entourage included Thomas More, while Erasmus accompanied Charles V.

The war began. Tournai returned to the Netherlands.

I perceive [Erasmus wrote] and the sight is a torment to me, that this war between the Germans and the French gets more and more bitter every day. What a calamity for the whole of Christendom that the two most powerful monarchs in the world should contend like this in such disastrous conflict! It would be a lesser evil if the question could be decided by a single combat between those whose interests are at stake. But what have citizens and country folk done to deserve this, who are robbed of their livelihoods, driven from their homes, dragged off into captivity, slaughtered and torn to pieces? The spirit of princes must be hard as iron if they consider this and let it be, stupid if they do not understand it, idle indeed if they do not think it worth a thought. I had some hopes of our new pontiff, in the first place because he is a theologian, and then because his high character has been obvious all his life; but somehow or other papal authority carries more weight in stirring up war between princes than in bringing it to an end.[1]

Erasmus's personal worries were no less insistent. His polemic against Edward Lee became sharper year by year. The recent edition of the *New Testament*, with expanded annotations, provoked chain reactions. When, in February 1520, Lee published his *Annotations on the Annotations*, Erasmus was angered and brought out three volumes of justifications in succession. He said to Justus Jonas:

My friends are to write letters highly critical of Lee, but taking care to praise English scholars and the great men in England who support them, and bearing down on Lee and no one else; and him they are to laugh at as a foolish, boastful, deceitful little man, rather than attack him seriously. I should like to see many letters of this kind put together, so that he may be overwhelmed all the deeper. I should like them to be collected from the learned writers and sent me by safe hand, and I will revise them myself and see to their publication.[2]

This somewhat trivial project was realized very successfully, but other theologians continued to criticize the *New Testament*.

The story of the *Antibarbari* illustrates the often perilous episodes in Erasmus's literary life. With all his heart he had maintained this demanding enterprise of showing by his work and his example the harmony between ancient culture and the Christian message. Erasmus's Christianity was not a disembodied religion. It was the coronation of a providential history, in which Athens, Rome and Jerusalem played their continuing roles.

Composed in its first form in 1489, put into practice many times, lost and recomposed, the book was finally published by Froben in 1520.

Thirty years was a long period of gestation! During this time given over to work and reflection, Erasmus's thought had matured, his vocabulary enriched, his style improved. He had made his work more incisive and effective. Moreover, he was preparing a new edition of his correspondence. He wanted to correct his letters, suppress certain passages, improve others. This thankless work wearied and displeased him, because he had many books in hand which he judged to be much more important. His *famuli* collaborated with so much zeal that he expressed his gratitude to them: 'If I had had to draw up a list of all those whose advice has been of great use to me for the edition of the *New Testament*, my *famuli* would have had to have the honour of being cited in my preface.'

Adrian Barland, the Louvain humanist and pedagogue, demonstrated his fidelity to Erasmus by publishing an anthology of Erasmus's letters. This was his response to a request from the printer Dirk Maartens, who wanted to place short and meticulous models of letters at the disposal of teachers and students. 'It will be thought', he wrote, 'that these letters had been written by Cicero himself'. This little book, published in 1520, was a pedagogical success.

Erasmus who, after Luther, was the greatest opponent of indulgences, wrote to Cardinal Wolsey on 7 August 1520, to recommend to him a poor Greek, a collector of indulgences for his monastery on Mt Sinai which had been ruined by the Muslims. The monk spoke Greek, but knew no Latin, and there are few Christians whom a love of Greek makes generous. Erasmus pleaded warmly on behalf of this strange ambassador from the schismatic East.

> The bearer of this letter, Christophorus Paleologus, is a monk of Mount Sinai, by the common consent of reliable judges a man of good family and a thorough Christian, and (as I have learned from the familiar intercourse with him) upright, modest, and not without wit. He is anxious to collect funds for the relief of his monastery . . . In this part of the world his harvest has proved most unproductive, either because we are a close-fisted lot, or because the whole system of indulgences begins to be everywhere exceedingly unpopular.[3]

These reflections were indeed typically Erasmian, combining consideration for persons with disdain for systems.

He replied without constraint to the poet Riccardo Sbruglio who had heaped praise on him.

> It is not unpleasant, to be sure, to receive praise from a man who is praised himself, but it is not expedient to proclaim in any casual

company what your affection for me has dictated to your heart, not to say for the moment that some of it was quite unsuitable. The man who suppresses what good qualities we have lays on us less of a burden than he who ascribes to us what we have not. Sometimes under the gadfly promptings of affection you hold forth with all your powers and fight with every sort of weapon against those who think Erasmus less important than you with your kind heart, would have them think him. Consider: what is the result, except to rouse them to speak more harshly of me than before, and lay a burden of ill will upon me, some of which perhaps may brush off on you? I have long grown used to criticism, and no less am I sated with praise and glory. Admitting openly that I know nothing, I do what I can. If my attempts are unsuccessful, at least in honourable and difficult enterprises one is normally given credit even for the attempt. If my foot slips, I have my consolation: I am a man, I share this fault with all my fellows. If anyone does better, I do not grudge this addition to the public stock of learning; nor do I think it to my discredit if, after I have outstripped many men myself, someone arises who in turn can outrun me. It will not make me one hair's breadth the better scholar, if I claim to know everything; nor am I any the less learned if, with Socrates, I profess to know nothing at all. Though, when all is said and done, how small a part of knowledge is comprised in all we know! For of what I know myself I will not speak.[4]

It is understandable that Erasmus had approved the publication of a similar letter which praised his modesty, without detracting anything from his renown. To Maarten Lips, he advocated: 'Take comfort . . . in the theology of Christ, which delights in good men and makes the best of bad ones.'[5]

Erasmus told Thomas More of an interview with the Louvain Carmelite Egmondanus.

Need I now go into details? Every single chance remark was seized upon for some foul slander, as is the way of quarrelling schoolboys and saucy fishwives; everything I had said was thrown back at me inside out. He brought up a letter I had written to Luther. 'In that letter', I said, 'I tell him what he ought to avoid.' 'On the contrary,' he replied, 'you show him how to write.' Even that, it seemed, would have been unwelcome, had there been less error in what Luther wrote; so anxious was he to see him destroyed, not set right. The thing he could not swallow was my having added 'I am not telling you what to do, but to continue doing what I know you do already.' When I explained that this was the courtesy of the speaker who disclaims any wish to instruct just when he most wishes to, he flared up again. 'How right!' he cried. 'This is just like you rascally rhetoricians – all soft soap and falsehood and lies!' I admitted with a smile that speakers do lie sometimes, but that even doctors of divinity have been known to do so too.[6]

The year 1520 was a particularly fortunate one for Erasmus. As adviser to the new Emperor, he was part of the imperial entourage at the time of the coronation at Aachen.[7] This ceremony did not seem to have impressed him and he retired to his tent. He did not participate in the Diet of Worms. Court life wearied him tremendously.[8]

His publications were considerable: new editions or re-editions, among them the *Antibarbari*, the works of St Cyprian, those of Irenaeus and various apologists. Drawn into polemic, he became more reserved and sometimes less optimistic. His serenity diminished, alas, or even faded away, when letters became justifications, replies, ponderous vindications of an argument destined to wipe out his enemies or reinforce his friends.

We also know Erasmus in 1520 thanks to Dürer's unforgettable portrait: the quivering face, the eyes half-closed, shielding the interior view, on the lips an enigmatic and somewhat distant smile. The model appeared ageless, but with a presence which defied age. He was over fifty years old and would scarcely change any more: his features were fixed, like his character.

Rumours grew that he would soon leave Louvain. At Paris Budé waited for Erasmus who would have liked to retire in solitude, if he did not decide to go back to England or Rome. He was at that time a passionate witness of the Lutheran tragedy. Hostile to all forms of repression, he was no less resistant to the schism which was approaching.

Could St John Chrysostom, patron of anti-Semitism, have inspired Erasmus's views with regard to the Jews? That influence is improbable for, if Erasmus scarcely loved the Jews, he clearly detested Judaizing Christians who contented themselves with an external piety like the Jews. That he called the observance of a religion of fear pharisaical and the theologians who supported this attitude rabbis in no way implies that he was anti-Semitic.[9] He clarified his position to the inquisitor Jacob of Hoogstraten: 'What was the object of such a vigorous campaign to make the Jews unpopular? Which of us does not sufficiently detest that sort of men? If it is Christian to detest the Jews, on this count we are all good Christians, and to spare.'[10] That text expresses 'a discreet but exasperated reproach' in this apostle of tolerance. Later Erasmus was to confirm the assimiliation which he established between the observances of the Jews and the external piety of Christians. 'What I call Judaism', he said 'is not the impiety of the Jews in their own time, but the anxious obedience of Christians with respect to their own observances.'[11]

In his long explanatory letter to Hoogstraten, Erasmus returned to other questions. He justified his efforts to soften the lot of ill-matched couples. Bodily separation was not sufficient to bring them peace.

He invited the responsible clergy to think carefully about the evils of acquiescence:

> I record my pity for people who are loosely held together by an unhappy marriage, and yet would have no hope of refraining from fornication if they were released from it. Their salvation I wanted to secure by some means, if it should prove possible, nor have I any wish for this to happen without the consent of the church. I am no innovator; I refer the whole question to the Church's discretion . . . I am no supporter of divorce; but I pity those who are set for perdition. Christian charity often wishes for something that is not possible, and it is often a pious act to wish for something that you cannot bring about. I point this out in brief and merely by way of comment, not as a matter of dogma; it is you who thereupon emphasize the word 'dogma' in order to get me into trouble. You trembled all over, according to your account, at what I said, so severely that you nearly collapsed in horror, and my brief comment, which I left to the judgment of the church, you describe as an attack on the church as a whole.
>
> After laying foundations such as these, which are so widely different from my true opinions, you prolong the discussion to great lengths, adducing every possible argument to prove that after a divorce remarriage is unlawful, as though I were unaware of the opinions of the early Fathers or the decrees of the church on this subject. But it is possible that the spirit of Christ may not have revealed the whole truth to the church all at once. And while the church cannot make Christ's decrees of no effect, she can none the less interpret them as may best tend to the salvation of men, relaxing here and drawing tighter there, as time and circumstances may require. Christ wished that all his people might be perfect, so that no question of divorce should arise among them; the church has endeavoured to secure the full rigour of the Gospel dogma from everyone. How can you be sure that the same church, in her zeal to find a way for the salvation even of weaker brethren, may not think that this is the place for some relaxation? The Gospel is not superseded; it is adapted by those to whom its application is entrusted so as to secure the salvation of all men. Nor is a thing superseded when it is better understood.[12]

This argument did not convince Hoogstraten, and the professors of the Theology Faculty at Louvain were no more favourable to the suggestions of Erasmus. When matters grew bitter, Erasmus let his indignation be known. The hypocrisy of the Dominican Vincentius Theodorici exasperated him.

> Ever since you moved to Louvain, you have never ceased to deliver wild attacks on my reputation at every opportunity, although never provoked by any injury, however slight. And at first I was unwilling to believe this.

Such conduct seemed unworthy, I will not say of a priest, of a preacher of the Gospel, of a theologian, or of a monk, but of a man. It is a habit of women, and of impudent and foolish women, to use their tongues as a weapon in order to relieve their feelings. Later, when so many reports arrived from all quarters of what you had said, at dinner in one place, in monasteries at another, at another in some tumbrel or hoy, I believed what I was told, but with the limitation that the whole thing, whatever it amounted to, was clearly negligible. And all the time, when we met you were all smiles, all friendly greetings, evidently supposing that what you scattered everywhere would never reach me.[13]

The success of the Trilingual College continued to infuriate the Louvain masters. Erasmus was the mentor of the College; he controlled the recruitment of the teachers. The humanist spirit threatened the old scholasticism. This success pleased Erasmus whose credit was considerable. His financial situation improved and allowed him to make constant use of the services of many secretaries, copyists and messengers. 'I now feel a regular grandee, keeping as I do two horses who are better cared for than their own master and two servants better turned out than he is.'[14]

The way Erasmus's household was run was scarcely appropriate to his needs. His horses carried him to Antwerp or Brussels. His secretaries recopied his works and participated in his research. They had some difficulty in following their master, who published book after book at breakneck speed. In 1521 there appeared through Dirk Maartens, two works of his youth: the *Poems*[15] and the treatise *Contemptio Mundi*.[16] This last work, begun about 1489, appeared at last, with a final chapter added which was not inconsistent with it, but which enlarged its significance. It was not the cloister that mattered for salvation, nor the number of spectacular mortifications, but a complete respect for vows. The world was not however canonized by Erasmus whose ideal was 'the monastery in the world', that is to say, the ordinariness of a secular life taken up with faith and generosity.

In September of the same year, Maartens printed Erasmus's *Apology*[17] against a Spanish theologian Diego López de Zúñiga who had criticized the Erasmian edition of the *New Testament*. This polemic was to be prolonged for some years. In November, Johannes Froben published Erasmus's *Apologies* in Basel.[18] In it we find the echo of his theological disputes with Lefèvre d'Étaples, Jacques Masson (Latomus), Jan Briaert and Edward Lee. If we add some *Paraphrases* and countless letters, we shall have an approximate idea of the humanist's intellectual activity in 1521.

That year – the last which Erasmus spent in the Netherlands – was equally productive in journeys and unforeseen events. First at Louvain, then at Antwerp, from the end of May until October, Erasmus and his library took up residence at the house of his friend the canon Pieter Wychmans, close to the Collegial Church of St Guidon of Anderlecht, near Brussels.

The simple life to which Erasmus aspired he found there for some blessed months. He loved the gentle caresses of spring and revealed their charm with humour.

> I used to think in the old days that it was merely for the pleasure of it that the Ancients spoke so highly of life in the country. Experience has now taught me that it is not so much enjoyable as healthy. Your friend Erasmus had nearly been done for in cities: so endless was the trouble with my digestion. Already I was involved with more than one physician; physic was prescribed for me and pills and enemas, powders, ointments, baths, poultices – everything. And all the time I had no leisure to be ill, so constantly was I called away, now here, now there, by business suddenly arising. And so I packed up my traps and mounted my horses. 'Where are you going?' my servant asks me. 'Wherever we are greeted by a healthy and life-giving climate,' was my reply. Scarcely had I spent two days here and my fever had departed to the devil and my digestion was sound again. I really seemed in this country to grow young again.[19]

The splendid letter which Erasmus addressed to his friend Justus Jonas was written at Anderlecht. In it we find this cheerful happiness and smiling serenity which accompanied his rediscovered health and regained balance. For the edification of his friend, Erasmus described and compared his great spiritual models, Dean John Colet and the Franciscan Jean Vitrier. Unforgettable sketches of two parallel lives, in the course of which the reader may recognize several themes dear to the humanist: praise of the simple, studious and charitable life; rejection of false piety; finally, the philosophy of Christ.

> You have before you, dear Justus, not a portrait but such a sketch as fits the narrow limits of a letter, of two men born in our own day who were in my opinion truly and sincerely Christians. It will be for you to choose out of them both what seems to you to help most towards a really religious life. If you now ask which I prefer, they seem to me to deserve equal credit, when one considers their different surroundings. It was a great thing that Colet in his station in life should have followed so steadfastly the call, not of his nature, but of Christ; yet Vitrier's achievement is more remarkable, in that he developed and demonstrated so much of the spirit of the Gospel in that sort of life, like a fish that lives in stagnant water and yet has no taste of the marsh about it. But in Colet there were some things which showed that he was only human; in Vitrier I never saw anything which in any way had a flavour about it of human weakness. If you take my advice, dear Jonas, you will not hesitate to add the names of

both to the calendar of saints, although no pope may ever write them into the canon. O blessed souls, to whom my debt is so great, assist by your prayers your friend Erasmus, who is still struggling with the evils of this life, that I may find my way back into your society, never thereafter to be parted from you.[20]

No less vivid was the praise of Thomas More in the letter which Erasmus addressed to Budé. He cited him as an example to the French humanist who was apt to complain of the hardness of the times for a father of a family.

More is to be congratulated. He neither aimed at it nor asked for it, but the king has promoted him to a very honourable post, with a salary to be by no means despised: he is his prince's treasurer ... I am the more delighted for More's sake at this attitude of his prince towards him for this reason, that whatever increase in authority or influence accrues to him, accrues, I believe, to the study of the humanities ... But to be a good scholar himself and give generous support to all other scholars is not the only way in which he honours liberal studies. He takes pains to give his whole household an education in good literature, setting thereby a new precedent which, if I mistake not, will soon be widely followed, so happy is the outcome ...

About a year ago, More took it into his head to give me a demonstration of the progress of their education. He told them all to write to me, each of them independently. No subject was supplied them, nor was what they wrote corrected in any way. When they had shown their drafts to their father for criticism, he told them, as though he took exception to their bad writing, to make a cleaner and more careful copy of the same words; and when they had done that, he did not alter a syllable, but sealed up the letters and sent them off to me. Believe me, my dear Budé, I never saw anything so admirable. In what they said there was nothing foolish or childish, and the language made one feel that they must be making daily progress. This charming group, with the husbands of two of them, he keeps under his own roof. There you never see one of the girls idle, or busied with the trifles that women enjoy; they have a Livy in their hands. They have made such progress that they can read and understand authors of that class without anyone to explain them, unless they come upon some word that might have held up even me or someone like me.[21]

Sadly, these childhood letters have not survived. What would we not give to read these Latin letters addressed to Erasmus by More's daughters?

Some weeks later, he was to confide in his compatriot Nicolaas Everaerts, 'the summer with us is so short that sometimes we have none at all, and we are aware that it is leaving us before we have seen it has arrived. Never before was it so clear to me that climate and not food dictates our life. This whole summer I have spent in the country, and never was anything a greater success.'[22]

From Anderlecht, experienced horseman as he was, Erasmus could easily travel to Brussels and Louvain. He was in Bruges in August for the meeting of the emperor and Cardinal Wolsey, Henry VIII's ambassador. On this occasion, he again saw again his friends Thomas More and Juan Luis Vivès for the last time. Finally he left Louvain for Basel on 28 October 1521 full of optimism, to open a new chapter in his career.

15

Erasmus and Luther:
The Clash of Two Reforms

The drama of Luther was to engage Erasmus in new conflicts.[1] The two men knew each other without having met or corresponded. The indulgences affair could have brought them together in common cause for, on this point, without having collaborated, their agreement was manifest: Heaven is not for sale! For the rest, they had scarcely any affinities. To be sure, Erasmus's religious evolution, like that of Luther, was characterized by a reflection on Scripture which brought deliverance from the burden of observances. They were equally opposed to scholastic theology and to monastic piety, but there were more problems which separated them than solutions which united them. Luther was not interested in humanism, while there was nothing of the orator in Erasmus. Luther was to find that Erasmus lacked godliness, while Erasmus was to remain put off by Luther's use of a personal experience for prophetic purposes.

Nevertheless, in 1516 Erasmus and Luther were close enough for their causes to be linked, and sometimes confused, by their friends as well as by their enemies. One of Luther's friends, George Spalatin, chaplain of the elector Frederick of Saxony, made the first move in writing to Erasmus on behalf of Luther.[2] It was a skilful letter, perhaps too skilful, with a summary of Lutheran positions on justification by works according to Saint Paul. Erasmus did not reply and, some months later, Luther confided in one of his supporters:

> I am reading our Erasmus but daily I dislike him more and more. Nevertheless it pleases me that he is constantly yet learnedly exposing and condemning the monks and priests for their deep rooted and sleepy ignorance; I am afraid, however, that he does not advance the cause of Christ and the grace of God sufficiently; here he knows even less than Stapulensis. Human things weigh more with him than the divine.[3]

The problem of indulgences divided the theologians of that time as it embarrasses those of the present day. The excessive influence of financial considerations in the everyday practice of indulgences could not but be a matter of concern to those who were trying hard to purify religion from anything smacking of superstition and magic. Despite the traditional doctrine which limited the effect of indulgences to the penalties due for sins already pardoned, the faithful believed all too often that for the price of alms, indulgences would wipe out the sins themselves and save souls. The larger the gift, the more effective would be the indulgences! Tendentious preaching exploited one of the purest sentiments of the Christian: concern for the salvation of deceased parents.

Leo X, the Medici pope, needed money to rebuild St Peter's in Rome. The treasury of the Holy See was empty, but the treasure of the Church was to help refill it. Faithful to a long tradition, the pope sent preachers throughout Christendom, to preach indulgences and invite the faithful to make extraordinary contributions.[4] Luther was scandalized by this preaching which he judged to be dangerous because it was ambiguous. He summarized his thoughts in certain propositions, the Wittenberg theses. From the time they became known, they caused a shock, and the new printery made Luther famous within a few days by spreading his bold thoughts across the world.

Luther clashed with the scholastic theologians. He did not speak their language, nor was his language understood by them. From this point, he envisaged a radical reform in theology. The Heidelberg Disputation of 1518, allowed Luther to assert his standpoint: 'Because men misused the knowledge of God through works, God wished again to be recognized in suffering. . . . Now it is not sufficient for anyone, and it does him no good to recognize God in his glory and majesty, unless he recognizes him in the humility and shame of the cross.'[5] His theology of the Cross was opposed to what he called the theology of glory; the former was preoccupied wholly with the crucified Jesus, the latter with Jesus glorified among the nations.

In his denunciation of the theology of glory, Luther aimed at Erasmus, without naming him.[6] Nevertheless, his opinion of Erasmus improved when he read these lines in the preface of the new edition of *The Handbook of the Christian Soldier*. He recognized himself in them: 'If one said, for example, that it would be safer to trust to good works than to papal dispensations, one is not condemning his dispensations in any case, but preferring what according to Christ's teaching is more reliable.'[7]

Luther seized this favourable moment and, on 28 March 1519, he wrote his first letter to Erasmus. He wanted to be able to gain his support, for he knew his immense reputation in the intellectual world, and dealt out compliment on compliment.

Often though I converse with you, and you with me, Erasmus my glory and my hope, we do not yet know one another. Is not this monstrous odd? And yet not odd at all, but a daily experience. For who is there in whose heart Erasmus does not occupy a central place, to whom Erasmus is not the teacher who holds him in thrall? I speak of those who love learning as it should be loved. For I am not sorry if among Christ's other gifts this too finds its place, that many disapprove of you; this is the test by which I commonly distinguish the gifts of God in his mercy from his gifts in anger. And so I give you joy of this, that while you are so highly approved by all men of good will, you are no less disapproved of by those who wish to secure the highest places and highest approval for themselves alone.[8]

Erasmus, who had no presentiment of Luther's remarkable destiny, gave no publicity to this letter. He knew that in Louvain the name of Luther was held in contempt. To be sure, he did not approve this intolerant attitude, but he neither could, nor wanted to, follow Luther. After mature reflection, he replied to him on 30 May, in a courteous letter which spoke of the sender as much as of the recipient.

Your letter gave me great pleasure: it displayed the brilliance of your mind and breathed the spirit of a Christian. No words of mine could describe the storm raised here by your books. Even now it is impossible to root out from men's minds the most groundless suspicion that your work is written with assistance from me and that I am, as they call it, a standard-bearer of this new movement. They supposed that this gave them an opening to suppress both human studies – for which they have a burning hatred, as likely to stand in the way of her majesty queen Theology, whom they value much more than they do Christ – and myself at the same time . . .

As for me, I keep myself uncommitted, so far as I can, in hopes of being able to do more for the revival of good literature. And I think one gets further by courtesy and moderation than by clamour. That was how Christ brought the world under his sway . . . We must take pains to do and say nothing out of arrogance and faction; for I think the spirit of Christ would have it so. Meanwhile we must keep our minds above the corruption of anger and hatred, or of ambition; for it is this that lies in wait for us when our religious zeal is in full course.

I am not instructing you to do this, only to do what you do always. I have dipped into your commentary on the Psalms. I like the look of it particularly and hope that it will be of great service.[9]

When the conflict between Luther and Roman authority entered its most difficult phase, Erasmus revealed his attitude to Luther to Albert of Brandenburg, Archbishop of Mainz. He asked for understanding and patience for the reformer.

I do not accuse Luther, I do not defend him, nor am I answerable for him ... It is, I imagine, my Christian duty to support Luther to this extent: if he is innocent, I should be sorry to see him overwhelmed by some villainous faction; if he is wrong, I would rather he were set right than destroyed; for this agrees better with the example Christ has given us, who according to the prophet quenched not the smoking flax and did not break the bruised reed. ... Men in whom gentleness was most to be expected seem to thirst for nothing but human blood, and are all agape for nothing so much as to seize Luther and destroy him. This is to play the butcher, not the theologian. If they wish to prove themselves eminent divines, let them convert the Jews, let them convert to Christ those who are now far from him, let them mend the standard of morality among Christians, which is as corrupt as anything even the Turks can show. ...

In the old days a heretic was listened to almost with respect and was absolved if he did penance; if he remained obdurate after conviction, he was not admitted – that was the extreme penalty – to communion with catholics in the bosom of the church. Nowadays the accusation of heresy is a very different thing; and yet on the slightest pretext at once they are all crying, 'Heresy, heresy.' In the old days a heretic was one who dissented from the Gospels or the articles of faith or things which carried equal authority with them. Nowadays if anyone disagrees with Thomas, he is called a heretic – indeed, if he disagrees with some newfangled reasoning thought up yesterday by some sophister in the schools. Anything they do not like, anything they do not understand is heresy. To know Greek is heresy; to speak like an educated man is heresy. It is, I admit, a serious crime to violate the faith; but not everything should be forced into a question of faith.[10]

To Willibald Pirckheimer, his friend in Nuremberg, Erasmus gave more freely of his views on Luther. 'I am heartily sorry to see a man of such gifts, who seemed destined to be like a great trumpet for proclaiming the Gospel truth, embittered like this by certain men's frenzied uproar.'[11] Erasmus's disappointment can be gauged in a letter to Maarten Lips: 'They will realize later that what I am supporting is not Luther but the peace of Christendom.'[12]

The clandestine publication of the letter to Albert of Brandenburg was particularly inopportune and contributed to making Erasmus's position in Louvain more delicate. In the face of the theologians' intransigence, he pleaded for Luther against those who dismissed him without trying to understand him, and made a schism inevitable. The question of indulgences was bypassed without resolution.

It is not too much to say that in these painful circumstances the ecclesiastical authorities were little disposed towards dialogue and clearly resistant to all changes. Erasmus kept calm and explained himself in this way to his friend the archbishop William Warham: 'As for me, I manage the whole business so as not to be wholly useless to wholesome learning and to the glory of Christ, and yet not to get myself mixed up in civil strife.'[13] Besides, Erasmus showed himself more prudent. He even went so far as to call on the printer Froben to stop publishing Luther's works. He repeated that he would write neither on Luther's behalf nor against him.

At Wittenberg the Professor of Bible developed his programme. He proclaimed the universal priesthood of believers and advocated the re-establishment of communion in two kinds. The number of his supporters grew from day to day. All those in Germany who were struggling against the authoritarianism of the Curia were with him. Over a few years Luther published a number of little treatises which had powerful and lasting echoes. He repeated that the Pope was not above the Bible. He denounced the system of benefices, the celibacy of priests, religious vows, scholastic theology and canon law, commercialized piety and ministerial priesthood.

Rome took the offensive. On 15 June 1520 Leo X listed and condemned Luther's heresies in the bull *Exsurge Domine*. All of his books were to be burned. He was to be excommunicated if he did not retract in sixteen days. Luther raised his voice and called the pope Antichrist.

Hopes for an honourable compromise were dashed when the Church hardened its doctrinal positions. Erasmus, who feared schism as much as he abhorred violence, addressed Luther with a sympathy tempered by aversion.[14] He was for him against those who rejected him without having read him, but he deplored the Reformer's lack of care in his decisions and lack of moderation in his language. In going too quickly too far, he was paralysing and weakening those who wanted a renewal of theology and piety without going as far as a religious revolution. The two men scarcely understood each other. They eyed each other scornfully, but did not seek a confrontation.

On 26 May 1521, the young Emperor Charles V promulgated the celebrated Edict of Worms which made Luther an outlaw. The Bull and the Edict disquieted Erasmus who was utterly opposed to the use of force in matters of faith. He was bold enough to declare: 'The burning of his books will perhaps banish Luther from our libraries; whether he can be plucked out of men's hearts I am not so sure.'[15]

Luther in no way lessened his criticism of Erasmus who, he said, 'seeks tranquillity in his writings and does not look towards the Cross.' Erasmus continued to hold back.

> Those who continue to support Luther have done all they possibly can to lure me into his camp. Luther's persecutors have tried to drive me into his party, raving against me by name everywhere in their public

utterances somewhat more offensively than they do against Luther himself. None of their tricks, however, have succeeded in moving me from my position. Christ I recognize, Luther I know not; the Church of Rome I recognize and think it does not disagree with the Catholic Church. From that Church death shall not tear me asunder, unless the Church is sundered openly from Christ.[16]

Erasmus complained of being torn between the reformers and the orthodox,[17] while Adrian VI, the new pope, a Netherlander and a friend of Erasmus, asked him, from 1522, to abandon his neutrality.

When you say in your letter that you fear lest some men's enmity and malicious gossip may have made us suspect you of a connection with the party of Luther, we wish to put your mind at rest in this regard. For though, to tell the truth, we have received reports on this subject from two or three persons perhaps who are not very well disposed towards you, yet by nature and on principle, and also in accordance with the pastoral office which we hold, we do not usually lend a ready ear to information reaching us to the discredit of learned men who are noted for their holiness of life . . . The affection however which we feel for you and the concern we have for your reputation and true glory prompt us to urge you to employ in an attack on these new heresies the literary skill with which a generous providence has endowed you so effectually; for there are many reasons why you ought properly to believe that the task has been reserved by God especially for you. You have great intellectual powers, extensive learning, and a readiness in writing such as in living memory has fallen to the lot of few or none, and in addition the greatest influence and popularity among those nations whence this evil took its rise . . . While you have the same vivid energy as a writer, your judgment is far more mature and the range of your knowledge far wider. Nor could you reasonably decline this task by maintaining, perhaps from some deeply ingrained modesty, that you are unequal to it.[18]

Erasmus replied respectfully, but evasively. He balked at the presence of anti-Lutheran militancy. He rebuked the rigour of repression and complained of being accused of heresy by preachers who were more hot-headed than enlightened. He had no trouble in showing that he had always opposed schism and factions.

Your Holiness suggests a remedy for these misfortunes. 'Come to Rome', you say, 'or write some really savage attack on Luther. Declare war on the whole of Luther's party.' In the first place, when I hear the words 'Come to Rome', the effect is just like telling a crab to fly. The crab answered 'Give me wings,' and I shall reply 'Give me back my youth, give me back good health.' How I wish my excuse on this point were not so unanswerable! It would take too long to set down all the reasons which have persuaded me to remain all this time in Basel. On one point I would dare to take my oath: if I had seen any course more likely to be of service to Christendom, I would have taken it even at the risk of my life. I never lacked the will to achieve something, only the hope of making any progress.[19]

After these considerations of a personal nature, Erasmus took up the issue and presented a spirited apology for religious liberty.

I perceive that many think this trouble should be healed by severity; but I fear the outcome shows that this plan has long been a mistake ... if it has been decided to overwhelm this evil by imprisonment and scourging, by confiscation, exile, excommunication and death, there will be no need of any plan from me. Not but what I see that a most humane nature like your own prefers a very different sort of plan, designed to heal the evils rather than to punish them. This will not be found abnormally difficult – if only all men were of the same nature as you, so that laying their private feelings on one side, to use your own words, they would whole-heartedly desire to promote Christ's glory and the salvation of Christian people. But if every man concentrates privately on his own advantage, if theologians insist that their own authority must be watertight at every point, if monks allow no reduction in their own privileges, if princes cling to all their own powers tooth and nail, it will be found very difficult to make any plan for the common good.

The first thing will be to investigate the sources from which this evil so often springs up afresh; for they must be set right before all else. And then it will not be found ineffective if once again a pardon is offered to those who have gone astray through the persuasion or influence of others; better still, an amnesty for all wrongs previously committed, which seem to have come about by some sort of destiny. If God deals with us on that principle every day, forgiving all our offences as often as the sinner shows himself penitent, is there any reason why God's vicegerent should not do the same? ... the world should be given some hope of changes in certain points where complaints of oppression are not unjustified. At the sweet name of liberty all men will breathe afresh.[20]

The liberty which Erasmus so heartily desired was not a liberty without qualifications. It required patience, precluded repression and rejected intolerance.[21] Faith could not be constrained. Faithful to his temperament as to his vocation, he wanted to write only to bring reconciliation. He refused controversy through love of concord, but the division was already too profound for one party or the other to take up a position 'above the fray'. Adrian VI does not seem to have replied to this unusual request: for him the fear of the executioner remained the shield of orthodoxy.

Erasmus's reserve was disturbing not only to Catholic radicals who accused him of disarming gestures. Capito, who was to finish his life in Lutheran circles, said it to him without beating about the bush: 'There are all sorts of stories spreading about you. Be careful, while you try to keep on good terms with both factions, not to get yourself disliked by both.'[22]

Meanwhile Erasmus was still waiting, always waiting. He paid tribute to the role of Luther who had 'begun a necessary work.' 'The world', he said, 'needed to be reawakened to evangelical truth, because it had been numbed by scholastic opinions, human constitutions and pontifical indulgences.' Luther, who knew nothing of this certificate of good conduct, judged Erasmus's caution severely; he did not understand his deeper motivations at all. His friend Ulrich von Hutten put a match to the powder by attacking Erasmus violently. Confrontation became inevitable and all hope of conciliation disappeared.

Erasmus replied first to Hutten:

> I love liberty. I neither wish to, nor can, serve any faction. . . . I cannot fail to condemn dissension and it is not within me not to love peace and concord. . . . What should I proclaim? If I condemn Luther completely, I see which party I shall bring help to, and how much evil I shall accomplish. If I approve completely, first I should be acting presumptuously, since I should be approving what perhaps I do not understand; secondly, I should ally myself with a faction which contains many people with whom I would not want to have any business. . . . If I divide my judgement, conceding some things to each party and rejecting other things, I should allow myself to be wounded by both sides and stir up nothing but fresh disturbances. Therefore it seems more prudent to stay still until the princes and the learned, abandoning their prejudices, seek those means which without disturbance may provide for the truth of the Gospels and the glory of Christ.[23]

Having lost all hope of making an ally of Erasmus, Luther wrote to him proudly, showing that he no longer expected anything of him but a prudent moderation. Basically, what did it matter to him, who was resisting both pope and emperor, to have one more opponent?

> To begin, I am saying nothing about the fact that you have behaved quite peculiarly toward us, so that your relationship with my enemies, the papists, would be unimpaired and safe. To continue, I was not especially offended by the fact that you have bitingly attacked and sharply needled [me] in several places in the booklets you have published in order to gain the favor of [my enemies], or to mitigate their fury against you. For we realize that you have not yet been given by the Lord such courage, or rather such a disposition, that you, together with us, could openly and

confidently fight these monsters around us; nor are we the kind of people who would dare to demand from you what would be beyond your strength. . . . I wish that a disposition which is worthy of your fame would be given to you by the Lord. If the Lord defers giving this to you, then I ask you, if you can do nothing else, in the meantime to be only a spectator of our tragedy. Only do not give comfort to my enemies and join their ranks against us. Above all, do not publish books against me, as I shall publish nothing against you.[24]

Erasmus's reply was measured, promising nothing, but not burning his bridges. He deplored the verbal extravagances of his correspondent and his irony surfaces again. 'Whatever you write against me gives me no great concern. When I consider the world, nothing could fall out more happily for me.'[25]

Luther and Erasmus were henceforth clear in their minds about their respective feelings. They had lost all their illusions. Duke George of Saxony, the unconditional supporter of the Roman position, wanted to throw Erasmus into the fray despite himself if necessary. He reproached him for pussyfooting too easily, for sparing Luther, and for thus favouring heresy and consequently betraying the Church.

Could such arguments touch Erasmus? He was too fearful of rooting out the good grain with the chaff. Meanwhile, because he could no longer remain in a state of uncertainty, he agreed to write a book against Luther's doctrines but, by one of those bold manœuvres of which he had the secret, he first published a new colloquy, *An Examination Concerning Faith*.[26] The title was ambiguous: there was no inquisitor in this dialogue.

Erasmus imagined a conversation between Aulus and Barbatius. Aulus, who expresses Erasmus's ideas, asks about the faith of Barbatius, who resembles Luther like a brother. Now Barbatius gives only irreproachable responses! Aulus notes their agreement on all articles of the faith. The joke which ends the dialogue does not detract from its demonstrative value at all:

AULUS: Well, I hope we'll have birds of good omen.

BARBATIUS: Oh, no: fish of bad odor – unless perhaps you've forgotten this is Friday.

AULUS: But that's not part of our bargain.[27]

We may note that it is no longer a question of freewill, indulgences or the pope in the Creed. In establishing agreement between Lutherans and Catholics on essentials, Erasmus made a final attempt at conciliation, but it was unsuccessful. His faith was clear and his loyalty prudent.

Like Montaigne after him – that other disciple of Socrates – Erasmus was not by nature sectarian.

More and more aware of his role in society, he was to feel himself constrained to take sides. Necessity, binding together a thousand reasons, obliged him to declare himself. In order not to pass for an accomplice or a coward, Erasmus finally took up the pen against Luther. His treatise was to make an enormous impact, for he denounced what, according to him, sharply separated the two doctrines on the question of grace and merit.

The book so long awaited appeared in September 1524. It was entitled *The Freedom of the Will* and analysed the liberty of man in relationship to God.[28] In defending the idea of liberty, Erasmus hoped for the support of the humanists. In leaning on Origen, who was more generous than Augustine towards human freedom, he wanted to avoid trusting in works as much as the fatalism which deprived man of the liberty to do good. He believed not in human initiative, but in man's humble co-operation with divine grace.

Erasmus stressed that God was not the author of evil and calmly and methodically defended the traditional position of the Church which accorded something to free will while leaving the greater part to the kindness of God. His theology was optimistic, while that of Luther, in wishing to accentuate the dependance of the creature, denied free will as a term without reality. With the first Epistle to Timothy (2.4), Erasmus repeated that 'It is the will of God that all men shall be saved', and he believed that man had a capacity for God.

In dealing with free will, Erasmus took up a difficult subject which brought him back to scholasticism and which was not very accessible to his preferred public. He applied himself to it nevertheless and his essay appeared to him to be as good as possible in a genre that was as mediocre as it could be. It was through this expedient that he approached Luther: 'There is hardly a more tangled labyrinth than that of "free choice", for it is a subject that has long exercised the minds of philosophers, and also of theologians old and new, in a striking degree, though in my opinion with more labor than fruit.'[29] The book clarified many issues:

> If we are in the path of true religion, let us go on swiftly to better things, forgetful of the things which are behind, or if we are entangled in sins, let us strive with all our might and have recourse to the remedy of penitence that by all means we may entreat the mercy of the Lord without which no human will or endeavor is effective.... This, I say, was in my judgment sufficient for Christian godliness, nor should we through irreverent inquisitiveness rush into those things which are hidden, not to say superfluous: whether God foreknows anything contingently; whether our

will accomplishes anything in things pertaining to eternal salvation; whether it simply suffers the action of grace; whether what we do, be it of good or ill, we do by necessity or rather suffer to be done to us.[30]

The offer of grace and freedom to accept it were for Erasmus inseparable terms in a theological correlation. 'A human eye that is quite sound sees nothing in the dark, a blind one sees nothing in the light; thus the will though free can do nothing if grace withdraws from it, and yet when the light is infused, he who has sound eyes can shut off the sight of the object so as not to see, can avert his eyes, so that he ceases to see what he previously saw.'[31] It is remarkable and revealing of his character that Erasmus had not yielded to the siege mentality of the time. He maintained that Luther was sometimes right and he did his best to take from the error that part of the truth which rendered it attractive, for to identify novelty with heresy would be to confuse ignorance with orthodoxy.

To Luther, who proclaimed the clarity of the Bible[32] in matters concerning salvation, Erasmus replied:

> What need is there of an interpreter when the Scripture itself is crystal clear? But if it is so clear, why have so many outstanding men in so many centuries been blind, and in a matter of such importance, as these would appear? If there is no obscurity in Scripture, what was the need of the work of prophecy in the days of the apostles? You say, 'This was the gift of the Spirit.' But I have the suspicion that just as the charismata of healings and tongues ceased, this charisma ceased also. And if it did not cease, then one must ask to whom it has been passed on. If to any Tom, Dick or Harry, all interpretation is uncertain.[33]

For Erasmus the Church can therefore explain Scripture. Nevertheless he did not deny in any way that the Church should obey Scripture, as Luther for his part had taught.

The Freedom of the Will was received favourably by Catholics in general, though some regretted that Erasmus had not treated Luther with greater severity. Erasmus explained himself, on 10 December 1524, in two letters addressed, respectively, to the doctor Henry Stromer and the theologian Philip Melanchthon. He tried to get them to understand that he was not rejecting everything in the Lutheran reform.

> Considering that the life of Christians was universally very corrupt, even if I had felt very badly about Luther, however I nearly decided that he 'was a necessary evil'. He who destroys him would also destroy what is best for this state of time. . . . I have written nothing about free will apart from my mind's judgement; I disagreed with Luther in many other matters,

but I feared doing battle, lest the fruit of this disorder should be destroyed by my work.[34]

To Melanchthon, who was at once Luther's friend and his own, Erasmus repeated the same argument in similar terms. He did not want to withdraw from the line on which he had settled at any price.

From the time he entered the conflict, and despite the depth of his ecumenical spirit, Erasmus could no longer play the role of mediator, which alienated him from both sides. His position was less original, but more distinct, if not less uncomfortable. An able dose of the critical spirit and of respect for tradition assured his inner equilibrium.

Luther replied to him forcefully and passionately. He relied on the anti-Pelagian writings of Augustine to affirm *The Bondage of the Will*.[35] The book printed under this avenging title came off the presses in December 1525. It was scornful of Erasmus, who was described as an Epicurean, a hypocrite, an atheist and a sophist! Luther took the opposite view point *vis-à-vis* the arguments of his adversary. He conceded him nothing and went so far as to declare that the Fathers of the Church who had upheld the theory of free will were no more faithful to the Scriptures than Erasmus. Time and time again Luther described Erasmus as a sceptic, and he added: 'The Holy Spirit is no Sceptic, and it is not doubts or mere opinions that he has written in our hearts, but assertions more sure and certain than life itself and all experience.'[36]

The polemic continued for some years, and separated for ever these two men who were united by a common will to reform. Highly technical, and sometimes very subtle, arguments were put forward by one side or the other. From a distance the faithful in both camps followed this difficult, obscure, not to say insoluble debate, on double predestination.[37] Luther continued to set against the theology of glory his theology of the Cross: God brings to death in order to make live; he condemns in order to liberate. As for Erasmus, he developed not a theology of glory, but a theology of freedom. He contrasted Luther's reasoning and his own in two striking formulas. 'To those who maintain that man can do nothing without the help of the grace of God, and that therefore no works of men are good – to these we shall oppose a thesis to me much more probable, that there is nothing that man cannot do with the help of the grace of God, and that therefore all the works of man can be good.'[38] Thus while Luther could not follow a Church which was clinging on to its traditions, Erasmus put his faith in an internal reform of the Church. He preached progress and patience at the same time. Belief in free will did not entail a denial of grace.

Amidst the crisis of institutions and confusion of spirits, Erasmus, as the perpetual mediator that he was, saw to it that courageous strength did not give way to a fearful withdrawal. He respected liberty too much to yield to fanaticism. He called for an open dialogue, without threats and without pretence. In any case he believed the violent repression of dissent to be cruel and disastrous; it was foreign to the seriousness of the situation and unworthy of the Gospel. Therefore he wanted to see civic tolerance of the Lutheran worship, without giving up hope for the necessary unity of all Christians.[39]

The relations between Luther and Erasmus, after they had become bogged down in polemic, were in the strictest antipathy according to the classical schema of the incompatibility of character. Luther declared that Erasmus was lacking in piety and even in sincerity: he called him *doctor amphibolus*. Erasmus reproached Luther for being excessive and unpredictable: *doctor hyperbolicus*. For Luther, Erasmus was a profaner, no longer even a Christian. For Erasmus, Luther was a blasphemer who adorned himself improperly with the evangelical label.

Nevertheless the faith of these two men of prayer was deep. More than evident in Luther, it was not lacking in Erasmus who could write to his opponent: 'I do not concede that you profess a more living attachment than mine to the purity of the Gospel, for which there is nothing that I would not endure.'[40]

Was Erasmus the precursor of the Protestant reformation? It was said of him while he was alive, and has been repeated until our own time that, 'Erasmus laid the eggs which Luther hatched.'[41] It is true that Erasmus had more or less influenced all the currents of reform. His criticism of abuses, his exegesis, his action in support of theology and piety left a permanent impression on reformers like Zwingli, Oecolampadius, Pellicanus, Bucer and Melanchthon. All of them in the end separated from him by separating themselves from the established Church.

Luther's case was different. If his religious evolution, like that of Erasmus, had been marked by meditation on the Scripture which had delivered each of them from the weight of observances, if they had an equal aversion to the university theology and monastic spirituality of their time, there was nevertheless a fundamental discord between them.

Between Luther and Erasmus, opposition of temperament showed itself strikingly, despite the coherence of some of their writings, in the way in which they took up questions: a radical reformism in the case of Luther, and with Erasmus a reformism which handled the Tradition and traditions carefully. Luther was a prophet and his discoveries were flashes of lightning. Erasmus was a man of knowledge with a critical spirit that was always alert. Luther had a sense of the tragic, Erasmus a sense of humour. Prophets don't know what to do with humour, and are paralysed by it. Critical spirits speak of their discoveries more freely than of their certitudes. Erasmus's theology was an open theology opposed to the decisive theology of Luther.

From the time that the Church's reform began, difficulties multiplied along with opposition.[42] For Luther, faith was the regulator of the Church. For Erasmus, the Church was at the same time the regulator of faith. He believed in ministerial priesthood as well as in the priesthood of the faithful. Luther believed in the Church, but he subordinated the institution to the event of salvation. For Erasmus there existed between the Church and faith an interdependence which could be illustrated by history. Too timid in Luther's eyes, Erasmus tried to reform the Church without shattering its providential foundations.[43]

Erasmus's unquenchable optimism clashed with the conservatism of Rome and the pessimism of Luther. Luther was dominated by a sense of sin. He put his mind at ease by reassuring others. His sincerity could not be doubted, but his objectivity was sometimes questionable and his oratory detracted from his prophetic role. He rose up justifiably against the abuses of his time, formalism, superstition and ignorance, and asserted an exclusive doctrine. In changing perspectives, he put into effect a religious revolution, making a clean sweep of questions of merit and devotion as well as of questions of tradition and hierarchy.

The expression 'clean sweep' graphically describes Luther's radical manner, by which he eliminated everything, apart from the Bible and the Fathers, which hampered the development and expansion of his ideas. In denying the supreme authority of the visible head of the invisible Church, he harshly contradicted the ecclesiology inherited from the Gregorian reform.

16

Settled in Basel

After receiving the pension which the emperor had granted him, Erasmus left Louvain and the Netherlands in order to distance himself from his enemies in the Faculty of Theology. He had chosen withdrawal to Basel so that he could be closer to the printer Johannes Froben who was devoted to him and to the Archbishop Christoph von Utenheim, who was no less so.[1]

As he had escaped from a stifling environment in leaving Steyn, so in leaving Louvain for Basel, Erasmus made a break with uncomfortable circumstances and set out on a new adventure. The journey, made on horseback, was exhausting. Close to twenty days to pass through Tirlemont, Maastricht, Aachen, Düren, Koblenz, Mainz, Worms, Speyer, Strasbourg, Sélestat and Colmar, before finally arriving in Basel on 15 November.[2] Journeys by stages, however, have certain advantages. On the way, Erasmus had taken up again with numerous friends. Delighted and exhausted, he descended on Froben before choosing a house for himself.[3] His health was indifferent and the stench of the stoves made him ill. One of his friends tells us 'that he could scarcely hold the pen between his fingers.'[4] When an attack of gout and stones had passed, he set to work again with determination.

To his friends and admirers Erasmus was at that time a great writer surrounded with an aura of literary fame. He was to make Basel the humanist capital: from London to Cracow and from Antwerp to Alcala a complex network of friendship had grown up. While the master published his books, he found time to correspond with the scholars of Europe. Despite his repeated promises, he was never to return to his homeland. His long wandering was over, he was at home in this old, grand and beautiful Germanic city, full of the colour of everyday life, its citizens and its artists, its Churchmen and its travellers. He spent eight fruitful years in Basel, and was to follow this with six years in Freiburg, before returning to end his days in Basel in peace and serenity.

The peaceful rhythm of daily labour favoured a good organization of work. Erasmus's time was divided between his lectures and the translation of his works. The *famuli* responded to him and received their instructions. The master knew enough German to give his orders to Margaret, his housekeeper, of whom he did not only speak in glowing terms, for she was 'light-fingered, a prowler, a drinker, a liar and a gossip'.[5]

He found diversion in the variety of his researches and publications. He sometimes listed with satisfaction what he had published in the year, what was still with the printer and what he had in hand. In Basel Erasmus consolidated the financial security which came with the success of his writings.

But great polemics pursued him. Sustained with more or less strength and constancy by popes, bishops and kings, Erasmus defended himself. On occasion, he launched attacks and added to his *Apologias*. Stunica in Spain, Lee in England, Titelmans in the Netherlands, Luther and Hutten in Germany, Pio in Italy, Bédier and Clichtove in France, were his major opponents.

In his publications, which took up most of his time, the collections of letters occupy a special place. In 1522 Erasmus put the finishing touches to a sixth volume which was being enlarged and continually delayed: *Letters to diverse correspondants*.[6] This recapitulative edition brought together all the letters published so far with an ample supplement which extended from 1489 to 1521. In all there were 612 letters, of which 158 were published for the first time. The edition would have been more interesting if Erasmus had not discarded numerous letters which, nevertheless, have happily been preserved. Prudence explains his refusal to publish the recent correspondence with Luther as well as the stinging letters to certain theologians. A letter from Leo X, of 15 January 1521, was also discarded, doubtless because it contained some reservations disagreeable to Erasmus's self-esteem.

Letters revised for printing, letters familiar or exemplary, they were addressed to friends, protectors, printers, sometimes to the great ones of the world, sometimes to modest schoolmasters. There are also to be found in this volume letters of thanks, condolence, recommendation, praise and remonstrance, and an occasional portrait. The edition again brought to life Erasmus's thought and career. A stage in his life had been reached. In seven years, he had published six volumes of his correspondence!

The development of Lutheranism affected him deeply and constrained him to an even more demanding caution. A difficult period began, difficult for the Church, which withdrew into itself, difficult for Erasmus who was searching for a third way between Reformation and Counter-Reformation.

At almost the same time his treatise *On the Writing of Letters* came off the press.[7] This book's story is like that of a novel. The first edition of the work went back to the last years of the fifteenth century and belongs to the young humanist's pedagogical work – careful to teach his disciples how to compose a fine letter in good Latin. This was the time when Erasmus was making a poor living from his lessons in Paris. For the benefit of his pupils he constructed valuable tools of trade which were later to become renowned manuals.

The treatise *On the Writing of Letters* testified to Erasmus's efforts to polish and refine style. A preface, clearly intended for this kind of work, dating from 1498, was addressed to Robert Fisher. Did the announced treatise already exist in manuscript when Erasmus composed this preface? A first edition had certainly been used by its author for the profit of his pupils. Why did he not immediately publish such a useful manual? Doubtless because Erasmus had not been able to find a publisher: in 1498, he was an unknown, and had to content himself with having his works recopied.

A manuscript copy fell into the hands of his friend Augustin Caminadus before the end of the year. When Erasmus took possession of it again, he corrected his text, and as he was in the meantime at a distance from Robert Fisher, he envisaged publishing the text at the author's expense and dedicating it to Adolph van Veere, son of his patron at that time and pupil of his friend Batt. Erasmus, meanwhile, had lost sight of this project, rushed off his feet by a thousand other tasks, when in 1513 he discovered, in an *Epistolary Art* of Jean Despautère, numerous fragments of his forgotten manuscript. His bad temper was as understandable as his desire to recover his property. Since the publication of *The Praise of Folly*, Erasmus had become a well-known figure. His confidence in himself had developed in keeping with this. When Froben suggested himself as publisher of the treatise, Erasmus nevertheless turned a deaf ear: the preparation of the Graeco-Latin *New Testament* and the edition of St Jerome interested him more and occupied him almost exclusively. He was to be brought back to the question by what can only be called unfair competition, even at a time when literary propriety was ill-defined and badly protected.

Two distinct forgeries of his work appeared, one in Germany, the other in England. Irritated by the off-handedness of the printers and stimulated by the success of the work, Erasmus replied with an amended text published by Froben, complete and in line with current tastes. The former preface was replaced by a vengeful letter, addressed to Nicolas Bérault.

After so many misadventures, the treatise *On the Writing of Letters*,[7] decorated with a frontispiece by Hans Holbein, began a glorious career.

Republished more than a hundred times, it was rich in advice and examples. No writer had more clearly explained to his readers the distinctions and variety of epistolary types. He had a high notion of a letter considered as a literary genre which 'depicts the customs, the destiny, the feelings and the conditions of private life', while maintaining the tone of conversation. 'For what subject cannot be committed to a letter? In them we feel joy, pain, hope and fear. In them we give vent to anger, protest, flatter, complain, quarrel, declare war, are reconciled, console, consult, deter, threaten, provoke, restrain, relate, describe, praise and blame. In them we feel hatred, love and wonder; we discuss, bargain, revel, quibble, dream, and, in short, what do we not do? 'He adds: 'a letter . . . is a mutual conversation between absent friends.'[8]

Erasmus's preferences were for simplicity of expression, a natural and familiar style, in respect of syntax. He resolutely abandoned conventional, artificial and impersonal formulas. Doubtless he had not always followed these wise recommendations, but nevertheless an epistolary treatise like this could only be written by a great letter writer.

The *Paraphrases* of the Gospels are among Erasmus's favourite books and those of his readers.[9] While the *New Testament* was a work intended for the learned, the *Paraphrases* were addressed to all those who read Latin.[10] Froben published this work of pastoral inspiration in four little volumes, from February 1522 to December 1523. They gave expression to a vital piety. Erasmus wanted to proclaim the Word of his Master. Jesus separated himself from the scribes and Pharisees to express his solidarity with the poor and the outcast, the weak and the sinful; he preferred mercy to sacrifice and he was the master of the Sabbath because he was master of the Law. He advocated pardon for all men of goodwill. Erasmus eagerly stressed the parables, those marvellous stories, more convincing than the most explicit teaching. He delighted in what was provocative in the Gospel: a world in which the weakest is the greatest, in which the prodigal child and the worker at the eleventh hour seemed to be privileged, in which the lost sheep was the most loved of the flock – in a word, a world turned upside down, the foolish world evoked in the final pages of *The Praise of Folly*.

In an irenic spirit, Erasmus dedicated the four *Paraphrases* to Charles V, Ferdinand of Austria, Henry VIII and Francis I respectively. Each contained exhortations for peace and against war. To Charles: 'There is no war, however just its cause or moderate its conduct, which does not bring in its train an immense procession of crimes and calamities!' To Francis I:

Matthew I had dedicated to my own prince, Charles; John, which I expounded immediately after Matthew, to Charles's brother Ferdinand; Luke, my third target, to the king of England; Mark seemed left for you, so that the four Gospels might be devoted to the four leading monarchs in the world today. I only wish that as your four names are joined with such symmetry in the one volume of the Gospels, so your hearts may be closely united in concord by the spirit of the gospel![11]

The *Paraphrase on the Gospel of St Matthew*[12] was strongly inspired by Origen. In it were to be found clear allusions to the problems of the time, and not only to war. With reference to the parable of the tares, Erasmus set forth his doctrine of tolerance: that dissidents should not be persecuted.

The religious ignorance of the faithful distressed Erasmus. Having exalted the Holy Scripture, he was eagerly looking towards the compilation of a kind of little catechism and the renewal of baptismal vows.

The main points of faith and Christian doctrine should be expounded to Christian folk every year with clear brevity and learned plainness, and lest they should be at all perverted by the fault of preachers, I would wish a book to be made by learned and virtuous men, and read out to the masses by a priest. I hope that it be put together not from human defects, but from Gospel sources, from the apostles' letters, from the Creed, which may have been written by the apostles, I know not; certainly it manifestly bears the authority and purity of the apostles. This could happen not unseasonably at Eastertide; and this would be better than rousing people with unsuitable and often obscene jokes, a custom which I know not what demon brought into the Church. For, admit, even if the people ought to be attracted and even roused by some pleasure, however to rouse laughter with games of this sort is the job of clowns, not of theologians. Indeed, it seems to me that it will be of benefit for this matter if baptized boys, when they have reached puberty, should be ordered to be present at readings of this sort, in which it may be explained to them clearly what the profession of baptism entails. Then they should be examined carefully in private by virtuous men, whether they understand enough and remember their instruction. If this examination is successful, they should be questioned whether they will confirm what their godparents promised in their name at baptism. If their reply is satisfactory, then that profession should be renewed publicly, together with their friends, with weighty, suitable, chaste, serious and splendid ceremonies, which are fitting for this profession, than which nothing can be holier. For what are human professions if not images of that holiest profession, that is, the recalling of Christianity, disfigured by the world? . . .

Comedies are now acted out in some churches, not exactly blamed by me, about Christ's resurrection, his ascent into heaven, the sending of the Holy Ghost. How splendid would the spectacle be, to hear the voice of so many young men dedicating themselves to Jesus Christ, so many young recruits swearing in his words, renouncing this world, which is filled with malice, abjuring and repudiating Satan with all his pomps, pleasures and works? To see new Christs, bearing the sign of their genealogy on their foreheads? To see the crowd of candidates proceeding from the holy font? To hear the voice of the rest of the congregation cheering and blessing Christ's young recruits? . . .

Then I should wish that the little book of Christian philosophy, of which I have spoken, be circulated generally; the pure Christ should be shown in it, not clouded over with Jewish ceremonies or people's commentaries or decrees; in short, not gloomy and harsh, but as he is, agreeable and full of love. Those who have been instructed with primers of this sort will not come completely raw to the reading of Holy Scripture. There are many people now in their fifties who do not know what they vowed at baptism, who do not even dream of what the articles of faith, the Lord's Prayer or the sacraments of the Church mean . . . We are Christians in name, habits and ceremonies rather than from disposition.[13]

This great page of eloquence illustrates the biblical reformism of its author and his desire for spiritual exegesis. Erasmus wanted the Christian people to know the Divine Word. This was the source of his insistence on correct religious initiation and personal engagement.[14] How could he not approve such a programme with his generous impulses and his understanding of concrete situations?

The *Paraphrase on the Gospel of St Matthew* had not passed unnoticed by the Faculty of Theology of the University of Paris, but the impression which it made on the minds of its critics was frankly unfavourable. The syndic of the Faculty, Noel Bédier, the Sorbonne's pursuer of heresies, was stirred by Erasmus's declarations. The novel aspect alone was noted and he was judged improper and subversive. What was positive in the thought of Erasmus, the renewal of the vows of baptism and the institution of a catechism, escaped him, or he took no notice of it. At the same time, Erasmus's plea for tolerance was rejected without reservation. 'It is part of the Catholic faith not only that one can, but that one must, punish heretical opinions by execution,' Bédier confidently declared.

We have evidence, nevertheless, that Erasmus's text had been read attentively, if not sympathetically. Bédier had scrutinized it very closely with pen in hand. He even took up certain expressions from the preface, then mounted his attack without further ado. Having correctly cited the text on the renewal of the baptismal vows, Bédier distorted its obvious sense. He reproached the 'new evangelist' with a grievous error. Erasmus taught, he wrote 'that it is necessary to repeat baptism, the sacrament which, by divine law, cannot be repeated.' The formulation was plain, clear and curt. It was indefensible since Erasmus had asserted the contrary when he said 'A second baptism is forbidden.'

Bédier continued on his way, neglected the context and explained why, with the whole tradition, he was an advocate of infant baptism: children who died without baptism were destined for eternal damnation. Today, because Augustinian pessimism no longer has the same currency among Christians as before, Bédier's arguments make the mind boggle. They did not convince Erasmus, but he was careful not to bring up this point, which was somewhat embarrassing in terms of his orthodoxy. He had not even invoked the existence of Limbo, doubtless because he did not believe in it. Nevertheless, stung into activity, accused of impiety, and even of heresy, he took up Bédier's censures and refuted them with as much firmness as indignation.[15]

Erasmus's first contact with Anabaptism went back to the very beginnings of the movement which was to acquire this name. It was in June 1522 that Balthasar Hubmaier, parish priest of Waldshut, one of the future leaders and martyrs of the sect, came to Basel. There he met Herman Buschius and Henricus Glareanus, and then he visited Erasmus, a friend of these friends. He gave a fine account of this interview: 'I talked a lot with [Erasmus] about purgatory and on those two passages from John 1: 'not of the will of the flesh nor of the will of man'. Erasmus kept himself for some time from purgatory, but at last, offering an obscure reply, he hastened to many other different matters. Erasmus speaks openly, but writes closely.'[16] This fragment of a letter is worth its weight in gold. In it we see the two men face to face, Bible in hand, taking each other's measure in a courteous discussion. Erasmus never spoke of his conversation with Hubmaier. To my knowledge, he was only to mention the latter's name twice, some time later, to report that he was an opponent of Luther and above all the 'doctor of Anabaptism'.

Erasmus wrote sensibly, Hubmaier declared. What work was he thinking of in such a comment? It is plausible to imagine that Hubmaier had read the preface to the *Paraphrase on the Gospel of Matthew* which had just appeared. This text has everything to fascinate a dissident, but without giving him full satisfaction. If the 'doctor of Anabaptism' had read this preface he would have found it worth while, but insufficient. The renewal of the baptismal vows is certainly praiseworthy, but it is not an actual baptism. What reassured the Catholics could only scare off the Anabaptists. Reading the writings of Erasmus without preconceptions does not allow the conclusion that he was captivated by Anabaptism. Only Bédier could imagine such a thing!

Later, Erasmus confided to his English friend Cuthbert Tunstall:

> For those they call Anabaptists have been muttering about anarchy for
> a long time: they also maintain other unnatural dogmas, which, if they

should break out, will make Luther seem almost orthodox. They also mutter that baptism is unnecessary for both adults and children. But if they should succeed in convincing others, as some are trying to, that there is nothing in the Eucharist except bread and wine, I do not see what they have left us of the Church's sacraments. Another type of madness prevails: they wish to be received as prophets.[17]

As we can see, Erasmus was rather badly informed and made no concessions to the new prophets.

In 1522 Erasmus published a little treatise which was to cause a great fuss, *On the Eating of Meat* (*De esu carnium*).[18] This open letter was addressed to Christoph von Utenheim, bishop of Basel. Erasmus laid before his friend his thoughts on the ecclesiastical rule of fasting. He insisted on its contingent character and on the fact that this rule should not be imposed as a matter of serious sin. Prohibitions of this sort were only the reflection of their time and the Church could adapt them to the present.

Erasmus had a sense of history. In his battle against the monolithic and intangible character of the human constitutions of the Church, he was not afraid to write that these rules have value only if they remain faithful to the norms of the Gospel. If they are too rigorous, they became inhuman. It is not a betrayal of Erasmus's thought to suggest that for him, what is inhuman is not Christian and that rigourism leads inexorably towards despair.

In stressing again his respect for the customs received from the apostles, he discusses the appropriateness of maintaining abstinence, fasting and priestly celibacy. These rules, instituted with true zeal can in the long term damage true Christian piety, which was emancipated from 'Judaic ceremonies'. Why should the Church be the only institution not to evolve? The Holy Spirit should not be invoked in order to justify standing still. On the contrary, it represents a promise of continued creativity.[19]

Erasmus insisted that there was no law of celibacy among the teachings of Christ. He followed this up by showing that continence was not essential for priesthood and that discipline has adapted to historic circumstances.

Long ago the Church abolished nightly vigils at the martyrs' tombs, even though they had been accepted by the general custom of Christians for several centuries. It transformed fasting, which used to be prolonged to evening, to noon, and changed many other things as occasion demanded. Why should we adhere to a human institution here so doggedly, especially since so many reasons exhort change? For first, a great number of priests live in bad odour, and celebrate those holy mysteries with an uneasy conscience. Secondly, their fruit is to a large extent destroyed because their teaching is despised by the people on account of their shameful life. But if marriage were allowed to those who cannot remain continent, they would live more tranquilly and preach God's word to the people with authority, and take care to teach their children more openly, nor would they be a reproach to each other. I do not say this to make myself a promoter or defender of those priests who have recently married without papal authorization, but I may advise the nobles of the Church to ask themselves whether it is advantageous for an old institution to be fitted to present usefulness. Meanwhile, I would also want the bishops to guard against the carelessness with which they accept any untried people so rashly into the priesthood.[20]

For Erasmus, in fact, candidates for the priesthood should be questioned carefully by their superiors. Above all, they should question themselves and examine their consciences to ensure that they were not committing themselves in a spirit of greed or easy living. Moreover, not without a trace of mischievousness, Erasmus warned the priests who thought to find refuge within marriage to reflect on it twice, 'for fear lest a double penitence should torture them, that of priesthood and that of marriage.[21]

Erasmus's doctrine on priestly celibacy is complete and coherent. He was not to change any of it, but to retain these views in the face of all obstacles. Now the outbreak of the Reformation made his views difficult to defend in the presence of Catholic opinion, offended by the marriage of dissident priests. We would be greatly mistaken in thinking that Erasmus was happy with this situation. In fact, this was not a question of the relaxation of the canonical rule, as he had wished, but a display of liberty won at Rome's expense.

For Erasmus, the adjustment of the priestly status should come from the Church, not from individuals. In criticizing these unions, he nevertheless did not declare them null, but he deplored the suspect manner in which they had been concluded. Besides, he disclaimed any involvement in these marriages without being sure whether the reading of his works could have influenced any dissident. For the priests who went over to the Reformation, marriage was a way of breaking with the system and leaving the former clergy. Erasmus did not understand it. He was amazed, or pretended to be amazed, that the new prophets resisted the enticements of the flesh no better. Would the new Gospel be inseparable from these new households?

The number of public holidays represented a risk of poverty for the most destitute workers. Erasmus, who had some awareness of social issues,[22] hoped for a reduction in these public holidays and even asked that in case of necessity the Sunday rest might be interrupted. Contrary to the view of his opponents, Erasmus did not contest the laws of the Church, but their restrictive interpretation and stifling application. For his part, he respected celibacy, he observed the restrictions of Lent, but he had obtained a dispensation from the fast.[23]

In Basel, Erasmus was safe from the great inquisitorial leaders. Well settled, in a comfortable house, surrounded by his *famuli*, not far from his friend, the printer Froben, he corresponded with all the literati of Europe and his prestige was immense. It was at this time that Spanish Erasmianism developed, Erasmianism without Erasmus.[24] The humanists praised him for having united profane letters and sacred letters.

In this spring of 1522, meanwhile, there were many reasons for uneasiness. 'During the winter months', Erasmus confided to his friend and protector Stanislas Turzo, bishop of Olomouc,

> some kind of pestilent rheum troubled me greatly for many days, and then returned after an interval and was worse and more prolonged than ever. Shortly before Lent, when I was more or less recovered, I was suddenly laid low by a stone in the kidneys. The fact is, the crazy habitation of my body, breaking down now in one place and now in another, gives its tenant notice that he must shortly flit, and this I almost think desirable, when I see the tragic mess we are making of this world of ours. All of which we owe to certain disputatious persons, of whom one party have some plans – I know not what – to re-establish the liberty of the gospel, while the others consolidate their rule by strengthening their defences even more.
>
> For my own part, I seem to see a way to put the interests of the Christian religion first without commotion. But to play that piece we should need princes devoted wholeheartedly to the public weal, and to the glory of the supreme prince, Jesus Christ, before whose judgement-seat every monarch however powerful must take his stand. I myself have never come to any agreement with any member of Luther's party; I have always tried to recall them to more moderate policies, in fear, of course, that things might end in civil strife. And yet there are people with the effrontery to traduce me even in the emperor's court as a supporter of Luther. Here, Luther's people grind their teeth at me because they say I disagree with him; they tear me in pieces in their public pronouncements and threaten me with venomous pamphlets on top of that. So to both sides I am a heretic![25]

In Rome, Paris and Zürich, friends were expecting him and pressed him to come. But journeys distressed him. He left Basel, in the autumn, with Beatus Rhenanus; he did not go beyond Constance, where Johann von Botzheim received him affectionately. During this stay he fell ill and had to return to Basel, whence he sent his impressions to his friend Marcus Lauwerÿns:

The situation of the place itself was full of charm too. Constance is dominated by a wonderful great lake, which stretches both far and wide for many miles and at the same time loses none of its beauty. Its attractions are increased by the forest-clad hills prominent in all directions, some distant and some near at hand. For at that point, as though wearied by its rocky headlong passage through the Alps, the Rhine seems to have found an agreeable resting-place to recuperate in, through the middle of which it makes its gentle progress; at Constance it gathers again into its proper channel . . . It is said also to be full of fish and of almost incredible depth . . . The Rhine glides for some distance past the city of Constance, and then, as though not serious and merely indulging its fancy, it makes an island, which is occupied by a well-known house of nuns; thereafter it runs together again and makes a smaller lake, which they call for some reason the Venetian lake.[26]

The following year Erasmus paid a visit to the archdeacon Ferry de Carondelet at Besançon. He then went to see another friend at Freiburg im Breisgau, the jurist Ulrich Zasius. He was not to go either to Rome or to Paris. To Zwingli, who offered him citizenship of Zürich, he replied that he wanted to be 'a citizen of the world.'[27]

17

Basel: The Daily Round of Work

Erasmus's life in Basel was organized in accordance with his work and for his work. Distractions were rare, apart from friends' visits. He had no pet, no distracting pastime, not even an artistic hobby. He had no holidays; his entire will was bent towards the completion of his works.

Luxury and frivolity were strangers to him, but not comfort, [1] nor even on occasion the pleasures of the table. Although he had been able to write to one friend: 'Since my youth I have taken food and drink as if it were poison', he was nevertheless able to give a lyrical description to another friend of the delights of Burgundy wine.

> On first tasting I did not much fancy it, but the night following showed its true colours; my digestion was suddenly so much mended that I seemed reborn – a new man ... I had previously tasted certain wines grown in Burgundy, but they were fiery and dry. This one was of a most agreeable colour – you might call it ruby-red, and the taste neither sweet nor dry but very pleasant ... so kind in fact to the digestion that even when taken in some quantity it did very little harm ... Happy indeed is Burgundy on this count if no other, and well does she deserve to be called a mother of men, now that she has such milk as this in her breasts.[2]

As for the pleasures of the flesh, they were a subject for humour. 'I was never a slave to venery, and indeed had no time for it under the load of my researches. If ever I had a touch of that trouble, I was set free from that tyrant long ago by advancing years, to which on this account I am most grateful.'[3]

The great Holbein painted three portraits of Erasmus at this time. The most beautiful, preserved at Longford Castle,[4] presents him full face, with a fine, serious and calm appearance, as if lit from within. The nose is long and generous, the thin lips seem to suggest a smile. His shaking hands are adorned with rings. He greying hair is escaping from a black hat, black like the fur coat which covered this sensitive, delicate and tireless humanist.

Ulrich von Hutten, who had thrown in his lot with Luther, incurred Erasmus's wrath – and he had his old friend expelled from Basel. In July 1523, Hutten loudly accused Erasmus of vanity, for, he said, he published his correspondence with the great men of the world to establish his reputation and increase his credit. Stung to the quick, Erasmus replied in a little work curiously entitled: *A Sponge to wipe away Hutten's Aspersions.*[5] It was, in fact, a defence of his correspondence. 'I do not publish', he said, 'a tenth part of the letters sent to me by princes and scholars. Sometimes I mention these letters to protect myself against the boldness of my enemies, for I have no other weapons with which to fight.' And he mentions the names of some illustrious correspondents: Charles, Ferdinand, Francis I, and Henry VIII! Hutten would like to have replied, but death took him off during the same year.

The book was an indictment as much as a plea. It appeared to be a vindictive work which scarcely added to the author's reputation, and it expressed a bitter disappointment.

> I see Lutherans, but I see little or nothing of the Gospel about them ... [Hutten] says one should be ready to die for the gospel, I would not refuse if the case called for it, but I am of no mind to die for the paradoxes of Luther. It is not a question of the articles of the faith but as to whether the Roman primacy was instituted by Christ, whether bishops by their constitutions can obligate anyone to commit a mortal sin, whether free will contributes to salvation, whether any work of man can be called good, whether the Mass can be called a sacrifice, whether faith alone confers salvation. These are subjects for scholastic disputation. Over such matters I would not take away any man's life nor do I propose to lay down my own. I would hope to be a martyr for Christ if I have the strength. I am not willing to be a martyr for Luther.[6]

The *Sponge* finally ended with a call for concord. Erasmus expressed a wish for the end of fighting and peace for consciences, but this hope was to be disappointed. The Lutheran conflict continued to fester: Erasmus committed himself to the struggle without enthusiasm, but not without vigour.

The success of the *Colloquies* and of his polemical works did not distract Erasmus from his more serious task of editing the works of the Church Fathers and the great classical authors. He published more texts than a philologist of our day reads during an entire lifetime.[7] After St Jerome, which appeared in 1516, and St Cyprian, in 1520, he published St Hilary in 1523, and this edition was to be followed by many others: St John Chrysostom, St Ambrose, St Athanasius, Arnobius, St Augustine, St Basil, and finally Origen in Latin, which was to come off the press after Erasmus's death. These thirty volumes are of uneven value in respect of the choice of manuscripts and the interest that Erasmus brought to their authors. It has even been suggested that the pseudo-Cyprian on martyrdom is a forgery of Erasmus.[8]

Pagan authors were not neglected, as behoved a humanist preoccupied with providing his peers with correct texts. In this domain, Erasmus was rarely the first editor, for the Italians had numerous editions of classical texts at their disposal. Nevertheless, Erasmus published selected works of Cicero, Seneca, Suetonius, Quintus Curtius, Quintilian and Terence. As well as these he translated Lucian, Euripides and Plutarch from the Greek.

All these editions, to which we must add the *New Testament*, required considerable work. Erasmus became a specialist in the 'hunt for manuscripts.'[9] He mobilized his friends and put his *famuli* to work. Rabelais himself wrote to Erasmus to tell him that he could procure for him a manuscript of Flavius Josephus, the great Jewish historian.[10]

Sometimes Erasmus made clear that he accorded greater importance to the oldest and most damaged texts.[11] For him, manuscripts were much more reliable in proportion to their age. He seemed not to know the golden rule in the classification of manuscripts: that the risk of error increases according to the number of intermediaries, that a copy made much later from an original is more valuable than an ancient copy of a copy.

The manuscripts which he assembled were collated, corrected and annotated. The adjusted text was sent off to the printer. The author corrected the proofs and, finally, the book was published; it was put up for sale at the Frankfurt book fair, then in bookshops. Erasmus made this long-drawn-out journey more than a hundred times and must have spent a considerable time in Froben's press. This superabundant production would have sufficed to assure the fame of a whole team. In Erasmus's case it illustrates an immensely fruitful relationship between philologist and patrologist.

Erasmus was conscious of getting older and thought about drawing up his will. Suffering from a stone, he obtained a dispensation from the fast and believed that death had never been so close. 'If it is hard to die once,' he wrote to Bishop Sadoleto, 'how much harder to die so many times and to be raised again to fresh torments?'[12] In this anguished and morose state of mind, Erasmus learned of the death of his Louvain friend, Jean de Nève. Soon after this, he addressed a moving letter to Joost Vroye, their mutual friend; it was printed and distributed some time later.

The *Letter on Death*[13] is a little treatise of twelve pages which appeared in 1522. This topical piece grew out of Erasmus's personal experience.

> But it is strange to recount the abhorrence with which ordinary people regard sudden death, to such an extent that there is nothing they pray God and the saints to deliver them from more frequently or with more feeling than from death sudden and unforeseen. . . . How much better it would be if those who are so much frightened of sudden death were to pray to heaven for a good life! What could be more foolish than to postpone amendment of life until one's deathbed! And how few people are made better by a long illness! – if indeed anybody ever is. . . . We are all born in the same way, but there are many different ways of dying. Let him choose for us whatever he will. No one can die badly who has lived well. . . . One should never despair of anybody; but all the same he learns very late to be a Christian who can no longer practise what he learns, and is very late in applying the remedy of confession when his soul hovers already on his lips.

Another passage replied to those who deplored the absence of the customary ceremonies of the Church in such circumstances. 'But there are no ceremonies, no holy water, no holy candle, no chrism, no sign of the cross, no crowd of mourners racked with sobs perhaps. . . . It is a wretched thing, they say, to die a solitary death. And yet the dead man is content if he has one angel to catch his poor parting soul and carry it to heaven.'[14]

Erasmus thus protested against the presence of intruders at the deathbed. He was to take up this critique, among others, many times, and with a great deal of spirit, in his *Colloquies*. At the end of the *Letter*, he was surely thinking of himself when he expressed an intimate conviction: 'The wisest course seems to me to be to seek security on this point in every way I can from Christ by prayers and by doing good up to the last day of my life.'[15] These two characteristics of Erasmian religion, loftiness of thought and solid good sense, are happily associated here.

In 1523, under the title *The Lord's Prayer*,[16] Erasmus published a paraphrase of the *Pater Noster*. That communal prayer occupied an important place in his religious thought, for it was the only prayer which Jesus taught to his disciples. Erasmus spoke of it often and returned to it often in his *Colloquies* and his *Paraphrases*. 'He who prays by reciting the Lord's prayer, prays with the whole Church,' he wrote. In 1517, he had devised 'a soldier's *Our Father*' to illustrate the contradiction between prayer and violent action.

In his 1523 meditation, Erasmus developed the seven requests of the Lord's Prayer with great loftiness of thought.

The terms of charity and godliness have pleased you more than those of fear: you prefer to hear 'Father' more than 'Lord'. You much prefer to be loved in return by children than to be feared by slaves. You loved first, and this itself is of your giving, that we love you in return. . . . But we cannot [renounce Satan's power] unless you grant strength to those who try, so that not our will, but yours, Father, works in us what your wisdom has decided is the best.[17]

Despite the success of *The Lord's Prayer* – or because of it – the Faculty of Theology at Paris was to condemn the French translation of this paraphrase, some months after it came out, for 'impiety'.

Close on its heels, Erasmus published the *Paraphrases* of the three other Gospels,[18] with their fine dedications to Ferdinand, Henry VIII and Francis I. The king of France had just addressed to Erasmus a letter written in his own hand, which Erasmus had reverently kept. 'I tell you that if you want to come here, you will be most welcome.'[19] Erasmus was flattered, but did not succumb. The circumstances were less good than in 1517. 'I would appear to pass over to the enemy,' he wrote to Willibald Pirckheimer. The enemy! The word is hard, but not out of place. The Habsburg-Valois War, which was to last intermittently until 1559, was entering upon a virulent phase.

The war was able to separate Erasmus from France, but it also reinforced his interest in peace. He replied to the letter from the King with the dedication of the *Paraphrase on the Gospel of St Mark* . In the preface he eloquently praised peace between Christian princes and condemned the territorial ambitions which provoked merciless wars. 'To maintain even an unjust peace is better than to pursue the most just of wars,'[20] he said. Erasmus was not afraid to reprimand rulers. He was not to disturb their conscience or their indifference. If there was one thing on which the great were in accord, it was the necessity of declaring war on peace. They were closer to the pagan Alexander than to the wise Solomon. Nevertheless Erasmus never gave up hoping for a reconciliation between the warring kings. He invited the Pope to re-establish peace, but he did not believe that the Church could depose unworthy kings, and he believed even less in papal theocracy.

It appears that Francis I did not reply to this unwelcome appeal by Erasmus. His thoughts at the time were directed towards Italy where his destiny was to be sealed. On 24 February 1525 he was defeated at Pavia and taken prisoner by Charles of Lannoy, the Emperor Charles V's general. Taken off to Spain, on 14 January 1526, he was to sign the Treaty of Madrid, in which he renounced French suzerainty over Artois and Flanders. The king promised everything that was asked of him, while deciding to do nothing about it when he was restored to freedom.

Not long after this treatise, which had proved unable to establish a true peace, Erasmus saluted the king on his return to Paris. He added, with some courage: 'Some have judged the clauses of this treaty to be harsh, not to say oppressive.' Such a declaration, once made public, could not but offend the subjects of Charles in Spain and the Netherlands, but Erasmus cared very little about this.

In this tense atmosphere, Erasmus confined himself to Basel. He now felt very much at ease, surrounded by chosen helpers, like the brothers Amerbach, Basil and Boniface, the latter a Professor of Law at the University. Erasmus found fame and security at the moment when his influence was about to be most challenged. The dedication of his books to great men was occasionally a source of not inconsiderable income. Sometimes he also offered a luxuriously bound book to someone from whom he expected a gift. In this way as the years passed, he received pieces of gold and silver, nuggets and rings, cups and goblets, horses and wine, furs and silk, not to mention candied fruits and other sweets. But the sales of his books became the major source of his income. In fact he achieved the amazing feat of living by his pen.[21]

Erasmus's reputation was so well established that his printers – Froben in Basel, Maartens in Louvain or Schürer in Strasbourg – argued over his manuscripts. Sometimes his works were even printed without his authorization, as we have seen in the case of the *Colloquies*, while translations and reprints became more and more numerous.[22] At this time Erasmus issued the provisional *Catalogue* of his publications[23] – provisional, but impressive in its richness and diversity. He designed a plan of his complete works in nine volumes.

Despite his reticence, Erasmus had not abandoned the publication of his correspondence. He remained in favour of an enterprise which responded to the wishes of most of his correspondents, who wanted to read their names in his collections of letters. What embarrassed him was the imprudence of some letters addressed at the beginning of the Lutheran crisis to old friends who had become irreconcilable enemies. But that didn't matter, for he made up his mind to censor them rigorously later. Meanwhile he continued to write, quickly and well. He was convinced of the necessity of revising all his works and not only his letters. As long as we live, we are always devoted to self-improvement and we shall not cease to make our writings more polished and more complete until we cease to breathe. No one is so good a man that he could not be made better; and no book has had so much work put into it that it cannot be made more perfect.'[24]

In his letters he often returned to the question of the danger of piling up dogmatic definitions. Though he believed in the development of dogma,[25] it was enough to define the truths contained in Scripture, without which salvation was not possible.[26] He gave a résumé of what appeared to him to be essential to the faith.

> The whole of the Christian philosophy lies in this, our understanding that all our hope is placed in God, who freely gives us all things through Jesus his son, that we were redeemed by his death and engrafted through baptism with his body, that we might be dead to the desires of this world and live by his teaching and example, not merely harbouring no evil but deserving well of all men; so that, if adversity befall, we may bear it bravely in hope of the future reward which beyond question awaits all good men at Christ's coming, and that we may ever advance from one virtue to another, yet in such a way that we claim nothing for ourselves, but ascribe any good we do to God. These above all are the things that must be implanted in the hearts of men. . . . If any man wishes to pursue more abstruse questions touching the divine nature or the substance of Christ or the sacraments, so that he may raise his mind on high and withdraw it from lowly things, he is welcome to do so with this restriction, that to believe what commends itself to this man or that should not at once become compulsory for everybody.[27]

To define the essential is good, but to go beyond it can become an evil. Erasmus attributed this evil to the 'impious curiosity' of theologians who believed that they could show everything and who tried to impose on the beliefs of the faithful explanations which, at best, were mere conjectures.

> On what pretext will we ask pardon for ourselves, we who formulate so many definitions about matters which could have been either ignored without loss of salvation or left in doubt? Or is he not destined to have fellowship with the Father, Son and Holy Spirit who cannot disentangle according to the method of philosophy what distinguishes the Father from the Son or the Holy Spirit from both?[28]

He went so far as to say:

> And this is certainly important for our religion, to revere everything in divine matters, but to assert nothing that has not been stated openly in the holy Scriptures.'[29]

> Such a dangerous inquisitiveness has generally arisen in us from the study of philosophy . . . Once faith was more a matter of a way of life than of a profession of articles. Soon necessity inspired the imposition of articles, but these were few, and apostolic in their moderation. Then the wickedness of the heretics made for a more precise examination of the sacred books, and intransigence necessitated the definition of certain matters by the authority of synods. Finally faith began to reside in the

> written word rather than in the soul, and there were almost as many
> faiths as men. Articles increased, but sincerity decreased: contention boiled
> over, charity grew cold. The teachings of Christ, which in former times
> were not touched by the clash of words, began to depend on the support
> of philosophy: this was the first step of the church on the downward
> path.[30]

With this vigorous indictment, Erasmus was trying to make the point that
the simple truth was in danger of being blurred behind the increasing
complication of scholastic formulas. Perhaps he was thinking of the
theory of transubstantiation?

For Erasmus, a disciple of St Jerome, the introduction of philosophy
into theology was a decadent factor, resulting in too many unnecessary
complications.[31] Religion is simple as long as it is not unwisely com-
plicated. The philosophy of Christ escapes all the criticisms deserved
by the philosophy of men. In a word, God is not the God of the philosophers, but the God of Jesus Christ. At the beginning of his career
Erasmus had already given this advice to the theologians: 'Let this be
your first and only aim; undertake this vow, and this alone: to change,
be seized, be inspired, be transformed into what you learn.'[32] Whether
they be critical or disenchanted, these reflections do not breathe fideism:
if faith is not rational, in the sense that it is not an object of demonstration, it does not follow that it is absurd. Faith is reasonable, it calls
for reflection and meditation.

Erasmus's attitude to theology is again found in his judgement of
knowledge. To question oneself, to hesitate, to know what one does not
know, all this is wisdom, for 'it is part of knowledge to recognize that
certain things are not for our knowing.'[33]

However, Erasmus did not think it necessary to reduce everything to
faith: faith does not give the Christian what reason allows him to discover. Erasmus's position *vis à vis* philosophy, and of knowledge, was
not anti-intellectual. He did not deny the legitimacy of philosophy, any
more than he denied the role of intelligence. Man's dignity rested on
his reason; it expressed itself in his conscience. Erasmus's aim, like that
of the author of the *Imitation of Christ*, was to put Christians on their
guard against the illusion of infinite and infallible knowledge, by denouncing vain knowledge and misplaced curiosity.

As he grew older, Erasmus felt that he was becoming more of a homebody. 'The last act of the play' had begun for him. He gave up long
journeys and, in the 1524 colloquy *The Old Men's Chat*, he had Glycion
say: 'I'm convinced I travel around the world more safely on a map.'[34]

Little by little, he gave up horse-riding.[35] In February 1524, he sold
two horses. In September, he confided to his friend Warham that the

horse which remained with him was good, if not beautiful. 'For he lacks all mortal sins, except gluttony and sloth; and he has been granted all the virtues of a good confessor: godly, prudent, humble, decent, sober, chaste and calm.' This casual and typically clerical jest was inspired by a hymn in the breviary. The word 'confessor' was intended in the liturgical sense: the saint who has confessed his faith, without dying for it.[36]

The confessor who pronounces absolution is in no way forgotten or neglected by Erasmus. He published a little treatise *On Confessing*, in 1524, some months after the publication of *On Prayer*. These two books had considerable success, not without offending some censorious scholastics.[37]

Fidelity to the Church did not prevent Erasmus from pleading once more for a lightening of ecclesiastical regulations. This double preoccupation was particularly apparent when he discussed the marriage of priests. Erasmus, as we have seen, was well suited to celibacy: perhaps he had more sensitivity than passion? In any case, he drew realistic conclusions from his observation of other priests.

> I have always declared very openly that marriage should not be annulled for priests subsequently ordained, if they cannot be continent, nor would I say otherwise if I were talking with the Pope; not that I should not prefer continence, but that I see hardly anyone who preserves continence. But meanwhile for what purpose is such a crowd of priests necessary? I never advised anyone to marry, but neither was I troubled by anyone wishing to marry.'[38]

If Erasmus pleaded untiringly for the marriage of priests, within the Church and with its blessing, he was outraged to see dissidents turn marriage into a challenge to the Catholic Church as Luther and Melanchthon, amongst others, had done. The number of these cases upset him and he refused to respect or approve them. It could be said that he had a foreboding of the harm these unusual unions would do to his ideas. This was not the way he had envisaged the emancipation of the priests. Because of this he developed an understandable ill humour and a tiresome aggressiveness.

At the beginning of 1525, at the request of the City Council of Basel, Erasmus addressed a long letter to them on how they should conduct themselves amidst the religious difficulties of the time.[39] It was a carefully constructed document, putting forward a well-modulated opinion. On the question of priestly celibacy, Erasmus's advice was explained in eight essential points. No recommendation would be justified in favour of priests who married without authorization. Superiors could take into consideration the case of those who entered mistakenly into the ecclesiastical life, but they should show themselves severe towards those who provoked others to rebellion. Great care was necessary with regard to married priests who were known to have had many concubines. The general principle remained: better a married priest than a priest with concubines. Ignorant and unworthy priests could also be married, but they should renounce the exercise of their priesthood and live as laymen. Educated priests who had taken orders in good faith and could be useful to the Church, though they were incapable of observing continence despite being virtuous in other respects, could be married while retaining their functions. Finally, vigilance was necessary to prevent unworthy men from abusing these measures. For Erasmus, priests in concubinage were at fault, but they were not necessarily bad pastors. This was a difficult, and even perilous, position to hold. Erasmus was overtaken and passed on the left by the dissidents, while on the right things were scarcely any better.

Rome remained deaf to his advice and suggestions; and though Erasmus had affirmed his opposition to Luther's radicalism, the Sorbonne had not changed its attitude and Noel Bédier, the most arrogant of Parisian theologians, listed his grievances. The first was having spoken ill of ecclesiastical celibacy. Erasmus replied mischievously that he had written an apology for celibacy. Then, pressed into a corner, he conceded approval of celibacy, while adding that the actual situation of the clergy, especially in England, inclined him towards marriage for priests.

The dispute continued and Bédier assembled his arguments in a volume of *Annotations* to which Erasmus replied with a volume of *Supputations*. In it he affirmed that ecclesiastical celibacy was not by divine right, which would have negated all his endeavours, and that, in consequence, the Pope and the Council had the power to dispense with it. Marriage for priests was a lesser evil, a remedy appropriate to the situation. Bédier obstinately considered Erasmus to be a dangerous opponent, and even classed him among the crypto-Lutherans. Josse van Clichthove, the French theologian of Flemish background, drew the same conclusion.

After lengthy polemics, Erasmus tried to raise the debate to a higher level, by stressing that marriage was a sacrament, but that virginity was not. It was no longer necessary to confuse celibacy and virginity; one was a legal category, the other a moral option. Erasmus recognized the superiority of virginity to marriage in principle, but held it to be an ideal not easily accessible to most mortals. Candidates for the priesthood who were too young and incapable of assessing the risks of their commitment should be put on guard. Moreover, Erasmus did not advise the ordination of married men because, at the beginning of the sixteenth century this was no longer a question – or not yet – and there was a plethora of priests. Nor had he thought of the possibility of a female priesthood.

If we consider Erasmus's declarations on priestly celibacy in their entirety, we can see that he was for ever searching for a solution to the problem of the priest living within the world. Moved by the unhappy situation of so many ecclesiastics who lacked a vocation and could not remain continent, he had wanted to soften the rigour of the laws on celibacy, as he had wanted, for comparable reasons, to soften the laws on the indissolubility of marriage. There was, however, no trace of the ideas of some theologians about the secularization of the Christian world and 'declergification'.

His position was an original one. It was moderate if compared with that of Luther, who denied ecclesiastical celibacy. Erasmus had never approved of unions made by priests who broke the rule. He asked of the Church understanding and leniency for those who could no longer keep the promises made at their ordination. On the one hand, he accepted the gift of virginal celibacy, sealed by an authentic and strong vocation. On the other hand, he wanted priests to be able to marry legitimately without being compelled to renounce their pastoral role, unless they had shown themselves to be truly unworthy of it. The Council of Trent, clinging to traditions, was unwilling to listen to Erasmus's plea. On this point, he was a voice crying in the wilderness.

18

The *Colloquies*: Chronicle of an Era

We have already noted the amazing success of the first *Colloquies*,[1] between 1518 and 1521. In order to stop the progress of counterfeits circulating under his name, Erasmus very quickly put in place a greatly enlarged and thoroughly transformed edition.[2] It appeared in March 1522 from the Froben press. Erasmus had forgiven Froben for the surreptitious publication of 1518, a reprehensible audacity, indeed, but one which remained beneficial to the author's fame. As a sign of reconciliation, the new edition was dedicated to the printer's son, Erasmius, the godson of the humanist. 'This book will help you not a little to acquire the rudiments of religion also, and on this score the uncounted host of children of your age will owe you a debt, as being the channel through which they get this great advantage.'[3]

The first formally recognized edition of the *Colloquies* began by presenting useful formulas for conversation. These formulas were laid out within dialogues in which moral and religious questions were approached with deliberate boldness. Therein Erasmus repeated proverbial expressions, familiar turns of phrase, a complete, precise and finely shaded vocabulary. *The Master's Orders* listed the numerous tasks of a *famulus*. Another dialogue described the games of Renaissance schoolboys. A third amounted to a critique of the system of benefices. A fourth warned against ill-considered vows.

The complete title of the volume clearly indicated the new and ambitious preoccupations of the author. *Formulas of familiar conversation, useful to young people, not only for polishing their style but also for directing their lives.* Each conversation was a comedy in one act in which Erasmus's verve and gaiety was given free rein.[4] This skilful presentation bestows a liveliness on *The Soldier's Confession.* Erasmus addressed himself to the issue of mercenary warfare of his time, and the theme of the dialogue was: What is gained in the soldier's job? The military profession was for Erasmus the school of villainy, a condition opposed to nature, good

sense, religion and humanity. He did not even believe in the sincerity
or courage of these combatants for whom the lure of gain and booty
was the sole motive. Three centuries before Stendhal, he emphasized
the soldier's inability to understand the action in which he was involved.

The mercenaries were merely the political instruments of the great
men of this world. This hateful exploitation of the people was encouraged by the court preachers. Erasmus was merciless against the
theologians who made a cut-and-dried apology for the 'right of war'.
He showed that their flock, these unhappy soldiers who went off for
adventure, had no religious sense. Their piety was superstitious, while
the theology of those who exhorted them in the name of a falsified
Gospel was crude. On both sides formalism took the place of religion:
this was what Erasmus could not accept. This is what he denounced at
his own risk and peril. So he too was a combatant – a combatant with
the pen – but he was to be paid only with rancour and hatred. As early
as 1517, Erasmus had written a little pacifist treatise, *The Complaint of
Peace.* Some years had elapsed and peace was no better received by the
masters of this world. Not being able to prevent war, Erasmus consistently
refused to allow it as a normal situation. Not being able to convince
those in power, he reached them by the sole weapon remaining to him,
irony.

HANNO. How is it you come back a Vulcan when you left here a
Mercury?

THRASYMACHUS. What Vulcans or Mercuries are you talking about?

HANNO. You left as though wing-footed; now you're limping.

THRASYMACHUS. The usual way to come back from war.

HANNO. What have *you* to do with war? You're more timid than a deer.

THRASYMACHUS. Hope of booty made me brave.

HANNO. Then you come back rich with plunder?

THRASYMACHUS. No, with an empty purse.

HANNO. So much the less luggage to weigh you down.

THRASYMACHUS. But I return laden with sins. . . .

HANNO. Tell me how the battle was fought and which side won.

THRASYMACHUS. So great was the tumult and the shouting, blast of
trumpets, thunder of horns, neighing of horses, and clamor of men
that I couldn't see what was going on; I scarcely knew where I myself

was. . . . What went on in my own tent I know; as to what happened in the battle I'm completely ignorant.

HANNO. Well, do you know how you got this lameness?

THRASYMACHUS. Damned if I know for sure. I think my knee was hurt by a stone or a horse's hoof.

HANNO. But I know.

THRASYMACHUS. You know? Did someone tell you?

HANNO. No, but I can guess.

THRASYMACHUS. Tell me, then.

HANNO. When you were scared and running away you fell down and knocked it on a stone.

THRASYMACHUS. Damned if you haven't hit the nail on the head! You've guessed right. . . .

HANNO. But you did refrain from sacrileges, I suppose?

THRASYMACHUS. On the contrary. Nothing was sacred there; no building spared, sacred or profane.

HANNO. How will you make amends for that?

THRASYMACHUS. They say you don't have to make amends for what's done in war; whatever it is, it's right.

HANNO. The law of war, perhaps.

THRASYMACHUS. Exactly.

HANNO. Yet that law is the greatest wrong. It wasn't devotion to your country but hope of spoils that drew you to war.

THRASYMACHUS. Granted; and in my opinion few men go there from any loftier motive.

HANNO. To be mad with many is something!

THRASYMACHUS. A preacher declared from the pulpit that war is just.

HANNO. The pulpit doesn't often lie. But war might be just for a prince, not necessarily you. . . . Weren't you worried about the destination of your soul if you fell in battle?

THRASYMACHUS. Oh, no, I was confident because I had commended myself once for all to St Barbara.

HANNO. Did she undertake to protect you?

THRASYMACHUS. Yes, she seemed to nod her head a little.

HANNO. When did this happen – in the morning?

THRASYMACHUS. No, after dinner.

HANNO. But then, I dare say, even the trees seemed to walk.

THRASYMACHUS. How he guesses everything. . . .

HANNO. I don't see how you can be absolved from such outrageous sins unless you betake yourself to Rome.

THRASYMACHUS. No, I know a shorter way.

HANNO. What is it?

THRASYMACHUS. I'll go to the Dominicans and strike a bargain there with the commissaries.

HANNO. Even for sacrileges?

THRASYMACHUS. Even if I had robbed Christ himself, yes, even if I had beheaded him, such liberal indulgences have they and such authority to arrange matters. . . .

HANNO. What priest will you choose?

THRASYMACHUS. One I know to be as shameless and easygoing as possible. . . . Enough for me that I believe myself absolved.

HANNO. But to believe that is risky. It may not satisfy God, to whom you're in debt.[5]

The fact that many of these dialogues were associated with a meal expresses the author's taste for conviviality.

The Religious Banquet is without doubt the longest of the *Colloquies*. It is a little drama with six persons illustrating the Erasmian agreement between the Gospel and ancient wisdom. The best of the ancients had cultivated admirable natural virtues; they had bequeathed to us the example of a philosophy at once profound and accessible. Christians should imitate them in what they can, and not take refuge in the attitude of spiritual upstarts!

Everything in this dialogue is of a peaceful kind, both the framework and the conversations. The house and gardens described by Erasmus are undoubtedly those of Johann Froben, his printer and friend. A lovely dwelling, perfectly harmonious, well made for generous and serene exchanges about evangelical perfection. Mythology, history and theology sustain courteous conversations, of a high spiritual tenor. A constant progression leads the spirit of the reader from the beauties of nature to those of art, from the pleasures of friendship to those of meditation, from the teaching of Plato to that of Christ.

Erasmus reveals himself here as subtle and firm in his critique of the world. He also shows himself to be a man of prayer and a student of the Bible in order to apply their fruits to the conversion of souls. The editor of the *New Testament* is, at the same time, the apostle who counsels all Christians to have direct and daily contact with the Good News.

But let us listen to Eusebius, the principal hero of the colloquy.

> On the contrary, whatever is devout and contributes to good morals should not be called profane. Sacred Scripture is of course the basic authority in everything; yet I sometimes run across ancient sayings or pagan writings – even the poets – so purely and reverently and admirably expressed that I can't help believing their authors' hearts were moved by some divine power. And perhaps the spirit of Christ is more widespread than we understand, and the company of saints includes many not in our calendar. Speaking frankly, among friends, I can't read Cicero's *De senectute, De amicitia, De officiis, De Tusculanis quaestionibus*, without sometimes kissing the book and blessing that pure heart, divinely inspired as it was. But when, on the other hand, I read these modern writers on government, economics or ethics – good Lord, how dull they are by comparison! And what lack of feeling they seem to have for what they write! So that I would much rather let all of Scotus and others of his sort perish than the books of a single Cicero or Plutarch.

And Nephalius replies: 'When I read such things of such men, I can hardly help exclaiming, "Saint Socrates, pray for us!"'[6]

For Erasmus, man in his fullness is the Christian formed by classical culture and transformed by the Gospel. The Word is sweet and terrible, it is at once a consolation and a demand.

To be sure, Erasmus often provided his critics with weapons. In this edition of 1522, a dialogue entitled *Rash Vows* set up a ridiculous pilgrim who was carrying a bag full of generous indulgences applicable to the dead. It wasn't long before the Carmelite Nicholas Egmondanus of Louvain declared that the *Colloquies* were heretical. To Joost Lauwereyns, president of the Grand Council of Mechelen, to the chancellor Van der Noot and the Faculty of Theology at Louvain, Erasmus was to say, from the month of July, that Egmondanus's accusations betrayed a hatred for the author and for literature. He made his views clear for the benefit of the Faculty: 'I do not condemn indulgences, though they have been accorded thus far more than enough indulgence.'[7] This clarity was to have no success in appeasing the guardians of faith and morality. Whether they were from Louvain or Paris, they did not understand the Erasmian manner of drawing attention to the essentials by laughing at the incidentals.

The Whole Duty of Youth, which was inspired by the precepts of John Colet, drew the portrait of a model adolescent, Gaspar, who prayed at home, on the road, and in church. He received the sacraments and tried hard to live his religion without giving in to superstition. From the moment of waking, he lifted up his heart to God.

> I give thanks for his having deigned to preserve me that night and I pray that during the entire day likewise he will bless me to his glory and the salvation of my soul; and that he who is the true light which knows no setting, the sun eternal giving life to all, nourishing and inspiring them, may be pleased to illumine my mind, that I may not by any means fall into sin, but by his guidance pass to everlasting life.

During the Mass, Gaspar associated himself with the sacrifice of the Redeemer.

> I give thanks to Jesus Christ for his inexpressible love in condescending to redeem mankind by his death; and I pray that he may not let his sacred blood be poured out for me in vain but that with his body he may always feed my soul, with his blood make my spirit live; that gradually, by growth in goodness, I a boy may become a worthy member of his mystical body, the Church; that I may never break that most holy covenant made with his chosen disciples at the last supper by means of the bread and cup distributed to them, and through them with all who are united by baptism with his company.[8]

These prayers, we may note, were in the mainstream of the purest Christian tradition.

This edition of the *Colloquies* in March 1522 was of fundamental importance. The formulas were not to vary any further, but the dialogues blossomed. Much more than a school book, the work became a collection of reflections intended for adults. From this point on, the *Colloquies* had found the secret of their success. From edition to edition, Erasmus was to take up his work again lovingly. He was to touch up his dialogues, to add others to them, until the end of his working life, so much so that it can be said that the history of the *Colloquies* became Erasmus's own history: countless editions and translations, forgeries, condemnations, corrections, apologies!

In this way the book moved from the didactic to the satiric, even the polemical, genre. Not without some artifice at times, it even took on the form of philosophy and theology, since it reflected all the author's preoccupations. Playfully, Erasmus touched on all the great problems of culture, morality and religion, through the petty conflicts of daily life. The present furnished him his subjects every bit as much as history. The *Colloquies* amused without ceasing to be true. We see and hear travellers, hotel keepers, soldiers, beggars, burghers, monks, women and children talking. Holbein had illustrated *The Praise of Folly*, and one would like to think that the *Colloquies* inspired Breughel, as the similarity between the Dutch writer and the Flemish painter has often been recognized.

The edition of the *Colloquies* of August 1523 presented six new dialogues. *Inns* conveyed Erasmus's experiences as a traveller, the man who had crossed the Alps on horseback and was able to compare the inns of France with those of Germany. The 'literary travels' had left him numerous memories – precise and often spicy ones. We should remember that it was in the course of this journey that Erasmus conceived *The Praise of Folly*. His curious, observant nature did not allow anything ridiculous pass in anybody at all. The history of manners pervades his testimony like a watermark. In it we see his horror at the German stoves as well as the menu of a hotel meal of the sixteenth century. We can note the parallel, too often repeated after him, of French cordiality and Germanic rusticity.

BERTULF. Why do most people like to linger two or three days in Lyons? . . .

WILLIAM. Because that's a spot the companions of Ulysses couldn't have been torn away from. The Sirens are there. No one's treated better in his own home than in a public house in Lyons.

BERT. What happens?

WILL. At the table some woman would always be standing by to enliven the meal with jokes and pleasantries (and the women there are awfully good-looking too). First the hostess would come and welcome us, bidding us be merry and accept with good grace whatever was served. After her the daughter, a lovely woman with such delightful manners and speech that she would cheer Cato himself. They would chat with us not as with strangers but as if with old familiar friends.

BERT. I know the politeness of the French. . . . But precisely what was the food like? Because stories don't fill your belly.

WILL. Really sumptuous; so sumptuous I wonder they can take guests for so low a price. And when the meal is finished they feast a man with funny stories, so he won't become bored. I fancied myself at home, not abroad.

BERT. What did you find in the bedrooms?

WILL. Girls: laughing, jolly, sportive girls everywhere. They asked of their own accord if we had any dirty clothes; they washed them and brought them back – clean. In short, we saw nothing there but women and girls except in the stable, though often girls invaded even that. They embrace the departing guests and take leave of them as affectionately as if they were all brothers or close relatives.

BERT. Maybe these manners suit the French. I prefer German ones as being more manly.

WILL. I've never seen Germany, as it happens, so please do be good enough to tell me how a guest is treated there.

BERT. Whether the method of treatment is the same everywhere I don't know. I'll tell you what I saw. No one greets the arrival, lest they seem to be on the lookout for a guest; that they consider base and degrading, unworthy of Germanic austerity. When you've shouted a long time, someone finally sticks his head out of the little window of the stove room (where they spend most of their time until midsummer), like a turtle from his shell. You must ask him if you may put up there. If he doesn't shake his head, you know there's room for you. . . . if the inn's one of the better-known ones, a servant does show you the stable and even a place for your horse – a very poor place, since the better ones are reserved for the use of later guests, especially nobility. If you ask why you hear instantly, 'If you don't like this, look for another inn.' . . . If you arrive at four o'clock, you still won't dine before nine and sometimes ten.

WILL. Why?

BERT. They don't prepare anything unless they see everyone's present, in order to serve them all in one operation.

WILL. Looking for a short cut. . . .

BERT. When the evening's already late and no more arrivals are expected, an aged servant with a white beard, cropped head, grim look, and dirty clothes makes his appearance. . . . Glancing about, he silently counts the people in the stove room. The more he sees there, the more energetically he fires up the stove, even though the weather's oppressively warm without it. Among these folk it's a principal part of good management to melt everybody in sweat. . . .

WILL. But nothing seems to me more dangerous than for so many persons to breathe the same warm air, especially when their bodies are relaxed and they've eaten together and stayed in the same place a good many hours. Quite apart from the belching of garlic, the breaking of wind, the stinking breaths, many persons suffer from hidden diseases, and every disease is contagious. Undoubtedly many have the Spanish or, as some call it, French pox, though it's common to all countries. In my opinion, there's almost as much danger from these men as from lepers. Just imagine now, how great the risk of plague.

BERT. They're brave fellows. They laugh at these things and pay no attention to them.

WILL. But all the while their bravery endangers the public.

BERT. What would you do? This is their custom and they're resolved not to depart from established ways.

WILL. Twenty-five years ago nothing was more customary among the Brabanters than public steam baths. Now these are out of fashion everywhere, for the new pox has taught us to let them alone.[9]

More incisively, *The Shipwreck* projects a scene of sailors and passengers confronted with a tempest. In the presence of danger, the most extravagant promises burst forth from all sides. The Virgin and the saints are summoned to help. If they save those in danger of shipwreck, they will enrich their sanctuaries. One woman alone neither cries out or weeps. Holding an infant tightly in her arms, she prays in silence. The narrator stresses the point that he had refrained from making false promises. 'I don't make deals with saints. [I] went straight to the Father himself, reciting the *Pater Noster*. No saint hears sooner than he or more willingly grants what is asked.'[10]

In this edition of 1523, Erasmus devoted four dialogues to woman and marriage. The condition of women occupied a place of importance in the author's thought, from prostitutes to cloistered nuns, including girls to be married, women badly married and model spouses.[11] He deplored unhappy unions and clandestine marriages every bit as much as enforced vocations.

From a reading of these colloquies, it is clear that Erasmus's thought on marriage had evolved. He had lost his fondness for the Platonic opposition between flesh and spirit. He seemed more understanding with respect to the problems of sexuality experienced by his contemporaries.

The most lively of these matrimonial dialogues is undoubtedly *Courtship*, which sets a scene of two young people, smitten with one another, but not equally in a hurry to crown their union. The text is interesting for its account of contemporary matrimonial ceremonies. In Erasmus's time clandestine marriages concluded without parental agreement or publicity were still valid. The Council of Trent was to remedy this, while safeguarding the freedom of those engaged. Erasmus seemed hardly sympathetic with an apologetic for a love which 'does not recognize laws.' Like Rabelais, he condemned ill-matched unions, in which he saw the source of disunion. He did not think that the approval of parents was without value, for, above all, he feared haste. Marriage was too important to be botched. This colloquy was to be bitterly criticized by Erasmus's opponents because it suggested very obviously that marriage was preferable to celibacy.

PAMPHILUS. Then don't provoke Nemesis: return your lover's love.

MARIA. If that's enough, I do return it.

PAMPH. But I'd want this love to be lasting and to be mine alone. I'm courting a wife, not a mistress.

MARIA. I know that, but I must deliberate a long time over what can't be revoked once it's begun.

PAMPH. *I've* thought it over a long time.

MARIA. See that love, who's not the best adviser, doesn't trick you. For they say he's blind.

PAMPH. But one who proceeds with caution is keen-sighted. You don't appear to me as you do because I love you; I love you because I've observed what you're like.

MARIA. But you may not know me well enough. If you'd wear the shoe, you'd feel then where it pinched.

PAMPH. I'll have to take the chance; though I infer from many signs that the match will succeed. . . . these omens assure me that we shall have a blessed, lasting, happy marriage, provided you don't intend to sing a song of woe for our prospects.

MARIA. What song do you want?

PAMPH. I'll play 'I am yours'; you chime in with 'I am yours.'

MARIA. A short song all right, but it has a long finale.

PAMPH. What matter how long, if only it be joyful.[12]

With *Marriage*, we go further forward. Erasmus, like his friend Vivès, was constantly preoccupied with the problems of Christian marriage.

His doctrine was simple. The theologian who called the man of the world to piety had to proclaim the eminent dignity of marriage. It was by that idea, among others, that Erasmus foreshadowed St Francis de Sales and his *Introduction to the Devout Life*. Erasmus was a feminist because he was a humanist and a Christian.

Although the little Erasmian treatise on marriage had no great repercussions, the colloquies devoted to marriage rapidly achieved success. The public favoured the stories, which amused them while instructing them, rather than dissertations which instructed them without entertaining them. But Erasmus was not a feminist like Anna Eleanor Roosevelt or Simone de Beauvoir. He had no system, no theory of the second sex – simply a pedagogy associating the better half of humanity with the progress of scholarship. The rest would follow. So it was an application of Christian morality: marriage exists, and is inseparable from the promotion of woman; but to those unhappily married, Erasmus could advise only tact.

Marriage, Erasmus said, was the general condition of men and women: no purpose could be served by complaining about it, since one had to be content with it. Here we find the central idea of Erasmian morality: concord. Concord between the nations, the Churches, the schools, and even between spouses. Spouses should improve themselves by a reciprocal effort of mutual goodwill. In an unhappy household, wrongs are usually on both sides, and it is up to the woman to gain or regain her husband's affection.

Erasmus called the woman who complained of marriage Xanthippe. By giving her the name of Socrates' grumpy companion, he did show prejudice in favour of the stronger sex – unless he was thinking, on the contrary, of a kind of rehabilitation of this unfortunate name. The clichés of bourgeois vaudeville were no strangers to his colloquy. It is true that Erasmus had not married and this suited him, for the society of women seemed foreign to him.

EULALIA. Greetings, Xanthippe! I've been dying to see you.

XANTHIPPE. Same to you, my dearest Eulalia. You look lovelier than ever.

EUL. So you greet me by making fun of me right away?

XAN. Not at all: I mean it.

EUL. Maybe this new dress flatters my figure.

XAN. Of course it does. I haven't seen anything prettier for a long time. British cloth, I suppose?

EUL. British wool with Venetian dye.

XAN. Softer than satin. What a charming shade of purple! Where did you get such a marvellous gift?

EUL. Where should honest wives get them except from their husbands?

XAN. Lucky you to have such a husband! As for me – I might as well have married a mushroom when I married my Nicholas.

EUL. Why so, if you please? Are you falling out so soon?

XAN. I'll never fall in with the likes of him. You see I'm in rags: that's how *he* allows his wife to appear. Damned if often I'm not ashamed to go out in public when I see how well dressed other women are who married husbands much worse off than mine.

EUL. Feminine finery, as St Peter the apostle teaches . . . consists not of clothes. . . . Harlots are decked out for vulgar eyes. We're sufficiently well dressed if we please one husband.

XAN. But meanwhile that fine gentleman, so stingy towards his wife, squanders the dowry he got from me – no slight one – as fast as he can.

EUL. On what?

XAN. On whatever he pleases: wine – whores – dice.

EUL. That's no way to talk.

XAN. But it's the truth. Besides, when he comes home drunk in the middle of the night, after being long awaited, he snores all night and sometimes vomits in bed – to say no worse.

EUL. Hush! You bring reproach on yourself when you reproach your husband.

XAN. Hope to die if I wouldn't rather sleep with a brood sow than such a husband!

EUL. Don't you welcome him with abuse then?

XAN. Yes – as he deserves. He finds I'm no mute.

EUL. What does he do to counter you?

XAN. At first he used to talk back most ferociously, thinking he'd drive me away with harsh words.

EUL. The bickering never came to actual blows?

XAN. Once, at least, the argument grew so hot on both sides that it nearly ended in a fight.

EUL. You don't say so!

XAN. He was swinging a club, yelling savagely all the while and threatening terrible deeds.

EUL. Weren't you scared of that?

XAN. Oh, no. When it came to my turn, I grabbed a stool. Had he laid a finger on me, he'd have found I didn't lack arms.

EUL. A new sort of shield! You should have used your distaff for a lance.

XAN. He'd have found he had an Amazon to deal with.

EUL. My dear Xanthippe, this won't do. . . .

XAN. That's true . . .

EUL. Whatever your husband's like, bear in mind that there's no exchanging him for another. Once upon a time divorce was a final remedy for irreconcilable differences. Nowadays this has been entirely abolished; you must be husband and wife till the day you die.

XAN. May heaven punish whoever robbed us of this right!

EUL. Mind what you're saying. Christ so willed.

XAN. I can scarcely believe it.

EUL. It's the truth. There's nothing left now but to try to live in harmony by adjusting yourself to each other's habits and personalities.

XAN. Can I reform him?

EUL. What sort of men husbands are depends not a little upon their wives.

XAN. Do you get along well with your husband?

EUL. Everything's peaceful now.

XAN. There were some difficulties at first, then?

EUL. Never a storm, but slight clouds appeared occasionally: the usual human experience. They could have caused a storm had they not been met with forbearance. Each of us has his own ways and opinions, and – to tell the truth – his own peculiar faults. If there's any place where one has a duty to recognize these, not resent them, surely it's in marriage.

XAN. Good advice.

EUL. It frequently happens, however, that good will between husband and wife breaks down before they know each other well enough. This above all is to be avoided, for once contention arises love is not easily recovered, especially if the affair reaches the point of harsh abuse. Things glued together are easily separated if you shake them immediately, but once the glue has dried they stick together as firmly as anything. Hence at the very outset no pains should be spared to establish and cement good will between husband and wife. This is accomplished mainly by submissiveness and courtesy, for good will won merely by beauty of person is usually short-lived.

XAN. But tell me, please, by what arts you draw your husband to your ways? . . .

EUL. My first concern was to be agreeable to my husband in every respect, so as not to cause him any annoyance. . . . I noted . . . what soothed and irritated him, as did those who tame elephants and lions or suchlike creatures that can't be forced.

XAN. That's the sort of creature I have at home!

EUL. . . . Trainers of horses have calls, whistles, caresses, and other means of soothing mettlesome animals. How much more fitting for us to use those arts on our husbands, with whom, whether we like it or not, we share bed and board for our entire lives. . . . If my husband seemed quite depressed and I had no chance to appeal to him, I wouldn't laugh or joke, as some women like to do, but I too put on a somber, worried look. As a mirror, if it's a good one, always gives back the image of the person looking at it, so should a wife reflect her husband's mood, not being gay when he's sad or merry when he's upset. But whenever he was more upset than usual, I'd either soothe him with pleasant conversation or defer to his anger in silence until he cooled off and an opportunity came to correct or advise him. I'd do the same whenever he came home tipsy: at the same time I'd say nothing except what was agreeable; I'd just coax him to bed.

XAN. Wives have an unhappy lot for sure if they must simply put up with husbands who are angry, drunk, and whatever else they please.

EUL. As if this putting up with things didn't work both ways! Husbands have much to endure from our habits as well. On occasion, however – in a serious matter, when something important's at stake – it's right for a wife to reprove her husband; trivial matters are better winked at.

XAN. What occasion, pray?

EUL. When he's at leisure and not disturbed, worried or tipsy, then she should admonish him politely. . . . and this very admonition should be seasoned with wit and pleasantries . . . After reproving him as I intended,

I'd break off that talk . . . For as a rule, my dear Xanthippe, our mistake is that once we've started to talk we can't stop.

XAN. So they say. . . . Whoever could do all this must be a philosopher. . . .

EUL. Tell me, finally: have you any enemies?

XAN. I have a stepmother – the genuine article – and a mother-in-law just like her.

EUL. Do they hate you so very much?

XAN. They'd like me to drop dead.

EUL. Have a thought for them, too. How could you give them greater pleasure than by letting them see you parted from your husband, living like a widow, nay worse than a widow? For widows may at least remarry. . . .

XAN. Do you think I'll succeed if I try?

EUL. Look at me. I'll vouch for it, and meantime I'll approach your husband and remind him too of his duty.

XAN. I approve of the plan, but watch out he doesn't suspect this plot; he'd raise hell.

EUL. Don't fear. I'll speak to him in such a roundabout way that he'll tell me himself what the trouble is between you. After that I'll draw him on very innocently, in my usual fashion and – I hope – make him more considerate of you.[13]

The theme of the conversation entitled *The Young Man and the Harlot* was borrowed from an old legend telling of the conversion of the sinner Thaïs. Well before Anatole France, and in a totally different spirit, Erasmus cleverly modernized the pious example bequeathed by the Middle Ages. Sophronius, the converter, was young and himself a convert. The lost woman, Lucretia, recognized in him one of her favourite clients, accepted the debate and finally gave in to his reasons. This colloquy moralizes, but without going to extremes. The characters are plausible. Sophronius speaks to Lucretia of the Erasmian translation of the *New Testament*. Shouldn't the Good News be known to prostitutes too?

SOPHRONIUS. Quit joking and treat the subject seriously, as it deserves. A girl with so many friends has no friend at all, Lucretia, believe me. Those who resort to you treat you not as a friend but rather as an object of contempt.... If you haven't yet caught the new contagion called the Spanish pox, you can't long escape it. If you do get it, you'll be the most miserable creature alive, even if you prosper in every other respect, even if you have fame and fortune. What will you be but a living corpse? You used to think obeying your mother burdensome; now you're at the beck and call of an utterly repulsive bawd. You were fed up with parental reproofs; here you must often endure beatings by drunken, maddened whoremongers. To do some of the housework at home in return for bed and board, disgusted you; here what commotions, what late hours you put up with!

LUCRETIA. Where has this new preacher come from?

SOPH. Now think it over. This bloom of beauty that draws lovers to you will soon fade. What a pitiable sight you'll be then! What dung heap will be more contemptible than you? You'll change from whore to bawd, a distinction that doesn't fall to everyone! And if it does come, what is there more wicked or more closely tied to devilish spitefulness?

LUC. Almost everything you say is true, my Sophronius. But where did you pick up this newfangled holiness? Generally you're the wildest playboy of them all. Nobody used to come here oftener or at more inconvenient times than you did. You've been in Rome, I hear.

SOPH. I have.

LUC. But ordinarily people return from there worse than they went. How come it happened otherwise for you?

SOPH. I'll tell you: because I didn't go to Rome for the same reason or in the same fashion. Others commonly go to Rome intending to return worse – and abundant opportunities for that purpose are at hand there. I set out with an honest chap by whose urging I took a book along instead of a flask: the New Testament, translated by Erasmus.

LUC. Erasmus? He's half a heretic, they say.

SOPH. You don't mean that man's reputation has reached even this place?

LUC. No name is better known to us.

SOPH. Have you seen him?

LUC. Never, but I'd like very much to see the person I've heard so many bad reports of.

SOPH. From bad men, perhaps.

LUC. Oh, no: from reverend gentlemen.[14]

It was at this time that a wicked forger, the Dominican Lambertus Campester, published an unexpected counterfeit of the *Colloquies* in Paris. He suppressed what seemed to him unorthodox and recast the remainder in the spirit of the out-of-date theology.

Erasmus protested angrily.

As long as there was nothing in the book but the merest trifles, it found surprising favour on all sides. When it began to be useful in many ways, it could not escape the poison-fangs of slander. A certain divine in Louvain, who is physically purblind and mentally even more so, detected in it four passages that were heretical. This book had another experience worthy of record. It was printed lately in Paris after the correction, which means of course the disfigurement, of several passages which were thought to glance at monks, vows, pilgrimages, indulgences and other things of the kind which, if they were to have the greatest influence with the public, would mean larger profits for that party. Even in this he displayed such folly and such ignorance that you would swear it was the work of some itinerant buffoon.... He pays such grovelling homage everywhere to France, to Paris, to theologians, to the Sorbonne, to the colleges, that no beggar could be more abject. So if he thinks something not complimentary enough to the French, he transfers it to the English, or instead of Paris he puts London. He adds some offensive remarks as though they were mine, in hopes of getting me into trouble with people whose high opinion of me causes him pain. In short, everywhere he cuts out, puts in, alters to suit himself, like an old sow covered in mud and rolling in a stranger's garden; all is filth, confusion, and upheaval.... And this stuff is printed in Paris, where it is a crime to print even the Gospels without a favourable verdict from the theologians![15]

In this declaration there was something more than anger. In rejecting the 'improvements' of his forger, Erasmus showed courage. He provoked and brought down wrath upon his own head.[16]

Between 1524 and 1533, the *Colloquies* doubled in number and size. They all bear witness to the talent and originality of their author. Among the most impassioned, *An Examination Concerning Faith* was written in a conciliatory spirit, at the beginning of the quarrel with Luther. As we have seen, it was an attempt to re-establish religious concord by leading Christian faith back to the essentials. *The Old Men's Chat* denounced the aberrations of an undisciplined and unhealthy piety. Speaking of an old pilgrim who had left wife and child to see Jerusalem, so that, he believed, he might die thus in peace, a character in the colloquy becomes indignant and exclaims: 'Unrighteously righteous old man!' On the other hand, the friar Conrad outlines the Erasmian doctrine of devotion to the saints, saying in the colloquy *The Well-to-do Beggars*: 'The most devout adorer of saints is the one who emulates them.' He mocks those who want to be buried in the Franciscan cowl: 'God recognizes a fool in Franciscan habit no less than one in a soldier's uniform.'[17] In *The Ignoble Knight* (1529) our author harshly criticizes the ambition which leads men to seek after nobility and fancy names and contrasts nobility of title with that of feeling.

The Abbot and the Learned Lady owes some of its charm to two friends of Erasmus. Thomas More, an exacting educator of his daughters, had made him aware of the importance of the education of women for the education of children. Like Juan Luis Vivès, Erasmus was delighted to see women benefiting from wider teaching. Magdalia was not a 'learned woman' such as Molière depicted a century later, nor was she a noble lady, but an intelligent, refined and cultivated middle-class woman. She triumphs easily over the large jovial Father Abbot who thinks only of drinking and eating well, rather than reading and getting his monks to read. Behind this joviality, the Abbot Antronius was an unfortunate individual, typical of those commendatory abbots who collected benefices without filling the offices. In his colloquy, Erasmus is not content with taking up the cudgels for the equality of the sexes; he vigorously denounces the decadence of the monasteries, one of the most serious abuses in the Renaissance Church.[18]

ANTRONIUS. You confuse growing wise with enjoying yourself. It's not feminine to be brainy. A lady's business is to have a good time.

MAGDALIA. Shouldn't everyone live well?

ANT. Yes, in my opinion.

MAGD. But who can have a good time without living well?

ANT. Rather, who can enjoy himself if he *does* live well?

MAGD. So you approve of those who live basely if only they have a good time?

ANT. I believe those who have a good time are living well.

MAGD. Where does this good time come from? From externals or from within?

ANT. From externals.

MAGD. Shrewd abbot but stupid philosopher! Tell me: how do you measure good times?

ANT. By sleep, dinner parties, doing as one likes, money, honors.

MAGD. But if to these things God added wisdom, you wouldn't enjoy yourself!

ANT. What do you mean by wisdom?

MAGD. This: understanding that a man is not happy without the goods of the mind; that wealth, honors, class make him neither happier nor better.

ANT. Away with that wisdom!

MAGD. What if I enjoy reading a good author more than you do hunting, drinking, or playing dice? You won't think I'm having a good time?

ANT. I wouldn't live like that.

MAGD. I'm not asking what *you* would enjoy most, but what *ought* to be enjoyable.

ANT. I wouldn't want my monks to spend their time on books.

MAGD. Yet my husband heartily approves of my doing so. But exactly why do you disapprove of this in your monks?

ANT. Because I find they're less tractable; they talk back by quoting from decrees and decretals, from Peter and Paul.

MAGD. So your rules conflict with those of Peter and Paul?

ANT. What *they* may enjoin I don't know, but still I don't like a monk who talks back. And I don't want any of mine to know more than I do.

MAGD. You could avoid that by endeavouring to know as much as possible.

ANT. I haven't the leisure.

MAGD. How come?

ANT. Because I've no free time.

MAGD. No free time to grow wise?

ANT. No.

MAGD. What hinders you?

ANT. Long prayers, housekeeping, hunts, horses, court functions.

MAGD. So these are more important to you than wisdom?

ANT. It's what we're used to. . . . I could put up with books, but not Latin ones.

MAGD. Why not?

ANT. Because that language isn't fit for women.

MAGD. I want to know why.

ANT. Because it does little to protect their chastity.

MAGD. Therefore French books, full of the most frivolous stories, do promote chastity?

ANT. There's another reason.

MAGD. Tell me plainly, whatever it is.

ANT. They're safer from priests if they don't know Latin.

MAGD. Very little danger from you in that respect, since you take such pains not to know Latin!

ANT. The public agrees with me, because it's a rare and exceptional thing for a woman to know Latin.

MAGD. Why cite the public, the worst possible authority on conduct? Why tell me of custom, the mistress of every vice? Accustom yourself to the best; then the unusual will become habitual; the harsh, enjoyable; the apparently unseemly, seemly.

ANT. I hear you.

MAGD. Is it fitting for a German woman to learn French?

ANT. Of course.

MAGD. Why?

ANT. To talk with those who know French.

MAGD. And do you think it unsuitable for me to know Latin in order to converse daily with authors so numerous, so eloquent, so learned, so wise; with counselors so faithful?

ANT. Books ruin women's wits – which are none too plentiful anyway.

MAGD. How plentiful *yours* are, I don't know. Assuredly I prefer to spend mine, however slight, on profitable studies rather than on prayers said by rote, all-night parties, and heavy drinking.

ANT. Bookishness drives people mad. . . . I've often heard the common saying, 'A wise woman is twice foolish.'

MAGD. That's commonly said, yes, but by fools. . . . If you're not careful, the net result will be that we'll preside in the theological schools, preach in the churches, and wear your miters.[19]

As we have seen, Erasmus does not hide his sympathy for the difficult position of those who are married. In *The New Mother*, Fabulla accuses men of drunkenness and brutality. Eutrapelus, the defender of the stronger sex, replies that only men have to go to war for their country. But Fabulla will have the last word: 'But quite often you same men desert your post and run away shamefully. And it's not always for your country, but more commonly for a paltry pittance, that you desert wife and children. You're worse than gladiators: you voluntarily surrender your bodies into the slavish necessity of killing, or being killed.'[20] Women give life, men give death.

George, the unfortunate hero of *The Funeral,* dies as he has lived, in the pretentious confusion of ceremonies. He is to be buried in a Franciscan habit, while Cornelius, a very Erasmian character, prepares for death with calm dignity, praying, reading his Bible, receiving unction and the last communion from the hands of his priest. He does not confess, for he had already confessed several days earlier, and his spirit is untroubled. His death, like his life, is edifying for those around him.[21]

On the occasion of the battle of Pavia, Erasmus recalled the rivalry of the Valois and the Habsburgs, putting an unusual speech into the mouth of a fishmonger; in it popular simplicity meets up with the wisdom of the Gospel. 'If I were Emperor, I'd conclude an agreement without delay with the king of France in this manner: "Brother, some evil spirit stirred up this war ... I grant you life and liberty." '[22]

Three years later, the war was still going on. The treaties that were signed brought only short truces. At this point Erasmus republished the dialogue *Charon,* named after the ferryman of Hades. In this he expressed himself with savage irony. The Habsburg-Valois War was displaying its horrors, and he could not but denounce its horrors. 'You've no reason to fear a peace within ten whole years', he makes the spirit Alastor say. These views were singularly prophetic. For every writer who was urging peace, there were a hundred who were fanning the fires of envy and hatred. In each camp, preachers gave assurance with equal conviction of the sanctity of their cause.

> There are some as helpful to our cause as the Furies themselves. ... Certain creatures in black and white cloaks and ash-gray tunics, adorned with plumage of various kinds. They never leave the courts of princes. They instil into their ears a love of war; they incite rulers and populace alike; in their evangelical sermons they proclaim that war is just, holy and right. And – to make you marvel more at the audacity of the fellows – they proclaim the very same thing on both sides. To the French they preach that God is on the French side: he who has God to protect him cannot be conquered! To the English and Spanish they declare this war is not the Emperor's but God's: only let them show themselves valiant men and victory is certain! But if anyone *does* get killed, he doesn't perish utterly but flies straight up to heaven, armed just as he was.[23]

Sadly, peace is not only persecuted, it has been declared dead.

Justly famous, the colloquy *A Pilgrimage for Religion's Sake* mercilessly denounces[24] the stupidity of pilgrims and the greed of those who dupe them. The first part is devoted to the delicate problem of the influence of the Virgin Mary on Jesus, as we shall see later. The second part of the dialogue, full of picturesque details, is based on Erasmus's personal recollections and tells of two English pilgrimages, one to Our Lady of Walsingham and the other to St Thomas of Canterbury. Everything is there to turn Christians away from these sanctuaries which are described as museums of superstition.

The colloquies of 1526, *A Fish Diet* and *The Funeral* are in the same vein. Their aim is to show, by significant examples, that even the most legitimate observances and devotions are only the means, and inadequate means at that, if they are not sustained by genuine piety. At the same time Erasmus defends himself from the charge of having ridiculed prayers addressed to saints. He pokes fun only at those who ask of heaven what they would not dare to ask of an honest man. He goes further in asserting that his dialogues serve God's cause. In short, if the *Colloquies* are not a book of piety as such, piety is never absent from them.

Erasmus was still young at heart when he published *The Epicurean* in 1533, the dialogue which crowned that year's volume. It was the conclusion of the collection, the synthesis of its author's religion – particularly of his morality. The inspiration derived from Valla is obvious here. Moreover, the responses of the conversationalists display the same verve as in the *Folly*, twenty-two years earlier.

It was not without consciousness of a paradox that Erasmus claimed to restore the true Epicureanism to Christianity. He rose up against the common prejudice which confused Christianity with the relaxation of morals. He paid homage to Epicurus for having considered peace of the soul to be the greatest good. Every man searches for happiness; none follows Epicurus' moral intention more perfectly than the Christian. Moreover, his doctrine was austere, like his life. It was the disciples of Epicurus who diverted his maxims from their original sense and it was to them that Epicureanism owed its dubious reputation. In fact, the apologia for Epicureanism here is only a process. Erasmus wants to give an invigorating image of Christianity, this living reality which he untiringly recalled to the attention of slumbering Christians.

HEDONIUS. Disease, hunger, watchings, labors, nakedness in themselves weaken one's physical condition. Yet not in these states only, but even at death itself cheerfulness keeps breaking through. Though the mind is in fact attached to a mortal body, nevertheless, since the mind is stronger, it somehow assimilates the very body, especially when spiritual energy is added to the impetuous force of Nature. Hence it is that we often see truly righteous men die with more cheerfulness than others feast.

SPUDAEUS. Yes, I've often wondered at that.

HEDON. But you should not think it wonderful that where God, the fount of all joy, is present, there insuperable happiness exists. What's strange about the mind of a truly righteous man rejoicing continually in a mortal body, since if that same man goes down to the depths of hell he will suffer no loss of happiness? Wherever is a pure heart, there God is. Wherever God is, there is paradise, heaven, happiness. Where happiness is, there is true gladness and unfeigned cheerfulness. . . .

SPUD. I only wish everyone were as convinced as I am.

HEDON. But if people who live agreeably are Epicureans, none are more truly Epicureans than the righteous and godly. And if it's names that bother us, no one better deserves the name of Epicurean than the revered founder and head of the Christian philosophy, for in Greek *epikouros* means 'helper'. He alone, when the law of Nature was all but blotted out by sins, when the law of Moses incited to lusts rather than cured them, when Satan ruled in the world unchallenged, brought timely aid to perishing humanity. Completely mistaken, therefore, are those who talk in their foolish fashion about Christ's having been sad and gloomy in character and calling upon us to follow a dismal mode of life. On the contrary, he alone shows the most enjoyable life of all and the one most full of true pleasure.

In this dialogue, published three years before his death, Erasmus seems to have wanted to affirm once again the essential thesis of Christian humanism and of the philosophy of Christ. Hence it is not surprising that Hedonius concludes the dialogue with these words:

> The shorter the time, the more passionately should he cry aloud. What can reach from earth to heaven is long enough with God: and even a brief prayer gets through to heaven, provided it is uttered with fervent force of spirit. The woman who was a sinner, in the Gospel, is said to have done lifelong penance. But with how few words the dying thief won paradise from Christ.[25]

Christian humanism believed what the Church believed: it accepted original sin, the weakness of fallen man, the necessity of grace and of asceticism, but it insisted on restored nature, it emphasized the grace offered to all and the easy yoke of Christ. *The Epicurean* takes up forcefully, and sometimes with malice, its author's most precious ideas: a profound agreement between Antiquity and Christianity, the philosophy of Christ, theological optimism.

Why had Erasmus chosen the name of Epicurus as a springboard? Perhaps quite simply because Luther had thrown this name in his face, and as a specific insult. It was characteristic of Erasmus to react to the taunt and to boast of it. In his *Table Talk* Luther had paid him back in kind, going so far as to say:

> In my will I shall forbid my sons to read his Colloquies, where Erasmus says godless things under fictitious and different characters, and puts to attack the Church and Christian faith.... He is a Democritus and an Epicurus, who rails subtly against religion. I prefer Lucian to Erasmus. For the former laughs at everything with open force, but the latter attacks everything sacred and all godliness, with every appearance of holiness and godliness. Therefore he is much more harmful than Lucian.[26]

A masterpiece of calculated boldness and of 'feigned innocence',[27] the *Colloquies* displayed the sense of the universal, so characteristic of their author. Erasmus found qualities of beauty and holiness even in paganism. He was attentive to the religious quarrels of his time, but he went beyond them in preaching peace to princes and piety to theologians.

Erasmus praised virtues, whether they were natural or Christian. He did not cut man off from his roots, while making clear that man in his fullness is the man transformed by the Gospel. After Plato, Lucian and so many others, Erasmus succeeded in raising his readers to his level without ever descending to theirs.

Throughout the sixty or so *Colloquies*, the most diverse ideas are circulated, asserted, and subtly harmonized. Erasmus's major themes were those of the most serious treatises: good literature, peace, the philosophy of Christ. They were taken up in the dialogues with an original presentation and a novel force. The literary genre adopted allowed him to show successively the for and against, to increase the picturesque features, to translate theories into situations and concrete actions.

The *Colloquies* clearly cannot be reduced to intellectual diversions or a collection of table talk or spicy anecdotes; or rather they are that and much more. Under their lively, often mocking and sometimes cutting form, these dialogues allow us to capture Erasmus's thought just as it was. They touch unashamedly on all the great preoccupations of the time, for all ages, all conditions and all professions.

Around these essential ideas, taken up again and again and deepened, minor themes were articulated, borrowed from everyday experience.

The *Colloquies* abounded in comments on social life, in variations on the problems of man and of the Christian. Erasmus's characters were alive, his situations real, his accounts consistent. He told a story well and, thanks to his gifts of observation and exposition, he painted his contemporaries in living colours. He had a genius for dramatization and his comedies in one act are full of humour and good nature, but also of feeling and wisdom. His style is never forced, but natural and relaxed.

Such are the *Colloquies.* In their definitive form, they were not merely the mirror of a life, the story of a mind and the journal of a soul, they were also the mirror of the life of the author's contemporaries. They left the reader amused, sometimes disconcerted, but never exploited. It is understandable that the *Colloquies* were one of the great literary successes of the sixteenth century. Despite the anathemas of the theologians, they won for Erasmus a public that was always increasing. They had even been 'picked up' by his opponents,[28] and to all their readers they had given an example of distinguished Latin and a taste for critical reflection. These readers found themselves questioned by Erasmus, who brought them back unfailingly to the question – that is to say, to the knowledge of their personal responsibility: this was the strong point of Erasmian morality.

Ecclesiastical criticism pursued the *Colloquies* from one edition to another. The Sorbonne condemned them in 1526, and its sentence was to be published in 1531. In the Netherlands, in England and in Spain, the alarm bells rang scarcely less loudly. In 1532 Erasmus replied in his *Declarations against the censures of the Faculty of Theology in Paris.* This weighty demonstration took up the censures point by point and refuted them.[29]

Erasmus defended his *Colloquies.* He wanted his book to be considered as a whole in which the assertions of some characters were corrected or modified by the replies of others. He painted men as they were so that they could be transformed into what they ought to be. His little theatre presupposed a perpetual dialectical confrontation of contrary thoughts, stances and attitudes: these were the scenes from daily life at the beginning of the sixteenth century.

Erasmus confessed to one of his friends that this book which entertained his readers and enriched his printers was a source of disappointment to its author. But he did not add what he could not forget: the *Colloquies* worked wonders for Erasmus's fame and the propagation of his ideas.

19

From *The Institution of Marriage* to *The Ciceronian*

Still hard at it, Erasmus had to sustain a threefold struggle: first against the theologians and monks who were disparaging good literature, then against the Lutherans whose position was radical and uncompromising, finally against the Italian humanists, who were unconditional supporters of pagan literature to the detriment of Christian literature.[1] He was not backward, however, in reminding Adrian VI's successor Clement VII of the disturbing situation of the Church.[2]

In Paris, Bédier continued to denounce Erasmus's 'heterodoxy'. Not content with attacking his *Colloquies*,[3] he wrote to him to list his errors:

> So I say, by virtue of the zeal with which I am roused for your salvation, that you have treated many things destructively and in a way likely to cause heavy scandal to the christian faith: example the celibacy of the clergy; monks' vows; fasting and the banning of the eating of flesh; observance of feast days; evangelical counsels; Holy Scripture to be translated into the vernacular; human laws and canonical hours; the divorce of the faithful; the symbols of the Church; and many other things of this sort.[4]

Bédier stressed the danger which he saw in the translation of the Scriptures into the common tongue and he denounced the group at Meaux inspired by Bishop Briçonnet and his Vicar-General Jacques Lefèvre d'Étaples. Erasmus replied in the same tone, accusing Bédier of injustice and bad faith. Moreover, he courageously defended Briçonnet and Lefèvre, who were reformers like himself.[5] He was undoubtedly still thinking of Bédier when, at the same time, he published a book on *Language* which showed that scandal-mongering and slander were responsible for the evils which tainted Christianity.[6]

Soon after, Erasmus received a visit from his old friend Jacques Lefèvre d'Étaples. The two men had got over their disagreements. Bédier had brought them closer by including them together in the same fierce condemnation. For his part, the humanist Polydoro Virgile sent to

Erasmus 'the price of a little horse which will carry him around where he wants to go'.

The years 1526 and 1527 were hard years for Erasmus, exposed as he was to the animosity of one group or another. Catholics reproached him for having taken refuge in a Lutheran town,[7] while some of Luther's followers published little Lutheran treatises under Erasmus's name.[8] Erasmus published two volumes against Luther refuting *The Bondage of the Will*,[9] while he crossed swords with Alberto Pio, the toughest of his Catholic detractors.[10] Finally, he published a little volume on the real presence in the Eucharist.[11]

Apart from polemics, Erasmus gladly returned to his programme for reform. He opened his heart to Simon Pistorius, counsellor of the Duke of Saxony:

> And, my Pistorius, you can boldly promise your prince about me, that (as I had begun to say), neither from conscience nor contrary to conscience have I ever held to, or ever shall hold to, any damned sect; nor do I do anything in my studies except yoke languages and good literature with more serious disciplines, so as to call scholastic theology, fallen in many to sophistical arguments, back to the well-spring of Holy Scripture: so that there might be fewer ceremonies in the habits of men, more godliness in their minds; so that bishops and priests might remember their duty; so that monks might truly be what they are said to be.[12]

The Institution of Christian Marriage, which appeared in Basel in August 1526, with a dedication to the Queen of England, Katharine of Aragon, was an important work in Erasmus's career.[13] He took pains to make clear the doctrine which he had expounded from 1518 in *The Praise of Marriage*, and illustrated in the more spicy of his *Colloquies*.

Erasmus certainly had a high ideal of conjugal union. He advised against rushing into it or contracting it without parental agreement. To spouses, he recommended that they should seek not only bodily pleasure, but also and more so, spiritual benefits: this is what he called a chaste marriage[14]. Moreover, he exalted fecundity and the family. When this programme was respected, marriage had, in his view, as much value as virginity consecrated to God. Moreover, Erasmus firmly opposed secret marriage and considered that dynastic marriages – political by definition – were often an insult to the dignity of the sacrament.[15]

Erasmus's matrimonial doctrine was consequently well structured. It did not gain the approval of the ecclesiastical world in general and of the religious in particular, who were sensitive only to Erasmus's critique of a certain kind of monasticism. To a Franciscan Joannes Gacchus, who had reproached him with denigrating his order, he replied by contrasting St Francis of Assisi with the Franciscans. He insisted on calling the religious back to the duties of their vocation. 'The Gospel teaches us to bless those who curse us, and you both curse and do ill to those who treat you well. While you rail thus against Erasmus, he does not cease to offer you what is better than all your cheese and eggs.'[16] And he went on to list his works of exegesis and patrology!

Erasmus, as we know, did not value the traditional linkage of observances with merits and eternal rewards. The notion of merit (like that of observance) was incontestably Christian, but scarcely evangelical.[17] It was grace alone which transformed Christians, but its gratuitousness made them afraid. It seemed to them more reliable to purchase their part of paradise and it was difficult for them to understand that Mary was 'full of grace' rather than full of merit.

In his *Paraphrase on the Gospel of St Matthew* Erasmus had written: 'No human work is good enough to be worthy of eternal life.' The Sorbonne was to condemn as heretical what Erasmus had not said, striking him with this censure: 'It is heretical to assert that man *with divine grace* cannot be worthy of heaven.'[18]

Erasmus expressed his anguish to Thomas More: 'If I should deal with the matter according to the spirit of monks and theologians, who attribute too much to the merits of men because of the advantage they gain from this, I would surely be speaking against my conscience and knowingly be obscuring the glory of Christ.'[19] Having said that, he did not deny merit, but did his best to give it a minor role, the role which it deserved.[20]

It was in 1526 that Albrecht Dürer finished his last portrait of Erasmus: an engraving which showed the humanist standing before his desk, wrapped up warmly in a large coat, a hat on his head and pen in hand. A bouquet of lily of the valley suggested springtime. The artist had reproduced in Greek the Erasmian sentence: 'His works paint him even better.' Despite the reservations of the model, who did not regard this engraving as a very good likeness, posterity has regarded this portrait as one of Dürer's finest works.[21]

Though Erasmus had chosen to live in Basel, on the frontiers of the Empire, he was not on that account any less loyal to the Emperor. But his loyalty and fidelity did not weaken his judgement which was always on the alert, or his unceasing calls for the re-establishment and protection of peace. He deplored the sack of Rome by the troops of Charles V in 1527. He held no brief for the Italians, but felt heartily sorry for the people who suffered from the horrors of occupation. He sent an open letter to Sigismund, king of Poland, a true manifesto for peace:

Indeed, war is sweet to those who have not experienced it; but he discerns it through darkness and from afar who puts a wicked peace before a just war ... I can desire rather than hope what (however) I think should especially be done for preserving the friendship of princes and the peace of the commonwealth, if princes can be persuaded to renounce their far-scattered dominions ... Now, it is neither godly, nor my intention that anything should detract from the authority of him whom Christ wished to be the head of his whole Church: however, if we wish to tell the truth, he should act more kindly, and the greatest princes would quarrel amongst themselves in wars of this sort less often, if the Pope himself, persuaded of the importance of peace should not enter into truce with any monarch, but should impartially offer himself as father to all.[22]

We should remember the project of Francis I for the institution of a royal college in Paris, as a counterbalance to the old Sorbonne. Erasmus and Budé could not but approve that initiative, yet Erasmus was to decline the honour of taking part in it.

An absurd controversy was soon to set the two humanists against each other. Budé reproached Erasmus for his commentary on the Epistle to the Galatians. Had it not been said, according to St Jerome, that the Galatians had borrowed their lightness of spirit from Gaul? Budé's chauvinism irritated Erasmus who, as far as he was concerned, willingly accepted being called 'the star of Germany'. He replied ironically to Budé's complaints.

You write that you were offended by my speaking of the French without enough flattery; nothing was further from my thought. I am almost neutral (as they say) towards all countries. However, if there is any one to which my mind inclines more, it is France. This has often brought wrath on my head, amongst my own people or amongst the English; especially when things were going badly for you with Julius, when the English were supporting the supreme pontiff. Read the *Panegyric*, in which I celebrate the return of Prince Philip from Spain. However, this seems the result of nature, not of judgement. For indeed, no country has been as ungrateful to me as France, apart from the liberal goodwill of my friends.

What I mention about the French in the preface to the Epistle to the Galatians reveals that it is not ill disposed, because I address the matter in fewer, gentler words than Jerome did. Even he made reference to this to show what was special about this Epistle ... In short, I did not expect that this matter would offend any Frenchman, much less you who, well acquainted with philosophy from childhood, ought to be free from these vulgar dispositions. And even if something a little harsh was said against the French [Gauls] of that time, what nation is not distinguished by some saying? Pindar and Plutarch even seem delighted by the saying about their being 'Boeotian bulls' (since both were Boeotians). I believe it is now almost 1,600 years since the Gauls moved to Asia, and formed Galatia: and it is not known from what part of Gaul they came. If anything was said against the Gauls of those times, does this appear to refer to all of

Gaul, which extended so widely? Even today do you not generally speak badly of the Normans, Manceaux, Bretons and Picards?[23]

Budé, who had little sense of humour, did not take in this advice and the correspondence between the two men dragged on painfully until the following year. Budé, moreover, could not understand how a humanist could decline the honour of coming up to Paris. Erasmus was letting him down! The future Collège de France was finally to be set up in 1530, without Erasmus or any of his followers. The name of Budé himself remains rightly associated with the foundation of the Parisian college, as that of Erasmus is inseparable from the history of the Trinlingual College in Louvain.

The Sorbonne, which no longer had any fear of displeasing the king, was publicly to condemn Erasmus's religious ideas in 1531. We know neither the deeper intentions nor the personal motivations of Francis I, but everything happened as if the king was finally abandoning this Erasmus, who had declined the royal College, to the vindictiveness of the Sorbonne.

At this time different religious groups were competing in Basel to express themselves freely and perhaps to seize power. The situation was in danger of becoming critical. Erasmus wrote to Warham on 29 May 1527: 'Here everything seems to be leading towards revolution, and I fear bloody disturbances.'[24]

Erasmus had never been a champion of the imperial idea. Quite the opposite! He condemned that idea as 'the source of all wars'. The Chancellor of the Empire, Mercurino Gattinara, asked him to provide a preface for the edition of a Latin work of Dante's, *De Monarchia*, to support his master's ambitions.[25] Erasmus could not approve of this woolly text which added nothing to the poet's standing. Above all, he could not share in Dante's political ideas, according to which the Empire was the guarantor of peace. On the contrary, for Erasmus the course of universal power was an explosive claim, an evil without a remedy. So he refused to publish this work and remained faithful to himself.

Religious problems fascinated Erasmus more. He did not cease to confront those who were promoting innovation with the agreement of the Church on essential doctrines, the *consensus Ecclesiae*. To a monk tempted by the world, he confided his deepest fears in the face of the rise of the Reformation. His disappointment made him bitter, extreme and unjust.

I fear lest you may be deceived by some people's tricks; today they boast grandly of 'evangelical freedom'. Believe me, if you knew more about it, you would loathe your life less. I see that a breed of people is emerging which my soul deeply abhors. I do not see anybody becoming better, but everybody worse, at least those I know. And so I am deeply grieved at having preached freedom of the spirit in my earlier writings. I did so in good faith, without any suspicion that such a breed would result. I was hoping for a decrease in human ceremonies, with a consequent increase in genuine piety. Now the ceremonies are discarded, but the result is not freedom of spirit, but an unbridled licence of the flesh. Some cities in Germany are filled with vagabonds – monks who have left the monastery, married priests, most of them starving and naked. All they do is dance, eat, drink and go whoring. They do not teach and do not learn.[26]

Erasmus explained his aversion for the innovators more moderately, but with as much passionate conviction to Martin Bucer. 'As things are, some people are not satisfied with any of the accepted practices; as if a new world could be built all of a sudden. There will always be things which the pious must endure. If anyone thinks that Mass ought to be abolished because many misuse it, then the Sermon should be abolished also, which is almost the only custom accepted by your party.'[27]

Erasmus was keen to share his feelings with his friend Willibald Pirckheimer about religious revolution. 'Wherever Lutheranism rules, literature dies . . . If the Lutherans had not torn the Eucharist to pieces or suppressed the Mass or destroyed images, and had begun by getting their own followers to lead a blameless life, a happier ending might have been expected. Now Luther is silent, Melanchthon is mellowing; but, as you say, the Phrygians are becoming wise too late.'[28]

Disappointed by the unforeseen course of the Reformation, Erasmus had thus resolutely and finally drawn away from the dissidents. He did not on that account remain any less the butt of the misunderstanding and suspicion of the Paris and Louvain theologians. On 12 November 1527, he tried to justify himself with a declaration to the Sorbonne: 'First, I bear witness before God, who sees into the depths of the human heart, that all ungodliness and whatever divides the harmony of the Christian flock is hateful to me; and that I shrink with all my heart from those who draw disciples to themselves, but whom the Church, the bride of Christ, does not recognize.'[29]

But his judges allowed him no respite. The Spanish Inquisition subjected his writings to a hostile examination.[30] The grievances of the Spanish monks recalled those of the Paris theologians, but the famous conference of Valladolid ended without any conclusion. Erasmus was nevertheless to reply to it with a vigorous *Apology*.[31]

'For unless I were ungodly,' he opened up against his detractors from the Sorbonne, 'I would not let it be said, nor shall I, lest anyone become ungodly by my example.'[32] Sometimes bitterness overcame him.

Nor have the voices of some of your people escaped me: 'When Luther has been destroyed, let us attack Erasmus.' So destroy Luther and then, if you like, attack Erasmus. Truly, when Luther was raging with impunity, you kept quiet, hiding like snails in your shell. By the command of the Emperor, the Pope and other princes, I joined battle with Luther, and in that region within whose borders he held most sway. When the enemy was rendered weaker by my war, my danger, my wounds, you, suddenly leaping from behind, attack the struggle, doing what, I ask? Do you envy the Catholic Church its victory? Or do you want to help the enemy?[33]

Protected by the Pope and the Emperor, Erasmus complained of having been stabbed in the back by Catholic authors while he was exerting himself against Luther. Haunted by these assaults, he contemplated drawing up a catalogue of his enemies,[34] just as he had often published the list of his friends and protectors. In a long letter he confided to Thomas More his weariness and disgust at the futile battles which he was obliged to conduct.[35] These incessant struggles summoned up all his energies and drained his strength. To preserve his work he reduced his activities.

... my health [he wrote to Juan Maldonado] is so frail and troublesome that I cannot conveniently live with anyone, unless I am forced to be a nuisance to him. Change of clothing, food cooked differently, or another kind of wine served,[36] change of place, sitting a little longer, or a harsher climate, throws me into my present condition and forces me to be in peril for my life.... To be as little nuisance as possible to many people, I have kept to myself, and contributed nothing to my friends' discussion, except, on certain days, one or two short afternoon hours. The weakness of my stomach from supper beggars description; I listen to a servant reading.[37]

The prospect of approaching death forced Erasmus to draw up his will.

In the name of the Lord, Amen. In the year 1527 after Christ's birth, following St Agnes' Day, at Basel, I, Erasmus of Rotterdam, doctor of theology and priest in the diocese of Utrecht, being in whole (by the grace of God) and sound mind, have declared by my own hand my last will concerning all my goods which I shall leave behind. As heir of these and as fideicommissarius, I designate Doctor Bonifacius Amerbach, as executors Beatus Rhenanus of Sélestat, Basilius Amerbach and Hieronymus Froben; willing and resolving:

First, that my heir should take for himself from my goods all my rings which he shall find described in the inventory; moreover, the spoon of pure gold and the gilded double cup, the gift of Duke George; as well as 100 crowns in money.

To Henricus Glareanus let him give all my linen, with my two best garments, the one violet, the other black, trimmed with sable fur (commonly called marten), and 50 crowns.

To Ludwig Baer, as a most faithful friend who will not disdain to help with our testament of fideicommissum, he will give an hourglass of pure gold.

To Basilius Amerbach, two silver trenchers, with silver flasks and a silver cup, with the image of Saint Jerome on the lid.

To Beatus Rhenanus two forks, one gold, the other silver.

To Hieronymous Froben, two purses, one with a silver band, the other with gilded silver.

To Johannes Froben, my bed-curtains, with two woven hangings.

To Sigismund, Froben's corrector, whatever is left of my clothes, and 26 common ducats, with a gilded spoon.

To Johannes Botzheim, canon of Konstanz, he shall give as a remembrance a silver spoon, with a figure of Saint Sebastian on it.

To Conradus Goclenius, all my gold and silver medals, and six silver cups which he now has.

The remainder of my silver or gilded vessels shall be spent on the publishing of my works by the will of my heir and the advice of the executors.

I sold my whole library some time ago to the noble Polish baron Jan Laski for 400 gold pieces, of which he has paid 200, except for the Greek books written by pen on parchment or paper, for which, if he wishes to own them, he shall settle separately, in accordance with my receipts.

In the publishing of my works, this is what I wish my heir and the executors to do: Let them see that all my compositions are printed by Johannes Froben, if that is possible, or by someone else, handsomely and as properly as can be done, divided in volumes, as I have described in my Catalogue. To help the printer more in this, I wish him to be paid, as soon as the work is begun, 300 florins a year, if he has finished it within four years, 400 if within three years. However, the works of Saint Jerome or of Hilary and the like, edited by me, will not be counted amongst these compositions, if it is not convenient for the printer: although I should desire this also, if he can do it for a fair price.

I do not wish the correctors to be allowed to add their own notes to my works: they should correct only errors caused by the printers' carelessness, or even my own, only if it be obvious, and they should do this as briefly as possible, after consulting amongst themselves. Great care should also be taken in printing citations of authors, books and chapters . . . In this area I especially want Henricus Glareanus, Conradus Goclenius, Beatus Rhenanus, Bonfacius Amerbach, Basilius Amerbach and Sigismund to be appointed. If they decline, I give my heir the right to find other suitable people. If Conradus Goclenius agrees to take charge of this business in Basel, I wish 100 crowns to be paid to him yearly for four years, apart from what the printer might give, if he wishes to give anything; to Glareanus 60 gold florins for the same number of years;

to Sigismund 40. My heir shall estimate his own and his brother's work according to his own judgement, if they wish to do it. Finally, since the work which each will be responsible for is unsure, I allow my heir, either by his own decision or by the judgement of the executors, to lessen or increase payment according to the work undertaken. However, I should not like more than three, or at most four, correctors to be employed; and if two are enough for the work, compensating for their small number with diligence, by so much will their payment be increased.

Indeed, in the agreement with the printer, I allow my heir, with the executors, to arrange the payment according to the merit of the edition and the number of volumes which he prints. I should not want less than 1,500. I desire Froben, or his eventual successor in the printing works, to be dealt with more lavishly. But if he is reluctant to undertake the business, let them perusade someone else. But if because of this, either my heir or the executors are put to any expense, I wish that this be deducted from the remaining money, so that whatever has been left as a legacy to anyone may remain intact.

Of each volume or part they will take care that twenty should be carefully produced so that when the work is finished, they send

one complete set to the Archbishop of Canterbury;
another to Cuthbert Tunstall, Bishop of London;
a third to Thomas More, baron, of England;
a fourth to John, bishop of Lincoln;
a fifth to Cambridge, to be placed in Queens' College, in the public library of the college;
a sixth, to John, Bishop of Rochester;
a seventh to Spain, to be placed in the imperial library;
an eighth to the Bishop of Toledo;
a ninth to Ferdinand, brother of the Emperor Charles;
a tenth to Bernard, Bishop of Trent;
an eleventh to Giambattista Egnazio;
a twelfth to the College of Busleyden, Louvain, to be placed in the library;
a thirteenth to be placed in the College at Lis;
a fourteenth to Tournai, to be placed in the college which Peter Coutrellus founded for languages and literature;
a fifteenth to Francis Craneveld, senator of the Council of Mechelen;
a sixteenth to Gand, for the abbot of Saint Bavon;
a seventeenth to Marcus Lauwerÿns, dean of Saint Donation's, to be placed in his college library;
an eighteenth to Nicolaas Everaerts, president of Holland, or whoever succeeds him;
a nineteenth to Herman Lethmaet the theologian;
a twentieth to the monastery at Egmond, to be placed in its library.

If any of these should have died, let my heir choose others as he wishes.

Concerning the agreement with the printers, let the matter be conducted secretly, lest any malignant spirit arises to interrupt the good work. In the number of the sets to be sent I wish my editions of Jerome and Hilary also to be included.

What remains when these things have been completed or added up should be given for godly uses, especially for helping young men of promise and for settling decent girls.

Let my heir take care of my burial with neither mean nor lavish expense, according to the rites of the Church, so that no one can complain. I owe no one anything; I have no [natural] heir; and I have been adequately authorized to draw up a will by an apostolic diploma, even concerning ecclesiastical goods.

To my servant Quirinus, if he is with me at my death, I wish 200 gold florins to be given for his faithful and long service.

These wishes I have expressed, being sound in body and health, on the year and day mentioned above, and for greater certainty I have written both copies with my own hand, and affixed to the document the special seal of my ring – the god Terminus – reserving my right to add, subtract and change everything completely, if I wish, according to public law.[38]

This document showed Erasmus to be a writer who was concerned for his work as well as a generous man who forgot neither his friends nor the poor.

The humanist's fortune was managed by an Antwerp banker, Erasmus Schets, a cultivated man who had foreign correspondents and who was present at the Frankfurt fair. His advice was valuable. The letters exchanged between the two men shed light for us on the preoccupations of a learned man who gradually became a rich man, without being able to master financial affairs. Erasmus in Basel was as ignorant about the laws on money as during his unhappy return from England in 1500, when the customs men at Dover had confiscated his money. From Antwerp, on 14 August 1528, Schets reminded his client and friend of the usefulness of letters of exchange.

As for the crowns or any other sort of moneys which they paid you in England, I do not know what loss may come to you. For exchange justifies the value of moneys, there valued more, here less. However, it is possible, as you say, that some profit from this money might accrue to you by exporting it. But the interdict stands in the way, as long as exportation is not allowed without the danger of confiscation, apart from the fact that during the journey there may be a chance that this money will be exposed to the dangers of the sea or of robbers. Therefore it is more secure to exchange these moneys.[39]

The great doctor Paracelsus, while staying in Basel, where he was to teach for several months at the University, met Erasmus in 1527 and described his illnesses to him with a perspicacity which astonished the sick man. Erasmus replied with gratitude and not without a touch of mischief:

> I wonder how you know me so thoroughly, having seen me once only. I recognize how very true are your dark sayings . . . As I told you, I have no time for the next few days to be doctored, or to be ill, or to die, so overwhelmed am I by scholarly work. But if there is anything which can alleviate the trouble without weakening the body, I beg you to inform me. If you will be so good as to explain at greater length your very concise and more than laconic notes, and prescribe other remedies which I can take until I am free, I cannot promise you a fee to match your art or the trouble you have taken, but I do at least promise you a grateful heart. You have resurrected Froben, that is, my other half: if you restore me also, you will have restored both of us by treating each of us singly. May we have the good fortune to keep you in [Basel]![40]

Unfortunately Paracelsus's attentions were insufficient to save Johann Froben, who died in the same year.

The spirit which pushed Erasmus towards classical antiquity was powerful, but not exclusive. His concern to return to the authentic Christian sources led him to add the study of Hebrew to that of Greek and Latin. *The Ciceronian: A Dialogue on the Ideal Latin Style* reveals his inmost wish to us.[41] Just as Erasmus had separated himself from the Reformers from the time that they had threatened to overturn the Church and construct a new one, so he kept his distance from the radical humanists who absorbed the poison of paganism with ancient culture. Erasmus wanted to protect his ideal, his conception of humanism – Christian humanism – against all deviations. Strangely enough, he chose as his target not the Epicurean culture of Horace, but Ciceronian idolatry. Now Erasmus liked Cicero, having edited his works and praised his morality. He counted himself among the disciples of the great orator. But who was a the true disciple of Cicero?

In 1527, Erasmus had already put together the ideas which were to nurture his treatise. He confided his deepest thoughts to Francisco Vergara, professor at the University of Alcala.

> There is also a new kind of enemy who has lately begun to spring out of ambush. They feel put out that good literature should treat of Christ, as if nothing could be elegant but what is pagan. To their ears Jupiter Best and Greatest sounds better than Jesus Christ the Redeemer of the world, and Conscript fathers than the Holy Apostles. . . . They praise Pontanus to the skies, while they turn up their noses at Augustine and Jerome. But I would rather have one ode of Prudentius singing of Jesus than a whole shipload of the poems of Pontanus, whose learning and eloquence in

other directions I do not despise at all. Among these people it is almost more disgraceful not to be a Ciceronian than not to be a Christian; just as if, were Cicero now alive, he would not speak differently about Christian matters than he did in his own day, when it was the main part of eloquence to speak to the point at issue. No one denies that Cicero excelled in the art of speaking, although not every kind of eloquence suits particular persons or subjects. What does this odious boasting about the term *Ciceronian* mean? Let me whisper what I think in a few words. Under this pretence they hide their paganism, which is dearer to them than the glory of Christ. It will not grieve me much to be blotted from the list of *Ciceronians*, provided that I can be inscribed in the ranks of Christians.[42]

The Ciceronian was a dialogue, like the *Colloquies*. It depicts three characters, Bulephorus, Nosoponus and Hypologus. The first of these expounded Erasmus's cherished ideas against Nosoponus. Hypologus was an indecisive and rather inconsistent person. His role was to give new impetus to the dialogue and to introduce a lighter tone into it. The publication of *The Ciceronian* in 1528 showed the evolution of Erasmus's thought. This dialogue is not a disavowal of his admiration for Cicero – and still less an abdication of Christian humanism – but the denunciation of a new paganism which, especially in Italy, hid behind the unchallengable reputation of the Roman orator.

Not without some injustice, and with a good deal of exaggeration, Erasmus took aim at an Italian coterie and distinguished between the pure Ciceronian and the pagan, 'Cicero's monkey'. A true disciple of Cicero is one who does today what a Christian Cicero would have done. Erasmus maintained all his respect for the great interpreter of pagan wisdom but, at the same time, he summoned ancient eloquence to the service of faith.

Those whom Erasmus dubbed Ciceronians in his view committed an error similar to that of so many Franciscans: the disciples betrayed the master by wanting to imitate him according to the letter and not according to the spirit. He protested against the superstitious purity which rejected Christian terminology. 'Shall he for Father of Christ say "Jupiter Optimus Maximus", for the Son, "Apollo" or "Aesculapius"? Shall he for Queen of Virgins say "Diana"; for church "sacred assembly" or "state" or "republic"; for the Christian faith, "the Christian persuasion"?'[43]

Throughout the length of the exchanges, and apart from personal utterances and attacks, *The Ciceronian* defines a reduced and slanted classicism. Reduced, in that it shakes off all traces of paganism. Slanted, in that if Cicero had lived in our day, Erasmus believed, he would have expounded today's philosophy. Thus Erasmus transposed the Roman inspiration of Cicero into a Christian inspiration, a committed humanism.

In canonizing Cicero *ad usum delphini*, Erasmus reoriented the teaching of Latin towards its definitive form. Cicero the model of eloquence, the arbiter of good taste and the precursor of Christianity, became the preferred author, the sure standard of the classical humanities of which the Jesuits were soon to make favoured champions. The story of *The Ciceronian* highlights Erasmus's pedagogical importance. This man who did not like to teach worked only for teachers, and consequently for their students.

Erasmus fought the Ciceronians and the writers who professed a kind of neo-paganism with equal vigour. He knew the myths and the parables of the Graeco-Roman world. At the beginning of his career, he introduced the gods into his letters and even into his religious poems. He evoked Diana and Venus. He borrowed from the ancients certain expressions coming from mythology. He would say that he had 'delivered to Vulcan' what he threw on the fire. He would write 'if it please the gods' where the Christian tradition wanted to recognize only 'if it please God'. Gradually, in the *Adages* among other works, he put these literary games behind him and put mythology in its historical place. He did not forget it, but he went beyond it, and reproached the Italian neo-pagans for not following his example. He went so far as to say that in Rome too many images of false gods were to be found and too few representations of Christian mysteries.

The Ciceronian was often badly understood. Some saw in it only a diversion allowing its author to escape from religious polemics. The Italians, who did not fail to denigrate Erasmus's style as insufficiently classical for their taste, gave vent to their indigation. Others ended up thinking that Erasmus had denied humanism.

It was nothing of the kind. On the one hand, in this strange quarrel between ancients and moderns, Erasmus resolutely took the part of the moderns, that is to say, humanists attentive to the evolution of the world. On the other hand, *The Ciceronian* abounded in striking suggestions. It was hard for certain humanists – Italians especially – but it created no amalgam, and recognized the value of humanism without excluding the Italians from it. Finally, if he claimed the right to constitute a personal style for himself, Cicero remained for him the greatest of the masters and the first model of good Latin style.[44]

The importance of the book remained its subject. Did the imitation of ancient models sum up humanism? To be sure, Erasmus was a supporter of imitation, his pedagogy demonstrated it abundantly, but he wanted people to learn to imitate the ancients in order to define themselves in relation to them.

Erasmus's enemies did not spare him: he wrote badly, they said, his cause was evil, and he criticized only those whom he envied![45] Erasmus received the judgement of his humiliated peers with disappointment. 'I see', he wrote, 'that nothing is safe any more but writing nothing!' Then he laughed when a forger showed himself incapable of imitating his style. He was to continue writing and was to change neither his advice nor his character.

The problems of style did not distract Erasmus from his religious preoccupations for long. In August he published a *Commentary on Psalm 85* which was a meditation on piety and, at the beginning of 1529, he dedicated *The Christian Widow* to Mary of Hungary.[46]

The thought of death sometimes assumes a cheerful form in his meditations. He recounts one of his dreams:

> Kneeling beside my bed, as I am accustomed to do, I was saying my prayers. Sleep fell on me while I was praying. For even while praying I seemed to myself to feel I know not what feelings, not quite human ones. As I was staying in a completely unknown land in a very uncomfortable inn, a youth of very handsome appearance appeared to me, with an expression so lively that it immediately made me glad only to look at him. He said, 'Why are you staying here, Erasmus? Your lodging is too uncomfortable.' I said, 'Because I am a traveller, and in a strange land.' 'Why then', he said, 'do you not hasten to depart from here?' 'I should do nothing more willingly,' I said, 'but I fear lest I should exchange an uncomfortable dwelling for one more uncomfortable.' He said, 'Yet, if you will follow me, I shall show you a very calm place, with no smoke spreading everywhere, no ceiling pouring with rain, no wall open to the winds, no cracks betokening ruin, no hissing snake or noisy jackdaw or grating magpie or braying ass or barking dog, to be a nuisance.' 'To such a dwelling.' I said, 'I should willingly travel'; and as soon as I was ordered to follow, I followed.
>
> He showed me a meadow of such pleasantness that no human speech could describe it; so I am not going to hold up the reader with an account here. In this meadow there were palaces everywhere, beside which the courts of kings would seem nothing but pig sties. Overcome by wondrous emotion, I wished to rush straight there. But the youth, stopping me with his left hand, said, 'Beware what you do. For each his own day waits: I shall briefly show you and lead you from here, Meanwhile, collect what baggage you need for this place.' 'What I need for this place?', I said. 'No Codrus is more a Codrus than me.' Then he said, 'The necessities for your journey consist precisely in that you have no need of any, for you will be coming to a host as good as he is rich.' He said these things and vanished.[47]

The meaning of this dream was as clear for Erasmus as it was consoling. His 'light slender baggage' was ready. He listed it with satisfaction: the works of St Jerome, the *New Testament* and the *Paraphrases*. Death would surprise him without frightening him.

20

Christis First

Luther's all too famous words to Erasmus – 'You are not pious' (*Du bist nicht fromm*)[1] are well known, and this summary judgement has often been accepted by Catholic opinion at large. Yet Erasmus's life was marked out by pious publications like the *Handbook of the Christian Soldier*, *The Preparation for Death* and, above all, *On Prayer*. The Christian ought to pray always and in every situation, whether he is asking for help or pardon, for God loves his children's prayers.[2]

This piety is very clear in *On Prayer*,[3] published in 1524. This was Erasmus's major contribution to the practice of piety, a little work of Augustinian inspiration and pastoral character on the role of prayer in the spiritual life. The book includes models of prayer and model prayers. Erasmus suggested fine developments on the prayer of Jesus, the Lord's prayer and the prayer of the disciples. The Bible and the liturgy offered Christians an almost inexhaustible choice for raising the soul towards God. Praying with the psalms constituted a favoured form of prayer. Erasmus insisted on this point and gave many examples. He equally recommended the use of liturgical prayers, preferably in the common language, which would help the laity to associate themselves with the priest during the Mass. At the same time, he listed and characterized the different hours of the breviary, a book which he knew by heart.

Intimate, personal prayer – if necessary, prayer without words, reaches God's heart if it is sincere. The solecisms of improvised formulas do not offend Our Father! Ejaculatory prayers recited before the Crucifix were no less valuable. The most banal and sometimes the most suspect of prayers – the prayer of petition – was welcomed by Christ, but it was appropriate to ask God only for what was understood explicitly or implicitly in the Our Father. That would exclude prayer for the satisfaction of a whim, but permit intercession for the dead.

It was legitimate to ask for a return to health, on condition of submitting oneself to the divine will, as Erasmus did in a moving text. 'Lord, Salvation of all the living, deliver me, if possible, from this evil which is in me, but let your will be done and not mine. If you, to whom everything is known, judge this illness necessary to my salvation, deal with me according to your holy will. Only give me the courage and the strength to stand the test and to resist temptation.'

The author of these lines was indeed a man of prayer. For him, because prayer was love, it was feeling; because it was knowledge, it should also be theology. Without this balance, piety grew weak and atrophied. Erasmus's battle against superstition and purely external piety alienated him from a number of Catholics who were too attached to traditional observances. Moreover, he cannot be reproached for not having exalted the liturgy. He was a man of his time and his major preoccupation remained inward piety.

When *On Prayer* appeared, Luther had already condemned the cult of the saints. Very sensitive to the frequent deviations of this cult, Erasmus nevertheless defended its legitimacy sensitively and firmly. His doctrine was subtle. Since Scripture neither ordained nor forbade the cult of the saints, it should neither be considered necessary nor held to be impious. Compared to the homage rendered to God, these devotions remained secondary, but they benefited from a long tradition which went back to the time of the martyrs and could not be prevented without scandalizing the faithful. The saints, those who were possessed by God, deserved respect, admiration and, above all, imitation. Their word was nothing other than a dialogue with God. As for the superstition of some devout persons, it ought clearly to be denounced, because it reduced confidence in God in favour of suspect procedures. Erasmus scented a basis of paganism under Christian cover: St Anthony had replaced Aesculapius and the Virgin Mary had dethroned Proserpine. Here, as elsewhere, he showed himself less attentive to traditions as such than to the good or bad use that men made of them. The right intention preserved the piety of the simple and it was necessary to tolerate what could not be suppressed without provoking an even greater evil.[4]

On Confessing[5] was a booklet published in Basel by Froben, probably for the fair in the spring of 1524, and was often to be republished. In his treatment of the sacrament of penance, Erasmus took on a very controversial subject. He laid out the advantages and the problems of auricular confession as imposed by the Fourth Lateran Council of 1215. This type of confession had not been instituted by Christ and a new Council could decide to suppress it for the good of the Church. In waiting for an eventual decision in this area, Erasmus recommended all Christians to submit themselves with good grace to the established usage. For the rest, he asked the Church for a softening of the rules so that penitents would not be overwhelmed by scruples and anxiety. He pleaded for contrition inspired by love rather than by fear.

The author attached several important letters to this treatise, which made it a little epistolary collection. Two letters from Adrian VI showed that Erasmus wanted to attach the posthumous patronage of the most religious pope of the Renaissance to the benefit of a work which was difficult and showed no respect for ecclesiastical usage.

Erasmus was primarily a theologian undertaking research rather than an advocate of pastoral care. There was, however, no contradiction between theological research and the pastorate. Theological research fed the pastorate and allowed it continually to build itself up. This complementarity, however, was not clear at any time. The difference in methods explained this tension. Theological research attempts to understand and explain the programme of salvation to the well informed, while the pastorate aims at edifying the faithful without weighing them down with exegetical and theological erudition.

Erasmus the theologian clashed, on the one hand, with the theologians who took up useless questions for the sake of their vain curiosity and, on the other hand, with preachers and monks (these were often the same men) who allowed nothing to be called into question and reproached him for ridiculing piety. Now Erasmus in no way wanted to play the role of the sower of tares: it was enough for him to invite the guides of Christian piety to make their own self-criticism.

Erasmus's Mariology was the touchstone of his piety, for it was a favoured domain of his thought and religious outlook. Through its manifestations, one can put a finger not only on Erasmus's piety and his faith, but also on his submission to the Bible, his faithfulness to the Church, and finally his theology and his critical Christianity. Though he wrote so much, he devoted no work to questions of Mariology. Nevertheless, Mary was so often cited in his work that a book could be made from the passages which concern her; nothing resembling a treatise, but observations which together would not be negligible, a book in which amusement would be blended with severity and fervour with irony.

The author reacted against the confusions of a proliferating, ambiguous and inadequate Mariology. He wanted to temper his expression and, better than many of his co-religionists, he denounced the dangers of superstition and what we call Mariolatry. He nevertheless repudiated all radicalism and endeavoured to save what was essential in Catholic piety. His success lay in stigmatizing abuses without ceasing to honour and venerate Mary. He reserved his most severe disapproval for the pastors, preachers and theologians who encouraged an ardour which had gone astray and was sentimental and commercialized.

There was no doubt that Erasmus, like any Christian of his time, had been initiated in his infancy into Marian piety. Among the rare writings preserved from his years as a student and a monk, we can find only one work devoted to Mary, an interminable Latin poem of more than 400 verses: a masterpiece written in his twentieth year.

In 1501, he reminded Anna van Veere, his patron at the time, that he had once sent her some prayers which, he had said, 'will enable you to call down from Heaven, as by magic charms (and even against her will, if I may so put it), not the poets' moon, but her who brought to birth the sun of righteousness.'[6] The text is strange at first sight, but is explained by the traditional allegory of Jesus and Mary represented by the sun and the moon. Erasmus enriched the image with a touch of surrealism in having the sun born from the moon. As for the 'magic charm', its mention is surprising, for Erasmus abhorred magic even more than superstition, with which he usually associated it.[7]

The *Paean* piles up praises of Mary, lists her titles, borrowed from ancient and medieval piety, not omitting mythological comparisons: Mary is Diana and Jesus is Jupiter! The *Supplication to the Virgin* was a text contemporary with the preceding one, but less subject to the learned rhetoric of humanism. The personal accents here are easily perceptible. Erasmus called the Virgin 'my salvation' and 'my refuge'. If he compared her to 'the most beautiful moon, sister and mother of the eternal sun', he also praised 'the intact Virgin' who knew neither the passions of sex, nor the pains of childbirth.[8] Finally, Erasmus endeavoured to compensate for these hyperbolic praises by calling to mind the One Saviour, a skilful call which associated Mary with Jesus without making her his equal, for this was the limit of his Mariology.[9] Moreover, he added to the two prayers addressed to Mary an eloquent *Prayer to Jesus, Son of God and of the Virgin*. It was in this last text that he boldly called Jesus 'Magus and enchanter'.

Erasmus's Marian piety was no less manifest in his great works. Thus it was that *The Praise of Folly* attacked Christians who dared 'to attribute to Mary a power almost as great as that of Jesus', instead of imitating her virtues. In 1512, he was to be seen in the famous sanctuary at Walsingham in Norfolk. He went there as a pilgrim and returned from there little edified.

The fifty-first verse of the second chapter of Luke posed a problem of interpretation to the editor of the *New Testament*, where the text specified that Jesus 'was subject' to his parents. In the name of common sense, Erasmus refuted those who tried to infer from it that Jesus still owed obedience to his mother. His opinion, which was entirely orthodox, had shocked those who held to the sovereign power of Mary, those strange theologians whose principal arguments came from the *Ave maris stella*.

Mary appears many times in the *Colloquies*. *The Shipwreck* irreverently cited the *Salve Regina*, that extraordinary poem made up of sighs, groans and appeals. Erasmus appears to be insensitive to the beauty of this song, one of the most accomplished works of Latin mysticism. However, he does not condemn the terms, but its use in relation to shipwreck, as if the domain of Jesus was heaven and of Mary the sea. 'Shipwrecked sailors', he said, 'were praying to the Virgin Mother, calling her the Star of the Sea, Queen of Heaven, Mistress of the World, Port of Salvation.' Erasmus detected in this exuberant piety a leftover from paganism. 'Formerly Venus was protectress of sailors, because she was believed to have been born of the sea. Since she gave up guarding them, the Virgin Mother has succeeded this mother who was not a virgin.'[10]

A Pilgrimage for Religion's Sake was a cruel satire about abuses noted in so many of the devout. The most spicy page added additional interest by making us read a 'letter of the Virgin Mary' against the deviations of her cult.

> I was all but exhausted by the shameless entreaties of mortals. They demanded everything from me alone, as if my Son were always a baby (because he is carved and painted as such at my bosom), still needing his mother's consent and not daring to deny a person's prayer; fearful, that is, that if he did deny the petitioner something, I for my part would refuse him the breast when he was thirsty.[11]

But the primacy of Christ did not signify the negation of Mary and the Virgin then addressed the Zwinglian iconoclasts: 'But me, however, defenceless, you shall not eject unless at the same time you eject my Son, whom I hold in my arms. From him I will not be parted. Either you expel him along with me, or you leave us both here, unless you prefer to have a church without Christ.'[12]

The ignorance of some of Erasmus's opponents explains some serious disputes, whether they confused philology and heresy, or did not understand Erasmus's theological thought, even when it was in its clearest form. Some Spanish monks were offended to read in his works that the Bible does not proclaim Mary's perpetual virginity. Now Erasmus was very precise on this subject. 'We believe in the perpetual virginity of Mary, although it is not expounded in the sacred books.' He went further. Like Thomas More, he acknowledged Mary's decision to maintain virginity throughout her life, but denied as a ridiculous fable the view that the Virgin had pronounced the three vows of the religious.

Erasmus analysed the Marian prayers. On the one hand, *The Little Office of the Virgin* seemed to him to suffer from a rather inappropriate attribution to Mary of biblical texts which related rather to the Church, or even of prayers which ought to be addressed to Jesus alone. On the other hand, he said, the rosary could be left in the hands of the simple, provided that they expected no miracles from it. A good pupil of the modern devotion, Erasmus refused to condemn any prayer whose intention was right.

A formula of prayer intended for after a meal: 'By the blessed entrails which were counted worthy to bear the Son of the Eternal Father' irritated Erasmus, who regarded it as respectful, but out of place in the cirumstances. He joked about it publicly, and this earned him indignant reproaches from Noël Bédier.[13] Erasmus was also scandalized by the excessive pomp directed to the glory of Mary in the churches. He fought for the defence of an authentic liturgy, denouncing the canticles chanted to the Virgin during the consecration contrary to ancient usage.

With the entire Catholic tradition, he believed in the virgin birth of Jesus as well as in the divine motherhood of Mary. Did he also profess the doctrine of the immaculate conception of Mary, a belief not yet officially defined, but very widespread, and which most humanists accepted? When he took up polemics with Lefèvre d'Étaples, he was content to scoff at the Scotists, his perpetual enemies, who declared that the opinion of the Fathers, who were generally not favourable to the immaculist doctrine,[14] was injurious to Mary. A little later, he complained of a Dominican friar who suspected him of being an enemy of St Thomas and a champion of the Immaculate Conception, at a time when the Dominicans were of another opinion.

It is clear that Erasmus, like St Thomas, did not proclaim himself an 'immaculist', but declared that the doctrine of the Immaculate Conception was 'more favourable' and 'more probable'. More favourable undoubtedly to the eminent dignity of Mary and more probable because more in conformity with the judgement of the Church. The judgement of the Church to which he referred was the immaculist definition of the Council of Basel in 1439, which recognized and confirmed an irresistible tradition adopted by the liturgy.

However, certain of the immaculists' arguments irritated Erasmus just as much. He rebuked those who reasoned as if Jesus was obliged to want his mother immaculate so as to honour her. Fundamentally for Erasmus, immaculism was not essential, as history clearly shows. Thus, at the end of his life, he could write: 'There is no one who is not conceived in sin: but as far as the Virgin is concerned, I make no pronouncement.'[15]

But he did not conclude from this in any way that the Virgin could not be invoked, and proved this in his writings.[16] At the request of his friend Theobaldus Bietricius, priest of Porrentruy, Erasmus published a *Votive Mass of Notre Dame of Loreto*,[17] the shortest work that he published in a single volume. The choice of this subject was disturbing. The *santa casa* of Loreto was then already the centre of an important popular pilgrimage. Who would not want to see and touch Mary's house? The miraculous translation of the *santa casa* was not a matter of doubt at this time. It would be necessary to wait for Canon Chevalier, at the beginning of our century, to demonstrate the hoax involved in this.

It is reasonable to think that Erasmus regarded Loreto with the mixture of respect and detachment which characterized his attitude to pilgrimages. He had not gone to Loreto, but he believed in the Madonna's miracles. The translation could only be for him a very ancient tradition, whose origin he did not know, but whose success he recognized.

Had Erasmus wished, by his homage to the Virgin of Loreto, to prove his orthodoxy, as some have insinuated? This preoccupation remains possible, but I prefer to believe that he had yielded to friendship and that he wanted to show his mastery in a genre as exceptional as the publication of a liturgy. To compose a Mass at the request of a modest priest, what a programme for a religious author! A fine opportunity, besides, to teach by example what ought to be a truly Catholic cult, putting the Virgin Mary in her place again in the work of redemption! What an incredible task – to praise Loreto, without provoking anyone and without weakness! In fact, he did not celebrate the *santa casa*. For him, even a votive Mass was always and above all else the memorial of the Lord and the most respectable private revelations were little enough in face of the revelation of Jesus Christ. His theological orientation can be recognized here as much as his natural reserve. From a writing of circumstance, an exceptional one from his pen, he drew an astonishing lesson about Marian piety which conformed to his deepest conviction. There was no concession to easy, superficial devotion! Mary was glorified only in respect of Jesus and in relation to Jesus.

The prayer of the Mass reveals the author's intentions. 'We venerate the Mother because of the Son.' The page in the Gospel was that of the marriage of Cana, a text which shows us the Virgin's kindness and humility. The sermon, added in the second edition, was no less Erasmian: Mary, servant of the Lord and model of availability. To crown the whole, he listed the four aspects of Marian devotion: praise, honour, invocation and imitation. 'The last of these is the most important, because without it these things are unfruitful, and this alone contains all the rest in itself.' Mary is Queen of Heaven because she is full of grace, but she is full of merits because she made herself the servant of the Lord.

One passage from the sermon raises a delicate problem: that of Mary's sufferings. The question had been discussed for centuries and the swooning of the Virgin remained a theme of preaching, notably at the time of pilgrimages. Erasmus, evoking Calvary, expressed himself thus:

She suffered at her son's suffering, but by force of character she restrained the human feelings of her heart, she smothered her sighs, she held back her flowing tears, and while the rest of the disciples fled in fear, she alone stood with John beside her son's cross. Those pictures, which show her fallen down and stricken with fainting, dead with suffering, are damaging. She did not wail, tear her hair, beat her breast, cry out that she was unhappy. She drew more comfort from the redemption of mankind than suffering from the death of her son.[18]

The last phrase of this quotation is significant. Here we see Erasmus taking up a scholastic argument, more easily to attack a too sentimental devotion.[19]

The Loreto Mass was well received by the Catholics. The archbishop of Besançon accorded it a flattering approval. Only Ulrich Zasius, despite his friendship for Erasmus, was not won over. He communicated to Boniface Amerbach, in a confidential letter, his admiration for the sermon and his reservations about the remainder. 'I leave Loreto to the Italians and venerate Mary in heaven', he declared. If Erasmus had known about this letter, he would doubtless have been annoyed, but he would have been soothed by seeing his friend giving spirited praise to the most personal aspect of the Mass, the sermon. He who was to devote his last years to a book on preaching left us few sermons: that of the Loreto Mass is a model of prudence and depth, and a most remarkable testimony to his pastoral sense.

As he got older, Erasmus became more sensitive to the good faith of simple souls. He did not accommodate himself more to superstition, but he tolerated what could not be corrected except at the cost of a terrible disorder.

Erasmus knew that devotion to the saints was relatively late, but that it had spread prodigiously. In a letter to Sadoleto, he outlined his position.

Far be it from me that veneration of the saints or the use of images should ever be condemned in my books. Here and there I reproach the superstitious or distorted devotion of saints: I consider it superstitious, when a knight about to go on military service promises himself that he will return unharmed if he pays his respects on bended knees to a image of Saint Barbara, and repeats little prayers in her honour, very like magic ones; I think it distorted, when we revere the saints through candles and paintings, while our whole life is a fight against their morals – since the devotion most pleasing to the saints is if someone imitates their godliness. I have never wanted to destroy paintings and symbols, since they are very important trappings of life, although I should want nothing to be seen in churches except what is worthy of that place. As to invoking the saints and adoring images, there is great dispute. First, it is agreed that there is no passage in the Bible which allows us to invoke saints, unless perhaps you want to twist where in the gospel parable Dives asks for Abraham's aid. But although in such a matter it can seem truly dangerous to make any innovation with the authority of Scripture, I never disapprove of invoking the saints, nor do I think that it ought to be disapproved of; just do not let there be any superstition, which I often point out, and not without reason; for I consider it to be superstition when everything is sought from the saints, as if Christ were dead; or when we ask for the help of saints in such a spirit, as if they were more easily persuaded than God; or when we seek special things from different saints, as if Catherine can do what Barbara cannot; or when we call on them, not as intercessors, but as authors of those good things which God grants us![20]

'Our salvation depends on Christ and the Virgin owes her own salvation to him,'[21] Erasmus says in one of the most striking of those formulas at which he was so adept.

On one point he corrected himself, perhaps without being aware of it, at any rate without acknowledging it. Whereas in his *Paean,* he had saluted Mary as a 'true Diana', in the *Ciceronian,* he was to ridicule pagan writers who called Jesus Apollo and his mother Diana. Erasmus was then no longer the young poet smitten with an antique mythology veneered onto Christianity.

Nevertheless, Erasmus employed, without any reservations, the invocations of the most traditional piety, those of the litanies. Very often, he called Mary the Virgin Mary or the Mother of Jesus. He called her also Mother of God, Mother of Mercy, Queen of all, New Eve, Queen of Heaven and earth. He compared her to the morning star, the aurora, the rainbow, the dove, the tree of life, the tower of David, the throne of Solomon, the Cedar of Lebanon and the rose of Jericho.

In the large range of Erasmus's Marian expressions, there was little place for the advocate. There was none for the mediatrix, the co-redemptrix, the mother of the Church, the mother of sorrows, the source of all grace. Erasmus regretted the application to Mary of expressions too suggestive of the Song of Songs, or again of the text of Ecclesiastes: 'I was created before all ages.' When Genesis spoke of the Ark of the Covenant, the accommodation to the literal sense did not, he said, permit attributing to Mary what belonged to the Church, while, in other cases the generous attribution was defensible, and the Virgin could be invoked under the name of the Gate of Heaven.

Erasmus's Mariology is complex, but coherent. It is uneven and polemical. Nevertheless, it is undoubtedly founded on the Bible, the Fathers and the judgement of the Church. Erasmus also accepted, without long debates, traditions which did not have their source in Scripture, provided that they were worthy of their object. He really discussed only the deviant Marian cult, stigmatizing the deformations which had entered it, just as he fiercely opposed the doctrine which placed Mary beside her Son if not before him.[22]

Christocentrism, which determined Erasmus's theology, imposed limits on him beyond which he was never to pass. 'Christ', he wrote, 'is the anchor of our salvation, Mary is not.' But this Christocentrism was not anti-Marian, for Erasmus wished for 'salvation through Jesus, but not without his Mother.'[23]

Erasmus's various reflections on piety unfailingly lead his reader to the essential aspect of faith in Christ. Authentic faith supports the pretentions of intellectualism no more than the weaknesses of superstition. It rejects the vanity of dilettantism just as much as the opium of habit. It cannot be a conquest of reason or a reward for merit. In the final analysis, if piety is a work of man, faith is a gift of God, which guarantees the awakening of an enlightened conscience. True piety cannot exempt the Christian from the obligations of love.

21

Freiburg: Voluntary Exile

The security which his stay in Basel gave Erasmus was precarious, on account of the rapid progress of the Reformation. The inconsiderate pressures exercised by the dissidents irritated him, the destruction of images in the churches shocked him, the harassment to which the clergy was subject scandalized him. The forbidding of the celebration of the Mass prevented him from the free exercise of his religious duties. Would he have to leave Basel? Erasmus withdrew from it little by little. He sold his library to the Pole Jan Laski, but on a deferred arrangement whereby he was able to enjoy its possession until his death.[1]

The disciples of Oecolampadius – who was still a friend of Erasmus – were the most threatening among the innovators. For their part, the Anabaptists survived despite the general hostility to them. The Cathedral Chapter migrated to Freiburg-im-Breisgau, while the bishop, Christoph von Utenheim, took refuge in the Jura.

Erasmus felt himself to be in danger and reconsidered the invitations which came to him from abroad. He did not wish to appear to approve of the Reformation. He was to find provisional protection in a neighbouring town, a Catholic and University town where his old friend the jurist Zasius was living and teaching: Freiburg-im-Breisgau.[2]

On 17 March 1529, Erasmus revealed his situation to Francisco Vergara:

> Meanwhile, I am undertaking a change of home, and I am forced to fly from the nest that I have been used to for so many years; for I fear lest at some time the treatment given to male and female saints should fall against me. Moreover, some people hold the most stupid, but wondrously stubborn suspicion that I am secretly connected with these sects, since everyone who is most addicted to them hates me very much. So the risk of death must be escaped at another risk of death.[3]

On 25 March 1529, he explained to Alfonso de Fonseca, the archbishop of Toledo, why he was going to have to leave his refuge in Basel:

I have settled in Basel to undertake something which might at least benefit the public with love of literature or godliness. The fact is that I have not abandoned myself to rest. However, I have not completely remained a silent spectator of this play. In conversations, letters and published books I have recalled or deterred many people, or at least calmed them down. Finally, I have joined battle openly with Luther, and accepted his poisoned darts with firm breast, and, with all my strength, have either repelled them or even turned them against him. . . .

I ought to change my residence: I know that I shall not do this without the greatest risk to my life. I have been used to this nest for so many years: but Christ will see to the outcome. Let me do what is right for a good Catholic person, so that godliness may be a stronger reason than safety; especially since to stay here, where it is not permitted to celebrate Mass or to share in the Lord's body, is nothing but to profess what these people profess. Oecolampadius is master of all the churches. Monks and nuns are ordered to go elsewhere, or to put off their holy garb. The same thing is happening in many other cities. Nothing traditional is done in the churches save what in some things a preacher of this sect once proclaims; then boys and girls sing a psalm to a German tune. These are only preludes. I am dreadfully afraid that paganism will follow Pharisaism. Luther holds several cities which think much the same as the Church about the Eucharist; but the other side has more, and it seems that it thinks it has the right to abolish the whole priesthood and monasticism. The Anabaptists, despite great number everywhere, have no church anywhere. They are praised for the innocence of their life before all other dissidents, but are also oppressed by the rest of the sects, not only by the Catholics.[4]

On Easter Tuesday, 30 March, Erasmus confided his worries to his close friend, Ludwig Baer:

I congratulate you with all my heart, because you are allowed to celebrate the Lord's resurrection, as is right, with spiritual rejoicing. Here we celebrate our Easter without an 'Alleluia', without a victory feast, although not without bitter herbs. Meanwhile it seems to me that we are sitting by the rivers of Babylon, so that we are not free to sing the Lord's song in a strange land. But I am alone merely in body; I am with you in spirit.

I was hoping to be at Freiburg before Easter Sunday, so that anyone asking for me here could be told what the angels replied to the godly women: 'He is risen, he is not here.' But around 15 March, for no obvious reason, a very persistent congestion, not without fever, seized me; so much that on some nights I was in great danger of choking with thick phlegm. I have hardly yet sufficiently recovered from this illness. However, every day I await the return of Hieronymus Froben from Frankfurt. It seems more prudent to wait for him; since by his help I shall leave here more safely, and he could be bringing letters, either from the Emperor's court at Brabant or from the Council of Speyer, which may force me to go somewhere other than Freiburg. It is better, I think, to change residence once than twice. However, I have sent ahead the most important of my meagre belongings, and the things thieves and robbers must look for, to be followed at the earliest occasion by the rest of my goods. Meanwhile, my bedroom is my church, until I am allowed to sacrifice to the Lord, like the Hebrews restored to the freedom of the desert: which I hope will happen very soon.[5]

Preparations for the journey went ahead. Erasmus bade farewell to various people. Some hours before his departure, he wrote again to Ludwig Baer and told him, with more spirit than emotion, the sad story of the Anabaptist priest Philip Schwitzer, undoubtedly to illustrate the confused situation of the religious struggle in Basel.

I don't know whether what is happening here is worthy more of Democritus' smile or Heraclitus' tears. You may judge. A travelling preacher came here. As soon as he paid his host the little amount he owed, he said, 'Farewell, and do penance.' He then went to the public and showed himself as a second Precursor, shouting in a clear and distinct voice, with a grave face, 'Do penance, do penance, do penance; the hand of the Lord is upon you.' For several days he walked through all the streets of the city repeating this proclamation. Entering the cathedral, he began to inveigh against the corrupt life of the canons. Many of them smiled at this, others ignored it. Finally, it is said, he entered the churches of Oecolampadius's followers, and inveighed a great deal against them, more freely and harshly, calling them, again and again, 'destroyers of souls'. Someone interrupted him: 'You there! you call us to penance; say what you think we ought to do, and how God may be appeased.' Then, as if inspired by heaven, gazing on the enquirer with a Gorgon's eyes, he said, 'Pharisee, why do you tempt me? The Spirit has not ordered me to say anything else.'

It is also said that he had acted as Precursor in Montbéliard. When he did not find anyone there who was willing to do penance, he was locked in a gaol for three months and did penance for everyone. When he was discharged from there, following the gospel injunction, 'to shake the dust from his feet', he changed his residence to here; when the word of penance was looked upon even less favourably here, he was ordered to gaol. When he was being led there, he called out 'Do penance' no less eagerly. One of his two guards said, 'If you are not quiet, you wretch, I shall punch you on the nose.' He called out even more, 'Do penance.' I don't know what happened in the gaol. It is agreed that he was dismissed on condition that he should not return within the jurisdiction of this state.

Then, I believe, he took himself to Lucerne, a city which is more hostile to new sects than any other. He performed the job of Precursor there for several days, and reminded us of John the Baptist also in that he was thrown into chains; he was unlike him in that John was beheaded, the other burnt – undoubtedly because an Anabaptist played the part of the Baptist so badly.[6]

Before his departure, Erasmus had a meeting with Oecolampadius. Some misunderstandings were dispelled but, pressed to remain in Basel, Erasmus held to his decision to leave. His precious objects, his books, his furniture, were already in Freiburg. On 13 April at noon, Erasmus finally took the boat to Neuburg and from there he reached Freiburg by road. Some friends, including Boniface Amerbach, accompanied him until his arrival, and then returned to Basel.

Erasmus was warmly received and accommodated with honour in a house owned by the municipality. The skies were calm, and his optimism seemed justified. But Erasmus was now over sixty years old and a frail, worn-out, sick man. The presence by his side of his old servant Margaret was a poor compensation. He kept her in his service because he was afraid to replace her with a servant who might prove still worse, but this did not prevent him from finding her unbearable and sour.

Erasmus was scarcely installed in his house *Zum Walfisch* when he put into Latin verse his farewell to Basel: 'Now Basel farewell; no other city for many years has showed kindlier hospitality than you. I pray that henceforth everything will be happy for you, and that no less happy guest than Erasmus ever arrives!'[7]

Would our traveller ever attach himself to Freiburg or make only a brief stay there? His hesitation was apparent. 'I have decided to remain here this winter,' he said to a friend, 'to fly with the swallows towards the city which God has prepared for me.[8] He thought of new travels, but gradually Freiburg kept him. Months passed. The swallows came and left again. Erasmus was still there. He was to live in this new refuge for many weary years.

Like many of his fellows, Erasmus was afraid of doctors. If he sometimes consulted them, he set the rules. He hated fish and his preferred remedy was Burgundy wine which he believed able to conquer gout! He believed that he could feel the weight of death on his shoulders and he wanted to complete his work without delay. His treatise *On the Education of Children* came off the press in the year that he settled in Freiburg. Matured over a long time, growing out of experience and learning, it was not to offend anyone's susceptibilities.

Nothing was superfluous, nothing was without importance in the education of children. It was still necessary to go beyond a concern for behaviour and the need for training, to arrive at education properly speaking. Erasmus was a prodigious pedagogical adviser. He appealed incessantly to the child's reason and the use of repeated exercises, desiring that even the very young should be instructed and informed as to human letters as well as divine precepts. 'Man is not born man, but becomes man.'

Erasmus undoubtedly possessed a wide range of knowledge. He wrote on medicine, history, and natural sciences, but he was not at ease in these subjects and his domain lay elsewhere. Most often he was content to borrow from these sciences moral anecdotes, eloquent examples, lessons, and, above all, the elements of Greek or Latin vocabulary. We can admire this charming and unexpected piece in which visual methods are ingeniously applied.

One illustration might show an elephant trapped in a snake's stranglehold, its forefeet entwined by the other's tail. This picture arouses the interest of the pupils – so what does the teacher do? He teaches his students that this large animal is called *elephas* in Greek and the same thing in Latin, except that we can also use the Latin inflexional forms, *elephantus* and *elephanti*. He next points out that part of the body with which the elephant picks up its food, [*proboskis*] in Greek and *manus* in Latin. He also tells his students that this animal does not breathe out through the mouth as we do, but through the trunk. He calls attention to the pair of tusks protruding on each side of the trunk; these are the source of the ivory so greatly valued by the rich, he says, and produces an ivory comb to illustrate his point. He also teaches his pupils that huge snakes such as the one depicted are found in India . . . And amid all these details, he also impresses upon his students that between the snake and the elephant there is, instinctively and constantly, a ruthless warfare. If there is a boy who happens to be an especially ambitious scholar, he may learn other facts as well about elephants and snakes.[9]

We should not smile too quickly or shrug our shoulders! On this page, Erasmus shows no literary pride. He did not invent, but he possessed no information at first hand. If he had never seen a dragon, neither had he seen an elephant. His knowledge of natural history was purely bookish. If the information about dragons was borrowed from folklore, that on elephants was correct and inspired by Pliny.

Erasmus's pedagogy was liberal, and rested on his confidence in nature. We need to understand the master's confidence in the nature of the pupil, a confidence expressed in all of his works devoted to education, from *The Method of Study*, in 1511, to *On Good Manners for Boys* in 1530. In this last essay, which was a genuine manual of good breeding, he gave advice on politeness and on hygiene, and even went into considerable detail. Erasmus was not one to mix his genres.[9] Even self-mastery is not a specifically Christian virtue. Civility is a training process leading to good habits, and acquires a deeper meaning only through a respect of persons.

The nostrils should be free from any filthy collection of mucus, as this is disgusting (the philosopher Socrates was reproached for that failing too). It is boorish to wipe one's nose on one's cap or clothing; to do so on one's sleeve or forearm is for fishmongers, and it is not much better to wipe it with one's hand, if you then smear the discharge on your clothing. The polite way is to catch the matter from the nose in a handkerchief, and this should be done by turning away slightly if decent people are present. . . . Attention must be paid to the care of the teeth, but to whiten them with fine powder is for girls, while brushing with salt or alum harms the gums. To brush them with urine is a custom of the Spaniards. Food particles should be removed from the teeth, not with a knife or with the nails, in the manner of dogs or cats, and not with a napkin, but with a toothpick of mastic wood, or with a feather, or with small bones taken from the drumsticks of cocks or hens. . . .

It is boorish to go about with one's hair uncombed: it should be neat, but not as elaborate as a girl's coiffure. It should be free from infections of nits and vermin. It is not polite to be continually scratching one's head in front of others just as it is unsightly to scratch the rest of the body, especially if it is done through habit rather than necessity. The hair should neither cover the brow nor flow down over the shoulders. To be constantly tossing the hair with a flick of the head is for frolicsome horses. It is not very elegant to brush back the hair from the forehead with the left hand; it is more discreet to part it with the hand.[10]

In *The Education of Children*, Erasmus appealed to his personal experience and delivered to us, in passing, some recollections of an excessively harsh education which he wanted to spare others.

If you follow my advice, or rather, I should say, the advice of that most penetrating of philosophers, Chrysippus, you will see to it that your infant son makes his first acquaintance with a liberal education immediately, while his mind is still uncorrupted and free from distractions, while he is in his most formative and impressionable years, and while his spirit is still open to each and every influence and at the same time highly retentive of what it has grasped; for we remember nothing in old age as well as what we absorbed during our unformed years . . .

A teacher can expect success in the classroom if he displays the qualities of gentleness and kindness and also possesses the skill and ingenuity to devise various means of making the studies pleasant and keeping the child from feeling any strain. Nothing is more harmful than an instructor whose conduct causes his students to take an intense dislike to their studies before they are sufficiently mature to appreciate them for their own sake. A prerequisite for learning is that the teacher must be liked. Gradually, after first enjoying learning because of their instructor, children will come to like their teacher for the sake of learning. . . .

There are people you could not mend by flogging even though you beat them to death; yet, if you use kindness and persuasion, you might lead them in any direction you pleased. I must confess that this was my nature when I was a boy. My teacher had more affection for me than for any other pupil, and on the pretext that he had conceived the greatest hopes for me, he kept a closer watch on me than on anyone else. Finally, wishing to ascertain for himself how well I could stand up to the rod, he charged me with an offence I had never dreamed of committing and then flogged me. This incident destroyed all love of study within me and flung my young mind into such a deep depression that I nearly wasted away with heart-break; the result was, at any rate, that I was presently seized with the quartan fever. When my teacher at last realized the mistake he had made, he expressed his regrets to his friends, saying 'I almost destroyed his character before I had learnt to understand it.' He was certainly not an insensitive, ignorant or, as far as I can imagine, a malicious person; he did recover his senses, but too late as far as I was concerned.[11]

The wonderful availability of children is advantageous for the acquisition of languages. 'Children have such a marked ability to pick up a foreign language that, for instance, a German boy could learn French in a few months quite unconsciously while absorbed in other activities. In fact it is the youngest who are always most successful.'[12]

With its thousand pages and thousand letters, the *Collected Letters* of 1529 was the most substantial of all those published by Erasmus.[13] Its preparation had been long and often painful. Erasmus was obliged to reconcile contradictory aims. He wanted to give the public a collection of his letters, but it appeared to him appropriate to sacrifice a large part of them. His recapitulatory volume should be at once an anthology and a documentary collection. In the end, he agreed to add to the letters already published what had been acquired in recent years: hundreds of letters! What could he do, except search for a middle way? This solution, perhaps wise, and certainly Erasmian, was not achieved without some hesitation, indeed, without some errors. The volume was to be huge without being complete. It was to be made up of model letters and to reproduce everything that had been published before, while adding 400 unpublished letters from recent years. Among the new letters, only some were addressed to Erasmus. All the others were from his own hand and were addressed to more than 200 correspondents of all nationalities.

Erasmus presented this publication to the reader in a familiar style. His feelings, like his intentions, were revealed there with simplicity.

I have mentioned before that none of my compositions is less pleasing to me than my Letters, and I have recounted the reasons for my opinion; nor is my mind different to me now from what it once was. Nevertheless, since Hieronymus Froben asserted that this whole work has already been requested strongly by scholars for two years, I have re-edited what had been printed, and have attached a substantial addition. . . .

It did not seem that the order should be changed; I have only divided the whole work into books, so that the reader may find what he is looking for more easily. Some friends have suggested to me by letter that they should be ordered chronologically; even if this had been easy, for certain reasons it did not seem a good idea. Also I decided not to adopt an order by subjects, because in this sort of writing the most pleasing thing is variety. Furthermore, if anyone wants such a thing, I have appended the day and year at the foot of each of them. In addition, I have prefixed an index, attaching the names of persons and page-numbers, to show distinctly who wrote to whom, and how many times he wrote. There are a number of letters which I would have liked to add, if I had had them at hand. But shifting residence was a reason that many have been lost which I should have preferred to be saved; indeed, everything was so mixed up that I looked for a large part of it in vain. I have decided to give this warning, so that if anyone perchance, when he has seen letters sent to other friends, of lesser status, is worried that there are none written to him, he should not suspect that I have done this out of bad will.

In these times I do not know what can be written that may not offend one person or another. However, I have striven, as far as my strength allowed, to omit, or at least to moderate, what might convey a lot of bitterness. I have freely left off from mentioning people by name; I wish that this could have happened everywhere! But this is not how to publish letters. I have left out solemn titles, which are not only pretentious, but even difficult and irksome to the reader: I pray that this not be taken adversely, as if it were done out of contempt. For who does not know that kings are most invincible, most serene; abbots venerable; bishops reverend; cardinals very reverend; popes most holy and blessed? Therefore such things as 'invincible majesty', 'very reverend lordship', 'most gracious highness' and 'reverend fatherhood', not only harm the purity of Latin style, but also burden the reader with superfluous and irksome details.[14]

Erasmus explains little about his collected letters. This preface, one of the last of its kind, is thus the more interesting. The humanist's rhetorical care – genuine prudence or innocence tinged with malice – shows clearly that the publication of his letters was risky. He accepted it because he could not avoid it. He published or republished his letters without classifying them in chronological order.

The comparison of the more recent letters with those of earlier years shows us an Erasmus frequently troubled by a feeling of failure, powerlessness, and even helplessness. His disappointment was the measure of his hopes. Everything that he loved was collapsing around him and the age of gold was fading into the distance, whether considered from the point of view of good literature or of Christian concord. His pessimism tended to lead him astray. He believed that the Protestant Reformation would kill good letters, forgetting the major role of Melanchthon in this area. He no longer even anticipated the admirable effort of the Catholic Reformation and he expected no great things of a Council that arrived too late. These errors of perspective were to cast permanent shadows over the end of his life, without, however, weakening his intellectual powers or his Christian conviction.

Moreover, virulent polemics returned. Erasmus composed vigorous apologies against Pio, Clichthove, Eppendorf, and Geldenhouwer.[15] This sterile activity wearied him and his health suffered. News which the couriers brought daily was hardly encouraging. In Spain, the good days of Erasmianism were over. The Inquisition regarded the partisans of Luther and the disciples of Erasmus with an equal contempt. In Paris, an unfortunate admirer, Louis de Berquin, who had translated Erasmus, went to the stake.[16] In Liège, the Inquisitor Dirk Adriaanszoon [Hezius], after a police raid, ordered books by Erasmus which had been found at the school of the Brethren of the Common Life to be seized.[17] At Freiburg, on the other hand, Erasmus feared a sedition provoked by dissidents. 'If any disturbance should happen,' he said, 'I shall be among the first victims of the followers of Zwingli and Luther; although I shall suffer this sooner than leave the Catholic Church.'[18]

This was why the persistence of calumnies directed at his piety exasperated him. He cited indignantly the words of the Spanish theologians who dared to say of him: 'He thinks lightly of the blessed Virgin'; 'He condemns the cult of the saints'; 'He thinks impiously about the Trinity.'[19]

After a crisis of despondency, Erasmus's optimism took over again. His will sustained him and his determination to work delivered him from his fears, just as it had already delivered him from the problem of his feelings. He willingly made an assessment of his work and to those who hoped for nothing more from his old age, he replied with triumphant humour.

How am I more feeble than these people? Budé is younger than me by two years; Bédier by perhaps four or five; Latomus by three. Up to this time I have been continually engaged in working, from which comes the greatest part of my ill-health and debility. As one old man, I maintain the burden of four strong youths. My eyes are not bleary, thanks be to God, although some people marvel that I have not been completely blind for a long time. I have never yet used reading glasses, neither by day nor by lamp-light. I have never used a staff, I walk quickly, on firm feet; my hands tremble less than a young man's. My stone becomes gentler every day, and, if I moderate my studious work, with God's help, I could live with unimpaired senses for fourteen years. But my way of life is in God's hands. Those who live with me do not think that my intellect or memory are greatly impaired. And where is that feeble old man, dead and buried?

But still, he has given you Jerome, Cyprian, Augustine. He now gives you Chrysostom, from whom (with Athanasius) he translates so much. He has illustrated many passages in the New Testament from Greek authors: let them read the index, and they shall understand how much this feeble old man has contributed to learning and godliness.[20]

Everything in this piece of bravura was true, except what had to do with Erasmus's health. His kidneys were making him suffer. He badly neglected his appearance. His mood sometimes showed its effects. Those close to him felt sorry for him, but his work continued unabated.

22

Freiburg: The Final Harvest

Erasmus's eirenic efforts did not go as far as participating in the Diet of Augsburg in 1530. He preferred to persuade by his writings and still hoped that the break would be avoided thanks to the generous efforts of Melanchthon, but he was to be a powerless witness of an imminent schism.

Erasmus reproached the innovators for the contradictions of their doctrine and deplored their imprecations against the Roman Church. 'Nor do you want these things to be cleansed, but to be destroyed. . . . but you rip out the tares with the wheat or, to speak better, you rip out the wheat instead of the tares.'[1]

At this time in his life, satisfaction and bitterness took turns. He had gained much affluence and spoke of it with a certain vanity to a Spanish friend, Cristóbal Mejía.

I have a room strewn with letters from learned men, magnates, princes, kings, cardinals, bishops. I have a chest filled with gifts of cups, flagons, spoons, clocks – several of which are of pure gold. There are many rings; and the number of all these things will be much greater unless I give many of the gifts again to friends who are devoted to study. Amongst those who give these things are many outstanding, not only in learning, but also in holiness of life, such as the Archbishop of Canterbury, the Bishop of London, the Bishop of Augsburg, and especially John, the Bishop of Rochester: who had escaped [my notice], as well as the bishop of Wroclaw, John Turzo . . .

Every day the number of my benefactors increases, although I have not sought anyone's benefaction, openly proclaiming that I had enough goods for my frugal life, which I do not regret – to the extent that I should sooner be deprived of something than add anything to it. However, such is their spontaneous generosity that, if I returned nothing to anyone (and I return several, except for the Emperor's pension), this alone would be enough to support my studies. I have always returned the gifts of those of moderate means whenever friendship would not be harmed; or I have accepted them for civility's sake, so as to repay them in abundance.[2]

Bitterness overcame him when his efforts to re-establish peace seemed to him to be useless. He counted his enemies and wept for the friends who had forgotten or betrayed him. He wrote that the summer of 1530 had been for him 'almost sterile'. This was only a figure of speech, for he had just finished the edition of his beloved Chrysostom and was to publish a fascinating illustration of ancient wisdom, the *Apophthegms*, in honour of the young Duke William of Cleves.

Despite his rheumatism, his stones and his gout, Erasmus found the strength and time to reply to his adversaries on the right and on the left: their uncompromising prose aroused his anger. Sometimes rancour blinded him; he passed from fear to suspicion and from misunderstandings to clumsy gaffes. Then his exasperation abated and his good humour triumphed.

The tactlessness of former friends who introduced extracts from his works into tendentious pamphlets compelled him to make careful, but quite essential, clarifications. This was the case with Gerard Geldenhouwer, a childhood friend who had gone over to the Reformation. Erasmus reasserted the facts firmly and not without irony in his *Letter against those who would be called evangelical*, addressed to Geldenhouwer in November 1529 and published in January 1530. Erasmus spoke first of personal matters and of Geldenhouwer's poverty, in response to which he did not neglect to send some pieces of gold, despite his own difficulties, the importance of which he exaggerated.

This, my poor body, has need of great expense; it was even frail in the flower of my life, so much more when old; my health is very poor, and my double illness is doubly incurable. For just as there is no cure for old age from doctors, so they say that the stone cannot be cured in old men. Already I have spent a good deal on servants, both those that I have now and those I have dismissed, on messengers and letter-bearers, on those who somewhat lighten my labours by their work – that is, those who go hunting for ancient manuscripts, who collate them and annotate them, who re-read and write out my own works. Furthermore, you would hardly believe how much loss of personal property I have suffered since I departed from Basel. For there, apart from other advantages, I had a house maintained at others' expense, provided with others' furniture; here everything must be provided for from my own money. Finally, as prices of goods increase beyond measure, my wealth decreases. The Emperor stages a very movable play, so that even his creditors do not now dare to appeal to him. So much is lacking from me, as a useless assessor and appellant, no less slow than ashamed, receiving my pension. . . .

Truly, my dear Vulturius, after you resolved to profess the evangelical life, I am amazed that poverty is irksome, when once the blessed Hilarion, when he had nothing to pay his passage, thought that it was glorious that without knowing it he had gained such evangelical perfection.... But what you mention about offending, I could not be angry with such a friend even if I wished to; I declare that it grieves me to see you in this mess you have got yourself into, and I would love to set you out of it.[3]

In this letter Erasmus wanted to express his separation from the Lutheran movement. He continued by making clear that he was in no way putting in question the prince's justice and his right to punish a heretic 'if he is truly a heretic', but that he recommended to Churchmen clemency and persuasion rather than the denunciation of the dissident to the secular arm. Finally he moved to the essential point by showing the happy accord of faith and works.

Let it be a matter of dispute whether good works produce faith or faith produces good works, or whether good works justify or not; it is certainly beyond dispute that without faith there is no hope of salvation for anyone; and from faith good works necessarily arise through charity, so that they profess faith shamelessly who do not pursue good works, and they promise themselves salvation in vain, who take pride in faith without good works. I am already afraid lest under that word many heathens arise amongst us, who may even be more free if they believe that there is neither heaven nor hell, and that souls do not survive the body's death. Yet meantime they profess free consciences. Perfect godliness has a peaceful conscience, but so has the greatest ungodliness. But I would prefer a restless conscience, which being constantly stirred by the seed of faith is not allowed to be quiet. It is an incurable evil which is not felt.[4]

And he developed his point of view in some virulent pages.

When Martin Bucer revived the discussion, Erasmus wrote to him soon after with the same firmness: 'I do not see with what countenance you expect this, when you so disagree amongst yourselves.'[5] In a reply to a Lutheran pamphlet, Erasmus bared his heart a little.' 'Neither my age nor my bad health obliges me to live in idleness. I work with my hands in order not to be a burden on anyone and to be able to come to the help of those in need.'

On his arrival in Freiburg, Erasmus had been able to have at his disposal part of the house *Zum Walfisch*, but he did not feel at ease there. Friends invited him to Rome, to Besançon, to Brabant. Was he going to remain in Freiburg or agree to leave again? In Antwerp Pieter Gillis on the one hand and Erasmus Schets on the other invited him to return to the country in which his friends were waiting for him. Erasmus remained doubtful. He knew that he no longer had any real friend at the court of Charles V except for Conradus Glocenius.[6] 'Is there nothing you do not promise' he replied to Schets, '. . . wines, a house, friends, what not? I beg you, where are these splendours which you promise?'[7] So he dismissed the idea of returning, without giving it up entirely, and took a surprising decision. 'But hear something about me that you may laugh at,' he wrote to Johann Rinck of Cologne:

> If anyone should tell you that Erasmus, already nearly seventy years old, has wed a wife, would you not make the sign of the cross three or four times? You would do so, I am sure, and quite rightly. Yet now, my dear Rinck, I have done something no less onerous, no less irksome, no less far from my nature and my studies. I have bought a house with a splendid enough name, but for an unequal price. Who should not now expect the rivers, reversing their course, to return to their sources, after Erasmus, who till now has for his whole life put his life as a writer foremost, has become a bidder, a buyer, a bargainer, a pledge-taker, a builder, and through the Muses has business with carpenters, blacksmiths, masons, glaziers? These cares, my dear Rinck, from which my nature has always recoiled, have almost killed me with weariness. I am still a tourist in my own house, because although it is large, it holds no nest to which I might safely entrust this poor body. I have prepared a single chamber, in building a smoke room, with ground and walls both covered, but because of stinking feet I have not yet dared to trust myself to it. However, I ought to depart shortly, since it is propitious and favourable.[8]

It was when he was finally installed in this house *Zum Kind Iesu* that Erasmus received his Freiburg friends Ulrich Zasius, Henricus Glareanus and Ludwig Baer, or friends from elsewhere, and it was there that he pursued his work.

One aspect of the problem of war with which Erasmus was preoccupied to the end of his life was the war against the Turks. When the Muslim danger was distant, Erasmus spoke of the crusade in scathing terms. From the moment when the threat became acute, or it was no longer a matter of Christians going to conquer the territory of the infidels, but of defending Europe against invasion, his tone changed. In 1526 the King of Hungary was killed at the battle of Mohacs. In 1529 the Turks were outside Vienna. In 1530 Erasmus published his *Consultation on the subject of War against the Turks*, a short reflection on the anxieties of the time.[9]

He remained faithful to what he had always taught, but he was more sensitive to the question of defending Europe. War was declared against the Turks. It was a fact and no longer a possibility. Erasmus understood that resistance to aggression could become inevitable. Reluctantly he resigned himself to a defensive war while refusing to call it a Crusade.

He was not among those who denied the possible necessity of legitimate defence, but he specified its conditions. It was necessary that it be conducted with humanity and lead to a peaceful evangelization. One would like to think that Erasmus was aware of the fragility of his solution. It must have cost him a great deal to make so many concessions to the war party. He made them, he said, for the safety of Europe, 'for the maintenance of the Christian peace'. But he weighed the risks of his involvement. 'I am afraid that, in having to combat the Turks, we may be reduced to becoming Turks ourselves.'[10]

His contemporaries were in no way mistaken about this. They had always considered Erasmus a defender of peace. Julius Pflug expressed the general view when he said to him: All friends of peace are looking to you alone.'[11] For the benefit of his old friend Johann von Botzheim, he commented on the most recent political news in which his interest had not waned.

Never has what the Emperor does been more secret than now, nor [has he been] more hidden anywhere than where he now lives in Brabant. Some of my friends have mingled purposely with the imperial courtiers, to fish for something: they could not sniff anything out. Everyone knows this, he hunts diligently, I think because of his health, worn out by so many and such long journeys, and so many audiences. It is a long journey from Spain to Bologna. There, besides ceremonies carried out with religious punctiliousness, he discussed higher matters in familiar conversations with Clement VII. After, there came the Diet of Augsburg, with the stupendous celebration of the Princes. From there he journeyed to Aachen, where King Ferdinand was designated King of the Romans. After such business was successfully finished, he relaxes his spirit a little in his Flanders, in whose bosom he was born. A vast sum of money is demanded, but I hear that it has not been agreed to by all parts of his dominion. People's opinion is divided for what use this may be, but nothing is certain. There are some who consider that he will return to Spain in autumn, in triumph through France; others think that these 'sinews of war' are being prepared against the Turks; a few conjecture that there will be a sudden attack against the champions of the sects. God knows what will happen![12]

More formally Erasmus described to the Cardinal of Trent, Bernhard von Cles, his fragile health and his determined labours.

With how much pleasure I read in your last letter that the most serene King of the Romans, Ferdinand, with many people listening, has adorned my name with such honourable mention that I do not need anyone else's praises before him. . . . I can hardly see what I might seek from King Ferdinand except what his outstanding goodness offers spontaneously.

Apart from my studies, for which I am glad to die, I am useless for any other job in life. High office would even be nothing more to me than a burden to a fallen horse. To accumulate goods when life's span is already at an end would be no less ridiculous than if someone were to give travelling-provisions when a journey had been completed. Frugality has always been pleasing to me, and now it is even necessary. However, I should desire a quiet old age ... To deter decline, to improve health – neither the Pope nor the greatest of princes, the Emperor, can do this. When I have both wishing me well, I wish that they could at least stop the mouths of detractors. But even this is not in their power.[13]

The year 1531 saw the death of two of the innovators, Zwingli and Oecolampadius, former friends who had became adversaries of Erasmus. Erasmus did not hide his relief and did not seem to be ashamed of this. He breathed more easily, but the *Chronicle*, published in Strasbourg by Sebastian Franck the same year, strangely embarrassed him. The author of this pamphlet, like others before him, used Erasmus's works and turned them against the Emperor and the Pope. Erasmus reacted sharply, calling for Franck's punishment. He was placated when the City Council of Strasbourg ordered that the *Chronicle* should be pulped.

Erasmus had never forgotten Terence, the great love of his youth. When, for a few months, he received at his house two young Poles, Johannes Boner and Stanislaw Aichler, as well as their teacher Anselmus Ephorinus, he was preparing the edition of the comedies of the great Latin poet. He was to dedicate this volume, published in 1532, to Johannes and Stanislaus Boner. Their father, the banker of King Sigismund and a faithful admirer of Erasmus, was to send him, by way of thanks, two superb gold medals.

Erasmus returned to religious questions with the bishop Jacopo Sadoleto. He could not fail to express his regrets. It should not have been necessary to give importance to Luther and his writings on indulgences, to throw oil on the fire. It should not have been necessary later to have recourse to the services of the almost universally odious monks, or provoke the horrible rage of the populace, or again to burn the books or the men.[14]

If he continued to correspond with his friends, and sometimes with his enemies, Erasmus no longer seemed to envisage a new recapitulative edition of his correspondence. However, he gathered together the letters sent out among his correspondents.[15] He had them recopied by his *famuli* and, on occasion, he retouched them cautiously. Andrea Alciati, a courageous friend who wanted to bring him to a greater serenity, had said to him frankly: 'Amongst those you have edited for these last four years, rare are those from which open declarations of revenge do not appear.'[16]

In March 1531, Erasmus sent to the printer Herwagen, in Basel, the letter which was to serve as a preface to the edition of the *Epistolarum floridarum*:

> I mention this, my dear Herwagen, so that you may be contented with what I now send you, not as I wish, but as I can. For I had to send this, or nothing. So I send you some flowery letters. I know that you are wondering why this is their title. But this is of no importance, make no mistake. This little work could hardly be undertaken during the troubled business of leaving one place and moving to another; so that from a great heap of letters I marked with little flowers those which it was useful to have printed, although I very rarely write any for this purpose.[17]

Flowery letters! Erasmus seemed to have made a play on words: little flowers drawn on the letters or flowers of style? The *Epistolarum floridarum*, which the printer had requested, appeared in September 1531. These 112 letters were mostly written naturally, without any emphasis and entirely unedited. They delighted both modest and famous friends who found among them the letter which Erasmus had addressed to them. They aroused the annoyance or anger of those who found in them the humanist's sometimes not very flattering remarks made public.

Erasmus himself did not really appreciate his collection. He confided his disappointment to Karel Utenhove: 'Recently, I re-read my so called "flowery" letters, and found them rather withered.'[18] Having said that, he again applied himself to the letters from the following year, in a volume printed in Freiburg and entitled: *Letters Old and New*.[19] This volume of 131 letters, of which only twenty-five were previously unpublished, was the last recapitulative collection published by Erasmus.

In between, his friends summoned him and proposed again that he return to Brabant. He hesitated, procrastinated and temporized. 'I fear three things,' he confided in his banker: 'first, that this poor body cannot bear the cold and windy climate; then, that the favour of Queen Mary may not be strong enough to protect me from the monks' attacks; finally, that the court may kill me, while here, hiding in my bedroom, I can support life, albeit poorly.' Then on 2 March 1532, he made a curious admission to Bucer: 'Old men seem suspicious to me, not so much from the fault of their age as from great experience of ills which they had never believed would come about. Sometimes it happens that while they think that there is a scorpion sleeping under every stone, they are wrong.'[20]

Despite his fears of being placed among the crypto-Lutherans, Erasmus did not give way. Indulgences, the source of abuse and misunderstanding, continued to irritate him, and he owed it to himself to say so. In 1532 he repeated it, clearly for the benefit of the Sorbonne.

No one doubts the power of the Pope, or even of individual bishops, to remit the penances imposed by men, and for weighty reasons and very moderately, lest the strength of Church discipline weaken: but whether this power extends to Purgatory has been doubted by many, even by godly people. Indeed, whether holy Councils have approved such indulgences is not sufficiently clear. It does not seem likely to me.[21]

Once more, competence and subtlety combined with Erasmus in a great talent for exposition and a genuine eloquence, doubtless with a little too much irony. He accepted indulgences because of the authority of the Church and recognized their stimulating role in calming the weakness of sinners, but he regretted that they had no scriptural or patristic base and that their advocates resorted to an indefensible casuistry. He also deplored the false security offered to the dying by indulgences little understood, as if they were an assurance for eternal life. Finally, he denounced the *de facto* connection established between the remission of punishment and the importance of alms. For him, the practice of indulgences obscured evangelical teaching on penitence and pardon. So he agreed to return to the preaching of 'love which covers a multitude of sins' as making the contrition of sinners perfect. One could say that Erasmus admitted the principle of indulgences because he did not put in doubt the treasury of Christ's merits, the communion of saints, or the power of the keys. He proclaimed the mercy of God and the mediation of the Church, but he feared everything which threatened true piety. For reasons similar to those of Luther, but not proceeding from the theses of 1517, Erasmus set himself against a system which too often justified the greed of the mighty and the exploitation of the weak.

The friendly relations between Thomas More and Erasmus had suffered no eclipse, but few of the letters which they exchanged at this time are preserved.[22] More had become Lord Chancellor of the Kingdom of England. When the ecclesiastical hierarchy gave the King full powers over the Church, he courageously resigned. In this critical situation which was to turn into tragedy, he did not forget Erasmus and continued to take his side.[23]

Rabelais, who had played a part in securing the loan of a manuscript to Erasmus, expressed his admiration to him on 30 November 1532:

You who have taught me, whose face is unknown to you and whose name is obscure, and so nurtured me with the pure breasts of your holy teaching that whatever I am and can do, if I did not owe to you alone what I have received, I should be the most ungrateful of all men today and in times to come. Therefore keep well perpetually, most beloved father, father and honour of your homeland, defender of literature, invincible champion of the truth.[24]

This enthusiastic praise may surprise us, yet it was deserved. Erasmus had prepared for Rabelais the pathway of satire and the 'Gargantua' was in the same vein as the *Colloquies*.

Between 1530 and 1532, Holbein, who was travelling around the continent, made more portraits of Erasmus. A large portrait, recopied many times by the artist, showed Erasmus, seated at his desk, a half-smile on a face visibly marked by suffering, the glance peaceable, but distant. On the little portrait on the medallion, the counterpart to that of Luther, Erasmus's face is that of an old man, but its glance astonishingly young under the very high arch of the eyebrows.[25]

The eighth edition of the *Adages* came off the Froben presses in March 1533. The volume carried, in a frontispiece, a portrait of Erasmus engraved on wood. Filled out much more than the preceding editions, it was dedicated to Charles Mountjoy, son of Erasmus's old friend and English patron. The author complained humorously of the length of his work: 'It is easy, I know, to write some adages, but it is difficult to write thousands!'

Over three years, from 1533 to 1536, Erasmus was to publish more religious works. He lived in deep inward peace which was not to desert him. His *Catechism* was an exposition of the Apostles' Creed, the Ten Commandments and the Lord's Prayer through questions and answers.[26] He wisely rejected the notion that the Creed had been composed by the twelve apostles article by article, but he maintained the apostolic authority of the doctrine taught in it. Possessed by his idea of an ancient summary of the faith which was to be developed by what followed after, he did not note that the Apostles' Creed and that of Nicaea were two different texts. He suggested that the gradual extension of the Creed was due to the necessity of combating heresy over the centuries.

Erasmus's piety, so disputed by those who have only worked through his satiric works, found unequivocal expression:

> Whoever turns his eyes to the crucified Christ with complete faith, so that he fears to crucify him afresh by doing those things which Christ died to wash away, there is hardly anyone so weak that he cannot accept the troubles of this age with a calm mind when he reflects on how many things Christ, who was free from all taint of crimes, suffered for us. Who may be found so inhuman and ungrateful that he would not love him in return, who first so loved, and incited him to mutual love by such favours?[27]

The success of the *Catechism* was immediate. All the copies offered for sale at the Frankfurt fair were sold in less than three hours and Froben republished the work in the same year.

The treatise *On Mending the Peace of the Church* was the most successful expression of Erasmian ecumenism, an eloquent plea in favour of the reunion of divided Christians.[28] It was dedicated to the German Julius Pflug, a longstanding friend of Erasmus. His zeal compelled him to implore Christians, Catholic and Protestant, to act for the *Unam Sanctam* before it was too late. It is in this little book that this admirable profession of faith is to be found: 'There is only one God, but there are diverse views of Him.'[29] Already, in his *Paraphrase on the Gospel of St Mark*, Erasmus had written: 'There is one universal Church, but there are many church communities. Christ is equally in all of them.'[30]

Erasmus described the struggle which pitted against each other those who were 'unwilling to accept changes' and those who wished 'nothing of the old to remain'. He chose devotion to the saints as an example.

> It is also a religious practice [he wrote] to believe that certain saints who while living were able to expel demons and recall the dead to life are still able to do this. Those who do not share this opinion should pray with sincere belief to the Father, Son and Holy Spirit, and should not disturb those who, out of superstition, implore the intercession of the saints. Superstition, which I must admit is quite widespread in the invocation of the saints, should be corrected. Yet we must tolerate the pious simplicity of some, even when there is a certain amount of error involved. If our prayers are not heard by the saints, Christ, who loves simple souls, will give us what we request through the saints.[31]

In this work, which was the synthesis of his Christian philosophy and his critical Christianity, Erasmus took up the essentials of his religious programme: the primacy of the Gospel, the mission of the Church, the purification of institutions and of piety. He added to it an appeal for mutual tolerance. Let the Catholics not anger the Lutherans by treating them as heretics! Let the innovators, for their part, tolerate popular piety! Let both sides hold to the essentials with faith and love, to avoid divisions! 'Most evils', Erasmus recalled, 'creep in little by little and on different occasions. They ought to be eliminated in the same way, provided this does not cause a disturbance. Otherwise they should be concealed until an opportunity presents itself for removing them.'[32]

In this approach to dogmatic questions, Erasmus asked for tact, but made no concession. He touched quickly on freewill, justification and the Eucharist.

> Concerning *The Freedom of the Will*, this is a thorny question rather than something that can be profitably debated. If it must be ironed out, however, let us leave it to competent theologians. . . . Let us agree that we are justified by faith, i.e., the hearts of the faithful are thereby purified, provided we admit that the works of charity are necessary for salvation . . .

As far as the Mass is concerned, whether there is superstition or corruption it should be reasonably corrected. I see no reason why the Mass itself should be suppressed. It consists of psalmody; the introit; the doxology; prayer and canticles; lessons from the prophets, and from the Apostles and from the Gospels; the creed; thanksgiving or, as it is called, the Eucharist, the commemoration of Christ's death; then prayer again, including the Lord's Prayer; after this the symbol of Christian peace; then the communion; the sacred canticle, and prayer. Finally the priest blesses the people and, as a group commended to his protection, bids them depart in piety and mutual charity. What is there in this that is not pious and does not arouse reverence?[33]

In the end, Erasmus submitted his reflections to the judgement of the Church, from which he hoped for a courageous and effective intervention.

I take this stand, not because what I say should be taken as absolutely certain or because I wish to dictate what the Church should do. It is rather that while awaiting a council we must cut off, so far as in us lies, the causes of dissension. Let us not do anything by force, and certainly do unto others what we would wish them to do unto us. Let us beseech heaven and earth, but in no way force anyone into a religion that repels him.[34]

To conclude the volume in the same spirit, a *Prayer for the Peace of the Church* recalled the central theme of Psalm 83, chosen as the argument for the treatise.

Except for Erasmus's wholehearted friends like Pflug and Witzel, *On Mending the Peace of the Church* did not receive the welcome hoped for. With Catholics as well as Protestants, the impression and even the accusation of indifference prevailed. Luther reasserted that he could not agree with a man who did not align himself with Scripture alone; later the Index was to condemn this work and judge it pernicious. Erasmus was not shaken by this. For him, concord was one of the marks of the truth of the Church, for peace and unanimity signified the presence of God among his own.[35]

Erasmus's moderation and prudence led him to recall the necessity for progressive and patient reforms in the Church.

Both parties stretch the rope so tight that it may break, to the misfortune of both: and this is the source of the world's disorder. They destroy all the images, that are both tasteful and useful. Let superstitious worship be destroyed, let images unbecoming or immodest for churches be destroyed, but gradually and without disturbance. They wish to throw out priests; let them do the deed, so that priests may be learned and godly, nor let anyone rashly be allowed to such an honour unless he is approved and worthy. There will be fewer: what then? It is better to have three good ones than 300 useless. They do not like the Church's worship. Much is sung and done in the churches that is not fit; let these faults be corrected, but gradually; let the worship remain. . . . Let those who are persuaded that the saints have no influence with Christ invoke the Father, Son and Holy Ghost in good faith. Let them honour the saints and let them worship them by imitating them; but let them not carp at those who honour and invoke them with godly affection. Let superstition be reproved; let affection be approved, which I think is not displeasing to Christ, even if it is deluded.[36]

In the same spirit, Erasmus showed his missionary preoccupations and spoke of the exploitation of tribes colonized by Christians. Faith only rarely entered into the calculations of the conquerors. He wrote to his Portugese friend Damião de Goes:

In your letter you lament with godly affection the ruin of the Lapps, whose worldly goods are stripped by Christian princes, yet are not allowed to grow rich with spiritual goods; they are oppressed by a human yoke, yet not taught to submit to Christ's gentle yoke. For those noblemen who measure victories by plunder prefer to rule beasts rather than men. Because of this, fewer nations which do not know Christ are joining the fellowship of the Church. They see that they are sought, not for Christianity, but for plunder and wretched slavery, and that bad morals are often found in Christians.

It is one thing to do business, but a very different thing to do the business of godliness. Wherefore, to state the case openly, it was not without distress that I read of the victories of that outstanding and fortunate general, who has plundered so many coastal cities, throwing into the sea what the ships could not carry off. But it would be better for me not to talk about military affairs, especially since I know too little about them and their circumstances. I shall say this in general: greed and the desire for ruling are not the least reasons that the Christian religion is caught in these straits. If they are tamed with gentleness and kindness, even wild beasts will eat out of one's hand; with harshness and unkindness even those which are gentle by nature are made savage.[37]

To Justus Decius, Erasmus denounced hoaxers who claimed to be his *famuli* or invented false letters to reap profit from them. 'I only warn you yourself to guard against such people, and to warn your friends to guard against them. How will I guard against them, you ask? If you believe none of their tales, unless they bring letters from me, signed by my own hand, and commending them by name.'[38]

Erasmus's position *vis à vis* the Anabaptists clearly reflected two of his fundamental principles. For the faith and practice of religion, hold to the essentials. For the solution of all problems, religious or otherwise, never turn to violence. In declaring to an unidentified correspondent: 'As for baptism, what the Church has preserved for so many centuries should be preserved,' he formulated a bold concession to peaceful Anabaptists: 'It could be left free to each parent, however, whether he prefers his child to be baptized straightway, or to leave it till adolescence, only meanwhile it should be instructed carefully in orthodox dogmas and holy morals.'[39] This unusual proposition aroused no reaction because its author had given it no publicity.

For Erasmus, baptism was essential, because it was in the Gospel. But the age required for baptism was secondary, because it was not in the Gospel. It is because baptism is the first of the sacraments that he favoured the repetition of its promises by the baptized who had arrived at the age of personal commitment. He would have been gratified if the Church had accepted his policy of openness, but the infant baptism professed by Rome had made impossible all conciliation or reconciliation.

As for violent Anabaptism, whose fate had been already sealed at Münster, Erasmus could only condemn it, while deploring the horrifying manner with which it was repressed: 'The Anabaptists ought not to be tolerated in any way. The Apostles order us to obey magistrates, and these people disdain to obey Christian princes. The sharing of goods should be out of charity, possession and the right of disposal should remain in the power of the owners!'[40]

His spirit of concord was shown one more time, when he said: 'If they disagree amongst themselves about the Eucharist, so that every day they produce ridiculous new opinions, how much wiser it would be to stay with the old doctrine, until either a General Council or divine revelation reveals something more certain.'[41]

One last time Erasmus took up his pen against Luther, in 1534, in a *Justification against the Errors of Martin Luther*,[42] a tightly argued message essentially concerned with peace and Christian unity. Concord was one of the marks of truth, of the truth of the Church in particular.

Had Erasmus, the anti-establishment theologian, become a conservative theologian? He gave this impression by his growing hostility to the Reformation and his firm defence of the threatened Catholic institutions. In fact, he had not rejected the idea of a dialogue between the parties and, if he was less lively in his expression, if his polemic had become less aggressive, he gave up none of his essential positions on the internal reform of the Church.

Old age is an incurable evil. Life carries us along and death awaits us. Erasmus realized this more every day. At Easter 1534, he had to say Mass in his room. His illness became more severe, sometimes intolerable. Circumstances lent themselves to the compilation of a *Preparation for Death*,[43] a true, spiritual testament of Erasmus. This meditation on death was presented as a meditation on the true life, alternating, in Erasmian manner, general considerations and practical advice.

The doctrine of the book was traditional. It went beyond the visceral fear of death, made a bet on the invisible and repeated with the Apostle: 'Death, where is thy victory?' Since death delivers the soul from the prison of the body, it was necessary, after having done what was possible to delay the day of reckoning, to accept it courageously, if not joyfully. In the *Handbook of the Christian Soldier*, Erasmus had already suggested the same ideas, the same attitudes. Here, there is a different emphasis. The meditation of the old man shows more serenity, a serenity due no doubt to the calming influence of age and spiritual depth.

From the first lines of its preface to Thomas Boleyn, a longstanding friend, who did not yet suspect the destiny of his daughter Anne, Erasmus proclaimed loftily that a good death was 'the very summit of Christian philosophy.'[44] Death was the gate of heaven, if preceded by a virtuous life.

> Therefore this meditation on death should be carried out throughout our whole life, and the spark of faith should be fanned continually, so that it may increase and be strengthened; joined to this, charity should entice hope, which will not cause any shame. We do not have any of these from ourselves, but they are God's gifts, to be solicited by frequent prayers and vows . . . Perhaps someone may think, 'At sometime I shall become a monk; then I shall bewail my badly led life; meanwhile I shall enjoy the world.' When life is present, who has promised you that will to desire repentance, to be embraced instead of pleasures? Or is anyone able to give himself that resolve? The sinner can succeed in returning to himself by Christ's grace alone. . . . It is certainly the desire of a Christian person that none of the sacraments be wanting, for they are great mental comforts and aids to our confidence; and it is a part of Christian uprightness to satisfy all justice, when it may; but it is more Christian to desire faith and charity, without which all is in vain.[45]

The book analysed the prayers most suitable for the Christian meditating on his final end. Erasmus cited the litanies of the saints, but he had little love for the invocation: 'Deliver us, Lord, from a sudden and unforeseen death.' He proposed a formula more in conformity with his thought: 'Deliver us, Lord, from an evil life.' For the occasion Erasmus gave examples of badly understood piety, like that of the Englishwoman who had paid very dearly for a priest – a bad priest, moreover – to say Masses on her behalf every day, during a year, in Rome, 'as if Roman Masses were better than British Masses.' He was disturbed by the false assurances given to those who were ill: they could only engender ridiculous illusions and painful disappointments. He felt sorry for those who placed their confidence in suspect customs, such as wanting to be buried in a monastic habit or making a reckless vow. Finally he condemned the thoughtlessness of the words addressed to the dying by friends under the influence, no doubt, of new doctrines. 'Those who say: "Believe that you will be saved and you will be saved", are doubly in error.'[46]

Despite all the ceremonies which prepared, accompanied and followed a believer's death Erasmus knew that Christianity was a religion of life and could not degenerate into a religion of death. It was life that mattered, it was for life that man existed, and a virtuous life remained the best assurance against eternal death.

To prepare for death is not to choose one's death, it is to accept the death which awaits us. By faith we already possess our hope, that hope which is not an alienation, but a realization. The dying man should pardon his enemies and accept the ordeal of suffering, finally count firmly on the help of the Church, the mystical body of Christ, and give back his soul to God in hope. To be sure, it was suitable to begin one's preparation in time, before the dimming of the intellectual faculties. It was when one was still lucid that one should receive the sacraments of penance and the Eucharist.

On the role and the place of the last rites, *The Preparation for Death* developed an opinion dear to its author – orthodox, although unusual. 'Indeed, I think that many people journey to their rest neither forgiven by a priest, nor having taken the Eucharist, nor been anointed, nor buried with Church rites; while others, with every ceremony solemnly performed, and even buried in church near the high altar, are carried off to hell. . . . The only conditions for a good death are burning faith and a brave will.'[47]

Certainly, Erasmus was in no way hostile to confession made to a priest. We do not know if he had heard confessions, but he himself confessed regularly and he bequeathed one of his jewels to one of his occasional confessors, Johann of Breisgau. To his friend Ludwig Baer, he had confided, in 1529, his respect for repentance: 'I never dared, or would dare, to approach Christ's table, or to leave this life without having confessed to a priest what weighed on my conscience.'[48] What he denied was the popular superstition which attributed a quasi-magical virtue to the sacraments, thus amounting to an attack on the dignity of man and the liberty of the Christian.

Erasmus believed that confession should be brief and sincere, and above all without ceremony! Once made, and made well, it was superfluous to repeat it and it was necessary to struggle against scruples and anxiety. And this gave him an argument more in favour of a virtuous life. 'Let our basic concern be to hate the faults confessed and to rediscover the frame of mind in which we were before we fell into sin. It is of prime importance to organize our lives in such a way that we never commit a serious sin. He who is capable of acting thus is exempt from the burden of confession.'[49]

Persuaded that if the priest gives absolution, it is God who pardons, Erasmus meanwhile advises confession to the sick who were in danger of death, but he dismisses the torture of the general confession proposed or imposed on the dying. It is useless for the sincere believer's peace of mind.

Though somewhat too long in its development, this text was of great religious depth, and was one of the most popular and the most widely diffused of Erasmus's works. Out of a meditation on death, it made a theme of spiritual life for the use of the pious Christian.

23

Return to Basel: Farewells

The years passed. Erasmus felt himself to be a long way from his youth and his first literary successes. Every day the task appeared more onerous to him, and his strength diminished. His whole aim henceforth was to end his work and his life worthily. Often sick and always tired, he was suffering from weakness, dependency and the humiliations of old age. More and more he felt himself to be alone.

Pirckheimer departed at the end of 1530. Warham, his friend and protector since the happy years in England, died in 1532. Pieter Gillis, who had been a link between Erasmus and More, followed him in 1533. In 1534 Mountjoy departed, one of his first pupils in Paris, the one who had drawn Erasmus to England.

The election of Alexander Farnese to the Papacy under the name of Paul III on 13 October 1534 encouraged Erasmus. He saluted the new Pope:

> Most blessed Father, the old man [Simeon] in the Gospels, cold in age, warm in godliness, remained alive for no other reason than that he might see the Lord's Christ: although I am like him only in old age, I have a certain feeling which is not completely unlike that. For I believe myself to be about to depart hence with a composed mind, now that after such storms of human affairs and whirlwinds of discords I see calm restored to the Church from heaven.[1]

In the silence of old age, Erasmus relived the vanished years, his rather sad childhood, the brutal death of his parents, his impassioned adolescence, his great friendships and perilous journeys. He turned the pages of his books and of his life. Silently he listened once more to *The Praise of Folly*, as if it were the work of a stranger reminding him that all is vanity. Where were the friends of yesteryear? Many were no longer of this world. What memories surrounded him! Some of the companions of his youth had become bishops and cardinals, while others had chosen to go over to the Reformation. Sadly, his faithful friends were so few and Erasmus read their letters once more with a melancholy spirit.

This obsession -- a temptation of unreason – threatened his always precarious equilibrium. Erasmus brought before the tribunal of his soul those who were opposed to his projects, and condemned them all once more. He had become a disappointed man, complaining and irritable, but he also remained a lucid man who tried to be reasonable and who ended by accepting in pure faith the aridity of the spirit, the irregularities of the memory, the constraints of old age, and in the end renunciation and death. His vitality was not found wanting and his courage astonished the few witnesses of his last years. Even more than throughout the rest of his life, he lived only for thought and by thought; or rather, thought alone at this time animated his worn-out body. His intellectual activity scarcely slowed down at all. What an alert intelligence was his! Again, and always until his last breath, he wrote to his friends, to the world, to God.

During the last years of his life, Erasmus suffered more and more in the flesh. Illness was his companion and held him captive. He was not very happy in Freiburg, which was too small a town for his liking, and he missed Basel, where the politico-religious troubles had eased. The Reformation was now established there, a Reformation without extremism. His nostalgia for the Netherlands became so much the stronger because he could not expect to return. Erasmus knew everything about death that the ancient and modern philosophers and theologians had taught him. This amounted to very little, nothing about *his* death, except that it was inevitable and menacing.

Though he worked with such perseverance, his work was slower and more painful. He slept badly, he wrote fewer letters, and these letters were shorter than before. He often had to dictate his correspondence and sometimes he was incapable of signing his letters. Used to a feeling of urgency, Erasmus worked feverishly, well aware of the work already accomplished. He saved his energies against the day when he could exert himself more. He managed his strength carefully, but not his sorrow.

Freiburg was to have been for Erasmus a haven and an exile. He decided, at the end of May 1535, to cast off for the last time and return to drop anchor in Basel,[2] the city he loved, where he was sure to benefit at the moment from a genuine personal toleration. He would be able to publish his most Catholic writings there without any obstacle. He was able to say to a friend: 'Believe me, the sects are no threat to me at all.' He found his old friends again and moved in to the house *Zum Luft* to oversee the printing of a new work.

Despite all his vicissitudes, hardly having finished his book on death, Erasmus in fact had taken up again enthusiastically a great project of his youth – a project for ever being deferred – the composition of a treatise on preaching. 'I am', he wrote to a friend, 'often and unhappily afflicted by gout, in both the hands and the feet. I have spent many days unable to write a word. I am forcing myself at the moment to conclude my work on preaching. I must fulfil my task earnestly after taking it up lightly. The volume is growing in proportion to my work on it.'

The volume appeared in August. It was heavy and laborious, the work of a whole lifetime.[3] It was a treatise of Christian rhetoric, enriched with wise advice and colourful anecdotes. Erasmus, who had so ferociously mocked bad preachers, displayed in it his pastoral care and missionary zeal.[4]

Against the Reformers who claimed a monopoly of preaching, he reminded all priests who had the care of souls that they should learn to preach well. He defined the rules of preaching; he specified its role in the life of the priest. On occasion he touched on religious art, and his ideas on this point were to be taken over by the Council of Trent. He did not condemn music in church, but he required that it should not be too intrusive at the expense of the sermon. Once again – and here the Council of Trent was not to follow him – he advocated the translation of the Gospel into the vernacular, to help preachers present the Word of God intelligibly. For the parish church truly to become the house of the people, it was necessary that the priest should speak there the language of his people. Meditation on the Gospel should go beyond a study of the text and be transformed into a questioning of the Christian. Erasmus believed that the Church would be present as long as there were people in it, but it should take care not to neglect the Gospel. The Word existed only to be announced, so that it might become light, warmth and nourishment.

It seemed at times less difficult, Erasmus observed, to talk to pagans rather than to Christians, since the latter were walled up in an impregnable self-assurance and shut off from any religious anxiety. The sermon was not an exercise in high acrobatic oratory, but a teaching, a witness and an evangelization, for the sacred orator had a mission to speak as a prophet during the Eucharistic sacrifice. The seriousness of the subject did not prevent some witticisms. 'If', Erasmus said 'elephants can be trained to dance, lions to play and leopards to hunt, surely priests can be taught to preach.'[5]

It was in Basel, to which he returned in 1535, that Erasmus received the Pope's reply. Paul III wrote in a kindly manner, expressing the desire that Erasmus should come to Rome to take part in the future

Council and he granted him the revenues of the Provost of Deventer. The Pope was thinking of bringing him into the College of Cardinals. Erasmus was flattered, but declined this belated dignity which would be for him only a purple shroud. He explained his refusal to Batholomaeus Latomus.

> Here is something to make you laugh. At the insistence of Ludwig Baer, the great theologian, I had written to Paul III. Before he handed over the letter, he spoke most enthusiastically about me. He had decided to enrol some learned men in the College of Cardinals, for a future Council. My name was put forward. But difficulties were put in the way: health incapable of undertaking the work, and meagre wealth. . . . Now they do this to load me with preferments, so that, providing the correct wealth, I may be presented with a purple cap. 'A gown for a cat', they say. I have a friend at Rome who is working particularly on this, warned in vain by more than one letter from me that I care for neither priesthood nor pensions, a man living for the day, every day awaiting death and often desiring it, so painful are my sufferings meanwhile. It is hardly safe to put a foot out of my bedroom, and even a donkey's sense would be too foolish for me. This poor body, thin and weak, can only bear warm air. And they wish to push one so afflicted out of here to beg for preferments and [cardinals' caps]. However, I am gratified by the supreme pontiff's mistake about me and his kindness towards me.[6]

In the same letter, Erasmus judged that it would be difficult to reunite a Council 'in such dissension of princes and countries'. Finally, he ended by a remark that was very Erasmian in its solicitude. 'I desire to know where the boy, whom I commended to you, lives. I request that meanwhile you address him lovingly. He has an excellent human father; he himself has a good disposition.'[7]

Moreover, bad news was not in short supply. The victims of intolerance – Protestants in France and in the Netherlands, and Catholics in England – were numerous. Fisher and More were beheaded in 1535 because they did not want to make themselves accomplices of Henry VIII, Head of the Church of England and schismatic King. 'In More', Erasmus lamented, 'I feel that I have died myself, as if there was one soul . . . for the two of us.'[8]

In 1535 Erasmus published a collection of prayers for all circumstances of life.[9] There is to be found an astonishing prayer of the unwilling combatant.

> Almighty Lord God Sabaoth, that is, of hosts, who through ministry of your angels guides both the wars and the peace of the nations, who granted to the young David both courage and strength, so that the weak boy, defenceless and untried in war, attacked and felled the giant Goliath

with a sling, I address my prayer. If this cause, for which I am forced to fight is just, first I pray that you turn the enemy's minds to the study of peace. May no Christian blood be poured on the earth, and no panic fear possess us. Let victory bring as little bloodshed as possible and with as little harm as possible. Let it come to those whose cause you approve, so that when the war is quickly finished, we may sing triumphal hymns to you with peaceful hearts![10]

For himself, Erasmus asks for benefit from illness and the favour of a Christian death.

Lord Jesus, sole Saviour of the living, eternal life to the dying, I submit and hand over myself completely to your most holy will, whether it pleases you that this little soul remain longer in the house of this poor body to serve you, or whether you wish me to journey from this world. . . . Grant your grace to my worsening illness, lest my faith waver, hope falter, charity become cold, human weakness be cast down by the fear of death; but, after death has seized my body's eyes, do not let my mind's eyes be turned from you, and, when the use of my tongue is gone, let my heart earnestly cry to you, 'Into your hands, Lord, I commend my spirit'.[11]

The book was véry classical in inspiration and some critics have wanted to see in it nothing but exercises in style. In its first part it put forward short prayers to the three persons of the Trinity and to Mary, prayers adapted to the seasons of the year and the necessities of the spiritual life: against temptation, in sadness, for communion, for a happy marriage, and so on.

The second part of the volume gathers together, in the spirit of the Modern Devotion, numerous ejaculatory prayers borrowed from Holy Scripture. These were 'arrows', little prayers and fervent invocations directed towards God. Erasmus was fond of these prayers for all occasions, these brief formulas which suited a man perpetually occupied, for whom work itself was also a prayer.

Finally, the reader rediscovers two long prayers to Christ, already published previously, such as the paraphrase of the Our Father. All Erasmus's prayers, without attaining the lyricism of Luther's prayers or the humour of Thomas More's, were clearly constructed and easy to read. This spiritual anthology, in the great Erasmian tradition, united elegance with eloquence. But were they just 'exercises in style'? They explained their author's religious ideas and pedagogical preoccupations admirably. The collection was to have a rapid and lasting circulation, thanks to numerous editions and translations.

If Erasmus showed himself to be preoccupied with his health, the finishing of his work and departure of his old friends, in the end the misfortunes of the Church and the world disturbed him even more. His horizon was singularly darkened by them, but he remained true to himself. To a sick disciple, Damião de Goes, he offered advice dictated by long experience.

I am amazed where this dizziness in the head comes from in a young man. Italy has excellent doctors, by whose advice you could banish this illness. You ought to guard against strenuous reading, especially after lunch and dinner; instead of reading, you should talk to learned people. Are you afraid of winter in balmy Italy? What would you do in Lapland? But if you are seriously afraid, take yourself to the sauna; you will be as warm as you wish.

And he continued, drawing on recent political events: 'There is also much discussion here about events in Africa: I expect new news from there sooner than good news. I am not very disturbed by such stories. Meanwhile lower Germany is completely destroyed by the Anabaptists. Münster has been taken. Everyone over twelve years old was killed, if the tale is true.'[12]

Instead of dreaming of the illustrious position to which Rome had invited him, Erasmus devoted himself to a simple friendly gesture. Some years before, he had discovered in Christoph Eschenfelder, who was employed on the city tollgate of Boppard, a faithful reader of his works, and here a new friendship had begun. Eschenfelder asked his friend to dedicate to him a commentary on a Psalm. Thus it was to the most humble of those who had not lost their faith in him that this honour fell: Erasmus dedicated to him the commentary on Psalm 14, composed in the midst of most cruel suffering. The *Purity of the Christian Church*[13] appeared in Basel in the course of February 1536.

This book is an illustration of true, inward piety. Some letters are attached to the commentary, making a final collection of letters of this small volume. The elegaic letter of Paul III took a prominent place in the collection. It irritated the humanist's intractable enemies. The Inquisitor Theodoricus Hezius wrote from Liège to the future cardinal Girolamo Aleandro:

Recently in Louvain I met the very learned doctor Jacques Masson [Latomus] who through his many important writings against the heretics and their friend Erasmus has given many proofs of his intelligence, knowledge and piety. He informed me that a new book by Erasmus is being sold in Louvain, including, among others, a letter from His Holiness Paul III to Erasmus himself, saluting him in an extraordinary manner not only for his firm doctrine and his eloquence, but for his rare piety and the uprightness of his conduct. The Pope, moreover, exhorts Erasmus to join him in defence of the Catholic faith leading up to, and during, the next general Council.[14]

Aleandro replied to Hezius in the same tone, promising him unreserved support.[15] The righteous indignation of the Liège inquisitor and of the Louvain theologian and future cardinal was enough to show that Erasmus's enemies had not been disarmed and that they still feared his influence at Rome.

Erasmus's situation was indeed novel and delicate, if not difficult: a Churchman isolated in the midst of dissidents. He explained it many times to different friends and one cannot say – as Luther did among others – that he wished for this situation. He accepted it, however, with a serenity which today still amazes those who are unaware of his problem in this domain.

Eustache Chapuys, Charles V's ambassador to London, wrote to him at length and in confidence. Telling him of the death of Katharine of Aragon, he explained to him how *The Preparation for Death* had sweetened the last moments of this unhappy queen.[16]

In February, Erasmus composed a new will, the will of a rich and generous man.

In the name of the Holy Trinity. I, Desiderius Erasmus, relying on the documentary authority of the Emperor, the Supreme Pontiff, and the Magistracy of the illustrious city of Basel, again specify my last wishes by this writing from my own hand, which I desire to have confirmed and ratified in every way, declaring null and void anything which I may have otherwise devised. First, in the certain knowledge that I have no legitimate heir, I constitute that pre-eminent man Bonifacius Amerbach the heir of my property, and as executors Hieronymus Froben and Nikolaus Bischoff. I have long since sold my library to Jan Laski of Poland, according to the terms of a contract on this point already made between us: however, the books are not to be delivered to him except on the payment to my heirs of 200 florins. If he shall fail in this contract, or if he die before me, then shall my heir be free to dispose of my books as he will. To Ludwig Baer I bequeath my gold watch; to Beatus Rhenanus a gold spoon together with a gold fork; to Pierre Vitré 150 crowns in gold, and the same sum to Philippus Montanus. I leave to my servant Lambert, if he shall be with me at my demise, 200 florins in gold, unless I have given him that sum previously. I bequeath to Johannes Brischius a silver bottle, to Paul Volz 100 florins in gold, and to Sigismundus Gelenius 150 ducats. To Johannes Erasmius Froben I leave two rings, of which one has no stone, and the other has a jewel which the French call a turquoise. To Hieronymus Froben I leave all my wearing apparel and household goods, whether they be of wool, of linen, or of wood; and in addition the cup which bears the coat of arms of the Cardinal of Mainz. To his wife I leave the ring which has the figure of woman looking backwards. To Nikolaus Bischoff I leave a goblet with a lid, which has verses inscribed on its foot; and to his wife Justina I bequeath two rings, one of which has a diamond, and the other a small turquoise. To Conradus Godenius I give a silver cup which has engraved on its top the image of Fortune. If any of these legatees had died in the meantime, what was bequeathed to them shall remain at the disposal of my heir. Besides these items which I have designated for him by this present writing, my heir shall receive whatever is left of the cups, rings or similar articles, and in addition the medals, insignia and Portugese crosses which bear engraved on them the heads of the King of Poland and Severinus Boner, and all such things of a similar nature. I leave to him also all the doubloons and larger coins. The money which I have on deposit with Conradus Godenius is to be left with him to expend in Brabant as I have directed. If there be any remaining in the hands of Erasmus Schets, let it be gotten from him, and also any other that may be over and above, and let my heir, according to his best judgement and with the advice of my executors, distribute it for the benefit of the poor and sick who are advanced in years, for maidens of a marriageable age, for young men of good promise, and generally for all those whom he shall deem worthy of assistance. This my last will I have written down with my own hand for greater faith, and have affixed the special seal of my ring, Terminus. At Basel . . . on the twelfth day of February, in the year of our Lord 1536.[17]

If one compares this text with that of the first will, it is a little different: Beatus Rhenanus is no longer among the executors of the will. Perhaps he had preferred to be relieved of this responsibility? Moreover, Erasmus omitted everything concerning the complete edition of his works. It seemed that he had hesitated for a long time in this regard. His friends, including Rhenanus, thought nevertheless that the grand design of their departed master, who had yearned with all his declining strength for a really complete edition of his works ought to be realized – not an expurgated or slanted edition, an *Erasmus Romanus* or an *Erasmus Wittenbergensis*, or even an *Erasmus grammaticus*. What was required was an Erasmus uncongenial to party loyalties, an Erasmus inexhaustible for future generations, an Erasmus changed by his own immortality.

Old age is not a shipwreck when it permits a man to finish his work. Erasmus was able to lay down his pen and envisage the future with serenity. He was not to have the quick death that he had wanted. We can follow, month by month, if not day by day, the irreversible decline of his health. At many periods of his life, he had believed death to be approaching. This impression returns as a fundamental theme in his rare confidences. Now, he was no longer mistaken. He described with a pitiless lucidity the evils from which he suffered. 'There is no hope that this poor body, broken by old age and work, will survive such torments any longer.'[18] Pessimism and resignation shared his spirit, just as stones and dysentery weakened his body. His head was heavy, his eyes closed. He had to give up his grand projects and clear the battlements that he had fortified with so much care. The play was ending, the old actor wanted to make his exit.[19]

The last winter was to be the longest and cruellest of all. Gout made it difficult for him to move. Visits exhausted him. He did not leave his bed, ate with difficulty and wrote only painfully when he could write at all. His room was peopled with the ghosts of departed friends. Requests were relentless.

And here comes so-and-so after lunch to greet me, and has kept me sitting by the fire for three hours arguing about dogmas of faith . . . and he had no intention of finishing before night. I interrupted his conversation and sent him away . . . Now these major torments are gone, but I am practically confined to bed, except for three hours around lunchtime and the same around dinner time.[20]

Between 16 March and 17 May 1536, he seemed to have been unable to write. He had apparently celebrated Mass at Easter, 16 April, in his room. He enjoyed a respite in May. Though suffering a great deal, he dreamed of a visit to Besançon and asked his *famulus* Gilbert Cousin to be there. The lull was of brief duration, and in June Erasmus was again obliged to stay in bed and suspend his work. 'Nevertheless,' he said, 'without this work life would be unbearable.' On 28 June, Erasmus wrote to his friend Conrad Goclenius, Professor at the Trilingual College in Louvain, in the last of his letters to have been preserved: 'Would that Brabant were nearer!'[21]

Erasmus had only two weeks to live, and these were sad and sombre days. He suffered in spirit as well as in body from knowing himself diminished, feeling himself lost. At certain moments he could no longer even read, but he did not stop thinking of his books and particularly of his dear Origen, the edition of which he was not to see. His immense intellectual output had finally come to an end.

Some of his friends made their farewells to the invalid in his house *Zum Luft*. Conrad Pellicanus first, then Hieronymus Froben, Bonifacius Amerbach and Nicolaus Bischoff. These last three came together to the bedside of the dying man who, coming to himself for a few moments, compared them to the friends of the unhappy Job, the model of unconditional faith.[22]

For Erasmus it was no longer a matter of the abstract or distant death of which he had spoken so well: here death had come real and near, more and more near. He prepared himself to die, since this was the only task remaining for him. He showed himself calm and patient. The time for great plans or endless disputes was gone, just as the temptations of rancour or vengeance had left him. Henceforth, no one would have to fear his pen.

To prepare oneself for death is to accept the empty space of days and sleeplessness of nights. He experienced, to the point of nausea, the loneliness, lassitude and vicissitudes of this final struggle. While his relative isolation preserved him from the humiliation of seeing his agony transformed into a spectacle, he recognized that he was a sinner and proclaimed his faith. He abandoned himself to prayer, which dispelled his fantasies and reassured his hopes. 'Though I walk in the valley of the shadow of death, I will fear nothing, for you are with me.'

Finally, on the night of 11 or 12 July 1536, these were the last words uttered with his last breath: *O Iesu, misericordia! Domine, libera me! Domine fac finem! Domine miserere mei! Lieve God!*[23] Watched over by a *famulus*, Erasmus died as he had lived, calling on God.

Erasmus's funeral was celebrated in an ecumenical spirit. His body, carried by students and accompanied by friends, who were joined by representatives of the city and the University, was placed in the Chapel of the Virgin in the Cathedral. A tombstone, with a long epitaph engraved on it, composed by Bonifacius Amerbach, today still recalls his incomparable work.[24]

24

Erasmus's Personality

In Erasmus's life there was no dominant external event. All his activity was of an intellectual order; it was devoted to research; it was translated into his books and his letters. Should he be seen as a man of the library, enclosed in his ivory tower? Certainly, books constituted his familiar setting, but he did not live only among his books. The world was present in his thought, and it was for the world that he continually wrote in order to remind it of the conditions of its well-being. Erasmus's destiny, considered in its successive phases, was remarkably varied; it was often unexpected and sometimes disconcerting. Nothing which resembles the uneventful life of an intellectual withdrawn into himself!

We can make this judgement if we review the major stages of his journey. It was in the monastery that Erasmus became a humanist and it was in the world that his passion for the philosophy of Christ burst forth. The Netherlands brought him a basic classical and theological education, then a taste for international problems. From France he received his University training, and he owed to it his contact with the world of the pre-Reformation. In England he discovered Florentine Platonism, and he went to Italy to improve his knowledge of Greek. Julius II confirmed Erasmus in his pacifism as well as in his reformism, while the Faculties of Theology made him an enemy of scholasticism. Thus the major features of Erasmus's training as humanist and theologian stand out before our eyes.

Like everyone else, Erasmus unified his aspirations very deeply – his ideas and his work. From his youth he had constructed a harmonious mental universe, bringing together theology and philosophy, art and learning, pacifism and loyalty, fervour and tolerance. A comprehensive vision of his life and work shows him to us struggling at the same time for and against philosophy, for and against theology, for and against the University and monasticism.[1] He was a son of his time, the Renaissance, but he transcended the preoccupations of his contemporaries.

Before all else, Erasmus aspired to the good use of things and judged the tree by its fruits. He was in full support of good philosophy, good theology and so on.[2] On the other hand, no one was more hostile than he to what he called bad theology, bad philosophy, decadent studies and piety that had gone astray, the latter, above all, when it was pressed into the service of war.

Here was a fine programme for such a frail and vulnerable man! He was to go to the limit of audacity and to live dangerously. He was not to abandon himself to gloom. He was to withstand all the tempests and to overcome the crises of mood or of discouragement. Calm followed after storms in his life, just as faith followed disappointment.

Many times, in his letters as in his *Apologies,* Erasmus described his actions and justified his work.

> I saw the saintly Doctors of the Church regarded, some of them, as obsolete and out of date, and all in a corrupt, confused, and filthy state. I saw the teaching of the holy Gospel almost overlaid with the petty comments of men, and the gospel texts buried in mistakes as though in brambles and tares. Of course at this point it was piety, and not a choleric nature, that made me emphatic. No gentle, peaceful voice could rouse the world from such deep lethargy.[3]

In 1527 he found the formula which defined it best and shows us the essence of Erasmianism.

> So I shall give you a summary of what I have always done in my books. I protest strongly against the wars with which for so many years we have seen nearly the whole of Christendom stricken. I have tried to recall theology, too greatly fallen into sophistical subtleties, to its sources and early simplicity. . . . I was there when ancient languages flourished anew, at least as far as I had strength.[4]

The realization of such a project demanded exceptional gifts and heroic perseverance. Erasmus's magnetism operated from his youth but, as personal as it was, his talent owed much to the influences he underwent. Among these beneficial contacts, we need to recall the intellectual current of humanism and the spiritual vigour of the modern devotion, the exegesis of the Fathers, finally the stimulating friendship of his models Jean Vitrier and John Colet. From the beginning of the century of the Renaissance and Reformation, Erasmus's plan was marked out: he devoted himself to good letters, to peace and to the renewal of the Church.

To be sure, we know Erasmus's work better than its author. We can reach the man only through his work, which was immense. I would have neither the impertinence nor the naïveté to pretend to summarize such a long story in a few pages. After so much research, there remains much that is unknown. The mystery of individual psychology escapes us and we, who know ourselves so badly, cannot pretend to know Erasmus better than ourselves. Just as the finest portrait does not restore the presence of the model who is no longer there, the finest analysis could only skim over the personality of the subject studied.

On his intellectual qualities, historians are clearly unanimous. Erasmus was an original thinker and a brilliant writer. His work was exceptionally rich. In his works we can observe a mingling of elegance and simplicity: the elegance and simplicity of an artist who had moreover the genius of improvisation. He excelled in all genres: familiar letters, polemical apologies, poems of piety, pedagogical dialogues, religious pamphlets, moral dissertations, translations and classical editions. Provocative in *The Praise of Folly*, he showed a pleasing erudition in the *Adages*, a studied facility in the *Colloquies*, while displaying his fervour in the *Paraphrases*.

But Erasmus did not escape from the common lot; he evolved and changed. He changed sometimes from one day to the other and he evolved as he became older. He was more friendly now than before, but his letters were harder and more prickly when he had received bad news. He was not the same at twenty years as at sixty. He would not have written the letters to Servatius Rogerus at the end of his life and he would not have been capable of composing his great works when he was still in his Dutch monastery.

To read his letters from Steyn for the first time is disconcerting. The traditional Erasmus – satiric author, skilful story teller, religious writer or formidable polemicist – cannot be recognized. Here we are in the presence of an unexpected Erasmus, sentimental, tortured and touching. Where is the real Erasmus? Here and there, to be sure. He was, at different ages, the same being who laughed or cried, who told stories or talked about himself, who taught or reprimanded.

Erasmus changed, but he did not change altogether. He was marked first of all by his origins. His birth was irregular and he was a orphan, with few means. Fame came later, this wine more heady than the best Burgundy in his cellar. Then affluence, the relative failure of his projects, bitterness, and finally, the calm of his last years. There was, however, a steady foundation in him, positive elements of intelligence and sensibility preserved to draw his psychological portrait, reserve resulting from his genius, which cannot be analysed or catalogued, but which posterity has recognized from the sixteenth century up to our own day.

Through the course of his life, Erasmus showed himself successively serious and cheerful, patient and anxious, temporizing and bold, strong and vulnerable, simple and refined, profoundly religious and ferociously anti-clerical. He was a free spirit, a vigorous contestant, an apostle on occasions, in turn impassioned and casual, reticent and garrulous. He was perpetually on the alert and his solitary destiny has something pathetic about it. In controversy he could show himself vindictive; his perspicacity was remarkable and his barbed thrusts caused harm. He had the temperament of an artist and the gifts of a writer, the rigour of a philologist and a touch of mysticism. He was at once ironic and eirenic, which did not fail to arouse awful misunderstandings, for he could not resist the pleasure of making an epigram and he managed to shock those whom he wanted to rally to his side.

Erasmus did not go unnoticed. He left no one indifferent. Those who knew him loved or detested him. His intelligence drew them, his subtlety disturbed them, his malice angered them. With him, boldness went further than circumspection, or even cunning. Generally discreet in the expression of his intimate life, he occasionally went astray in vain polemics. Weak and sickly, he admitted that his health, in great measure, depended on his character and his mood. His prudence sometimes took time off, and his malice had wings and claws. He had the stature of a thinker and the weaknesses of a man of letters who was a past master in the art of evasion.

These contradictions appear irreconcilable to those who think it necessary to have recourse to psychoanalysis to throw a new light on Erasmus's character.[5] Psychoanalytic explanation is surely legitimate but, in the absence of adequate documents, psychoanalysis applied to history – psycho-history – has not so far managed to draw a very firm outline of the unconscious structures of Erasmus's personality. The fact that he had imposed on himself throughout his life a severe discipline of work despite his frail health prevents us from describing him as psychotic, while it cannot be suggested either that he suffered from a persecution mania. He did not see enemies where there were none. His enemies existed and showed themselves. Erasmus always had a quick reply for them, and defended his reputation – sometimes, it is true, with a marked acrimony. I see no more reason to believe – there is no documentation for it – that Erasmus took delight in the role of dispenser of justice or victim. The paranoid attitude attributed to him by some seems no better established than his homosexual tendency, so impenetrable does the obscure and hidden part of him remain to us. Though it is easy to assert of almost all theories that they agree with *some* facts, a hypothesis is only verified if all the arguments against it are refuted.[6]

Classical psychology remains more capable of clarifying the complexities of biography, in a limited but reliable degree. Its results are more modest, but more solid. The complexity of Erasmus's personality enriches it and adds to its appeal. It becomes clearer when one knows him better, that is to say when one gives him the floor and listens to him patiently. The portraits of Erasmus by Metsys, Dürer or Holbein help us to see him as his contemporaries saw him. But while they illuminate his character for us, they are less valuable than his letters.

Erasmus endured solitude better than community life. His morality appears to be good. Celibacy did not embitter him; he weighed up its advantages and did not stress its drawbacks. His friends and his books, his work and his piety filled his whole life. That life drew him from country to country and from city to city. A celibate free in his movement is readily mobile, even when he leaves with his library, as was the case with Erasmus. His mobility provoked an admiring or envious wonder in his correspondents. Thomas More replied to those who treated his friend as unstable: 'Is it the last word in piety to remain for all time without moving, encrusted on the same rock like an oyster or a sponge?' When he had gained financial independence, he was to settle in Basel, then Freiburg. He had been a nomad only out of necessity, and one cannot speak seriously of his instability.

Erasmus's writings depict throughout a passionate, sensitive and susceptible individualist, with a total independence of spirit. 'Without liberty, life is not life at all', he proclaimed. Or again: 'If I see my liberty threatened, I will give up everything.' He was not one of those who always say yes to their superiors. He did not take the wishes of the Pope or the Emperor as orders. For him, obedience did not suppress responsibility, because it did not abolish reason. He never accepted the idea of declaring white what he saw to be black. A free man knows when he must obey and when he should say no. A scholarly dose of critical spirit and respect for traditions assured his spiritual equilibrium. Rarely euphoric, he passed through periods of depression and exaltation, but took himself in hand with determination.

As Erasmus changed over the years, he had the temperament of a pioneer, but not the spirit of a conqueror. He distrusted excesses as much as extremes. It was said of him that he was too clever. True, he was not clumsy, but he was above all prudent and measured in his speech. He inclined towards reserved attitudes and reflective processes of thought. Those who accuse him of being faint-hearted forget the boldness of his pen and the conscious or unconscious provocativeness of his most famous writings.

The need for friendship was both Erasmus's strength and his weakness. Deprived of familial affection, he loved to be loved. To love was his nature. He was faithful to his friends and was unsparing with his advice, even if they had not asked for it. In difficult moments, friends formed a watchful guard around him. When they disappeared as the years went by, Erasmus suffered and reflected nostalgically on the gaps caused by death. With him the heart was no hindrance to the spirit.

He said of himself that he was 'born for love' and 'a man with few friends'. It was not out of pride that he revealed himself only to a chosen few, it was because he believed friendship to be a serious and deep feeling, not related to a superficial camaraderie. He had nothing of the popularity seeker about him, he was no friend of the whole human race. He had nothing of the gregarious spirit, any more than of the party spirit.

One must admire his sense of dialogue, his fidelity to the humanist ideal and to religious commitment, and finally, his prodigious application to work. Nothing could break down his joy at being harnessed to a task which he had chosen for himself. His perseverance and his courage were perhaps the most moving aspects of Erasmus's personality. He was one of those fragile beings who can do the work of four men with invincible determination. All that he knew, all that he had, all that he was, he invested in his work. He remains for us an astonishingly energetic teacher.

Some have thought that a good part of that energy was spent in the search for material gain. It is true that Erasmus, an orphan since his adolescence, entered upon life without a large personal fortune. His tutors pushed him towards the religious state that they considered the most advisable for a needy intellectual without relatives. When he left the monastery, Erasmus was poor. Being a secretary and a tutor brought him an irregular income. Finally, patrons and printers assured his subsistence. Erasmus succeeded little by little, and not without difficulty, in living by his pen. At forty-five years of age, he was affluent, but without having succeeded in ridding himself of a difficult future. He was to die rich.

Erasmus scarcely tells us anything of his inward life – he was too secretive to unburden himself – but his piety is in no doubt. It is enough to read the numerous prayers that he had composed to recognize in him a man of spiritual greatness and even a 'yearning mystic.'[7] If he yielded to vanity when he spoke of his literary successes, he was humble when he spoke of his relations with God. He does not seem to have tried out the spiritual favours which crown the mystical life. He speaks of them as a well-informed theologian, refusing to consign religion to an everyday greyness.

He had never denied his priesthood, though he broke with the life of the monastery. He passed his life as a free priest, avoiding all scandal. He married the Word, and asked nothing for himself. He had no longing for marriage, and remained faithful to his priestly commitment.

Did this commitment show his orthodoxy? This is a question that is difficult to deal with in a decisive way. As far as I am concerned, if I have no doubt as to Erasmus's orthodoxy, it is above all because he affirmed it strongly and frequently. Some of his enemies and biographers have denied this profession of faith, judging that it hid a profound scepticism and that Erasmus attacked Christianity while pretending to respect it.

Now it has often been observed that 'the burden of proof, in history as before the law, rests with him who wants to prove something that is contrary to the overt evidence.'[8] In accordance with proper methods, the declarations of a normal man about himself should be believed until there is proof to the contrary. I have never met this proof in the case of Erasmus and gratuitous accusations cannot take their place any more than rash interpretations. At the same time, I do not see that one could seriously pretend that Erasmus, though inwardly satisfied with his relationship with Christ, should consider approval of the hierarchical Church to be insignificant. This hypothesis has not been demonstrated any more than the preceding one. It is highly improbable since, for Erasmus also, 'Christ and the Church are one.'

Might we describe Erasmus as a saint? This question – often posed – is disconcerting enough for those of us who know human beings only from the outside – their visible behaviour, sometimes even the person that they construct for posterity. How can we avoid presenting an apologia? How can we distinguish scandal-mongering from calumny? Where are the secret virtues and the hidden vices?

All that we can reply is that Erasmus scarcely resembles the pious images of traditional sainthood. His brow was not illuminated by a halo. Of those he greatly admired – St Paul and St Jerome – there was nevertheless something we must remember: the impatience of St Paul and Jerome's vanity as an author. Certainly Erasmus had these two character traits, but did he, on the other hand, possess the asceticism of Jerome and the heroic virtue of Paul? Like his master Origen, Erasmus had rather the style of a doctor, but, also like Origen, he was not like a saint in a stained-glass window. Despite his ardent zeal for the cause of the Gospel, despite the strength of spirit with which he welcomed suffering, he was not a saint.

He had his weaknesses; he was ironic, wounding in his words, difficult to live with, an egotist even, combining the knowledge of how to please with the ability to do so. His susceptibility was the price paid for his sensibility. He was no courtier at all, and could not be imprisoned with collars or large sashes. This little priest was not born on his knees and we must recognize in him great courage in his work as a writer, in his campaign of reform, in his scorn for honours and finally in the condition of illness and the constraints of age. Half Oedipus and half Don Quixote, Erasmus was an Oedipus without Antigone and a Don Quixote without Sancho Panza.

Erasmus had his grandeur and his limits. He knew himself to be a sinner, but he believed that a sinner was always a Christian – a poor Christian, as long as he loved God. Death was to find him true to himself. He was among those theologians who, as he said it, must prove their doctrine by their behaviour. 'Anyone who cannot love Erasmus as a Christian, though a feeble one, must adopt what attitude he pleases towards him. I for my part cannot be different from what I really am.'[9]

Despite his trials, failures and disillusionments, he held on. He did not become a miser, and he persevered in the path he had traced out for himself. It was his faith, an intrepid faith, a faith of the warrior, that permitted him to triumph over the disappointments of the man of thought and the weaknesses of a man of action. For him, closer to Pascal than to Voltaire, grace always abounded. He was an optimist, but he was not blind: among the serious faults in history, he pointed to a steady lack of education, the permanence of war and a certain decline in Christianity. Against these evils which weighed down a world which was losing its bearings, he had struggled until his last day, through his love of good letters, his pacifism and his demanding Christianity.

Erasmus's words on death prefigured an end which was foreseen and prepared for with care. The unusual aspects of this solitary death can only scandalize those who suspect laxity in all nonconformity. Despite appearances, in his death, as well as in his life, he was inspired by a Christianity which was adult and responsible, free from fear, always seeking. His idea of death brought together pagan wisdom and Christian hope. Socrates was his model, the Stoics his masters, it is true, but he never forgot that, in the face of death, a life given to God is the greatest of securities. The philosophy of the ancients had taught him that it was suitable to die with dignity; the philosophy of Christ had convinced him that he must die in hope.

25

The Assessment of a Life's Work: Literature, Peace, the Philosophy of Christ

The love of literature showed itself exceptionally early in Erasmus. His studies prepared him for the mastery of Latin and an apprenticeship in Greek. Invoking Basil, Augustine, Jerome and Cyprian, he praised antiquity, without approving the depraved customs of the pagans. He exalted *bonae litterae*, good letters. They were good because they were beautiful and he dreamed of inculcating through them *boni mores*, good habits, in his disciples. The propaedeutic function and the moral value of classical culture were beyond question for him, from the moment when, pen in hand, he began to analyse the texts as explained by the masters and at times to expurgate them discerningly.[1]

None of the triumphs of science or art left him indifferent. Nothing would be too much in his peaceful arsenal, though he had no ambitions of becoming a universal man, like Paracelsus or Copernicus. Conquered by the key idea of the Renaissance, return to the sources, Erasmus insisted eloquently on the irreplaceable value of a text read in its original language.

> Fruit tastes better when you have picked it with your own hands from the mother tree; water is fresher if you draw it as it bubbles up from the actual spring; wine is pleasanter when you have drawn it from the cask in which it was first laid down. In the same way the Scriptures have about them some sort of natural fragrance, they breathe something genuine and peculiarly their own, when read in the language in which they were first written.[2]

The understanding of Christian humanism developed progressively in Erasmus. To sing of the wonders of God well, he needed the Muses' inspiration and all the charms of style. More than anyone, he stressed the profound agreement between antique and Christian ideals; there was no gulf, but rather historical continuity, between Antiquity and

Christianity. The religion of Christ realized to the full the most elevated moral impulses of the Ancients: from that point there should flow among Christians the spirit of optimism, of moderation and adaptation, the will to be man in perfection. Erasmus celebrated the harmony of nature and grace just as he admired the union of antique culture and Christian philosophy.

Against the 'barbarians' he made himself the champion of textual criticism, and he applied that method to the Bible as well as to the classical authors.[3] Why study the Gospel in the Vulgate alone, despite its errors, when one has a Greek text which is both older and purer? Every theologian ought to be first of all a cultivated man, a humanist. Philology is no threat to exegesis, but makes it possible. Humanism's desire is that Latin and Greek be studied in the best authors – the ancients – and in the best texts of those authors, freed of prose or verse commentaries. Here were the *humaniores litterae*, centred on literature. Erasmus understood better than others that the roots of European civilization were in Athens, Rome and Jerusalem. To cut oneself off from these roots would be to kill humanism and to undermine Europe's heritage.

A defender of studies, Erasmus taught very little himself. He respected the calling of the teachers, and praised it, but this was not his calling, because he could not abandon scholarly research to devote himself to the necessary popularization for teaching. He was content for the most part to be a pedagogical adviser, a teacher of teachers. To hear him talk, it was never too early to undertake the education of children. He carefully compiled books for introducing the young to culture. He published examples of letters, of models of conversation, of summaries of grammar and he endeavoured to enrich the Latin vocabulary of future humanists, while improving their pronunciation. His *Method of Study* was the manifesto of a modern pedagogy moving from words to things and planning a deeper study of the best Greek and Latin authors. 'In principle, knowledge as a whole seems to be of two kinds, of things and words. Knowledge of words comes earlier, but that of things is the more important.'[4]

There was no classical author with whom Erasmus was unacquainted. In his very first letters the great writers of Antiquity hold a leading place, and he was never to abandon them. It was to them that he owed his perfect knowledge of the Latin language which allowed him to create for himself a style that was personal, lively, colourful, adaptable and forceful. Whether it was a question of philology, theology or pedagogy, Erasmus profited fully from the amazing progress of printing which he called 'an almost divine tool'. His numerous books, often reprinted, spread his ideas across Europe with impressive speed.

He used Latin and sometimes Greek. He would have loved to have known Hebrew, but he started too late in life. Nevertheless, what he could not achieve for himself he wanted to offer others by organizing the Trilingual College in Louvain, for the three sacred languages. He haughtily ignored modern languages. He did not know Machiavelli, and did not read Luther in German. As for Rabelais, who called himself his disciple, there is nothing to indicate that Erasmus knew *Pantagruel.* When Gaguin published the *History of the French*, Erasmus praised him for having chosen to write in Latin. For him modern languages were not literary, but merely utilitarian. To be sure, he understood French and German, and was to rediscover his native Dutch in the hour of his death; but he was in no way a polyglot. Only Hebrew, Greek and Latin deserved in his eyes to be called the mother tongues of the West.

In this respect Erasmus did not share the aspirations of the Renaissance. He did not foresee the prodigious expansion of the modern languages, nor understand their literary value. He guessed none of their importance in terms of nationhood, unless he neglected them for this very reason. He still dreamed of Latin as a universal language, adaptable and living, as distant from Ciceronian as from scholastic Latin. Historically he remained the first champion of classical humanism and the last of the great Latin writers.[5]

As a poet or as a prose writer Erasmus was first of all a humanist who imitated glorious models. So, in his first writings, there was a perceptible search for ornaments and effects in expression. Yet he never slavishly imitated the style of Cicero's period whose moral thought he admired and he gradually disengaged himself from rhetorical artifice. His style then became more polished and personal and acquired a unique charm.

Erasmus skilfully made use of the concrete details and images of daily life; he was sensitive to the magic of words – above all when they were set in a beautifully printed page. Quotations were never a pretence or padding for him, but a deliberate choice to illuminate and reinforce the discourse. His prose was nimble and musical. He played with assonance and alliteration; he used the repetition of a similar sound, without overdoing it. He obtained unexpected effects from verbal accumulation or verbal antitheses, from the use of diminutives, from the balancing of clauses and the complementarity of phrases.

In the writings of this learned priest, there is no trace of ecclesiastical unctiousness or pedagogical weight. Erasmus united 'the graces of style' with 'universal knowledge', as one of his correspondents said to him.[6] He attained freely and effortlessly, with apparent disorder, a calm casualness and a very sure skill in digression. He moved easily from simple verbal effects to oratorical display. He proceeded by successive approaches or by calculated allusions, with some detours at times, indeed with somersaults. The sharpness of his analysis was most often wrapped in feigned sweetness or subtle irony, except when he had to recourse to risqué images or brilliant paradoxes.

Erasmus composed easily, too quickly on occasion, and he scarcely ever read over what he had written. 'I venture to say that almost all my works have been dashed off rather than published. Many times what I had in hand I wouldn't keep even an hour, going so far as to hand pages still damp with ink to the typesetters.' When he made corrections, he would add to his text more frequently than take something out. He wrote with as much temper as wit, giving himself fully to what he was writing.

All genres were familiar to him, from religious poetry to satiric prose. He excelled in essays, dialogues and letters. His prose revealed a perfect knowledge of the task of the writer and, beyond that, an ever-sparkling personal inspiration.[7] When he forced a point, he preserved a natural tone. A good storyteller,[8] he depicted characters more easily than scenes; he described neither Rotterdam nor Basel and, when he spoke of the sea, it was only to recall its dangers.

Erasmus was a master of understatement and studied omission. He used every stylistic device with virtuosity. His prose was nevertheless transparent even in its most allusive innuendos because his thought was clear. He was obscure only when he wanted to be,[9] and sometimes disconcerting, but never incoherent.

His letters bring him infinitely near to us. All of them demand to be read. Some are touching, some edifying, some amusing, some jarring, some threatening. Others are lyrical, emphatic, laconic, humorous. None of them is ridiculous, absurd or preposterous. The most beautiful were published at his own expense.

Erasmus taught his readers the distinction and variety of types of letters. His masters were Cicero, Pliny the Younger, Petrarch, Aeneas Sylvius and Angelo Poliziano. He had a high opinion and an incomparable experience of familiar and descriptive correspondence which 'displays the writer's character and fortunes and sentiments, like a picture and both private and public affairs.'[10] And he maintained a conversational tone throughout. In a word: he had all the qualities of a brilliant journalist! But he rarely wrote under the impact of events or in the heat of immediate reaction. He tempered his emotion better than his irony.

Boldness and prudence characterize Erasmus's letters as a whole, with here and there a clashing blend of candour and malice, for example when, in a letter to Pope Adrian VI, he praised the 'sweet name of liberty'. This was in 1523, the year of the first martyrs of the Reformation.

Into his most serious letters he introduced stinging touches and sharp allusions. In this he remained faithful to one of his principles: to speak of serious things with a smile, and to speak of light things with gravity. It was better to treat trifles seriously than to utter trifles on serious subjects.[11]

From his youth, Erasmus loved to write letters. His passionate need to communicate spread and blossomed in them. Throughout his life, he was to write with this facility, with that happy exultation that comes from work well done and work of one's own choice. With pen in hand, he feared no one, and his enemies knew this and were afraid of it. In his letters even more than in his other writings, we see Erasmus alive, we hear the echo of his great hopes and his petty calculations, his disappointments and his regrets, his sufferings and his joys, but also of his genius.

Erasmus's pacifism is one of the most original aspects of his work. It was the dream – sometimes the nightmare – which had haunted his days and nights.[12] It seems to me impossible to understand Erasmus's deep motivations in this area unless we remember the Gospel teaching of brotherly love, for this teaching, then common throughout the West, from the heads of state to the most humble of their subjects, was the sole barrier to nationalism. The general indifference into which that doctrine has fallen for centuries undoubtedly constitutes the most serious, and the most bloody, setback to Christianization. On the other hand for Erasmus and his peers, the Gospel remained a living and enlivening reality whose demands must be unceasingly recalled to Christians.

Erasmus always set himself against war, sometimes with very important nuances in the appreciation of political facts. All his statements are linked together and form an extension of his personal meditation. From his youth, he pleaded for peace. When he began to become known, his major interventions were tied to the history of the Netherlands. His last writings on war recalled the great confrontations of the Habsburg-Valois war.

If Erasmus spoke easily of European countries, it was because he had travelled widely. He was in the Netherlands in his youth and maturity, at Basel and then at Freiburg in his old age. He had spent three years in Italy, six in England and more in France. He observed, and noted the qualities and the faults of each people. As a general rule, Erasmus claimed to be Dutch with the Dutch, and German with the Germans. He praised England to the English and France to the French. This shows clearly that national rivalries were not worthy of his attention. What counted first in his eyes was the country of birth. He gave his entire loyalty to the Netherlands, though he bitterly emphasized the faults of his compatriots in the South as well as in the North. He also belonged to the Empire, that is to say at once to the German world and to the Holy Roman Empire. At the same time he regarded Basel as his homeland. Being born in the Empire and ending his days in Basel did not prevent Erasmus from speaking of England and of France alternately as his home country. If he criticized the French, and even more the Italians, he held an almost entirely favourable view of the English.

On occasion Erasmus made a distinction between Italy and its capital. When he said of Rome that it was the 'common fatherland', he was thinking of eternal Rome, ancient and Christian Rome. In this sense, Rome was his fatherland. The expression 'common fatherland' was an expression of a profound conviction. The man who talked in this way could not be the citizen of a historical fatherland. His homeland was where he felt most at ease. It was indeed everywhere he was loved and as long as he was loved. *Ubi bene ibi patria!*

This attachment to human beings and relative indifference to institutions was very Erasmian. Nations quarrelled over Erasmus, but he gave himself to all and belonged to none. His paradoxes give us an exact account of his vocation. He was not allergic to the principle of patriotism. When he spoke of Charles V, his emperor, we can note the power of his loyalty, but also assess its limits, for he had no hesitation in declaring the conditions of the Treaty of Madrid too severe and he refused to support the idea of universal monarchy through his writings.

If Erasmus habitually praised the countries through which he travelled, he was steadfast in avoiding any indication of his preferences. He preferred to hold several nations together in the same esteem or in equal admiration. He praised the agreement signed in 1520 by Charles V and Henry VIII just as, in 1529, he praised the Ladies' Peace which reconciled the Emperor and the King of France. He dedicated his *Paraphrases* on the four Gospels even-handedly to the four great rulers of his time – Charles, Ferdinand, Francis and Henry.

As he grew old, Erasmus became more sensitive to the question of the defence of Europe, this 'little end of the world that it left to us'. He went much further when he spoke out, with calm boldness, against the exploitation of national names. These names were 'very stupid labels', because they had become the names of factions. They separated and divided, whereas the scholar, the Christian and the man ignored frontiers. Among his contemporaries, Erasmus emphasized those whom the brotherhood of studies brought together.[13]

In short, Erasmus's homeland was first of all his birthplace, then the land which made him welcome, finally and above all the Christian world, Europe, the 'republic of letters' and the whole of humanity, waiting for the heavenly homeland. In him all these ideas came together and were fulfilled. He was by choice a rootless man. For this apostle of peace, nationalism was incompatible with Christianity and humanism. 'My own wish is to be a citizen of the world, to be a fellow-citizen to all men – better still a pilgrim. If only I might have the happiness of being enrolled in the city of heaven.'[14] This justly famous statement acquires its full value if we remember that for Erasmus, as for St Augustine, 'the Christian is he who considers himself a foreigner in his own house and his own country', a stranger who has here no permanent resting place.

The 'common homeland' dear to Erasmus was not of this world, and it was war that he met along the way. He condemned it without respite and without reservation time and time again. Throughout these declarations, some features remain unchanged: war is a bad risk; it brings with it the most frightful evils; it is a perversion of nature and a betrayal of the Gospel. On these essential points Erasmus was never to relent. He struggled resolutely for the restoration and maintenance of peace. His rare concessions went no further than the principle of a defensive war. Peace was not only the absence of war; it encompassed a teaching activity, a religious ethic, a positive policy.

We should not find recipes for preserving peace in his writings. He wanted to change the human heart, and appealed to the human conscience. Erasmus found lyrical accents to evoke the irrepressible horror of war and the wonderful attraction of peace. War could not but leave behind ruin and mourning, lives wounded and souls bruised. In the course of his meditation, Erasmus seems to carry the weight of the world, an upside-down world in which life is despised, and death dealt out or suffered. Not indifferent to the distress of the nameless masses, he gave expression to his compassion in a long cry of grief, so that the princes responsible might recognize their errors with sincerity and overcome them with courage.

As an alert moralist, he eloquently compared war and peace. When he came to the necessary remedies for a disordered world, he had less to say, and he who wrote so much has left us no trace of a political philosophy. Apart from conversion to the Gospel, he could only appeal to experience and good sense. He left the task of transforming laws to the statesmen and jurists; it was enough for him to touch hearts and awaken consciences. It belonged to men to build the peace which God inspires.

Erasmus's advice, we know, was aimed principally at kings and their ministers, to whom he proposed a code of good conduct. Sadly, princes sometimes become tyrants, unsparing of the blood of others and devoid of the most elementary humanity. They surround themselves with sycophantic ceremonial, furthering the exaltation of glory and the personality cult. These are nevertheless the ones whom Erasmus wanted to transform by persuading them to listen to the one who utters the words of eternal life. He addresses himself to kings as if they had already been won over to the cause of peace. He pretends to believe in the sincerity of the great ones of this world in their declarations of reciprocal friendship, just as he takes their professions of Christian faith seriously. Wasn't this the best tactic for him, and even the only one possible?

Repelled by the worldly success of arms, courts and crowns, Erasmus excelled in undermining military glory. He did not ask that the fire of heaven should fall on armies, but pleaded insistently that the leaders of these armies should be converted and that they should accept the risks of peace which were the risks of faith. He did not consider war a providential scourge, but condemned it with all Christian moralists. National antagonism aroused the worst follies of war. War devoured the countryside, destroyed towns, squandered finances and destabilized the State. How could the Christian princes be made to understand that God had not created men so that they could be led to a massacre as herds of animals are led to an abattoir?

Sovereign rulers had showered Erasmus with respect, but recognized no practical or lasting significance in his teaching. They had betrayed peace. Erasmus felt himself to be more and more powerless. 'I can only express my desires. No more!'[15] He feared that these same kings, lost in warlike folly, had stopped being what they wanted to be in order to become a monstrous curse. These lapsed Christians were neither a gift from heaven nor the salt of the earth. They disappointed Erasmus so much the more when they had more power. They disappointed him through their warlike attitude, their intolerance and, in the final analysis, by the lack of depth in their personal religion.

Erasmus reminded the Pope that he was the Father of all and that he should not ally himself with one ruler against another. His unique role in this domain was to serve peace by admonishing men of little faith locked up in a fear that made them ruthless. Apart from kings and great men, Popes and theologians, Erasmus also wanted to reach public opinion in his time and in the centuries to come. War had come as if it were fated; resistance to violence had become a necessity, as Erasmus knew. Although tolerating a defensive war, he did not omit to remind us of the rights of conscience and the strength of gentleness. Christian Europe could not be content to be reunited by fear. More than a Europe of nation states, it should become a Europe of brothers.

Erasmus did not see or know this united, peaceful Europe, and did not convince theologians any more than kings. Machiavelli had made more disciples than he. Should we conclude that he had been only 'a voice crying in the wilderness'? To this objection we have a perfect right to reply that Erasmian pacifism was a Utopia, in the highest sense of the term, in that this pacifism was centred on the Gospel: Christianity, because it is an invitation to go beyond oneself, is a Utopia, an effective Utopia. Now Erasmus wanted to apply to international relations the virtues which Christ required in personal relations: this was the origin of his attraction to non-violence and his appeal for an impossible peace. He never went back on this moral extremism, but he must have fully recognized the weight of human reality. His acceptance of legitimate defence, with all his well-known reservations, proceeded from this realism.[16]

Erasmus drew from within himself the indispensable faith to believe, in spite of all, in the wisdom of men, if not of nations, for he counted more on human beings than on nations. Machiavelli's profound pessimism had not reached him. As a spectator involved in an inexpiable drama, he rejected the glamour of uniforms, and unrelentingly called into question the false reasons which permitted wars and justified the worst forms of injustice.

Erasmus wanted to build a coherent theology of peace on biblical, especially New Testament, foundations. Devotion to peace is not a supererogatory work. Not to respect peace, not to live in peace, is to misunderstand the Gospel, for peace is the true effect of love. Jesus, 'Prince of peace', bequeathed to men of goodwill that peace which was the fruit of the Spirit, whose benefits were for enemies as well as friends. The apostolic preaching was called the 'Gospel of peace' by St Paul. 'Peace on earth' is a divine saying whose echo has come down to us despite the tumult of arms.

The theology of peace means an end to hatred and fear in favour of love and trust. 'Where would the kingdom of Satan be if there were no war?' 'He who preaches Christ preaches peace,' this 'divine benefit'. Erasmus clearly explained his views in relation to the Crusade, a war which shamelessly made a show of religious motivation. He was insistent, affirming that no compromise was possible with war and that aggression was the negation of Christianity. It was not to the violent, but to the peacemakers, that Jesus promised blessedness.

Moreover, the theology of peace had an eschatological dimension in the sense that it was at once a project too demanding to be realized in this world and an ideal too stimulating not to be able to help man raise himself above himself. The theology of peace also had a communal dimension: in the same way that the Bible encompassed sociological and theological ideas in its vision, the theology of peace according to Erasmus embraced man's misery and God's plan in the same perspective. This is why it seems legitimate to specify that the theology of peace is, in perspective, a theology of liberation, for peace postulates an active brotherhood – indeed a heroic solidarity. The notion of liberation is a fundamental Christian value. There is no lasting peace without justice, just as there is no justice without love. 'Christ's soldier', according to Erasmus, was at once a militant for peace and a defender of freedom.

Erasmus the moralist has been the guilty conscience of Europe. In the history of political philosophy, he took on the role of a fore-runner, though his noble thought brought no institution into being. He was a committed pacifist, who defended peace, good or bad, in the name of Christian universalism. For him, morality alone could save the world from self-destruction. His lessons have lost nothing of their urgent topicality, and all those who call for the subordination of politics to morality today are his disciples.

The philosophy of Christ occupied a central place in Erasmus's thought, as it did in his writings. It agreed with his conception of the mystery of Jesus in the life of his disciples. It would be impossible to take account of Erasmus's campaigns on behalf of literature and peace without taking account of this essential doctrine.[17] He called the philosophy of Christ a synthesis of theology and spirituality, a synthesis fashioned out of knowledge and love, nourished by meditation, prayer and renunciation, crowned by union with God. The philosophy of Christ demanded a personal approach to the Gospel and increased familiarity with its message. It was a return to the sources.

Erasmus borrowed the term 'philosophy of Christ' from the Greek Fathers, his favourite authors. For them, as for him, the expression was purposely paradoxical. It certainly amounted to a philosophy, that is to say a body of wisdom, a collection of co-ordinated principles, and not an irrational message that only held good for the illuminati. It was not a philosophy like any other, for it was not human, but divine. It was not only intellectual but, despite its name, it remained accessible to the simplest Christians. It brought God within the range in the heart. It required at one and the same time inwardness and brotherhood. It was life within life.

Erasmus used the expressions 'philosophy of Christ', 'Christian philosophy', 'heavenly philosophy' and 'philosophy of the Gospel' interchangeably. The Gospel was indeed the source of that transcendent and unifying doctrine with its key ideas about the Spirit which enlivens and love which edifies. To him, nothing was simpler than this philosophy which was remote from the philosopher's judgements and the ideas of this world, which alone reached the goal of happiness which all men sought. 'In this kind of philosophy,' he said, 'located as it is more truly in the disposition of the mind than in syllogisms, life means more than debate.'[18]

The philosophy of Christ transformed Erasmus's life. His piety, his bearing, his vision of the Church and of the world were marked by this doctrine and owed their deep agreement to it. With visible partiality Erasmus highlighted the truths of the faith which seemed to him the most expansive, the most joyful, the most human. He believed what the Church believed. He admitted the weakness of fallen man and the necessity of grace and penitence, but he insisted on redemption and the restoration of human nature. He believed in the mysterious activity of the Holy Spirit in every baptized Christian and exalted the grace that is offered to all and the light yoke of Christ. He was among those for whom nothing could any longer be as before since the time that God, through the Incarnation, had entered into human history.

Erasmian religion 'is summed up essentially in the personal act of a Christian responding to the invitation of his Lord.'[19] His faith was the faith of a seeker – which in no way resembled the religion of everyman – a burning faith, but an everyday struggle, an approach ceaselessly frustrated by the harshness of the journey.

Erasmus was neither a fanatic nor a triumphalist. In his religious conflicts, his intention was always to mediate. He did not aim to create a new Church, between Rome and the Reformation, but he explored a third way between Reformation and Counter-Reformation. His position was doubly uncomfortable, for he was suspected by the radicals of each camp. Both accused him of cowardice when he wished to provoke an intensity of dialogue and openness, for he wished for a reform different from the Reformation and a catholic reform other than the Counter-Reformation.

He did not dream of an easy religion, but of a religion that was less strained, more personal, less formalist, more lively, a religion in which obedience to the Beatitudes transcended respect for the Ten Commandments. This is why he was opposed to the spiritual comfort of resigned or lazy Christians; the asceticism which he preferred for men and women living in the world was not an accumulation of hagiographic performances, but the courageous acceptance of daily trials.

Moreover, Erasmus did not see the Church as a pyramid of functions and grades: it was the community of the baptized, the people of God, the mystical Body of Christ. For him, the Word of God should be meditated on according to New Testament ecclesiology which exalts service. These first truths, forgotten truths, Erasmus repeated untiringly.

Christocentrism was the golden rule of Erasmus's spirituality as well as of his theology. This spirituality was his throughout all his adult life. It was this that he so earnestly desired and proposed for all Christians. It was neither popular piety nor monastic piety, but a thrust towards a Christianity relaunched, joyfully discovering the purity of its origins. His piety, on the one hand, was illuminated and animated by faith. On the other hand, it spread its influence according to the variable demands of love and by respecting differences. He was glad to invoke the examples of his friends John Colet, Jean Vitrier and Thomas More, two clerics and a layman who represented fascinating models and unforgettable champions of the Christian philosophy.

The philosophy of Christ was present in all the choices Erasmus made. It was thanks to the philosophy of Christ that his humanism escaped the contagion of paganism. In the books of Antiquity, he did not recognize the last word of wisdom, but only the first, that which prepared the way for a better knowledge of Revelation. He loved the ancient authors, but never gave them an absolute value. He attended their school not to identify himself with them, but to define himself in relation to them.

With his books, Erasmus raised a cathedral, of which prayer was the keystone. This great seeker ploughed the whole field of letters. He believed, with a calm faith, that everything that was good in human affairs came from God and returned to him. In leading literature to God, Erasmus did not, however, intend to humble or enslave it, but to illuminate and enhance it. No apologetic concern guided him, but he obeyed a true theology of knowledge which restored literature to its origin and its end. For him, humanism would not have attained its fullness if it had not culminated in Christian humanism.

Likewise, if Erasmus made himself the champion of the three sacred languages, if he clearly misjudged the potentialities of the modern languages and literatures, this was because he always accorded primacy to faith over politics, to religion over the nation. To be sure, languages interested him, since he was a philologist, but they interested him above all as messengers of the Word.

> I would that [the Scriptures] were translated into all languages so that they could be read and understood not only by the Scots and the Irish but also by Turks and Saracens. . . . Would that, as a result, the farmer sing some portion of them at the plow, the weaver hum some parts of them to the movement of his shuttle, the traveller lighten the weariness of the journey with stories of this kind![20]

The influence of the modern devotion is clearly recognizable here.

Erasmus was a pacifist and internationalist for reasons other than those of natural morality or political science. He admitted these motivations, but went beyond them. The Christian, for him, because he was a Christian, could not but follow the ways of peace, despite national barriers. The philosophy of Christ gave an evangelical foundation to his pacifism. 'I say', he declared, 'that the whole Christian philosophy, that is, the Gospels and the apostles' letters, discourages man from war. Why should we be astounded at this, when they always encourage mutual peace and love, even of enemies? But if all Christians were such as Christ wished them, there would be no war amongst them, nor even quarrels.'[21]

Finally, Erasmus's ecumenism follows naturally from his fidelity. Christian disunity was a scandal and reunion a priceless good. The ecumenical spirit modified the relations of Christians among themselves profoundly. It was because the Council of Trent lacked this spirit that it preferred anathema to dialogue, and did not follow the Erasmian pathway of concord. Through fear of indifference and contagion, it enlarged the gulf which separated Catholics from Dissidents.

Ecumenism crowned and gathered up the theology of peace and continuity. The horror of divisions,[22] anchored in Erasmus's psychology, found support and confirmation in his religious vision of the world. Disorder leads to disaster. The worst of disorders, that of the spirit, threatens the peace of hearts and of peoples. Peace and unanimity are the signs of the presence of God in the Church.

Beyond controversial issues, Erasmus sometimes softened his positions without compromising his principles. He had certainly learned and suffered, yet nevertheless always remained faithful to himself, to his realizations of the *Handbook of the Christian Soldier* and *The Praise of Folly*. After the Lutheran explosion, he had to mute some of his expressions, but he did not change course. Between the suspect piety of the popular Church and the paralysing constraints of the authoritarian Church, he did not crumble, but remained loyal to the faith of his youth. He put his talent to the service of his convictions, until his last breath. His faith helped him to surmount temptations, solitude and misunderstanding. To say emphatically that Erasmus was first and foremost a Christian is not a salvage operation, but simply a matter of giving him his due.

If Erasmus's success on the pedagogical plane is indisputable, he suffered more than one reverse in other areas. He never reached the stage of creating a single European culture by making Latin a universal language. He was not able to stop war in the name of Christ. Martin Luther and Ignatius Loyola, equally shocked by his freedom of expression, agreed in doubting his piety. 'I am', he declared, 'a Ghibelline to the Guelfs and a Guelf to the Ghibellines.' His projects of religious reform foundered on conservative opposition from Rome: whether it was a matter of pilgrimages, relics, indulgences, marriage, the reading of the Bible in the common tongue, or the renewal of baptismal promises, his ideas were generally misunderstood. His defence of the rights of man, of the Christian and the theologian were a failure. Was Erasmus to be, as he himself said, a 'polygraph preaching to the deaf'?

Certainly not! He failed because he was right too soon, but the fervour with which he defended his policy of openness, though it did not touch his contemporaries, touches us today.

26

The Erasmian Message: From the Critique of Christianity to Critical Christianity

To all those able to follow him, Erasmus offered much more than a revision of traditions. He asked for an inward change. He hoped for the return of a Christianity 'pure and simple', a religion of love and not constraint, a Christianity which was not unhealthily preoccupied with definitions and anathemas. It was not a new religion, a 'Gospel without dogma', reserved for the initiated,[1] not was it a spiritualized moralism, even less a flight into illuminism. If he made appeal to the critical spirit, he asked for a committed faith which held nothing back.

How did Erasmus, the apostle of Christian unity, so often assume the role of ruthless censor of his Church? The reply to this question must be sought in history, for the Church of the Renaissance had inherited from the Middle Ages a powerful organization, a stifling clericalism and a formalistic piety. We have heard Erasmus rise up vigorously against countless abuses and insupportable controls.

He denounced a pharisaical religion, made up of routine practices and works drained of their spirit, the religion of false piety or mistaken Christians. He was not critical of ceremonies as such, but of treating ceremonies as ends rather than as means. He did not even condemn indulgences; what bothered him was the assurance of eternal life that they represented for most of the faithful, as if practices and devotions had value in themselves, when it was divine grace alone that transformed them. One could even speak of an obscuring of the faith when, for too many Christians, salvation was reduced to an accumulation of observances, without any perception of the relationship of these observances to the conversion of the heart. In all his struggles, Erasmus always returned to essentials, to inward religion and to the Gospel. For him, faith was not a herbarium of dried-out, tasteless, colourless plants.

Erasmianism as a religious outlook was not a schism or a sect. Approved by some, opposed or ignored by others, it was just one current of opinion permeating Catholic circles, an awakening of piety, a new style of engagement, a movement heralding Catholic Reform.

From the heritage of fifteen centuries, Erasmus accepted the development of piety, along with that of dogma. He rejected only superstitious deviations and ridiculous distortions perpetuated by a fervour which was unworthy of its object. He dismissed a childish and credulous religiosity hanging on to reassuring formulas because this behaviour was fatal to a spiritual life founded on the risen Christ. By their number, these practices devoured the time of Christians and got in the way of the essential mission of the Church: the proclamation of the Gospel. As a result, he combined an unceasing appeal to personal prayer with the merciless satire of commercialized pilgrimages, doubtful relics and imprudent vows. To the touching or bizarre folklore of private devotions he opposed the admirable procession of liturgical feasts that he had sung of in his verses.

In his critique of an adulterated piety, Erasmus reserved his most lively sarcasm for those who supported an ambiguous devotion. He was horrified at all exploitation of the credulity and anxiety of the simple; he said this without beating about the bush and repeated it fearlessly. He also knew that devotion to the saints was relatively late, but that it had proliferated amazingly. When the believer implored the Virgin or asked for the intercession of the saints, it was always God who responded and who gave. Prayer was essentially theological: to pray from the depths of the heart was to speak to God Himself. In every respect, Erasmus's critique linked up again with his theology.

Erasmus suffered from this tension, but it was not bad temper that possessed him; rather, he was consumed by love. He wanted the face of the Church to be beautiful, sweet and smiling, the face of a mother eternally young. Set amidst the disorder of spirits and institutions, he looked for solutions, dreamed up remedies. The purification of Christianity, which he sought with all his strength, with all his soul, postulated a change in theology, as well as in piety and discipline. He took no pleasure in offending simple souls, not even theologians or preachers. His critique was at all times as constructive as it was incisive.

Before Luther – and later against Luther – Erasmus entered the lists and spent himself without respite for the reform of religious institutions.[2] In this aim, he wanted first of all to renew the theological sciences by a return to the sources. Beyond that, he anticipated and embarked upon the restoration of the pastorate. Theologians after his own heart would have to know the three sacred languages and they would reflect on the Bible in the company of the Fathers of the Church.

There was to be no theology without exegesis and no exegesis without a preliminary knowledge of the pagan literature of Antiquity, its vocabulary and its grammar. This propadeutic alone made possible the synthesis of classical culture and Christian thought which we call Christian humanism.

Erasmus had a very lively, existential view of religion, and consequently of theology. This is why he reacted violently against the deviations of speculative theology which reigned then in the schools – the scholastic theology whose decadence was self-evident. He held Aristotle responsible, the pagan thanks to whom the admirable patristic theology had been supplanted by a quibbling dialectic. He added to the harmful influence of scholastic theology the damage wrought by canon law, the Talmud of the Christians. On either hand the simplicity of the Gospel was stifled under the mass of propositions, decisions and distinctions, put forward like oracles by theologians and canonists who believed themselves to be the world's censors.

His concern to spread his convictions came up against inertia, and even hostility. On the one hand, satisfied Christians could not understand the meaning of Erasmian reformism, and held it against him for denouncing their weaknesses. On the other hand, the boldness of the humanist's language appalled the theologians who replied in aggressive, and sometimes unsubtle, sermons, while the popes and the bishops accorded Erasmus constant favour.

Though he always declared that the reform of abuses and the adaptation of discipline should be made by the Church itself, at an opportune time and without upheaval, Erasmus frightened the doctors. On his way, in the Faculties of Theology and in the mendicant orders, he met Churchmen who, if they had forgotten nothing of what had been taught them, seemed to have learned nothing since they began teaching. They were the guides and interpreters of popular piety, but they confused tradition with the status quo, and unanimity of hearts with minds no longer active. Erasmus despised those who presented themselves as 'God's specialists'. Among them or at their side, the monks of the mendicant orders were the preferred targets of Erasmian irony. Did they not subscribe, thanks to the threefold vows, to an etiquette of sanctity, while they did not always live according to the spirit of Jesus? It was even the case that they set more store by their rule than by the Gospel! The monastic profession – Erasmus insisted – was not a panacea. Vows were to be respected, but it was through baptism that every Christian was dedicated to God. Besides, these ecclesiastical conservatives – conservers of the opinions of their schools and also of their privileges – easily became heresy hunters, the forerunners of the Inquisition, which was not such as to make them more sympathetic to their clear-eyed observer. Erasmus struggled for a Christianity with a human face.

In place of the ponderous, threatening scholastic theology, Erasmus called fervently for an open theology which, in its loyal quest, would not be crushed by the magistracy. The dross accumulated over the centuries had to be removed so that the Word of God might remain eternally young. Erasmus preached humility to the theologians, but not as if it were advice to naturalists or mathematicians: there was a humility proper to theology, the object of which was a mystery, the mystery par excellence. Since this mystery was inscribed in Revelation, theology is first of all Biblical; it is also patristic, for it was history and tradition, the Church's conscience on the march; finally, it was mysticism, because it ought to raise itself to the spiritual meaning of Scripture, to taste it by the heart as much as by the spirit. Such a method could only make clear the errors of the past, and especially the misguided accumulation of dogmatic definitions.

Theology had spoken too much! The Church was suffering from a theological verbosity. Erasmus held as responsible for this evil the 'impious curiosity' of theologians who believed that they had explained everything – the Trinity, transubstantiation, the resurrection of the body – and who wanted to impose on the faith of believers explanations which, at best, were only conjectures. Theology was dangerous when it became a rational game living by its brainwaves and formulas.

Erasmus detested class-consciousness, whether of theologians, monks or courtiers. Class-consciousness annulled that self-criticism which was indispensable to a healthy social life. He wanted to see the advancement of the laity and the emancipation of women and proposed a universal Christianity, acceptable to both laity and clergy. In this spirit, he enhanced the status of marriage and taught that every baptized Christian should be able to read the Scriptures in his or her mother tongue.

Erasmus recommended to the care of the Church two categories of Christians who seemed to him to need attention: priests with no true vocation and the unhappily married. For both he asked for a softening of discipline. Priests incapable of maintaining celibacy should be allowed to marry. He was not naïve enough to believe that marriage would overcome all the difficulties of the priestly life. It was enough to hope that it would smooth out some of them and bring the priests closer to the laity, for marriage was the common state and providential destiny of the majority of men. For husbands and wives who were ill-matched, Erasmus made a strong plea, with the same lack of success. He brought into the open the formalism and the burden of the prohibitions which were stifling them. In short, Erasmus wanted to relieve Christians from the bonds which were too heavy for them and which bound them to outdated traditions. What the Church had created in these areas it could unmake or modify.

Erasmus's suggestions were often in accord with Luther's, yet Erasmus did not become a Lutheran. Against the innovators he declared himself a renovator. He remained faithful to the Popes of the Renaissance while criticizing them. He supported the Mass and the sacraments, while advocating a return to their original purity. He denounced Christianity in order to awaken souls. He was in no way a 'Christian without the Church', and refused to separate himself from the Roman Church whose abuses he denounced: 'Neither life, nor death', he wrote, 'can detach me from the the Church'. He remained unceasingly, until his last breath, the watchful censor of the Church – in the Church – for he loved the Church, which was both his mother and his Cross.

Erasmus cannot be reproached for not having taken the lead in a fiercely anti-Lutheran reforming movement. His personal charisma was that of a seeker, not a leader. He gambled on the reform of the Church by the Church, a never-ending work, undertaken in courage and patience, in faith and hope. Erasmus knew that the Church that he saw was sick, short-sighted, and somewhat deaf, but he wrote this significant phrase: 'So I bear with this Church until I see a better; and it is forced to bear with me, until I become better.'[3]

Beyond his indictment of a certain kind of Christianity, we can discern Erasmus's plan: his 'critical Christianity', inspired by Valla among others. This expression was not that of the humanist,[4] although the idea ran throughout in his work. These two words comprehend first of all 'Christianity', a Christianity in no way weakened by his analysis; and 'critical', that is to say, not a camouflaged scepticism, but a manner of thinking and acting fashioned out of intellectual independence, of questioning without aggressiveness, of resourcefulness and clear-sighted faithfulness. In all, a Christianity illuminated by history, an original analysis which was not opposed to believers' zeal, but to their lack of awareness. Critical Christianity profited from the critique of Christianity to gain in purity, force and depth.[5] It amounted to an enlightened, clear-sighted and well-informed Christianity. It was the last word in Erasmianism.

While Christian humanism has opened the way to the criticism of Christianity and to critical Christianity, the latter flourishes in the philosophy of Christ of which Erasmus spoke so often and with such poetic force. In short, critical Christianity and the philosophy of Christ are two convergent and complementary aspects of the Erasmian religion, one more intellectual, the other more mystical. Their harmonious association cannot but make Christians more Christian.

Handled roughly by his colleagues in theology, censured by the Sorbonne, threatened by the Inquisition, but protected by the Popes, in his old age Erasmus knew both fame and disillusionment. There was the fame of being the prince of humanists, one of the renewers of Catholic theology; and the disillusionments, so bitter for this irenic man, who was constrained to be a powerless and wounded witness of the atrocious battles of the Church and its peoples, to see Luther separate himself from Rome and Rome closing its ears to the valid claims of the Reformation.

If on the one hand Erasmus's reformism was demanding, on the other hand his tolerance horrified the princes as much as the Churchmen. In time of war, moderates passed for traitors or innocents, and on this point Erasmus defended himself badly. He was no popular orator like Luther, no Church leader like Calvin, no founder of an order like Ignatius Loyola. He had more friends than partisans or disciples and it was enough for him to be a forerunner. Where he had sown, others would reap.

Erasmian irenicism was not to prevail at all at the Council of Trent, any more than his brand of reform. But this assembly appears to have followed Erasmus, without naming him, in his plan for a preaching that was at once learned and pious, as well as in the battle against popular superstition and the ignorance of the clergy. By contrast, the putting on the Index of all his works in 1559 – posthumous revenge of the theologians humiliated by Erasmus – compromised and retarded his liberating influence by imprisoning their author for three centuries in the hell of ecclesiastical libraries. Among his contemporaries and successors, many Catholics considered Erasmus to be a threat to the Church, though his vocation was to be vigilant in the service of the Church. It does not seem superfluous to recall that Luther's brutal challenge to Erasmus has been curiously accepted by the bulk of Catholic opinion.

Erasmus, moreover, was the child of his own work. For too long, history has only seen him in terms of *The Praise of Folly*, or rather in terms of what has been made of this difficult book. It is the accusation of indifference which has stifled the Erasmian message for so long. By a strange irony of this kind this same accusation was to clear the way for the relative success of Erasmus in the Age of Enlightenment. The sceptical Erasmus seemed to triumph in collective understanding until the renewal of Erasmian studies in the twentieth century.

Catholic Reform was carried out without him.[6] From 1543, the works of Erasmus were burned by the executioner in Milan. Nevertheless his ideas, though kept in the dark, were never entirely stifled, but continued to live an underground existence. Despite Luther, Protestant countries took over from Catholic countries and welcomed the spiritual heritage of Erasmus. For its part, the schismatic Church of England adopted Erasmus's religious writings,[7] while Melanchthon and Castellio praised him.[8] Bonifacius Amerbach, as a good disciple of Erasmus, maintained a climate of relative tolerance in Basel. The Jesuits tried hard to 'salvage' the pedagogical works of the master. Among his own, Erasmus, this *enfant terrible* of the Roman Church, continued to annoy the prophets of misfortune and the ardent admirers of triumphalism. It was only at the end of the seventeenth century that he emerged from the purgatory of writers out of favour and that his ideas again found an audience which would continue to grow and to extend while becoming more refined.[9]

The criticisms addressed by Erasmus to the Christians of his time have not all lost their topicality. Despite the admirable work of Catholic Reform and of the Second Vatican Council – an Erasmian Council if there ever was such a thing[10] – Catholicism remains still partially attached to the traditions of popular piety with all the good and less good features this carries with it. Each time prophets proclaim a message from the Virgin, the masses set off, the clergy follows, with more or less reluctance. Pilgrimages move crowds better supervised than before, but sometimes just as noisy. Indulgences are still announced in our Cathedrals. Finally, the 'faith of the coalman' still has its devotees and the Bible has not achieved the place which it deserves in the religious culture of our age.

A symbol of contradiction in his own time, Erasmus gradually became a factor of unity. His ideas circulated across the world, without it even being known sometimes that they originated from him. Opposed during his life, forgotten during the second half of the sixteenth century, he has approached closer to us now that he is identified not merely by striking phrases, but by and through his works as a whole. He is now studied and analysed in the same way that he had asked for his revered authors – Greek or Latin, pagan or Christian – to be studied.

Erasmus is recognizable not only as the prince of humanists, but as one of the most original spirits of the Renaissance, one of the first thinkers of the modern age, and the herald of a new intellectual liberty. Erasmus survives in his works – *The Praise of Folly* and the *Colloquies* have been translated into many languages – and in a spiritual inheritance as varied as his own genius. His ideas have entered into the common patrimony of humanity.

Erasmus the Christian and the theologian has emerged from the shadows to which the Age of Reformations and the Age of Enlightenment had relegated him: he constantly embarrasses some of his readers, who try to find in him the artist and the spiritual man in opposition to each other. Whatever one can say, there were not two Erasmuses, that of the *Folly* and that of the *Paraphrases*, that of the satire and that of the pastoral, the one a Voltaire, the other a Fénelon. Or rather, there are twenty varied Erasmuses who find their basis in a single self-same passion. Should I dare to suggest that Erasmus's anticlericalism, which had alienated him from countless readers, is a permanent paradox and a salutary catharsis?

Religious passion gave to his life a fundamental unity and makes its way throughout his books: the same faith explains reactions that are apparently opposed. If Lucian was sometimes found as a water mark in his theological books, the Gospel was always present in his secular works. The doctrine of the *Folly* no more contradicted that of the *Paraphrases* than the witness of the faithful Christian denied the boldness of the open theologian.

Though Erasmus is not an easy author, his message is better understood today than before. Despite some aberrant interpretations,[11] our century as it draws to its close feels itself to be in agreement with him on several points: the awareness of a civilization in peril, a brotherly search for peace, the formation of a European spirit, a concern for rational education, classical culture, ecumenism, conciliar and postconciliar reforms, and finally Christian humanism and critical Christianity.

Surprising, many-sided and inimitable, there is only one Erasmus, and he remains among us for ever.

Appendix: Chronology

c. 1469	Erasmus born at Rotterdam.
1478	At school in Deventer.
1484	Erasmus, an orphan, enters school at S'Hertogenbosch.
1487–1492	Erasmus in the monastery at Steyn. Initiation into humanism. Servatius Rogerus.
1492	Erasmus ordained priest.
1493	With the agreement of his superiors, Erasmus leaves Steyn to become secretary to Hendrik of Bergen, bishop of Cambrai.
1495	He enters the College of Montaigu in Paris, and pursues courses at the Sorbonne.
1496	A sick man, he leaves Montaigu and lives by his teaching.
1499–1500	Invited by his pupil Lord Mountijoy, Erasmus spends a wonderful year in England. Thomas More and John Colet.
1500	First edition of the *Adages*.
1501	Erasmus meets Jean Vitrier at Saint-Omer. By the publication of Cicero's *De Officiis*, Erasmus inaugurates his career as a philologist and editor of classical texts.
1502	Death of Hendrik of Bergen. Erasmus in Louvain.
1504	*Panegyric* for Philip the Handsome. *Handbook of the Christian Soldier*.
1505	Second stay in England.
1506–9	Discovery of Italy: Turin, Bologna, Venice, Rome.
1509–14	New and longer stay in England, interrupted by several journeys on the Continent.
1511	*The Praise of Folly*.
1512	*Foundations of the Abundant Style*.

1515	Basel. First volume of his correspondence.
1516	The *New Testament* in Greek and Latin. *The Education of a Christian Prince.*
1517	*The Complaint of Peace.* Last visit to England.
1518	Erasmus living generally in the Netherlands. *The Praise of Marriage.*
1519	Luther. The great polemics begin.
1520	The *Antibarbari.*
1521	Studious relaxation at Anderlecht. Erasmus leaves the Netherlands and settles in Basel.
1522	The *Colloquies. On the Art of Writing Letters.*
1524	*The Freedom of the Will.* Break with Luther. Erasmus edits the Church Fathers.
1526	*The Institution of Christian Marriage.*
1528	*The Ciceronian.*
1529	*The Education of Children.*
1529–35	At Freiburg.
1533	*On Mending the Peace of the Church.*
1534	*The Preparation for Death.*
1535	Return to Basel. *On Preaching.*
1536	Erasmus dies in Basel on the night of 11–12 July.

Abbreviations

ASD	*Opera Omnia Desiderii Erasmi Roterodami, Amsterdam,* 1969–
LB	*Erasmi Opera Omnia,* ed. J. Le Clerc, 10 vols., Leiden, 1703–6
Allen	*Opus Epistolarum Des. Erasmi Roterodami,* ed. P. S. and H. M. Allen, 12 vols. Oxford, 1906–58
Holborn	*Desiderius Erasmus. Ausgewählte Werke,* Munich, 1933
CWE	*The Collected Works of Erasmus,* Toronto, 1974–
ARG	*Archiv für Reformationsgeschichte*

Notes

CHAPTER 1: CHILDHOOD AND YOUTH

1 Allen (*Opus epistolarum Des. Erasmi Roterodami,* vol. 1, Oxford 1906, p. 578) chose 1466 as the date of birth. He was followed for a long time, and still is by E. W. Kohls, 'Das Geburtsjahr des Erasmus', in *Theologische Zeitschrift,* 22 (Basel, 1966), 96–121, 347–59, and by J. P. Gleason, 'The Birth Dates of John Colet and Erasmus', in *Renaissance Quarterly,* 32 (1979), 73–6. The date of 1467 has its defenders: A. C. F. Koch, *The Year of Erasmus' Birth* (Utrecht, 1969) and N. van der Blom, 'Une nouvelle vision sur l'année de naissance d'Erasme', in *Humanistica Lovaniensia,* 20 (Louvain, 1971), 69–79. Finally, the date of 1469 has been quite generally accepted since the work of R. R. Post, 'Quelques précisions sur l'année de la naissance d'Erasme', in *Bibliothèque d'Humanisme et Renaissance,* 26 (1964), pp. 489–509, and 'Nochmals Erasmus' Geburtsjahr', in *Theologische Zeitschrift,* 22 (1966), 319–33. For the record, J. Huizinga (*Erasmus and the Age of Reformation,* trans. from the Dutch by F. Hopman, New York, 1957, p. 5) hesitates between 1466 and 1469.

2 In the judgement of history, Erasmus was a learned commoner. He was 'of' Rotterdam, just as Leonardo was 'of' Vinci. Pieter was three years older than Erasmus. Cf. Allen, *Ep.* 1436, V. 428, l. 38, to Gerard Geldenhouwer, c. April 1524. On Erasmus's father, a copyist in Italy in 1458, see a note of A. Sottili in the *Wolfenbütteler Renaissance Mitteilungen* of August 1982, pp. 86–8. This note partly confirms the data of the *Compendium vitae* cited later. See also J. Ijsewijn in the same journal of December 1985, pp. 127–9. Erasmus's relations with his brother are not well known; they seem to have been difficult.

3 In the *Colloquium senile,* Glycion, who speaks like another Erasmus, declares that he is no more concerned about his death than about the date of his birth. Cf. *ASD* I. 3. 380, ll. 157–8. Erasmus's friend, Beatus Rhenanus, wrote to Hermann von Wied that he knew the day of Erasmus's birth (SS Simon and Jude, 28 October), but not the year. Cf. Allen, *Ep.* III, I. 55, ll. 77–9, (1536).

4 The *Compendium vitae* is reproduced in Allen, *Ep.* II, 1. 47–52. Notwithstanding its apologetic orientation, the documentary value of this text is great, except for Erasmus's origins. Cf. R. Crahay, 'Recherches sur le *Compendium vitae'* in *Humanisme et Renaissance,* 6 (1939), 7–19, 135–53.

5 Allen, *Ep.* 187 A, III. xxix, 1. 5, 4 Jan. 1506. Erasmus, son of a priest! This is the gratuitous and repeatedly reproduced assertion of J. J. Mangan, *Character and Influence of Desiderius Erasmus of Rotterdam,* vol. 1 (New York, 1927), pp. 4–5.

6 In 1495 we find *Herasmus Roterdam.* Cf. Allen, *Ep.* 45, 1. 149, the subscription on the letter to Gaguin. In 1496 *Herasmus Rotterdammensis* and *Desyderius Herasmus.* Cf. Allen, I. 155 and 161 (the headings of two prefaces) Cf. M. O'R. Boyle, 'The eponyms of Desiderius Erasmus' in *Renaissance Quarterly,* 30 (1977), 12–23.

7 N. van der Blom, *Erasmus en Rotterdam,* (Rotterdam, 1969). Erasmus was not able to forget the Dutch, as is shown in his treatise of 1528 *De recta latini graecique sermonis pronuntiatione* (ed. M. Cytowska, in *ASD* I. 4, (Amsterdam, 1981). Cf. J. Chomarat, *Grammaire et rhétorique chez Érasme,* vol. 1, pp. 107–25, (Paris, 1981). In his *Adages,* Erasmus writes: 'Holland is the place which I must always praise and honour for it is she who has given me birth' Cf. *LB* II. 1048 B.

8 P. Mestwerdt, *Die Anfänge des Erasmus* (Leipzig, 1917); R. L. De Molen, 'Erasmus as Adolescent' in *Bibliothèque d'Humanisme et Renaissance,* 38 (1976), 7–25. S. Cavazza, 'La formazione culturale di Erasmo', in *La Cultura,* 13 (Rome, 1975), 20–47. J. D. Tracy, 'Bemerkungen zur Jugend des Erasmus', in *Basler Zeitschrift für Geschichte und Altertumskunde,* 72 (1972), 221–30. In the *Carmen Alpestre,* Erasmus says in passing that he played with nuts in his childhood. Cf. C. Reedijk, *The Poems of Desiderius Erasmus* (Leiden, 1956) p. 286, 1. 89 (No. 83). See also J. Hoyoux, 'A game of Erasmus' in *Humanisme et Renaissance,* 4 (Geneva, 1937), 78–80. It is well known that one section of the *Colloquies* is devoted to play.

9 On the modern devotion, see a whole number of *Ons geestelijk erf,* vol. 59, Antwerp, 1985. See also L.-E. Halkin, 'La *Devotio Moderna* et l'Humanisme' in *Actes du IVᵉ Colloque de Montpellier 1975* (Montpellier, 1977) pp. 103–12. On the connections between the modern devotion and Jean Gerson, cf. J.-P. Massaut, *Josse Clichtove* (Paris, 1968), vol. 1, pp. 114–27.

10 R. L. De Molen, 'Interior Erasmus', in *Leaders of the Reformation* (Toronto, 1984), pp. 11–42. See also L.-E. Halkin, 'La jeunesse d'Érasme' in *Moreana,* 22 (1985), 109–23.

CHAPTER 2: A HUMANIST IN THE MONASTERY

1 Erasmus would certainly not have appreciated the relative pessimism of a book for the use of religious, but apart from this, the agreement is remarkable. See Mestwerdt, *Anfänge des Erasmus,* p. 78. J. B. Pineau (*Érasme, sa pensée religieuse,* Paris, 1923, pp. 68–70) is not serious in suggesting that Erasmus was an opponent of the *Imitation.*

2 Allen, *Ep.* 1436, V. 429, ll. 71–3, to Gerard Geldenhouwer, Basel, c. 2 Apr. 1524.

3 On Erasmus's friends see Y. Charlier, *Érasme et l'amitié* (Paris, 1977). On his studies at Steyn: Ch. Béné, *Érasme et saint Augustin* (Paris, 1969), pp. 28–58. The chronology of Erasmus's movements is particularly uncertain for the crucial years. See J. D. Tracy, *Erasmus. The Growth of a Mind* (Geneva, 1972), pp. 29 and 31.

4 Letter to Cornelis Gerard (1489), trans. from *Collected Works of Erasmus*, vol. 1, p. 36, ll. 10–14 (hereafter *CWE*); Allen, *Ep.* 23, I. 104, ll. 5–12.

5 Letter to Servatius Rogerus (1488), trans. from *CWE* 1, p. 17, ll. 18–23; Allen, *Ep.* 13, I. 86, ll. 16–20.

6 Letters to Servatius Rogerus (1487) trans. from *CWE* 1, p. 6, ll. 2–17; p. 9, ll. 2–23, 27–32; p. 12, ll. 32–42; p. 13, ll. 70–7; p. 14, l. 95. Allen, *Ep.* 4, I. 77, ll. 1–16; *Ep.* 7, I. 79–80, ll. 1–32; *Ep.* 8, I. 81–3, ll. 27–36, 61–8, 85–6. Erasmus himself recalls that 'youth is accustomed to being enflamed with a burning friendship for some comrades.' Allen, *Ep.* 447, II. 301, ll. 350–1. Some have even believed in a 'latent homosexuality' in Erasmus. See N. H. Minnich and W. W. Meissner, 'The Character of Erasmus' in *the American Historical Review*, 83 (1978), 598–624. I have studied this question, analysed the letters and shown the weakness of the arguments of these two authors in my article, 'La psychohistoire et le caractère d'Érasme', in *Storia della storiographia* (Milan, 1985), vol. 8, pp. 75–90.

7 Letter to Servatius Rogerus (1488) trans. from *CWE* 1, p. 21, ll. 41–4; Allen, *Ep.* 15, I. 89, ll. 38–41.

8 D. F. S. Thomson, 'Erasmus as a Poet', in *Commémoration nationale d'Érasme* (Brussels, 1970) pp. 187–210.

9 L.-E. Halkin, 'La piété d'Érasme', in *Revue d'histoire ecclésiastique*, 79 (1984), 671–708. See also E. F. Rice, Jr., *Saint Jerome in the Renaissance* (Baltimore, 1985), pp. 113–36.

10 This precept was borrowed from St Jerome. On the poets from Gouda, see J. Ijsewijn, 'Erasmus ex poeta theologus', in *Scrinium Erasmianum*, vol. 1, p. 382; Reedick, *Poems*, p. 170 (No.15).

11 On the expression of monastic piety in Erasmus, see R. Bultot, 'Érasme et Épicure', in *Scrinium Erasmianum*, vol. 2, pp. 224–5.

12 Letter to Jacob Batt, 1499. Allen, *Ep.* 95, I. 223, ll. 6 and 18. On Erasmus and plainsong, see J. Cl. Margolin, *Recherches érasmiennes* (Geneva, 1969), p. 94. About March 1502, Erasmus asked for a psalm-book. Cf. Allen, *Ep.* 169, I. 379, l. 4, to Pierre de Courtebourne.

CHAPTER 3: THE HARD APPRENTICESHIP OF FREEDOM

1 In 1493, according to all the evidence. Allen, *Ep.* 33, I. 128, introduction, from Willem Hermans, 1493(?). It appears that Erasmus at first accompanied his patron, whose actual journeys are not well known to us. Erasmus's itinerary has been reconstructed by M. Scherpenberghs, 'Les Voyages d'Érasme', unpublished paper, University of Liège, 1986.

2 In 1512, Aleander wrote to Erasmus: 'You never, as I hear, stayed very long in one spot', trans. from *CWE* 2, p. 217, ll. 12–13; Allen, *Ep.* 256, I. 503, l. 10. Thomas More defended Erasmus without difficulty; cf. H. Gibaud, 'Thomas More. Réponse à un moine', in *Moreana*, 27–8 (1970), 77.

3 Allen, *Ep.* 173, I. 381–4, preface, Louvain, 13 Feb. 1503.

4 M. M. Phillips, 'Erasmus and the Classics', in *Erasmus*, ed. T. A. Dorey (London, 1970), pp. 1–30; M. Cytowska, 'Érasme et les auteurs classiques', in *Eos*, 72 (Wroclaw, 1984), 179–187; P. P. Gerosa, *Umanesimo cristiano del Petrarca* (Turin, 1966); M. O'R. Boyle, *Christening Pagan Mysteries. Erasmus in Pursuit of Wisdom* (Toronto, 1981).

5 Béné, *Érasme et saint Augustin*, pp. 64–73.

6 Trans. from *CWE* 1, p. 71, ll. 11–23. Allen, *Ep.* 37, I. 36, ll. 9–18. Allen dates this letter to 1494, Béné (*Érasme et saint Augustin*, p. 61) places it rather in 1493.

7 *ASD* I. 1. 1–138, (ed. K. Kumaniecki). See J. D. Tracy, 'The 1489 and 1494 versions of Erasmus's Antibarbarorum Liber', in *Humanistica Lovaniensia*, 20, (Louvain, 1971), 81–120; S. Cavazza, 'La cronologia degli Antibarbari', in *Rinascimento*, 25 (Florence, 1975), 141–179; Chr. Christ-von Wedel, *Das Nichtwissen bei Erasmus* (Basel, 1981), pp. 21–30.

8 *ASD* I. 1, p. 83, ll. 17–18; p. 110, ll. 14–16; p. 112, ll. 17–23.

9 Charlier, *Érasme et l'amitié*, p. 88.

10 Trans. from *CWE* 1, p. 82 ll. 7–15; Allen, *Ep.* 42, I. 144, ll. 4–11 (1495).

11 Trans. from *CWE* 23, p. 76, ll. 26–8; *ASD* I. 1, p. 98, ll. 17–18. *Sic vive tanquam cras moriturus, sic stude quasi semper victurus. Occupabit mors, sed malo occupet studentem quam cessantem.* The same idea is to be found in a letter of 1529 to Charles Utenhove: Allen, *Ep.* 2209, VIII. 268, ll. 193–4. Erasmus had doubtless read by then the chapter *De meditatione mortis* – from *The Imitation of Christ* (I. 23), but he did not cite any passage from it.

12 Trans. from *CWE* 23, p. 54, ll. 37–8; *ASD* I. 1, p. 78, ll. 9–10. On the Socratic sense of not knowing, cf. *ASD* I. 1, p. 88, l. 26.

13 *ASD* I. 1, p. 130, l. 36.

14 Trans. from *CWE* I. 79, ll. 153–7; Allen, *Ep.* 39, I. 142, ll. 130–1, 138–41, c. Oct. 1494.

15 Allen, *Ep.* 48, V. 160, ll. 23–4, to Nicholas Werner, Paris, 13 Sept. 1496. I use the word 'Sorbonne' as a convenience, although it is not exactly right.

16 Allen, *Ep.* II, I. 50, ll. 103–5; *Ep.* 124, I. 285, ll. 6–8 to Batt, 12 Apr. 1500; *Ep.* 296, I. 565, ll. 17–19 to S. Rogerus, 1514; *Ep.* 447, II. 302, ll. 371–3, 388–91, 399–407, to Lambert Grunnius, 1516 – *ASD* I-3, pp. 531–2, ll. 1320–78; J. D. Tracy, *Erasmus. The Growth of a Mind.* (Geneva, 1972), pp. 27–8; A. Rabil, *Erasmus and the New Testament*, (San Antonio, 1972) p. 33.

17 Allen, *Ep.* 1, I. 37, l. 15; p. 146, introduction; *Ep.* 1996, VII. 400, ll. 15–19, Hector Boece to Erasmus, 26 May 1528.

18 Allen, *Ep.* 45, I. 148–52, towards the beginning of October 1495. See L.-E. Halkin, *Erasmus ex Erasmo*, p. 19. J. Huizinga, *Erasmus and the Age of Reformation*, p. 58. On Gaguin, see Massaut, *Josse Clichtove*, I. 144–66.

19 Trans. from *CWE* 1, p. 92, ll. 2–5, 27–31, 33–46. Allen, *Ep.* 146, I. 153–4, Paris, c. 7 Oct. 1495.

20 Allen, *Ep.* 124, I. 287, ll. 48–50, to Batt, Paris, 12 Apr. 1500.
21 Allen, *Ep.* 1, I. 19, ll. 34–6.
22 On the stench of the streets of Paris in this period, see M. Reulos, 'Paris au temps d'Érasme', in *Colloquia Erasmiana Turonensia* (Paris, 1972), 1. 82.

CHAPTER 4: PARIS: THE ATTRACTIONS AND BURDENS OF A TUTORSHIP

1 Allen, *Ep.* 48, l. 160, l. 29, to Nicholas Werner, Paris, 13 Sept. 1498. We know nothing more of Erasmus's first library.
2 Chomarat, *Grammaire et rhétorique*, 1. 184–92.
3 Trans. from *CWE* 6, p. 218, ll. 21–24. Allen, *Ep.* 909, III. 465, ll. 17–20, Louvain, 1519. It refers to the preface to the *Familiarium Colloquiorum Formulae*; see *ASD* I–3, pp. 73–4, ll. 14–17.
4 E. F. Rice, 'Erasmus and the religious tradition 1495–1499', in *Journal of the History of Ideas*, 11 (1950), 387–411.
5 *De casa natalitia Iesu*, Paris, Anoine Denidel, Jan. 1496 – text in Reedijk, *Poems*, p. 224 (No. 33).
6 Trans. from *CWE* 1, p. 94, ll. 4–16. Allen, *Ep.* 47, I. 155–6, ll. 2–15, 8 Nov. 1495.
7 Trans. from *CWE* 1, p. 103, ll. 102–4; Allen, *Ep.* 49, I. 163, ll. 85–90, to Hendrik van Bergen, Paris, 7 Nov. 1496.
8 Trans. from *CWE* 1, 98, ll. 26–9; Allen, *Ep.* 48, I. 159–60, ll. 22–4, Paris, 13 Sept. 1496.
9 Trans. from *CWE* 1, pp. 137–8, ll. 80–90; Allen, *Ep.* 64, I. 192, ll. 74–82, to Thomas Grey, Paris, c. August 1497. Tracy, *Growth of a Mind*, p. 23. Gryllard is a fictitious name.
10 Trans. from *CWE* 1, p. 107, ll. 19–20; Allen, *Ep.* 51, I. 166, ll. 15–17, to Hendrik van Bergen, 1497. See L.-E. Halkin, 'Erasmus docteur', in the *Mélanges André Latreille* (Lyons, 1972) p. 42; Allen, I. 591. The problem seems insoluble. See R. Stupperich, 'Zur Biographie des Erasmus', in *Archiv für Reformationsgeschichte*, 65 (1974), 70 and 30.
11 *ASD* V. 1, p. 339, ll. 1–3 (*De preparatione*, ed. A. Van Heck). See also Allen, *Ep.* 1794, VI. 478, ll. 31–32, to Guillaume Budé, 1527; *Adagia* (ed. S. S. Menchi, Turin, 1980), pp. 70 and 240.
12 *ASD* IV. 3, p. 156, l. 498 (*Moria*, ed. Cl. H. Miller). See J.-P. Massaut, 'Erasme et saint Thomas' in *Colloquia Erasmiana Turonensia* (Paris, 1972), 2. 581–611. See also Allen, *Ep.* 108, I. 246–7, ll. 30–7, to Colet, 1499.
13 *ASD* I. 3, p. 455; Holborn, *Desiderius Erasmus ausgewählte Werke*, p. 69, l. 8 (*Enchiridion*).
14 *ASD* IV. 3, p. 190, l. 159 (*Moria*); Ch. Béné, 'Les Pères de l'Église et la réception des auteurs classiques', in *Die Rezeption des Antique*, (ed. A. Buck), Hamburg, 1981, p. 48; M. Cytowska, 'Erasme et la philosophie antique', in *Antiquité vivante* (Skopje, 1976), 26. 457; M. O'R. Boyle, *Christening Pagan Mysteries. Erasmus in Pursuit of Wisdom* (Toronto, 1981).
15 Allen, *Ep.* 1002, IV. 33, ll. 8–12, to Nicholas Bérauld, 1519; *Ep.* 1381, V. 319, ll. 302–4, preface of 1523; *Ep.* 2284, VIII. 379, ll. 33–7, to Balthasar Mercklin, 1530.

16 Allen, *Ep.* 108, I. 246–7, ll. 19–36, to Colet, 1499. Tracy, *Growth of a Mind*, p. 109.

17 M. Cytowska, 'Érasme grammarien', in *Eos*, 64 (Wroclaw, 1976), 228–9; M. M. Phillips, 'Erasmus and the Classics', in *Erasmus*, ed. T. A. Dorey, (London, 1971), pp. 1–30. On the meaning of the words *grammaticus* and *grammatice*, in Erasmus, see Chomarat, *Grammaire et rhétorique*, 1. 183.

18 Trans. from *CWE* 1, pp. 113–15, ll. 1–31; Allen, *Ep.* 56, I. 172–3, II. 1–27, 35–65, Paris, 1497.

19 Trans. from *CWE* 1, pp. 118, ll. 45–47; Allen, *Ep.* 58, I. 176, ll. 42–3, Paris, 1497.

20 Allen, *Ep.* 61, I. 182, ll. 41–9, Paris 1497; *Ep.* 1745, VI. 404, ll. 1–10, Basel, 1526.

21 Trans. from *CWE* 1, p. 133, ll. 15–24; Allen, *Ep.* 63, I. 189, ll. 13–23, Paris, 1497.

22 Trans. from *CWE* 1, p. 133, ll. 9–12; Allen, *Ep.* 62, I. 88, ll. 8–10.

23 Trans. from *CWE* 1, pp. 111–13, ll. 9–59; Allen, I. 170, ll. 8–50. Erasmus returned to this quarrel in letters 59 and 60 which, it seems to me, could as well have been addressed to Christian Northoff as to Robert Fisher or Mambaer.

24 Allen, *Ep.* 4, I. 57, ll. 29–47.

25 Trans. from *CWE* 1, pp. 105–6, ll. 4–7; Allen, *Ep.* 50, I. 164–5, ll. 3–6.

26 L.-E. Halkin, 'Érasme pèlerin', in *Scrinium Erasmianum* (Louvain, 1969), 2. 249. Three years later, afflicted again with the illness, he repeated his confidence in St Geneviève.

27 Trans. from *CWE* 1, p. 128, ll. 125–38; Allen, *Ep.* 61, I. 184, ll. 117–30, Paris, August 1497.

28 Trans. from *CWE* 1, p. 151, ll. 6–11; Allen, *Ep.* 75, I. 202, ll. 5–8, to Arnold of Bosch, Paris, c. April 1498.

29 Allen, *Ep.* 1, I. 7, l. 22; A Jacob, 'L'Édition érasmienne de la Liturgie de saint Jean Chrysostome', in *Italia medievale e umanistica* (Padua, 1976), 19. 291–324.

30 Trans. from *CWE* 1, pp. 99–100; Allen, *Ep.* 96–100, I. 235–6, c. 1499.

31 Trans. from *CWE* 1, p. 151, ll. 15–23; Allen, *Ep.* 75, I. 202, ll. 13–21, to Arnold of Bosch, Paris, c. April 1498.

32 Trans. from *CWE* 1, p. 165, ll. 74–5; Allen, *Ep.* 81, I. 214, ll. 68–9, to Willem Hermans, Paris, c. December 1498.

33 Trans. from *CWE* 1, p. 181, pp. 5–9; Allen, *Ep.* 92, I. 228, ll. 6–8, Willem Hermans to Servatius Rogerus, February 1499.

34 Trans. from *CWE* 1, p. 170, ll. 92–113; Allen, *Ep.* 53, I. 219, ll. 80–98, to Willem Hermans, Paris, 14 Dec. 1498. By 1497, Erasmus had had to defend himself against the calumny of Thomas Grey's tutor: Allen, *Ep.* 58, I. 177, ll. 89–95.

35 Trans. from *CWE* 1, pp. 168–9, ll. 58–60; Allen, *Ep.* 53, I. 218, ll. 51–2, to Willem Hermans, 14 Dec. 1498.

36 Between Calais and St Omer. See J. Hadot, 'Érasme à Tournehem et à Courtebourne', in *Colloquia Erasmiana Turonensia*, vol. 1, p. 321, l. 100 (letter 93).

37 Trans. from *CWE* 1, p. 185, ll. 111–18; Allen, *Ep.* 93, I. 232, ll. 100–6, Tracy, *Growth of a Mind*, p. 96.

CHAPTER 5: ENGLAND: A SECOND HOMELAND

1 M. Pollet. 'Érasme en Angleterre', in *Colloquia Erasmiana Turonensia*, 1. 163. I shall make further borrowings from this article. See also R. Marcel, 'Les découverts d'Érasme en Angleterre', in *Bibliothèque d'Humanisme et Renaissance* (Geneva, 1952), 14. pp. 117–24. Erasmus has been translated and commented on severely by G. Marc'hadour and R. Galibois, *Érasme de Rotterdam et Thomas More* (Sherbrooke, 1985).

2 Erasmus to Richard Whitford, 1 May 1506, Trans. from *CWE* 2, p. 113, ll. 12–14; Allen, *Ep.* 191, I. 422, ll. 9–11.

3 Trans. from *CWE* 1, p. 193, ll. 17–26; Allen, *Ep.* 103, I. 238–9, ll. 17–22, to Fausto Andrelini, from England, summer, 1499.

4 The scene is described by Erasmus in 1523 in his famous letter to Botzheim: Allen, *Ep.* I, I. 6, ll. 4–28. The letter (autumn, 1499) in Allen, *Ep.* 104, I. 239. The poem *Prosopopeia Brittanniae*, in Reedick, *Poems*, p. 248 (No. 45). Erasmus was to judge his verse with a certain severity, while emphasizing its merits: Allen, *Ep.* 113, I. 261ff, to John Sixtin, Oxford, 28 Oct. 1499.

5 Trans. from *CWE* 1, pp. 235–6, ll. 18–32; Allen, *Ep.* 118, I. 273, ll. 15–27, December 1499.

6 P. I. Kaufman, 'John Colet and Erasmus' Enchiridion', in *Church History*, 46, (1977), 296–312.

7 Trans. from *CWE* 1, p. 201, ll. 50–9; Allen, *Ep.* 107, I. 244, ll. 40–9.

8 Trans. from *CWE* 1, p. 199, ll. 13–17, 25–8; Allen, *Ep.* 106, I. 242, ll. 11–23, Oxford, October 1499; see Béné, *Érasme et saint Augustin*, p. 110.

9 Trans. from *CWE* 1, p. 205, ll. 108–10; Allen, *Ep.* 108, I. 248, ll. 95–7.

10 This 'disputation' of 1499 was published in 1504 in the *Lucubratiunculae* of Erasmus under the title *Disputatiuncula de tedio, pavore, tristicia Iesu, instante crucis hora* (Antwerp, 1504, new style dating). Preface and extracts in Allen, *Ep.* 108–11, I. 245–53. Complete text in *LB* V. 1265–94. Analysis by G. Fokke, *Christus verae pacis auctor et unicus scopus. Erasmus and Origen* (Louvain, 1977) pp. 61–177. On the relationship between Erasmus and Colet see A. Godin, *Érasme. Vies de Jean Vitrier et de John Colet*, (Angers, 1982) On Colet's orthodoxy, see Béné, *Érasme et saint Augustin*, pp. 105ff. Chantraine, *Mystére et philosophie*, pp. 53ff, 280ff, Tracy, *Growth of a Mind*, p. 84.

11 J.-P. Massaut, *Critique et tradition* (Paris, 1974), p. 62. As we shall see, Erasmus was to follow this same theological line at the time of his conflict with Lefèvre. This doctrine would not prevent him from protesting against overly expressive representations of the Passion. See M. Bataillon, *Érasme et l'Espagne* (Paris, 1937), p. 202. Erasmus never forgot Christ crucified, *ASD* V. 1, p. 256, ll. 486–95 (*Explanatio Symboli*).

12 Allen, *Ep.* 109, I. 252, l. 116. Erasmus was to expound the same idea in the preface of the *Paraphrase on the Gospel According to St. Matthew*, in *LB* VII, col. xx 3 V°. The second citation after Pineau, *Érasme. Sa pensée*, p. 264.

13 Trans. from *CWE* 1, p. 230, ll. 25–29; Allen, *Ep.* 116, I. 268, ll. 22–6.

14 Trans. from *CWE* 1, pp. 231–2, ll. 53–82, 109–10; Allen, *Ep.* 116, I. 269, ll. 46–93, to John Sixtin, Oxford, November 1499.

15 Allen, *Ep.* 113, I. 265, ll. 148–52, to John Sixtin, Oxford, 28 Oct. 1499. In this passage Erasmus remarked that his Muse had been dead for ten years.

16 Chantraine, *Mystère et philosophie,* p. 356. Godin, *Érasme lecteur d'Origène* (Geneva, 1982) p. 14. The contrary thesis was put forward forcefully by J. Ijsewjn, 'Erasmus ex poeta theologus' in *Scrinium Erasmianum,* 1. 380ff.

17 Erasmus was to stop calling himself a poet. His poetry was, besides, inferior to his prose. It is marked more by ingenuity than by inspiration, and his models, Spagnuoli and Andrelini among others, are scarcely any better. See Allen, *Ep.* 1581, VI. 100, ll. 524–8, to Bédier, 1525.

18 Trans. from *CWE* 1, p. 246, ll. 2–7, 23–33; Allen, *Ep.* 120, I. 282, ll. 1–30, Tournehem, February 1500.

19 Allen, I. 591. See D. F. S. Thomson and H. C. Porter, *Erasmus and Cambridge* (Toronto, 1963); E. Rummel, 'The use of Greek in Erasmus's letters', in *Humanistica Lovaniensia* (Louvain, 1981), 30. 55–92.

20 Allen, III. xxix. Only in 1517 was he to be authorized to leave the order in which he had made his profession.

21 Trans. from *CWE* 1, pp. 117–18, ll. 18–25; Allen, *Ep.* 194, I. 427, ll. 15–21.

22 Trans. from *CWE* 2, p. 147, ll. 12–24, 26–30, 92–3; Allen, *Ep.* 215, I. 450, ll. 11–27, 27 May 1509.

23 Charlier, *Érasme et l'amitié,* p. 41.

24 Trans. from *CWE* 2, p. 186, ll. 58–68; Allen, *Ep.* 237, I. 478, ll. 50–60, 29 Oct. 1511.

25 Trans. from *CWE* 2, p. 187, ll. 4–6; Allen, *Ep.* 238, I. 480, ll. 2–4, 2 Nov. 1511.

26 Trans. from *CWE* 2, p. 262, ll. 6–9; Allen, *Ep.* 262, I. 513, ll. 5–10. The votive poem was published in 1515 in the *Lucubrationes.* Text in Reedijk, *Poems,* p. 303 (No. 92).

27 *ASD.* I. 3, p. 483, ll. 468–77.

28 Between 1512 and 1514. See K. Bauer, 'John Colet und Erasmus von Rotterdam', in *ARG,* Ergänzungsband 5 (Leipzig, 1929), pp. 173–5. See also *ASD* V. 1, p. 154, ll. 155–7 (*Modus orandi*).

29 *ASD* I. 3, p. 257, ll. 790–5 (*Convivium religiosum*); pp. 486–9, ll. 590–703 (*Peregrinatio*).

30 This was also the attitude of his friends More and Colet. See G. Marc'hadour, *Thomas More et la Bible* (Paris, 1969), p. 421.

31 *De ratione studii,* ed. J.-Cl. Margolin, *ASD.* I. 2 (Amsterdam, 1971), pp. 111–51, first edn, Paris, 1951.

32 *De copia verborum,* 1st edn., Paris, Bade, 1512; *LB* I. 3–110. See Margaret Mann Phillips, 'Erasmus and the art of writing', in *Scrinium Erasmianum,* 1 (Leiden, 1969), 335–50.

33 Trans. from *CWE* 24 (Literary and Educational Writings 2, ed. C. R. Thompson), p. 675, ll. 18–21.

34 Trans. from *CWE* 2, pp. 232–3, ll. 41–53; Allen, *Ep.* 263, I. 516, ll. 35–45, Paris, 19 May 1512.

35 Thomson and Porter, *Erasmus and Cambridge*, p. 14.
36 Trans. from *CWE* 4, p. 57, ll. 65–6; Allen, *Ep.* 457, II. 331, ll. 58–9, 27 Aug. 1516.
37 Trans. from *CWE* 2, p. 267, ll. 49–61; Allen, *Ep.* 282, I. 542, ll. 42–53, 28 Nov. 1513.
38 Allen, Introduction to *Ep.* 255, I. 501; G. Lawarrée, 'Érasme et l'argent', unpublished paper, University of Liège, 1973. Erasmus was to present a beautiful eulogy to Warham in 1535: *LB* V. 810 E.
39 Text, translation and substantial commentary by A. Prévost, *L'Utopie de Thomas More* (Paris, 1978).
40 Thomas More, Letter to Martin Dorp, original and translation in *The Complete Works of St. Thomas More*, vol. 15 (ed. D. Kinney, New Haven, 1986), pp. 2–3, ll. 13–21.
41 Trans. from *CWE* 4, p. 117, ll. 86–7; Allen, *Ep.* 481, II. 372, ll. 77–9.
42 Trans. from *CWE* 5, p. 12, ll. 52–7; Allen, *Ep.* 597, III. 6, ll. 47–52.
43 Trans. from *CWE* 5, pp. 828–9, ll. 6–8; Allen, *Ep.* 829, III. 295, ll. 4–6.
44 A. Gerlo, *Érasme et ses portraitistes* (Nieuwkoop, 1969), pp. 9–17.
45 Trans. from *CWE* 4, p. 368, ll. 8–17; Allen, *Ep.* 584, II. 576, ll. 6–14.
46 Trans. from *CWE* 5, p. 18, ll. 56–8; Allen, *Ep.* 601, III. 11–12, ll. 50–1; cf. Marc'hadour et Galibois, *Érasme de Rotterdam*, pp. 78ff.
47 Trans. from *CWE* 5, p. 106, ll. 2–5; Allen, *Ep.* 654, III. 76, ll. 1–4.
48 Trans. from *CWE* 5, p. 147, ll. 14–16; Allen, *Ep.* 683, III. 104, ll. 12–15.
49 Trans. from *CWE* 5, pp. 149–50, ll. 15–25; Allen, *Ep.* 684, III. 105–106, ll. 11–22.
50 M. Delcourt, *Érasme*, 2nd edn. (Brussels, 1986), p. 107.
51 Trans. from *CWE* 7, pp. 19–22, ll. 137–48, 172–201; Allen, *Ep.* 999, IV. 16, ll. 131–86, to Hutten, 1519.
52 R. J. Schoek, 'Telling More from Erasmus', in *Moreana*, 23 (Angers, 1986), 11–20.
53 Erasmus said it again in 1516: Allen, *Ep.* 392, II. 264, l. 20, to Rieger.

CHAPTER 6: PARIS AND LOUVAIN: FROM THE FIRST *ADAGES* TO THE *PANEGYRIC*

1 Paris, June 1500, enlarged edition by edition until it became an extensive anthology of more than 4,000 proverbs in 1536; critical edition in progress by F. Heinimann and E. Kienzle: *ASD* II. 5; II. 6ff. See M. M. Phillips, *The Adages of Erasmus* (Cambridge, 1964).
2 Chr. B. Beuermann, 'Le renouvellement de l'esprit par l'adage', in *Bibliothèque d'Humanisme et Renaissance*, 47 (1955), 347–55.
3 Trans. from *CWE* 1, pp. 257–8, 260–3, ll. 19–23, 49–58, 129–48, 169–72, 185–90; Allen, *Ep.* 126, I. 290–4, ll. 15–19, 110–38, 143–62, c. June 1500.
4 Trans. from *CWE* 1, p. 190, ll. 2–18; Allen, *Ep.* 101, I. 236, ll. 1–16, Paris, May 1499.
5 Trans. from *CWE* 1, pp. 249–50, ll. 25–8; p. 252, ll. 69–74; Allen, *Ep.* 123, I. 285, ll. 22–5, Paris, c. March 1500; *Ep.* 124, I. 286, ll. 61–4 Paris, 12 Apr. 1500.

6 L.-E. Halkin, 'Érasme et les langues' in *Revue des langues vivantes*, 35. 570–1 (Brussels, 1969). Chomarat, *Grammaire et rhetorique*, 1. 306–11. E. Rummel, 'The Use of Greek in Erasmus' letters', in *Humanistica Lovanensia*, 30 (Louvain, 1981), 55–92.

7 Trans. from *CWE* 1, p. 254, ll. 14–44; Allen, *Ep.* 125, I. 288–9, ll. 11–35, spring 1500. Erasmus takes up an ancient theme dear to Petrarch: P. De Nolhac, *Pétrarque*, p. 43. This letter also brings to mind the development of Erasmus's library. See F. Husner, 'Die Bibliothek des Erasmus', in *Gedenkschrift zum 400. Todestage des Erasmus* (Basel, 1936) pp. 228–59.

8 Trans. from *CWE* 1, pp. 295–7, ll. 41–60, 79–97; Allen, *Ep.* 138, I. 321, ll. 36–86, Orleans, 11 Dec. 1500.

9 Trans. from *CWE* 1, pp. 301–2, ll. 41–6; Allen, *Ep.* 139, I. 326, ll. 34–9, Orleans, c. 12 Dec. 1500.

10 Trans. from *CWE* 2, pp. 26–7, ll. 65–75; Allen, *Ep.* 149, I. 353, ll. 56–65, c. 16 Mar. 1501.

11 Trans. from *CWE* 1, p. 268, ll. 11–12; Allen, *Ep.* 128, I. 298, ll. 10–11, to Batt, Paris, July 1500.

12 Trans. from *CWE* 1, p. 291, ll. 54–5; Allen, *Ep.* 136, I. 317, ll. 49–50, 9 Dec. 1500.

13 Trans. from *CWE* 2, pp. 15–16, ll. 109–33; Allen, *Ep.* 145, I. 344, ll. 95–116, Paris, 27 Jan. 1501. See L.-E. Halkin, 'Érasme docteur', in *Mélanges André Latreille* (Lyons, 1972) pp. 39–47.

14 On the relations between Erasmus and Vitrier, see A. Godin, *Érasme. Vies de Jean Vitrier et de John Colet* (Angers, 1982) pp. 24–45. It is likely that Erasmus made the acquaintance of Vitrier in 1501 at the latest.

15 Trans. from *CWE* 2, pp. 11–12, ll. 2–22; Allen, *Ep.* 144, I. 341, ll. 1–17, Paris, 26 Jan. 1501. Erasmus sent 100 copies of the *Adages* to England to be sold there. At the end of 1504 he had received nothing. See Allen, *Ep.* 181, I. 405, II. 61–71, to John Colet, Paris, c. December 1504.

16 Allen, *Ep.* 171, I. 380, ll. 10–15, to Nicholas Werner, Louvain, September 1502. It was perhaps a question of some lessons to be given in Greek. See also R. Giese, 'Erasmus's knowledge of the vernacular languages' in *Romantic Review*, 18. 5 (New York, 1937). On Erasmus's studies at Louvain, see Allen, *Ep.* 181, I. 403, Introduction.

17 Ed. O. Herding, in *ASD* IV. 1, pp. 23–93, (Amsterdam, 1974). See also V. de Caprariis, 'Il Panegyricus di Erasmo a Filippo di Borgogna', in *Rivista storica Italiana*, 65 (1953), 199–211; J. D. Tracy, *The Politics of Erasmus* (Toronto, 1978), pp. 17–22; Allen, *Ep.* 179, I. 397, ll. 139–43, to Nicholas Ruistre, c. February 1504.

18 Trans. from *CWE* 27, p. 7; *ASD*. IV. 1, p. 72, ll. 500–1.

19 Trans. from *CWE* 27, p. 53; *ASD* IV. 1, p. 72.

20 See *CWE* 27, p. 36; *ASD* IV. 1, p. 56, ll. 935–47. Erasmus was not always a Francophile, as is evidenced in his *Prosopopeia Brittanniae* of 1499. See Reedijk, *Poems*, p. 248 (No. 45). He was to find the same sentiments in 1513 in his *In Fugam Gallorum* which which recalled the French defeat of Guinegate: Reedijk, *Poems*, p. 304 (No. 93).

21 Trans. from *CWE* 27, p. 56; *ASD* IV. 1, p. 75, l. 596.

CHAPTER 7: AN INTRODUCTION TO THE DEVOUT LIFE: *THE HANDBOOK OF THE CHRISTIAN SOLDIER*

1 The first edition of the *Enchiridion* appeared in the *Lucubratiunculae*, Antwerp 1503 (old style dating): text in H. Holborn, *Desiderius Erasmus Ausgewählte Werke*, Munich, 1933, pp. 1–136. The English translation in *CWE* 66, pp. 1–127, from which the quotations in this chapter are taken, is based on the 1519 Schürer edition. See also R. Stupperich, 'Das Enchiridion des Erasmus' in *ARG 4*, 69, pp. 5–23. M. M. de la Garanderie, *Christianisme et lettres profanes*, Lille-Paris, 1976, vol. 1, pp. 21ff.; Béné, *Érasme of St Augustin*, pp. 181ff.; Godin, *Érasme, Lecteur*, pp. 21ff.; H. de Lubac, *Pic de la Mirandole*, Paris, 1974, pp. 209ff., 395ff.; On Erasmus's spirituality see J.-P. Massaut, in the *Dictionnaire de spiritualité*, Paris, 1969, vol. 7, cols. 1006–28. On the Sorbonne censures against the *Enchiridion* and Erasmus's other books, see F. Higman, *Censorship and the Sorbonne, 1520–51*, (Geneva, 1979). See also R. De Molen, *The Spirituatity of Erasmus*, Nieuwkoop, 1987.

2 The *Handbook* is a work which emphasizes the role of the human will.

3 Holborn, *Desiderius Erasmus*, p. 32, l. 32.

4 Trans. from *CWE* 66, pp. 61–2. (*LB* V. 25A); Holborn, *Desiderius Erasmus*, pp. 63–4. See also Allen, XI. 183, ll. 467–8 (No. 3032) to Johannes Koler, Basel, 1535.

5 Trans. from *CWE* 66, pp. 31 (*LB* V. 5E); Holborn, *Desiderius Erasmus*, p. 29, l. 23; p. 30, ll. 13–14; p. 67, l. 5; p. 38, ll. 25–6; p. 83, ll. 25–85.

6 Trans. from *CWE* 66, pp. 79–80 (*LB* V. 35E).

7 Trans. from *CWE* 66, p. 81. (*LB* V. 36F); E. W. Kohle, *Die Theologie des Erasmus*, Basel, 1966, pp. 78 and 102.

8 Trans. from *CWE* 66, pp. 82, 63–4, 72–3 (*LB* V 36F).

9 Trans. from *CWE* 66, p. 71 (*LB* V. 30F).

10 Trans. from *CWE* 66, p. 72 (*LB* V. 31D).

11 Trans. from *CWE* 66, p. 64 (*LB* V. 26E); Holborn, *Desiderius Erasmus*, p. 87, ll. 2–3; p. 66, ll. 7–10; p. 74, ll. 25–7; p. 75, ll. 35–7; p. 74, ll. 33–4; p. 66, II. 26–32. Cf. *LB* V. 167 A-B (*Exomologesis*); L.-E. Halkin, *Erasmus pélerin*, pp. 239–58; Halkin, 'La place des indulgences dans le pensée religieuse d'Erasmus' in the *Bulletin de la Société de l'histoire du protestantisme français*, 129. 143–54; L. Bouyer, *Autour d'Erasme*, Paris, 1955, p. 149. The undoubted abuses do not allow us, however, to conclude that popular piety was in decline. Cf. B. Moeller, 'Frömmigkeit in Deutschland um 1500', in *ARG* Gütersloh, 1965, vol. 56, pp. 5–30 (Eng. trans. in H. C. E. Midelfort and M. U. Edwards, *Imperial Cities and the Reformation*, Philadelphia, 1972). Without putting in question the profound nature of popular piety in the Middle Ages, we may ask two questions: does the large number of chapels show a true preaching of the Gospel on the part of the Church? Have the saints sometimes attained a greater place within piety than Jesus Christ?

12 Trans. from *CWE* 66, p. 113 (*LB* V. 56C) Holborn, *Desiderius Erasmus*, p. 120, ll. 7–13. It should be noted that Erasmus ignored the obsession with satanism, so frequent at his time.

13 *LB* IX. 954 D-E (*Declarationes ad censuras*) Holborn, *Desiderius Erasmus*, p. 146, ll. 6–12 (*Paraclesis*) *LB* VII. 1046 C-E (*Paraphrasis in epistolas duas Pauli ad Timotheum*).

14 Trans. from *CWE* 66, p. 127 (*LB* V. 65B).

15 This is the meaning of the famous passage from the *Handbook*: 'Being a monk is not a state of holiness' (*CWE* 66, p. 127, LB V. 65B); cf. Holborn, *Desiderius Erasmus*, p. 135, ll. 8–9.

16 Trans. from *CWE* 66, p. 28 (*LB* V. 32E).

17 Trans. from *CWE* 66, p. 81 (*LB* V. 4B); Holborn, *Desiderius Erasmus*, p. 76, ll. 29–35; p. 70, ll. 11–28; p. 26, l. 27 – p. 27, l. 11.

18 Trans. from *CWE* 66, p. 84 (*LB* V. 38E); Holborn, *Desiderius Erasmus*, p. 88, ll. 21–32.

19 J. Étienne, *Spiritualisme érasmien et théologiens louvanistes* (Louvain, 1956), p. 16; Bataillon, *Erasme et l'Espagne*, p. 211; R. H. Bainton, *Erasmus of Christendom* (New York, 1969), p. 65.

20 G. Marc'hadour, *Thomas More ou la sage folie* (Paris, 1971), p. 21.

21 As J. Dagens said.

22 The word is P. Mesnard's.

23 St Ignatius, however, was to assert that the *Handbook* did not further the cause of piety. Cf. M. Rotsaert, 'Les premiers contacts de saint Ignace avec l'érasmisme espagnol', in the *Revue de l'histoire de la spiritualité* (Paris, 1973), 9. 443–63; J. C. Olin, *Luther, Erasmus and the Reformation* (New York, 1969), pp. 114–33.

24 Trans. from H. A. Oberman (ed.), *Forerunners of the Reformation* (New York, 1966), pp. 312–13; cf. Allen, *Ep.* 181, I. 404, ll. 30–1, Paris, 1504; *Ep.* 182, I. 406–12. The volume was published by Josse Bade: Chomarat, 'Les Annotations de Valla' in the collective work *Histoire de l'exegèse au XVIe siècle* (Geneva, 1978), pp. 202–28; J. H. Bentley, 'Lorenzo Valla and Erasmus' in the *Sixteenth Century Journal*, 8 (1977), 9–27.

25 Chomarat, *Grammaire et rhétorique*, 1. 321ff.

26 Trans. from *CWE* 2, p. 87; Allen, *Ep.* 181, I. 405, ll. 36–8.

27 Trans. from *CWE* 3, p. 63; Allen, *Ep.* 324, II. 50–1, ll. 31–2.

CHAPTER 8: ITALY AND THE RETURN TO THE SOURCES

1 Trans. from *CWE* 5, 365, ll. 142–4; Allen, *Ep.* 809, III. 267, ll. 124–5. See L.-E. Halkin, 'Érasme en Italie', in the *Colloquia Erasmiana Turonensia* (Paris, 1972), 1. 38–53. On Erasmus's stay in Italy see also P. O. Kristeller, 'Erasmus from an Italian Perspective', in *Renaissance Quarterly*, 23 (1970), 1–14; E. Garin, 'Erasmo e l'Umanesimo italiano', in *Bibliothèque d'Humanisme et Renaissance* 33 (1971), 7–17; S. Seidel Menchi, *La cultura italiana di fronte a Erasmo*, in *Eresia e Riforma nell' Italia des Cinquecento. Miscellanea* (Florence, 1974), 1. 71–2; M. P. Gilmore, 'Italian reaction to Erasmian Humanism', in *Itinerarium Italicum*, ed. H. A. Oberman and T. A. Brady (Leiden, 1975), pp. 61–115; J. W. O'Malley, 'Preaching for the Popes', in *The Pursuit of Holiness*, ed. C. Trinkaus and H. A. Oberman (Leiden, 1974), pp. 408–40;

W. J. Koster, 'Een brief van Arsenius aan Erasmus', in *Hermeneus*, 11 (1939), 17–20.

2   Trans. from *CWE* 2. p. 125, ll. 3–4. Allen, *Ep.* 203, I. 433, ll. 2–3, to Servatius Rogerus, Bologna, 16 Nov. 1506; cf. *Ep.* 118, I. 273, ll. 3–4, to Robert Fisher, 5 Dec. 1499; Chomarat, *Grammaire et rhétorique*, 2. 840.

3   Trans. from R. H. Bainton, *Erasmus of Christendom* (New York, 1969), p. 79, from the original in C. Reedick, *The Poems of Desiderius Erasmus* (Leiden, 1956), pp. 280ff.; cf. J.-Cl. Margolin, 'Le chant alpestre d'Érasme' in *Érasme dans son miroir et dans son village* (London, 1987) pp. 37–9; Thomson, *Erasmus as a Poet*, pp. 201–5.

4   Halkin, 'Érasme docteur', pp. 39–47.

5   Trans. from *CWE* 2, p. 128, ll. 41–3; Allen, *Ep.* 205, I. 435, ll. 38–9, to Jérôme de Busleiden, Bologna, 17 Nov. 1506.

6   The very harsh pamphlet *Julius Exclusus* was to be published in 1518 anonymously, doubtless because Erasmus was careful in handling Leo X, Julius II's successor; ed. W. K. Ferguson, *Erasmi opuscula* (The Hague, 1933), pp. 65–124.

7   We have already cited the critical edition of the *Adages*. On the adage 'Man is only a bubble', inspired by the Scriptures, see H.-D. Saffrey, 'Homo bulla', in *Epectasis: Mélanges Danielou* (Paris, 1972), pp. 533–44. On the learned Greeks in Venice and their relations with Erasmus, see D. J. Geanakoplos, *Greek Scholars in Venice* (Cambridge, Mass., 1962), pp. 256–78.

8   Trans. from *CWE* 2, p. 145, ll. 2–8. Allen, *Ep.* 212, I. 447–8, ll. 1–7.

9   *ASD* I. 2, pp. 637–9 (*Ciceronianus*); O'Malley, *Preaching for the Popes*, pp. 408–30, believes that it is unnecessary to generalize from Erasmus's severe judgement. See L. Gualda Rosa, 'Ciceroniano o cristiano? A proposito di Tommaso Fedra Inghirami', in *Humanistica Lovaniensia* (Louvain, 1985), 34. 52–64.

10 Allen, *Ep.* 3032, XI. 182, ll. 417–33, to Johannes Koler, c. August 1535.

11 *ASD* II. 6, p. 184, l. 490 (*Adagia*).

12 Allen, *Ep.* 1, I. 37, ll. 2–7. These texts, which are now lost, were models of discourse *in genere suasorio*. Erasmus composed others like them.

13 Allen, *Ep.* 1558, VI. 45, ll. 21–6, to Pirckheimer, 1525; *Ep.* 2018, VII. 431, ll. 54–7, to Alfonso Valdès, 1528.

14 Allen, *Ep.* 2465, IX. 206–7, ll. 10–35, to Alexander Steuchus, 27 Mar. 1531. No letter from Rome has reached us! See G. J. Hoogewerff, 'Erasmus te Rome', in *De Gids* (Amsterdam, 1959) 2. 22–30.

15 Trans. from *CWE* 3, p. 94, ll. 36–41; Allen, *Ep.* 334, II. 74, ll. 34–8, to Cardinal Grimani, 1515. See also Allen, *Ep.* 540, II. 486, ll. 48–50, to William Latimer, 1517; *Ep.* 2209, VIII. 264, ll. 30–1, to Charles Utenhove, 1529; *Ep.* 3032, XI. 177, ll. 210–32, to Johannes Koler, 1535.

16 Allen, *Ep.* 1358, V. 276, ll. 10–12.

CHAPTER 9: A RELIGIOUS PAMPHLET: *THE PRAISE OF FOLLY*

1   The Graeco-Latin title *Encomium Moriae* is a play on words on More and *Moria*, 'folly'. The first known edition was printed in Paris by Gilles de

Gourmont in 1511; critical edition by Cl. H. Miller in *ASD* IV. 3 pp. 71–195; Eng. trans. in *CWE* 27, pp. 77–153. From the countless studies I shall cite only: S. Dresden, 'Sagesse et folie d'après Érasme', in *Colloquia Erasmiana Turonensia* (Paris, 1972), 1. 285–99; M. Screech, *Ecstasy and the Praise of Folly* (London, 1980); J.-Cl. Margolin, 'Parodie et paradoxe dans l'Éloge de la Folie', in *Érasme, le prix des mots et de l'homme*, No. 5, pp. 27–57; D. G. Watson, 'Erasmus' Praise of Folly and the spirit of carnival' in *Renaissance Quarterly*, 32 (1979), 333–53; C. H. Miller, 'Styles and mixed genres in Erasmus's Praise of Folly', in *Acta conventus neo-Latini Guelphenbytani* (Wolfenbüthel, 1985), pp. 277–87; Z. Pavlovskis, *The Praise of Folly. Structure and Irony* (Leiden, 1983); L.-E. Halkin, 'Un pamphlet religieux au xvie siècle', in *Actes du colloque international Érasme* (Geneva, 1990), pp. 109–25.

2 The 1514 edition, as Screech has observed, was augmented by many passages which accentuated the religious inspiration of the book. Moreover Miller, its eventual editor, has shown in his critical notes that Erasmus did not invent the absurdities and incongruities that he denounced, but that he had actually read or heard them.

3 Trans. from *CWE* 27, pp. 83–5; *ASD* IV. 3, pp. 67–70, ll. 1–25, 42–67.

4 Trans. from *CWE* 27, pp. 86–8; *ASD* IV. 3, p. 72, ll. 23–9, p. 74, ll. 62–73.

5 Trans. from *CWE* 27, pp. 138–9; *ASD* IV. 3, pp. 172–4, ll. 788–97, 802–11.

6 Trans. from *CWE* 27, p. 135; *ASD* IV. 3, p. 168, ll. 675–86.

7 Trans. from *CWE* 27, pp. 125–7, 146–7; *ASD* IV. 3, pp. 144–6, ll. 361–75, 381–98; pp. 148–50, 408–23; pp. 185–6, ll. 48–56.

8 Trans. from *CWE* 27, pp. 130–1; *ASD* IV. 3, pp. 158–60, ll. 524–37.

9 Trans. from *CWE* 27, pp. 132–5; *ASD* IV. 3, pp. 162–8, ll. 587–610, 646–55, 660–1.

10 Trans. from *CWE* 27, p. 124; *ASD* IV. 3, pp. 140–2, ll. 304–12.

11 Trans. from *CWE* 27, p. 99; *ASD* IV. 3, p. 96, ll. 464–71.

12 Trans. from *CWE* 27, p. 114; *ASD* IV. 3, pp. 122–4, ll. 961–73.

13 Trans. from *CWE* 27, pp. 115–16; *ASD* IV. 3, p. 126, ll. 23–7.

14 Trans. from *CWE* 27, pp. 149–52; *ASD* IV. 3, pp. 189–93, ll. 141–3, 159–81, 226–57. The prophet cited is Isaiah 64:4. Erasmus might have borrowed the 'divine Folly' from Marsilio Ficino; see P. O. Kristeller. 'Erasmus from an Italian perspective', in *Renaissance Quarterly*, 23 (1970), 11; M. A. Screech, 'L'Éloge de la Folie et les études bibliques d'Érasme', in *Réforme et Humanisme*, Actes du IVe Colloque (Montpellier, 1977), pp. 149–65.

15 Chantraine, *Mystère et philosophie*, pp. 212–13.

16 Erasmus may have known Olivier Maillard. Cf. Chomarat, *Grammaire et rhétorique*, I. 132.

17 I Cor. 1: 18 and 26; 3: 18–19. See *ASD* IV. 3, pp. 186–8, ll. 67–140. The author of *The Imitation of Christ* (I. XVII. 2) spoke no differently: 'You must become fools for Christ.' And Luther: 'He who would be saved must become a fool.' Cf. M. Lienhard, *Martin Luther* (1983), p. 339. In the *Enchiridion*, Erasmus had already denounced the *sapientia carnis quae inimica est Deo*. Cf. Holborn, *Erasmus ausgewählte Werke*, p. 78, ll. 33–4.

18 Froben's edition of the *Folly*, in 1515, was printed in 1,800 copies. By 17 April all except sixty were sold. See Allen, *Ep.* 328, II. 64, ll. 47–8.

19 Marc'hadour, *Thomas More ou la sage folie,* p. 28.
20 *ASD* 1V. 3, p. 178, ll. 907–910.
21 Allen, *Ep.* 337, II. 93, ll. 91–2; *ASD* 1V. 3, p. 193, l. 257; see also p. 190, l. 158: 'Do not fear words: rather weigh up reality.'
22 Allen, *Ep.* 337, II. 103, ll. 468–9. On the diverse interpretations of the *Folly,* see J. Huizinga, *Erasmus and the Age of the Reformation* (New York, 1957), pp. 69–78; R. H. Bainton, *Erasmus of Christendom,* pp. 90–7. Chomarat, *Grammaire et rhétorique,* pp. 970–1001. A fine tribute to the *Folly* by Paul Volz in 1515 may be found in Allen, *Ep.* 368, II. 159, ll. 1–10 (*CWE* 3, p. 189).

CHAPTER 10: FROM THE *FOUNDATIONS OF THE ABUNDANT STYLE* TO *THE EDUCATION OF THE CHRISTIAN PRINCE*

1 Trans. from *CWE* 2, pp. 168–9; Allen, *Ep.* 225, I. 466, ll. 11–18.
2 Trans. from *CWE* 2, p. 235; Allen, *Ep.* 265, I. 518, ll. 6–9 (1512).
3 Trans. from *CWE* 3, p. 49; Allen, *Ep.* 315, II. 38, ll. 11–18 (1514).
4 Trans. from *CWE* 2, pp. 280–1; Allen, *Ep.* 288, I. 552–3, ll. 21–59 (1514).
5 Trans. from *CWE* 2, pp. 294–5; Allen, *Ep.* 296, I. 565, ll. 12–22 (1514). Erasmus never published this letter, but the text because known from 1515 by clandestine printing. See Halkin, *Erasmus ex Erasmo,* p. 78, n. 46.
6 Trans. from *CWE* 2, p. 303; Allen, *Ep.* 296, I. 573, ll. 236–7.
7 Allen *Ep.* 301, II. 6, ll. 14–32, to Mountjoy, Basel, 30 Aug. 1514. The promised *Paraphrase* appeared in 1517 and Erasmus's devotion to St Paul eloquently expressed itself therein: Allen, *Ep.* 710, III. 138–9, ll. 49–87.
8 Trans. from *CWE* 3, pp. 32–3; Allen, *Ep.* 305, II. 24, ll. 240–1.
9 M. M. Phillips (ed.), *The Adages of Erasmus,* Cambridge, 1964.
10 *Adagiorum Chiliades* (Froben, Basel, 1515), Preface.
11 Phillips, *Adages,* pp. 269–72.
12 *ASD* II. 5, pp. 160ff. The Silenus is inspired by Pico della Mirandola; cf. H. de Lubac, *Pic de la Mirandole,* Paris, 1974, p. 24.
13 Eng. trans. in Phillips (ed.), *Adages,* pp. 308–53.
14 Phillips (ed.), *Adages,* pp. 321–2.
15 Phillips (ed.), *Adages,* p. 338.
16 Phillips (ed.), *Adages,* p. 331.
17 Phillips (ed.), *Adages,* pp. 344–8.
18 *Aut fatuum aut regem nasci oportere,* I. iii. 1, *LB,* 2, 106C, Eng. trans. in Phillips (ed.), *Adages,* pp. 213–29.
19 *Scarabeus aquilam quaerit,* III. vii. 1, *LB* 2. 869A, Eng. trans. in Phillips (ed.), *Adages,* pp. 229–63.
20 *Felix qui nihil debet,* II. vii. 98, *LB* 2. 637D.
21 *Spartam nactus est, hanc orna,* II. v. 1 *LB* 2. 551E, Eng. trans. in Phillips (ed.), *Adages,* pp. 300–8.
22 Trans. from *CWE* 3, pp. 102–3; Allen, *Ep.* 335, II. 82, ll. 76–7; 83, ll. 109–10, 133.
23 Allen, *Ep.* 386, II. 189–92 (1514).
24 Trans. from *CWE* 3, pp. 114–15; Allen, *Ep.* 337, II. 93, ll. 86–94.

25 Trans. from *CWE* 3, pp. 124–5; Allen, *Ep.* 337, II. 101–2, ll. 413–32.
26 Trans. from *CWE* 3, p. 130; Allen, *Ep.* 337, II. 106, ll. 605–8.
27 Halkin, *Erasmus ex Erasmo*, p. 27.
28 Trans. from *CWE* 3, p. 87; Allen, *Ep.* 333, II. 70, ll. 41–2.
29 Trans. from *CWE* 3, p. 244 (*Ep.* 391A in this edition); Allen, *Ep.* 364, II. 154, ll. 22–30.
30 *ASD* V. 2 pp. 30–80, ed. A. Godin. On the many commentaries on the psalms, see Béné, *ASD* V. 2, introduction to the edition; Chomarat, *Grammaire et rhétorique*, 1. 665–710.
31 *A.S.D.* IV. 1, pp. 136–219, ed. O. Herding.
32 It was in the preface to the New Testament that Erasmus called Charles 'princeps Burgundionum'. Cf. L.-E. Halkin, 'Érasme entre François I et Charles Quint' in the *Bulletin de l'Institut historique belge de Rome*, 44. 309 (Brussels and Rome, 1974). See also Pasquier de la Barre, *Journal d'un bourgeois de Tournai*, ed. G. Moreau (Brussels, 1975), p. 193.
33 Trans. from *CWE* 3, p. 249; Allen, *Ep.* 393, II. 206, ll. 41–9, c. March 1516. Erasmus did not hesitate to describe Alexander as a 'hero of international banditry'. Cf. Allen, *Ep.* 704, III. 129, ll. 24–5, 4 Nov. 1517.
34 *ASD* IV. 1, p. 163, ll. 845–8.
35 It seems amazing that neither Erasmus nor Machiavelli cites the other. Cf. Telle, *Érasme et le septiéme sacrement*, p. 43. On the relationship between the *Education of the Christian Prince* and More's *Utopia*, see Herding, *ASD* IV. 1, p. 129, n. 103.
36 Trans. from *CWE* 27, p. 251; *ASD* IV. 1, p. 180, ll. 460–2.
37 Trans. from *CWE* 27, pp. 287–8; *ASD* IV. 1, p. 219, ll. 643–8.

CHAPTER 11: THE *NEW TESTAMENT*

1 *Erasmus Roterodamus. Novum instrumentum*, repr. of the 1516 Basel edition, with introduction and critical notes by Heinz Holeczek (Stuttgart, 1983); H. Gibaud, *Un inédit d'Érasme. La première version du Nouveau Testament copiée par Pierre Meghen (1506–1509)*, Angers, 1982; A. Rabil, *Erasmus and the New Testament*, San Antonio, 1972. H. J. de Jonge, 'Novum Testamentum a nobis versum. The essence of Erasmus's edition', in *Journal of Theological Studies*, NS 35. 394–413. On the *Annotations*, see Chomarat, *Grammaire et rhétorique*, 1. 541–86; Godin, *Érasme, Lecteur*, pp. 127–31; A. Reeve, *Erasmus's Annotations on the New Testament. The Gospels* (London, 1986). See also J. H. Bentley, *Humanists and Holy Writ* (Princeton, 1983); J. Aldridge, *The Hermeneutic of Erasmus* (Richmond, 1966). A. J. Brown, 'The date of Erasmus's translation of the New Testament', in *Transactions of the Cambridge Bibliographical Society*. 8, 351–80 (Cambridge, 1984); E. W. Kohls, *Die Theologie des Erasmus*, 1. 126–43; 2. 116–18.
2 Erasmus used a manuscript of the Apocalypse lent by Reuchlin. He described it as so ancient that it might have belonged to the apostolic age, but modern scholars attribute it to the twelfth century. Cf. Allen, *Ep.* 373, II. 165, Introduction.

3 Cf. Bainton, *Erasmus of Christendom* ch. 6.

4 M. O'R Boyle, *Erasmus on Language and Method in theology* (Toronto, 1977) pp. 3–31; Marc'hadour, *Thomas More et la Bible*, pp. 124–36; Chomarat, *Grammaire et rhétorique*, 1. 41.

5 This manuscript was found for him. Erasmus gave in, but posterity has followed Erasmus's first inclinations. Cf. J. H. Bentley, 'Erasmus, Jean Le Clerc, and the principle of the harder reading', in *Renaissance Quarterly*, 31. 314ff.

6 *LB* 6. 1024F. The Council of Trent was to persist in holding to the Pauline authorship of this Epistle.

7 A. Motte, 'Le Christ dans les Paraphrases d'Érasme sur les Évangiles', unpublished paper, University of Liège, 1985.

8 *LB* 6. 30C. Reeve, *Erasmus's Annotations*, p. 30. Always, in his annotation to the second part of the same verse ('Turn the other cheek') Erasmus affirmed that this last invitation should not be taken literally; it only prescribed great patience, and consequently did not leave the way open to justify a radical theory of the acceptance of injustice.

9 Allen, *Ep.* 373, II. 170, ll. 175–80, Preface of 1515. Calvin was to speak no differently in his famous *Treatise on Relics*.

10 *LB* 6. 118E. See also *LB* 9. 1161C–F (*Responsio ad Albertum Pium*).

11 Holborn, *Erasmus*, p. 159 (*Methodus*).

12 Translation from J. C. Olin, ed., *Christian Humanism and the Reformation* (New York, 1965), pp. 92–106; pp. 102, 96–7; P. Mesnard, 'La Paraclésis d'Érasme', *Bibliothèque d'Humanisme et Renaissance*, 13. 7–42. A complete *Letter on Evangelical Philosophy* (postface) was to complete this teaching: *LB* 6. f°×4 v°. See also S. Cavazza, 'Erasmo e la philosophia Christi', in *Ragione e civilitas*, ed. D. Bigalli, (Milan, 1986), pp. 47–58.

13 Holborn, *Erasmus*, p. 173, ll. 30–1; p. 115, ll. 1–3.

14 Seidel Menchi, *Erasmo da Rotterdam*, p. 274, ll. 1213–14. Cf. R. H. Bainton, 'Erasmus and the persecuted' in *Scrinium Erasmianum* (Leiden, 1969) 2. 197–202.

15 C. Labaye, 'Érasme et les ordres mendiants', unpublished paper, University of Liège, 1979.

16 Trans. from *CWE* 5, p. 309; Allen, *Ep.* 778, III. 225, ll. 149–52, to Guillaume Budé, Louvain, 22 Feb. 1518. On the whole affair and its reverberations see J.-P. Massaut, *Critique et tradition* (Paris, 1974), pp. 61–6; M. Mann, *Érasme et les débuts de la Réforme française*, p. 24.

17 Trans. from *CWE* 6, p. 29; Allen, *Ep.* 844, III. 332, ll. 59–60.

18 Trans. from *CWE*, 3. 312; Allen, *Ep.* 423, II. 258, l. 47. See also Erasmus's letter to Fisher, *Ep.* 413, II. 244.

19 Trans. from *CWE*, 4. 49; Allen, *Ep.* 456, II. 325, ll. 130–5, to Henry Bullock, 22 Aug. 1516.

20 On this theme see E. W. Kohls, *Die Theologie des Erasmus* (Basel, 1966); R. Padberg, *Erasmus als Katechet* (Freiburg, 1959), pp. 115–16; L. Bouyer, *Autour d'Érasme* (Paris, 1955); J.-P. Massaut 'Humanisme et spiritualité chez Érasme', in *Dictionnaire de spiritualité* (Paris, 1969), vol. 7, cols 518–39; Chantraine, *Mystère et philosophie*, p. 370; M. Hoffmann, *Erkenntnis und Verwicklung des wahren Theologie nach Erasmus* (Tübingen, 1972), pp. 100, 227.

21 Chantraine, *Mystère et philosophie*, p. 263. See also, *LB* 7. 23A–27B (*Paraphrasis in Mattheum*).

22 Trans. from *CWE* 4. 91; Allen, *Ep.* 474, II. 354, l. 15, Antwerp, 2 Oct. 1516.

23 Trans. from *CWE* 4. 96; Allen, *Ep.* 476, II. 357, ll. 23–4, to Pieter Gillis, Brussels, 6 Oct. 1516.

24 See Allen, *Ep.* 739, III. 169, n. 9.

25 *Epistolae aliquot illustrium virorum ad Erasmum Roterodamus et huius ad illos.*

26 Trans. from *CWE* 3. 308–9; Allen, *Ep.* 421, II. 255–6, ll. 136–44, Antwerp, c. 19 June 1516.

27 M.-M. de la Garanderie, *La Correspondance d'Érasme et de Guillaume Budé* (Paris, 1967), pp. 57, 60, 67, 82.

28 Trans. from *CWE* 4.5; Allen, *Ep.* 446, II. 290, ll. 53–9, London, 9 Aug. 1516.

29 Allen, *Ep.* 475, II. 355, l. 14, 6 Oct. 1516; *Ep.* 503, II. 423, ll. 8–16, to Ammonio, 29 Dec. 1516.

30 Trans. from *CWE* 4. 96–7; Allen, *Ep.* 476, II. 357, ll. 37–71, Brussels, 6 Oct. 1516.

CHAPTER 12: THE AGE OF GOLD

1 Trans. from *CWE* 3, pp. 261, 269; Allen, *Ep.* 541, II. 487, ll. 8–9; *Ep.* 542, II. 492, ll. 1–6.

2 Trans. from *CWE* 3, p. 211; Allen, *Ep.* 566, II. 527, ll. 33–40.

3 P. G. Bietenholz, *History and Biography . . . of Erasmus* (Geneva, 1966), pp. 331–4.

4 Allen, *Epp.* 517–19, II. 433–8. On the prebendary of Courtrai see G. Lawarrée, 'Érasme et l'Argent', unpublished paper, University of Liège, 1973.

5 *LB* 10. 1662 B-C (*Spongia*) *ASD* IV. 2 p. 80, l. 445 (*Querela*); Allen, *Ep.* 2291, VIII. 392, II. 55–7 (1530).

6 M. M. de la Garanderie, *Christianisme et lettres profanes* (Lille–Paris, 1976) p. 259.

7 *ASD* I. 2, p. 49, ll. 18–19 (*De Pueris*), ed. J.-Cl. Margolin; Allen, *Ep.* 2079, VII. 543, ll. 13–20 (1528). This letter allows us to accord more importance to the little colloquy of Claudius and Balbus (*ASD* I. 3, p. 137), on the defective pronunciation – according to Erasmus – of Latin by the French. Erasmus undoubtedly learned to speak French with great difficulty. In 1500 he spoke 'in bad French' to Anna van Veere. Cf. Allen, *Ep.* 124, I. 287, l. 50, to Jacob Batt. On the other hand, a letter of 1517 or 1519 showed that he knew the nuances of the French language: Allen, *Ep.* 660, III. 83, ll. 6–8.

8 Allen, *Ep.* 2079, VII. 543, ll. 13–20; L.-E. Halkin, 'Érasme et les langues', in *Revue des langues vivantes*, 25 (Brussels, 1969), pp. 576–7.

9 Trans. from *CWE* 4, p. 205; Allen, *Ep.* 522, II. 445, ll. 40–97; see M. M. de la Garandarie, *Christianisme et lettres profanes*, pp. 98ff.

10 Trans. from *CWE* 4, pp. 248–9; Allen, *Ep.* 534, II. 478, ll. 20–9.

11 H. De Vocht, *The Foundation and the Rise of the Collegium Trilingue Lovaniense* (Louvain, 1951) 1. 60.

12 In 1523 Francis I again made a new attempt, with no more success. See Allen, *Ep.* 1375, V. 307, ll. 8–9.

13 *ASD* IV. 2, pp. 59–100, ed. O. Herding.

14 Trans. from *CWE* 4, p. 246, ll. 10–14; Allen, *Ep.* 533, II. 476, ll. 6–12.

15 Trans. from *CWE* 27, pp. 309, 300, 303.

16 In 1501 the future Charles V was engaged to Claude, daughter of Louis XII. In 1504, he was engaged to Mary of England. In 1513, Louis XII married Mary of England. In 1515, there was a plan to marry Charles and Renée, another daughter of Louis XII. In 1526, Charles V married Isabella of Portugal. Cf. E.-V. Telle, 'Érasme et les mariages dynastiques' in *Bibliothèque d'Humanisme et Renaissance,* 12. 7–13. Tracy, *The Politics of Erasmus,* pp. 90ff.

17 Trans. from *CWE* 27, p. 306.

18 Trans. from *CWE* 27, p. 315.

19 Trans. from *CWE* 27, pp. 309–10; *ASD* IV. 2, p. 84, ll. 540–50.

20 Trans. from *CWE* 27, pp. 320–1; *ASD* IV. 2, p. 98, ll. 872–88.

21 Trans. from *CWE* 4, pp. 378, 382; Allen, *Ep.* 586, II. 583, l. 127; II. 585, ll. 231, 224–5.

22 Trans. from *CWE* 5, p. 233; Allen, *Ep.* 734, III. 164, ll. 24–5, 42–50, to Capito, 1517.

23 A. Motte, 'Le Christ dans les Paraphrases d'Érasme sur les Évangiles', unpublished paper, University of Liège, 1985.

24 On the detail of this affair, see L.-E. Halkin, 'Érasme de Rotterdam et Érard de la Marck', in *Hommages à la Wallonie* (Brussels, 1981), pp. 237–52.

25 Trans. from *CWE* 5, pp. 251–2; Allen, *Ep.* 746, III. 178, ll. 3–13.

26 Trans. from *CWE* 5, pp. 270–1; Allen, *Ep.* 757, III. 193, ll. 1–32.

27 On this difficult journey see H. Gibaud, 'Les tribulations d'Érasme, de Bâle à Louvain', in *La Correspondances d'Érasme et l'epistolographie humaniste* (Brussels, 1985), pp. 25–36.

28 *Auctarium selectarum aliquot epistolarum Erasmi Roterodami ad eruditos* (Basel, 1518).

29 *LB* 10, 1662B-C (*Spongia*).

30 *Aliquot epistolae sanequam elegantes.* Cf. Halkin, *Erasmus ex Erasmo,* pp. 45, 48; Bietenholz, 'Érasme et le public allemand', in *L'Humanisme allemand* (Paris, 1979), pp. 81–98.

31 Trans. from *CWE* 4, p. 110; Allen, *Ep.* 480, II. 369, ll. 238–9 (1516).

32 *CWE* 4, p. 182, ll. 15–17; Allen, *Ep.* 512, II. 429, ll. 11–15.

33 Trans. from *CWE* 5, p. 16; Allen, *Ep.* 600, III. 10, ll. 32–33.

CHAPTER 13: FROM LOUVAIN TO ANTWERP VIA BASEL AND COLOGNE

1 M. A. Nauwelaerts, 'Érasme à Louvain', in *Scrinium Erasmianum* (Leiden, 1969), 1. 3–24.

2 H. De Vocht, *History of the Foundation and the Rise of the Collegium Trilingue Lovaniense,* 4 vols. (Louvain, 1951–5); Allen, *Ep.* 531, II. 463, l. 147, to Budé, Antwerp, 1517.

3 Ed. J.-Cl. Margolin, in *ASD* I. 5, pp. 385–416. The text was repeated in 1522, with modifications, in the *De conscribendis epistolis*: *ASD* I. 2, pp. 400–29. The *Encomium matrimonii* in the French translation by Berquin was to be condemned by the Sorbonne in 1525. Cf. E. V. Telle, *Érasme et le septième sacrement* (Geneva, 1954). See also Telle, *Le Chevalier de Berquin. Déclamation de louenges de mariage* (1525), pp. 153ff, edition and commentary (Geneva, 1976); Payne, *Erasmus*, pp. 109–25; Fr. Foccroulle, 'Érasme et l'idéal du mariage', unpublished paper, University of Liège, 1986.

4 *ASD* I. 5, p. 402, ll. 217–18.

5 Trans. from *CWE* 25, p. 137; *ASD* I. 2, p. 418, ll. 3–10. This text includes an addition of 1522. Cf. L.-E. Halkin, 'Érasme et le célibat sacerdotal', in *Revue d'histoire et de philosophie religieuses*, 57 (1977), 497–511; Reeve, *Erasmus' Annotations*, pp. 53–4.

6 Trans. from *CWE* 5, p. 330, II. 5–6; Allen, *Ep.* 786, III. 240–1, ll. 23–4, to John Colet.

7 Trans. from *CWE* 5, p. 390, II. 3–16; Allen, *Ep.* 818, III. 287, ll. 1–14.

8 Trans. from *CWE* 6, p. 73, II. 15–16, 27–8; Allen, *Ep.* 858, III. 362, ll. 21–2.

9 Trans. from *CWE* 6, p. 74, II. 39–48; Allen, *Ep.* 858, III. 363, ll. 39–42. See Chantraine, *Mystère*, p. 99.

10 Trans. from *CWE* 6, p. 73, l. 9; Allen, *Ep.* 858, III. 362, ll. 4–5.

11 Trans. from *CWE* 6, pp. 85–6, ll. 444–61; Allen, *Ep.* 858, III. 373, ll. 420–36. In 1527 Erasmus was to return to this subject, which was very dear to his heart, and to declare that to malign one's neighbour in a sermon was as dreadful as to administer poison with the Eucharist: Allen, *Ep.* 1891, VII. 210, ll. 292–4, to Joannes Gacchus.

12 *Auctarium selectarum aliquot epistolarum.* Many editions followed.

13 H. Gibaud, *Un inédit d'Érasme* (Angers, 1982).

14 Trans. from *CWE* 6, p. 126, II. 288–92; Allen, *Ep.* 867 III. 401, ll. 267–72.

15 This second edition of the New Testament appeared in Basel at the beginning of 1519. Text of the *Ratio seu methodus compendi perveniendi ad veram theologiam*, in Holborn, *Erasmus*, pp. 177–305. We follow closely the commentary of Chantraine, *Mystère et philosophie*, pp. 155–210. An outline of the *Ratio* had accompanied the first edition of the *Novum Testamentum* (1516) under the title *Methodus*: Holborn, *Erasmus*, p. 150.

16 Holborn, *Erasmus*, p. 210, ll. 33–6.

17 *ASD* I. 3, p. 751, ll. 379–80. (*Colloquia*). For the reform of theology 'the work of Erasmus is fundamental': R. Guelley, 'L'evolution des méthodes théologiques', in *Revue d'histoire ecclésiastique*, 37 (1941), 31.

18 *LB* 6. 934.

19 *Familiarium colloquiorum formulae.* This little volume, revised and developed continuously was to be normally designated by the title *Colloquia*. Ed. L.-E. Halkin, F. Bierlaire and R. Hoven, in *ASD* I. 3, pp. 29–714.

20 Beatus Rhenanus, *Ep.* 80; *ASD* I. 3, pp. 29–30.

21 On the history of these editions, see F. Bierlaire, *Érasme et ses Colloques. Le livre d'une vie* (Geneva, 1977); E. Gutmann, *Die Colloquia familiaria des Erasmus* (Basel, 1968).

22 Trans. from *CWE* 6, p. 326, II. 9–18; Allen, *Ep.* 952 III. 555, ll. 7–15.
23 G. Chantraine, 'L'Apologia ad Latomum', in *Scrinium Erasmianum*, 2. 51–75. The text of the *Apologia* in *LB* 9. 79–104. See also J. Étienne, *Spiritualisme érasmien et théologiens louvanistes* (Louvain, 1956), pp. 163ff.
24 *Apologia pro declamatione de laude matrimonii*, in *LB* 9. 105–12.
25 Allen, *Ep.* 948, III. 544, ll. 110–33, to Petrus Mosellanus.
26 *Farrago nova epistolarum* (Basel, Froben, 1519).
27 Trans. from *CWE* 6, pp. 56–8, ll. 3–30; Allen *Ep.* 854, III. 353, ll. 1–26.
28 Trans. from *CWE* 6, p. 127, ll. 12–25; Allen, *Ep.* 868, III. 402, ll. 12–22.
29 P. G. Bietenholz, 'Érasme et le public allemand', in *L'Humanisme allemand* (Paris, 1979), pp. 79–86.
30 Trans. from *CWE* 7, pp. 126–7, ll. 245–56; Allen, *Ep.* 1039, IV. 118, ll. 228–39.
31 Trans. from *CWE* 7, p. 36, ll. 6–11; Allen, *Ep.* 1002, IV. 33, ll. 4–8.
32 On this point I am close to P. de Vooght, 'Un épisode peu connu de la vie d'Érasme: sa rencontre avec les hussites bohèmes en 1519–1521', in *Irenikon* 47 (1974), 27–47. The letter to Slechta: Allen, *Ep.* 1039, IV. 118, ll. 228–38.

CHAPTER 14: POLEMICS IN LOUVAIN AND RELAXATION AT ANDERLECHT

1 Trans. from *CWE* 9, p. 92, ll. 41–54; Allen, *Ep.* 1284, V. 64, ll. 38–49, to Nicholas Bérauld, Basel, 25 May 1522. On 'Plus oultre': Allen, *Ep.* 1437, VI. 434, ll. 108–11 (1530).
2 Trans. from *CWE* 7, p. 255, ll. 4–12; Allen, *Ep.* 1089, IV. 233, ll. 4–9, Louvain, 9 Apr. 1520. Chr. Charlier, 'Érasme et Lee', unpublished paper, University of Liège, 1980.
3 Trans. from *CWE* 8, p. 29, ll. 25–9, 31–3; Allen, *Ep.* 1132, IV. 325, ll. 19–30, Louvain, 7 Aug. 1520. See also Allen, III. 1, n. 6.
4 Trans. from *CWE* 8, pp. 85–6, II. 16–38; Allen, *Ep.* 1159, IV. 378, ll. 14–34, 13 Nov. 1520.
5 Trans. from *CWE* 7, p. 145, ll. 6–8; Allen, *Ep.* 1048, IV. 136, ll. 5–6.
6 Trans. from *CWE* 8, p. 96, ll. 188–201; Allen, *Ep.* 1162, IV. 388, ll. 171–84, c. November 1520. For the record, 'Our Masters' is the title given to professors of theology.
7 See above, Ch. 10, p. 101.
8 Allen, *Ep.* 1255, V. 7, ll. 113–16; *Ep.* 2133, VIII. 108, ll. 89–91; *Ep.* 2645, X. 19, ll. 38–9.
9 Chantraine, *Mystère et philosophie*, pp. 301ff; G. Kisch, *Erasmus' Stellung zu Juden und Judentum*, (Basel, 1969); C. Augustijn, 'Erasmus und die Juden', in *Nederlands Archief voor Kerkgeschiedenis*, 60 (1980), 22–38; S Markish, *Érasme et les juifs* (Lausanne, 1979); A. Godin, 'L'antijudaisme d'Érasme', in *Biblothèque d'Humanisme et Renaissance*, 47 (1985), 537–53.
10 Trans. from *CWE* 7, p. 49, ll. 147–50; Allen, *Ep.* 1006, IV. 46, ll. 139–43, Antwerp, 11 Aug. 1519; see J. Chomarat, *Grammaire et rhétorique*, 2. 1147. Erasmus did not appreciate the Talmud, the Cabbala, etc. Cf. Allen, *Ep.* 798, III. 253, ll. 20–3, to Capito, 1518.

11 *ASD* IX. 1, p. 74, ll. 245–6 (*Scholia*), ed. C. Augustijn.

12 Trans. from *CWE* 7, pp. 49–50, ll. 180–5, 188–213; Allen, *Ep.* 1006, IV. 47–8, ll. 171–202. See also Holborn, *Erasmus*, pp. 207–8 (*Ratio*).

13 Trans. from *CWE* 8, p. 176, ll. 11–23; Allen, *Ep.* 1198, IV. 463–4, ll. 8–20, Louvain, c. March 1521.

14 Trans. from *CWE* 8, p. 215, ll. 46–8; Allen, *Ep.* 1205, IV. 407, ll. 40–2, Antwerp, 24 May 1521. Cf. F. Bierlaire, *La Familia d'Érasme* (Paris, 1969), p. 45.

15 *Progymnasmata quaedam primae adolescentiae Erasmi.*

16 *De contemptu mundi*, in *ASD* V. 1, pp. 1–86, ed. S. Dresden. See Chomarat, *Grammaire et rhétorique*, 2. 941ff. Dresden shows clearly that Chapter 12, though written later than the rest, was written in the same spirit.

17 *Apologia respondens ad ea quae in Novo Testamento taxaverat Iacobus Iopis Stunica,* ed. H. J. De Jonge. On this matter, see Bataillon, *Erasme et l'Espagne*, pp. 123ff.

18 *Apologiae Erasmi Roterodami.* Cf. L.-E. Halkin, 'Une édition rarissime des Apologies d'Érasme en 1521', in *Bibliothèque d'Humanisme et Renaissance*, 45 (1982), 343–8. It is curious that this volume does not reproduce the *Apologia* against Stunica published in September. It was to figure in the second edition of the *Apologiae* in February 1522.

19 Trans. from *CWE* 8, p. 269, ll. 2–14; Allen, *Ep.* 1223, IV. 552, ll. 1–11, to Goclenius, Bruges, 12 Aug. 1521. The various places where Erasmus lived have almost all disappeared. His admirable house at Anderlecht is so much the more moving.

20 Trans. from *CWE* 8, pp. 243–4, ll. 674–92; Allen, *Ep.* 1211, IV. 526, ll. 617–33. This letter of 13 June 1521 was published and discussed by A. Godin, in *Érasme. Vies de Jean Vitrier et de John Colet* (Angers, 1982).

21 Trans. from *CWE* 8, p. 295, ll. 25–7, 42–4, 54–8, 69–84; Allen, *Ep.* 1233, IV. 577, ll. 63–77, Anderlecht, c. September 1521.

22 Trans. from *CWE* 8, p. 311, ll. 10–14; Allen, *Ep.* 1238, IV. 591, ll. 6–11, Anderlecht, c. October 1521.

CHAPTER 15: ERASMUS AND LUTHER: THE CLASH OF TWO REFORMS

1 On the relationship between Erasmus and Luther the bibliography is considerable. I shall cite only G. Chantraine, *Érasme et Luther* (Paris, 1981); M. Lienhard, *Martin Luther* (Paris, 1983), pp. 149–61; C. Augustijn, *Erasmus von Rotterdam* (Munich, 1986), pp. 108–42; E. W. Kohls, *Luther oder Erasmus* (Basel, 1978); M. O'R. Boyle, *Rhetoric and Reform. Erasmus's Civil Dispute with Luther* (New Haven, 1983); id., 'Erasmus and the Modern Question: Was he semi-pelagian?' in *ARG* 75 (1984), 59–77; J. W. O'Malley, 'Erasmus and Luther. Continuity and Discontinuity as key to their conflict', in *Sixteenth Century Journal*, 5 (1974), 47–65; J. C. Olin, *Luther, Erasmus and the Reformation* (New York, 1969).

2 A. Godin, 'Érasme et Luther d'après leur correspondance' in *Mélanges de la Bibliothèque de la Sorbonne* 5 (1985), 7–9. Spalatin's letter is dated 11 Dec. 1516.

3 Trans. from *Luther's Works* (American edn) 48 (Philadelphia, 1963), p. 40; original in *Martin Luthers Briefwechsel* (Weimar, 1930)1, p. 90. ll. 19–20; 2, p. 387, ll. 5–6. I do not know what text of Erasmus is the target, perhaps the *Ratio sive methodus*. Erasmus never rejected the theology of the Cross. See, inter alia, *ASD* V. 3, p. 256, ll. 486–91 (*Explanatio symboli*).

4 L.-E. Halkin, 'La place des indulgences dans la pensée religieuse d'Érasme', in the *Bulletin de la Société de l'histoire du protestantisme français*, 129 (1983), 143–54.

5 Trans. from *Luther's Works* (American edn) 31 (Philadelphia, 1957), pp. 52–3; cf. Lienhard, *Martin Luther*, p. 57. After this disputation, Bucer believed that he could say that Erasmus and Luther were in accord on all fundamental questions. Cf. N. Peremans, *Érasme et Bucer* (Paris, 1970), p. 32.

6 Luther saw the theologian of glory as he saw Erasmus. Cf. *Martin Luthers Werke*, 1 (Weimar, 1983), p. 614, l. 1727.

7 Trans. from *CWE* 6, p. 85, ll. 430–3; Allen, *Ep.* 858, III. 372, ll. 405–8, to Paul Volz, 1518; *Ep.* 933, III. 518, ll. 18–22, from Luther, 28 Mar. 1519.

8 Trans. from *CWE* 6, p. 28, ll. 2–12; Allen, *Ep.* 993, III. 517, ll. 1–10.

9 Trans. from *CWE* 6, p. 391, ll. 2–11, 43–6, 54–61; Allen, *Ep.* 980, III. 605, ll. 1–10, 52–5.

10 Trans. from *CWE* 7, pp. 110–15, ll. 63–4, 72–7, 117–23, 252–65; Allen, *Ep.* 1033, IV, p. 101, ll. 57–8, 64–8; p. 102, ll. 102–18; p. 105, ll. 229–41. Erasmus justified this letter and the one he had sent to Luther in a long plea which he addressed to Cardinal Campeggio: Allen, *Ep.* 1167, IV. 400–11, 1520.

11 Trans. from *CWE* 8, p. 42, ll. 96–8; Allen, *Ep.* 1139, IV. 337, ll. 86–9. (1520).

12 Trans. from *CWE* 7, p. 210, ll. 6–8; Allen, *Ep.* 1070, IV. 193, ll. 4–5.

13 Trans. from *CWE* 8, p. 214, ll. 37–40; Allen, *Ep.* 1205, IV. 497, ll. 32–4, 1521.

14 See his letter to Pierre Barbier: Allen, *Ep.* 1225, IV. 563–4, ll. 342–6, 1521.

15 Trans. from *CWE* 8, p. 72, ll. 179–81; Allen, *Ep.* 1153, IV. 366, ll. 157–8, 1520. See also *Ep.* 1166, IV. 398, ll. 53–6, 1520.

16 Trans. from *CWE* 8, p. 171, ll. 29–36; Allen, *Ep.* 1195, IV. 459, ll. 23–30, to Luigi Marliano, 1521.

17 *CWE* 9, p. 46; Allen, *Ep.* 1267, V. 32, ll. 21–8, to Stanislaus Thurzo, 1522.

18 Trans. from *CWE* 9, p. 205, ll. 14–21, 24–32, 69–72; Allen, *Ep.* 1324, V. 145–6, ll. 12–67, from Adrian VI, 1522.

19 Trans. from *CWE* 9, p. 438, ll. 136–46; Allen, *Ep.* 1352, V. 260–1, ll. 118–27, to Adrian VI, 22 Mar. 1523.

20 Trans. from *CWE* 9, p. 438, ll. 170–2, 181–206; Allen, *Ep.* V. 261, ll. 158–82.

21 Renaudet, *Erasme, sa pensée religieuse*, p. 209.

22 Trans. from *CWE* 9, p. 166, ll. 1–3; Allen, *Ep.* 1308, IV. 116, ll. 1–2.

23 *ASD* IX. 1, p. 162, ll. 14–24; *Spongia*, ed. C. Augustijn.

24 *Luther's Works* (American edn) 49 (Philadelphia, 1972), pp. 77–80.

25 Trans. from *Erasmus*, ed. R. De Molen (London, 1973), p. 146; Allen, *Ep.* 1443, V. 445, ll. 4–28 (1524); Erasmus replied on 8 May (*Ep.* 1445).

26 *The Colloquies of Erasmus*, ed. C. R. Thompson (Chicago and London, 1965), pp. 177–89. On this colloquy, see Bierlaire, *Érasme et ses Colloques*, p. 254; Chantraine, *Mystère et Philosophie*, p. 54.

27 Trans. from *Colloquies*, ed, Thompson, p. 189.

28 The *De libero arbitrio* in *LB* V. 1215–48; Eng. trans. of this work, together with Luther's reply, *De servo arbitrio*, in E. G. Rupp (ed), *Luther and Erasmus on Free Will*, Library of Christian Classics, 17 (Philadelphia and London, 1969); Godin, *Erasme*, pp. 469–90; Allen, *Ep.* 1489, V. 358, ll. 48–9, to John Fisher; *Ep.* 1634, VI. 201, l. 31, to Pius; see, among others, E. W. Kohls, 'La position théologique d'Érasme et la Tradition dans le *De libero arbitrio*', in *Colloquium Erasmianum* (Mons, 1968), pp. 69–88; Rabil, *Erasmus and the New Testament*, pp. 163–6. On God's desire for the salvation of all, see *LB* IX. 1117F. Cf. Augustijn, *Erasmus von Rotterdam*, p. 129.

29 Rupp (ed.), *Luther and Erasmus on Free Will*, p. 35; *LB* IX. 1219B (*De Libero arbitrio*).

30 Rupp (ed.), *Luther and Erasmus on Free Will*, p. 39.

31 Rupp (ed.), *Luther and Erasmus on Free Will*, p. 91.

32 J. M. McConica, 'Erasmus and the grammar of consent', in *Scrinium Erasmianum*, 2 (1969), 77–99; C. Christ von Wedel, *Das Nichtwissen bei Erasmus* (Basel, 1981), p. 101; C. Augustijn, 'Hyperaspistes I: la doctrine d'Érasme et de Luther sur la claritas Scripturae', in *Colloquia Erasmiana Turonensia* 2 (1972), 737–48.

33 Rupp (ed.), *Luther and Erasmus on Free Will*, p. 44.

34 Allen, *Ep.* 1522, V. 290, II. 12–67; *Ep.* 1523, V. 594 (1524).

35 The *De servo arbitrio*, in *D. Martin Luthers Werke*, Weimar edn, XVIII. 551–87, Eng. trans. (see above, n. 28); also in *Luther's Works* (American edn) 33 (Philadelphia, 1972), 3–295.

36 Rupp (ed.), *Luther and Erasmus on Free Will*, p. 109.

37 Melanchthon himself – who had appreciated the importance of the *De libero arbitrio* – feared that the theory of double predestination led to despair. Calvin replied to him vigorously. Cf. F. Wendel, *Calvin* (London, 1963), pp. 269–70.

38 Rupp (ed.), *Luther and Erasmus on Free Will*, p. 85.

39 Without giving up hope for a return to unity, Erasmus accepted the notion of civil tolerance with respect to Lutheran worship. Cf. J. Lecler, *Toleration and the Reformation* (London, 1960) 1. 129, 133.

40 Allen, *Ep.* 1445, V. 451, ll. 1–2.

41 Allen, *Ep.* 1258, V. 609, ll. 11–12; *Ep.* 2900, X. 258, ll. 62–9; *Ep.* 2956, XI. 21, ll. 39–40. On the other hand, it seems difficult to connect Erasmus with liberal Protestantism, with J. Lindeboom, *Erasmus van Rotterdam* (Utrecht, 1936), p. 44.

42 J.-P. Massaut, 'L'ecclésiologie d'Érasme entre la Réforme protestante et la Réforme catholique', in the *Bulletin de la Société d'histoire moderne*, 78 (1979), 2–8.

43 The conflict which had sharply opposed Erasmus and Luther was to be pursued and perpetuated among their disciples. Erasmus was to see more of his own (Hutten, Volz, Jonas, among others) abandon him and go over to the other camp, but he was to continue his relationship with them for as long as possible.

CHAPTER 16: SETTLED IN BASEL

1 Later Erasmus was to say that he had left the Netherlands to avoid being put in charge of an inquisition into Lutheranism. Cf. Allen, *Ep.* 1792, X. 199, ll. 17–23, to Nicholas Olah, Freiburg, 19 Apr. 1533. In 1523, he recognized that he was in Basel to bring himself closer to Froben: Allen, *Ep.* 1342, V. 205, l. 86, to Laurinus, 1 Feb. 1523. The whole of this long letter is full of curious details about Erasmus's friends, and on invitations and gifts received.

2 Allen, *Ep.* 1242, IV. 598–9.

3 P. Roth, 'Die Wohnstatten des Erasmus in Basel', in *Gedenkschrift Zum 400. Todestage des Erasmus* (Basel, 1936) pp. 270–80.

4 A. Horowitz, 'Briefe des Claudius Cantiuncula . . .' in *Sitzungberichte der philosophisch-historischen Classe der kaiserliche Akademie der Wissenschaften* (Vienna, 1879), 93. 441. On Erasmus's horror of stoves: Allen, *Ep.* 1248, IV. 609, ll. 8–12.

5 Allen, *Ep.* 2735, X. 124, ll. 50–1, to Quirinus Talesius, Freiburg, 31 Oct. 1532.

6 *Epistolae ad diversos* appeared with the date 1521. Cf. Halkin, *Erasmus ex Erasmo*, p. 104.

7 *Opus de conscribendis epistolis*, ed. J.-Cl. Margolin, in *ASD* I. 2, pp. 205–579; Eng. trans. in *CWE* 25. Cf. L.-E. Halkin, 'Le Traité d'art épistolaire d'Érasme', in *Moreana*, 21 (1984), 25–32.

8 Trans. from *CWE* 25, p. 71; *ASD* I. 2, p. 309.

9 J. Coppens, 'Les idées réformistes d'Érasme dans les préfaces aux *Paraphrases du Nouveau Testament*', in *Scrinium Lovaniense* (Louvain, 1961), pp. 344–71.

10 On the success of the *Paraphrases*, see Godin, *Érasme, lecteur*, pp. 354ff.

11 Trans. from *CWE* 49, p. 2.

12 Published in 1522: *LB* X. 1833A.

13 *LB* VII, Preface. The project of a summary of Christian doctrine had already figured in the celebrated letter to Volz. Cf. Allen, *Ep.* 858, III. 365, ll. 139–48. Erasmus was to realize his wish in the *Explanatio Symboli* of 1533.

14 On the matter of renewing baptismal promises, Bucer echoed Erasmus's views of 1539. Cf. Kohls, 'Érasme et la Réforme', in *Colloquia Erasmiana Turonensia*, 2. 843. From the Catholic side support was to come later. St Charles Borromeo advocated its use in 1582 and Pius X extended it to the whole Church at the beginning of the twentieth century, without any reference to Erasmus.

15 Noel Bédier, 'Annotationes in Fabrum Stapulensem et in Des. Erasmus', fo. 238 (Paris, 1526).

16 Allen, *Ep.* 1292 V. 76, Introduction.

17 Allen, *Ep.* 1369, V. 295, ll. 38–45. In 1533 he again condemned the sect in the *Ecclesiastes: LB* V. 934DE. As a matter of interest, Menno Simons owed some of his ideas to Erasmus, as C. Augustijn has shown in 'Erasmus and Menno Simons' in the *Mennonite Quarterly Review*, 1986, pp. 497–508.

18 *Epistola apologetica de interdicto esu carnium* (Basel, Froben, 1522) in *ASD* IX. 1, pp. 19–69, ed. C. Augustijn. In the letter to Volz, Erasmus had recalled

that Christ prescribed nothing in this domain: Allen, *Ep.* 858, III. 373, l. 413.

19 An astonishing kinship of sentiment in the intervention of a Mexican bishop, 27 Oct. 1964, at the second Vatican Council. 'The spirit of liberty and of love of which St Paul and St Thomas speak is not facilitated by heaping up purely ecclesiastical precepts. The laws of the Church should aim at nothing else than to promote and direct love, not to govern or support from the outside, in such a way that love falters and sin proliferates' (cited by R. Laurentin, *L'Enjeu du concile* (Paris, 1965), 4. 187).

20 *ASD* IX. 1. 28, ll. 232–48.

21 *ASD* IX. 1. 28, ll. 254–5.

22 On Erasmus's sense of society, see Margolin, *Le Prix des mots et de l'homme*, IX (London, 1986), 85–112. See also *ASD* V. 3, p. 310, ll. 851–65 (*De sarcienda*).

23 Allen, *Ep.* 1079, IV. 206, l. 5, to Sylvester Gigli, 1520; *Ep.* 1533, V. 263, ll. 55–6, to Zasius, 1523. Erasmus did not like fish, which was seldom fresh in his time: J. Hoyoux, 'Le carême et l'hygiène au temps d'Érasme', in the *Bulletin de l'Institut archéologique liégois*, 67 (1950), 111–20.

24 Bataillon, *Érasme et l'Espagne*, p. 167.

25 Trans. from *CWE* 9, 46, ll. 9–31; Allen, *Ep.* 1267, V. 32, ll. 7–28, 21 Mar. 1522.

26 Trans. from *CWE* 9, 379, ll. 419–42; Allen, *Ep.* 1342, V. 213–14, ll. 381–402.

27 *CWE* 9, p. 185, l. 2; Allen, *Ep.* 1314, V. 129, I. 2; *ASD* IV. 1 p. 75, l. 596 (*Panegyricus*).

CHAPTER 17: BASEL: THE DAILY ROUND OF WORK

1 G. Lawarrée, 'Érasme et l'Argent', unpublished paper, University of Liège, 1973.

2 Trans. from *CWE* 9, pp. 382–3, ll. 507–27; Allen, *Ep.* 1342, V. 213, ll. 381–408, to Marcus Laurinus, 1523.

3 Trans. from *CWE* 9, p. 424, ll. 380–3; Allen, *Ep.* 1347, V. 249, ll. 349–53, to Joost Vroye, Basel, 1 Mar. 1523.

4 Gerlo, *Érasme et ses portraitistes*, p. 48; C. Reedijk, 'Hercules, Holbein, Heckscher', in *Mededelingen van de koninklijke Academie voor wetenschappen, letteren en schone kunsten van Belgie*, Klasse der letteren, 47 (1985), 93–106.

5 *Spongia adversus aspergines Ulrici Hutteni* (Basel, Froben, 1523), ed. C. Augustijn, in *ASD* IX. 1, pp. 91–210.

6 Trans. after Bainton, *Erasmus of Christendom*, p. 178; *ASD* IX. 1, p. 188, ll. 587–96; p. 190, ll. 635–46.

7 P. Petitmagnan, 'Érasme éditeur des textes', in *Colloquia Erasmiana Turonensia*, 1. 218; Chomarat, *Grammaire et rhétorique*, 1. 452–74.

8 S. Seidel Menchi, 'Il trattato pseudo ciprianico *De duplici martyrio*', in *Rivista storica italiana*, 90 (1978), 709–43.

9 Chomarat, *Grammaire et rhétorique*, 1. 480; L. D. Reynolds and N. G. Wilson, *D'Homère à Érasme* (Paris, 1984), pp. 107–10.

10 Allen, *Ep.* 2743, X. 130, ll. 1–3, Lyons, 30 Nov. 1532.

11 Allen, *Ep.* 997, IV. 9, ll. 15–18, to the Chapter of Metz Cathedral, Louvain, 14 July 1519.

12 Allen, *Ep.* 1555, VI. 39, ll. 28–9.

13 This letter to Joost Vroye (Gaverius) was to be published with the *Exomologesis*: text in Allen, *Ep.* 1347, V. 237–50, 1 Mar. 1523.

14 Trans. from *CWE* 9, pp. 414–16, ll. 72–5, 82–5, 105–7, 86–9, 130–2, 137–9; Allen, *Ep.* 1347, V. 237–50, 1 Mar. 1523.

15 Trans. from *CWE* 9, 425, ll. 408–10; Allen, *Ep.* 1347, V. 249, ll. 378–80. 1 Mar. 1523.

16 *Precatio Dominica in septem partes distributa* (Basel, Froben, 1523) in *LB* IX, 1219–28. It is noteworthy that Margaret, the eldest daughter of More, translated the *Precatio* into English in 1524. The soldier's 'Our Father' is to be found in *ASD* IV. 2, p. 84, ll. 540–50 (*Querela Pacis*).

17 *LB* IX. 1219-D, 1224B.

18 A. Rabil, 'Erasmus' Paraphrase of the Gospel of John', in *Church History* 48 (1979), 142–55.

19 Allen, *Ep.* 1375, V. 307, ll. 8–9.

20 *CWE* 49, p. 3.

21 Lawarrée, 'Érasme et l'argent', pp. 84ff.; J. Hoyoux, 'Les moyens d'existence d'Érasme', in *Humanisme et Renaissance*, 5 (1945), 7–59; E. Bernstein, 'The Antwerp Banker Erasmus Schets and Erasmus of Rotterdam', in *Erasmus in English*, 14 (1985–6), pp. 2–10.

22 One example among several: in Erasmus's lifetime, there were twenty-one pirated editions of his *Paraphrasis Elegentiarum Laurentii Vallae*: *ASD* I-4, p. 203, ed. Heesakkers and Waszink.

23 *Catalogus lucubrationum*, edns in 1523 and 1524; text in Allen, *Ep.* 1, I. 1–46; C. Reedijk, *Tandem bona causa triumphat* (Basel, 1980), pp. 12–14. The *Catalogus* was to be completed in 1530 by a letter to Hector Boece: Allen, *Ep.* 2283, VIII. 372–7.

24 Trans. from *CWE* 9, p. 352, ll. 1483–7, *Ep.* 1341 A.

25 Allen, *Ep.* 1006, IV. 48, ll. 192–3, to Jacob Hochstraten, 1519: 'Sed fieri potest ut non omnia semel aperuerit Christi spiritus Ecclesiae', Bouyer, *Autour d'Érasme*, p. 130.

26 Lecler, *Toleration and the Reformation*, 1. 126.

27 Trans. from *CWE* 7, pp. 126–7, ll. 245–61; Allen, *Ep.* 1039, IV. 118, ll. 228–43; cf. Lecler, *Toleration and the Reformation*, 1. 126.

28 Trans. from *CWE* 9, p. 250, ll. 175–80; Allen, *Ep.* 1334, V. 176, ll. 166–70, to Jean de Carondolet, 1523; *ASD* IV. 3, p. 151, notes 431–2 by Cl. H. Miller.

29 *ASD* V. 1, p. 146, ll. 867–8 (*Modus orandi*).

30 Trans. from *CWE* 9, p. 251, ll. 184–5, 386–96; Allen, *Ep.* 1334, V. 176, ll. 172–4; V. 180, ll. 362–72, to Jean de Carondolet, 1523. See also Pineau, *Érasme. Sa pensée religieuse*, p. 262.

31 J.-P. Massaut, 'Érasme et Saint Thomas', in *Colloquia Erasmiana Turonensia*, 2. 584; Allen, *Ep.* 1232, IV. 574, ll. 81–2, to Nicholaas van Broekhoven, 1531; *Ep.* 2933, IX. 339, ll. 109–12, to Severinus Boner, 1531; *Ep.* 2643, X.

15, ll. 121–42, to Joannes Dantiscus; *LB* X. 1392F. Erasmus believed in the real presence, but thought the scholastic doctrine of transubstantiation to be of no use.

32 Holborn, *Erasmus*, p. 180, ll. 22–4 (*Ratio*).

33 Trans. from *CWE* 3, p. 125, ll. 441–2; Allen, *Ep.* 337, II. 101, l. 419, to Martin Dorp, 1515. This earlier letter, already cited, abounds in cutting remarks on misplaced curiosity in matters of faith.

34 Trans. from *Colloquies*, ed. C. R. Thompson, p. 195; *ASD* I. 3, p. 380, l. 166.

35 Allen, *Ep.* 2192, VIII. 224, l. 61, to Jacob Fugger, 7 July, 1529.

36 All this according to G. Machadour, 'Le Nouveau Testament dans la correspondance d'Érasme', in *La correspondance d'Érasme et l'epistolographie humaniste* (Brussels, 1985), p. 68.

37 See below, ch. 20.

38 Allen, *Ep.* 1459 V. 483, ll. 95–101.

39 Allen, *Ep.* 1539, VI. 10, ll. 116–50.

CHAPTER 18: THE *COLLOQUIES*: CHRONICLE OF AN ERA

1 *Colloquia*, in *ASD* I. 3, ed. L.-E. Halkin, F. Bierlaire and R. Hoven; Eng. trans. by Craig R. Thompson, *The Colloquies of Erasmus*, Chicago and London, 1965.

2 In 1534, Erasmus was to boast of having carried out the work quickly. See *ASD* IX. 1, p. 478, ll. 986–9 (*Purgatio*). He was perhaps exaggerating a little. On the history of the book and its editions, see F. Bierlaire, *Érasme et ses Colloques: le livre d'une vie* (Geneva, 1977).

3 Trans. from *CWE* 9, p. 37, ll. 13–16; Allen, *Ep.* 1262, V. 16, ll. 11–14, Basel, 28 Feb. 1522. Erasmius Froben, who preferred the muses of commerce to the commerce of the Muses, was not to be a credit to his godfather.

4 Erasmus's gaiety did not appear only in the *Colloquies*. See *ASD* IX. 1, p. 478, ll. 991–3 (*Purgatio*). On the themes of the *Colloquies*, see F. Bierlaire, *Les Colloques d'Érasme: réforme des études, réformes des moeurs et réforme de l'Église au XVIe siècle* (Paris, 1978); E. Gutmann, *Die Colloquia familiaria des Erasmus* (Basel, 1968).

5 Trans. from *Colloquies*, ed. Thompson, pp. 12–15.

6 *Colloquies*, pp. 65–8.

7 Cf. *CWE* 9, p. 123, ll. 63–4.

8 *Colloquies*, pp. 33–8.

9 *Colloquies*, pp. 147–50.

10 *Colloquies*, p. 142.

11 On the matrimonial dialogues, see É. V. Telle, *Érasme et le septième sacrament* (Geneva, 1954).

12 Telle, *Érasme et le septième sacrament*, pp. 93–4.

13 Telle, *Érasme et le septième sacrament*, pp. 115–27.

14 Telle, *Érasme et le septième sacrament*, pp. 156–7.

15 Trans. from CWE 9, pp. 305–9, ll. 302–13, 346–54, 418–19.

16 Delcourt, *Érasme*, pp. 49–51.

17 *Colloquies*, pp. 200, 209, 215.
18 This idea is expounded forcefully in a letter to Juan Vergara: Allen, *Ep.* 2133, VIII. 108, ll. 110–11, Basel, 1529.
19 *Colloquies*, pp. 219–23.
20 *Colloquies*, p. 271. On Erasmus and women, see E. Schneider, *Das Bild der Frau im Werke des Erasmus von Rotterdam* (Basel, 1935); E. H. Waterbolk, 'Erasmus kiest de Vrouw', in *Genie en Wereld Erasmus* (Hasselt, 1971), pp. 197–212.
21 The Colloquy *The Seraphic Funeral* was to be written in the same tone. See also Chomarat, *Grammaire et rhétorique*, 1. 626.
22 *Colloquies*, p. 326.
23 *Colloquies*, pp. 391–2.
24 L.-E. Halkin 'Le thème de pèlerinage dans les Colloques d'Érasme', in *Actes du Congrès Érasme* (Amsterdam, 1971), pp. 88–98. Lefèvre d'Étaples thought no differently: Mann, *Érasme et les debuts de la Réforme française*, p. 50.
25 *Colloquies*, pp. 545–51.
26 Cited by J. Boisset, *Érasme et Luther* (Paris, 1969), p. 21. See also C. Augustijn, *Erasmus von Rotterdam* (Munich, 1986), p. 143. Luther found the doctrine of the *Colloquies* 'impiissima': see *Luthers Tischreden*, Nos. 817 (I. 397) and 4899 (IV, p. 573). It is true that Luther no longer found any piety in Erasmus's theological works: *Luthers Briefwechsel*, VII. p. 32.
27 *ASD* I. 3, p. 9.
28 Bierlaire, 'Des Colloques d'Érasme aux Dialogues du Père Antoine Van Torre', in *Les Études Classiques* (Namur, 1973), 41. 50–1; R. Crahay, 'Une utilisation d'Érasme dans la pédagogie protestante', in *D'Érasme à Campanella* (Brussels, 1985), pp. 40–74.
29 Bierlaire, *Les Colloques d'Érasme*, pp. 201–303.

CHAPTER 19: FROM *THE INSTITUTION OF MARRIAGE* TO *THE CICERONIAN*

1 Allen, *Ep.* 1479, V. 519, ll. 118–22, to Haio Hermannus, 31 Aug. 1524; *Ep.* 1488, V. 534, l. 1014, to Warham, 4 Sept. 1524.
2 Allen, *Ep.* 1414, V. 391, ll. 59–73, 31 Jan. 1524.
3 Bierlaire, *Les Colloques d'Érasme*, p. 217.
4 Allen, *Ep.* 1579, VI. 83, ll. 89–96; VI. 85, ll. 154–6, Paris, 21 May 1525.
5 Allen, *Ep.* 1581, VI. 87–107, Basel, 15 June 1525; M. M. de La Garanderie, *Christianisme et lettres profanes*, I. 241–53; M. Veissière, *L'Évêque Guillaume Briçonnet* (Provins, 1986), p. 325.
6 *Lingua*, Basel, Froben, August 1525, ed. F. Schalk, in *ASD* IV. 1, pp. 233–370.
7 Allen, *Ep.* 1702, VI. 330, l. 15, 1526.
8 S. Seidel Menchi, 'Le traduzione italiane di Lutero nella prima meta del cinquecento', in *Rinascimento*, 17 (1977), p. 56.
9 *Hyperaspistes*, 2 v (Basel, Froben, 1526 and 1527): *LB* X, 1249–1536. Cf. Chantraine, *Érasme et Luther*, p. 65.

10 M. P. Gilmore, 'Erasmus and Alberto Pio', in *Action and Conviction in Early Modern Europe* (Princeton, 1969), pp. 299–318; Renaudet, *Érasme*, p. 52; Bierlaire, *Érasme et ses Colloques*, pp. 283–85.

11 *Detectio praestigiarum* (Basel, Froben, June 1526) ed. C. Augustijn, in *ASD* IX. 1, pp. 232–62. Cf. Renaudet, *Érasme*, pp. 54, 345.

12 Allen, *Ep.* 1744, VI. 404, ll. 148–59, c. September 1526.

13 *Christiani matrimonii institutio* (Basel, Froben, August 1526); *LB* V. 615–714. See Telle, *Érasme et le septième sacrement.*

14 *LB* V. 697F-698A; IX. 1085F–1086A; *ASD* I. 2, p. 420, ll. 13–22; p. 422, ll. 10–13.

15 E. V. Telle, 'Érasme et les mariages dynastiques', in *Bibliothèque d'Humanisme et Renaissance* 12 (1950), 7–13.

16 Allen, *Ep.* 1891, VII. 207, ll. 156–9, 16 Oct. 1527. On the outcome of this affair, see Allen, *Ep.* 2045 VII. 480, ll. 191–9. See also C. Labeye, 'Érasme et les ordres mendiants', unpublished paper, University of Liège.

17 The word 'merit' is not in the New Testament, but the idea can be found here and there.

18 *LB* VII. 105A IX, 885F (*Responsiones*).

19 Allen, *Ep.* 1084, VII. 8. ll. 75–8.

20 *LB* IX. 883C, 888B–F (*Responsiones ad censures*); VI. 226C (*Novum Testamentum*); Holborn, *Erasmus*, p. 61 (*Enchiridion*); *LB* IX. 465D (*Prologus*); V, 500D (*De amabili*); *ASD* V. 2, 376, ll. 609–16 (*Enarratio*).

21 Gerlo, *Érasme et ses portraitistes*, pp. 35–9. Erasmus often worked standing up, as he wrote to John Francis in the same year: Allen, *Ep.* 1759, VI. 423, ll. 50–51.

22 Allen, *Ep.* 1819, VII. 63–4, ll. 151–3, 173–7, 197–202, 15 May 1527.

23 Allen, *Ep.* 1840, VII. 93–4, ll. 11–44, 22 June 1527.

24 Allen, *Ep.* 1831, VII. 78, ll. 8–9, 29 May 1527.

25 Allen, *Ep.* 1790A, VI. 470, ll. 1–8, March 1527; J. M. Headley, 'Gattinara, Erasmus and the imperial configuration of humanism', in *ARG* 71 (1980), 64–98.

26 Allen, *Ep.* 1887, VII. 199, ll. 6–20, 15 Oct. 1527; Tracy, *Politics of Erasmus*, pp. 323–6.

27 Allen, *Ep.* 1901, VII. 233, ll. 96–101. On Bucer and Erasmus see N. Peremans, *Érasme et Bucer* (Paris, 1970).

28 Allen, *Ep.* 1977, VII. 366, ll. 40–70, 20 Mar. 1528.

29 Allen, *Ep.* 1902, VII. 235, ll. 15–18, 12 Nov. 1527.

30 Bataillon, *Érasme et l'Espagne*, pp. 250–65.

31 *Apologia adversus monachos quosdam Hispanos* (Basel, Froben, 1528); *LB* 9. 1015–94.

32 Allen, *Ep.* 1902, VII. 235, ll. 15–18, 12 Nov. 1527.

33 Allen, *Ep.* 1891, VII. 211, ll. 350–9, to Joannes Gacchus, c. 17 Oct. 1527; the reply from the Sorbonne in Allen, *Ep.* 1902, VII. 236, l. 63, 12 Nov. 1527.

34 Allen, *Ep.* 1858, VII. 137, l. 366, to Robert Aldridge, 23 Aug. 1527. For the outcome of this project, see Allen, *Ep.* 2045, VII. 475–83,to Martin Lipse, 5 Sept. 1528.

35   Allen, *Ep.* 1804, VII. 5–14, 30 Mar. 1527. See F. Rastier, 'Les métamorphoses de l'ennemi, in *Orpheus* 16 (1969), 129–46.

36   Later, Erasmus was to say that he had drunk no more wine, unless it was strongly blended, at least from 1527: Allen, *Ep.* 2192, VIII. 224, ll. 67–71, to Anton Fugger, 7 July 1529.

37   Allen, *Ep.* 1805, VII. 20, ll. 274–86, to Juan Maldonado, 30 Mar. 1527.

38   Allen, VI. 503–6. See Lawarrée, 'Érasme et l'argent', pp. 366ff; Reedijk, *Tandem,* pp. 17–20.

39   Allen, *Ep.* 2084, VII. 442, ll. 20–2. See E. Bernstein, 'Erasmus' money connection', in *Erasmus in English,* 14 (1986), 2–10.

40   Trans. after Huizinga, *Erasmus and the Age of Reformation,* pp. 242–3; original in Allen, *Ep.* 1809, VII. 28, ll. 1–5, 9–18 (1527).

41   *Ciceronianus sive de optimo genere dicendi* (Basel, Froben, March 1528), ed. P. Mesnard, in *ASD* I. 2, pp. 583–710. Cf. Chomarat, *Grammaire et rhétorique,* 2. 815–40, with a fine praise of the imitation, p. 1172. On the Ciceronianism of the fifteenth century, see E. Garin, *La Renaissance* (Verviers, 1977), pp. 61, 64.

42   Allen, *Ep.* 1885, VII. 193–4, ll. 121–39. Cf. P. Bietenholz, *History and Biography in the work of Erasmus* (Geneva, 1966), pp. 62–6.

43   *ASD* I. 2, p. 697, ll. 8–10.

44   Ch. Béné, 'Érasme et Cicéron', in *Colloquia Erasmiana Turonensia,* 2. 571–9; M. Cytowska, 'Érasme et les auteurs classiques', in *Eos* 72 (Wroclaw, 1984), 185, 187; H. De Lubac, *Exégèse médiévale* 4 (Paris 1964), 462, 481, 482.

45   The protestations were to come from Italy and France (Scaliger, Budé, Dolet, etc.). Cf. É. V. Telle, *L'Erasmianus sive Ciceronianus d'Étienne Dolet* (Geneva, 1974), p. 57; R. Autlotte, 'Une rivalité d'humanistes: Érasme et Longueil', in *Bibliothèque d'Humanisme et Renaissance* 30 (1968), 549–73.

46   *Conciolais expositio in psalmum LXXXV,* ed. C. S. Rademaker, in *ASD* V. 3, pp. 329–427; *Vidua christiana* (Basel, Froben); Allen, *Ep.* 2095, VIII. 48, ll. 25–6.

47   Allen, *Ep.* 2095, VIII. 48, ll. 25–53, Preface.

CHAPTER 20: CHRIST FIRST

1   This historic statement was cited by Béné, *Érasme et saint Augustin,* p. 149. See also the *Dictionnaire de théologie catholique* 5 (Paris 1913), 395. I draw the reader's attention to my article 'La piété d'Érasme', in the *Revue d'histoire ecclésiastique* 79 (1984), 671–708; J.-P. Massaut, 'Humanisme et spiritualité chez Érasme', in the *Dictionnaire de spiritualité* 7 (Paris, 1969), cols. 1006–28.

2   *ASD* V. 1, p. 126, ll. 174–5; *LB* V. 500F (*De sarcienda Ecclesiae concordia*).

3   *Modus orandi Deum,* in *ASD* V. 1, pp. 120–76, ed. J. N. Bakhuizen van den Brink.

4   *ASD* V. 1, p. 156, ll. 197–215; p. 172, ll. 797–9.

5   *Exomologesis,* in *LB* V. 146. See J.-P. Massaut, 'La position œcuménique d'Érasme sur la pénitence', in *Réforme et Humanisme,* Actes du IVᵉ Colloque (Montpellier, 1975), published 1977, pp. 241–81.

6   Trans. in *CWE* 2, p. 17, ll. 160–2; Allen, *Ep.* 145, I. 345, ll. 137–41, Paris, 27 Jan. 1501. The 'supplications' to Mary figure in *LB* V. 1227–40. Cf. L.-E. Halkin, 'La mariologie d'Érasme', in *ARG* 68 (1977), 32–55.

7   There are numerous texts in Erasmus about the danger of the magical spirit to piety.

8   In 1528, in his *Apologia adversus monachos quosdam Hispanos*, Erasmus was to affirm that there was only a 'pia credulitas' there. Cf. *LB* IX. 1085B.

9   *LB* V. 1237D. In his *Apologia* of 1528, he again took up the same short affirmation: 'In Christo fixa est nostrae salutis ancora, non in Virgine': *LB* IX. 1087B. See also *ASD* V. 1, p. 100, ll. 121–2 (*Liturgia*).

10 Trans. from *Colloquies*, ed. Thompson, p. 141; *ASD* 1. 3 p. 327, ll. 71–7; V. 1 p. 155, l. 181.

11 *Colloquies*, p. 289.

12 *Colloquies*, p. 291; *ASD* 1. 3, p. 474, ll. 123–128.

13 *ASD* V. 1, p. 172, ll. 785–6 (*Modus orandi*).

14 *LB* IX. 61E (*Apologia ad Iacobum Fabrum*). On the opinion of Lefèvre d'Étaples see G. Bédouelle, *Lefèvre d'Étaples et l'intelligence des Écritures* (Geneva, 1978), p. 197.

15 *ASD* V. 2, p. 298, ll. 160–1 (*De puritate*). See also Allen, *Ep.* 1334, V. 186, ll. 614–15, 1523.

16 E. F. Rice, 'Erasmus and the religious tradition', in the *Journal of the History of Ideas*, 11 (New York, 1950).

17 *Virginis Matris apud Lauretum cultae liturgia* (Basel, Froben, November 1523, in *ASD* V. 1, pp. 87–109, ed. L.-E. Halkin.

18 *Virginis Matris*, p. 104, ll. 242–8.

19 *ASD* V. 1, pp. 155–6 (*Modus orandi*).

20 Allen, *Ep.* 2443, IX. 162–3, ll. 201–26, 1531.

21 *LB* IX. 1166A (*Apologia ad pium*), 1531.

22 *LB* IX. 570B (*Supputatio errorum Bedae*) and 1087B (*Apologia ad monachos quosdam Hispanos*). See also *ASD* IV. 3, p. 142, l. 996 (*Encomium Moriae*).

23 *LB* V. 1237D (*Obsecratio*). It might be suggested that Erasmus's Mariology made him the precursor of Muratori and of the Catholic Enlightenment.

CHAPTER 21: FREIBURG: VOLUNTARY EXILE

1   Allen, *Ep.* VI. 504 (*Testament*).

2   N. Pinet, 'Érasme à Fribourg (1529–1532)', unpublished paper, University of Liège, 1969; N. Piroton, 'Érasme à Fribourg (1532–1535)', unpublished paper, University of Liège, 1973.

3   Allen, *Ep.* 2125, VIII. 89, ll. 5–11, 17 Mar. 1529.

4   Allen, *Ep.* 2134, VIII. 111, ll. 114–21; 113, ll. 196–215.

5   Allen, *Ep.* 2136, VIII. 116, ll. 1–25.

6   Allen, *Ep.* 2149, VIII. 137, ll. 4–37; L.-E. Halkin, 'Érasme et l'anabaptisme', in *Les Dissidents du XVIe siècle*, pp. 67–8.

7   Reedijk, *Poems*, p. 345 (No. 123); Allen, *Ep.* 2196, VIII. 231, ll. 33–6, to W. Pirckheimer, Freiburg, 15 July 1529.

8 Trans. from *CWE* 26, p. 337, *De pueris statim ac liberaliter instituendis* (Basel, Froben, September 1528), ed. J. Cl. Margolin, in *ASD* I. 2, pp. 21–78. See also his *Le Prix des mots et de l'homme* (London, 1986), pp. 370–391.

9 *De civilitate morum puerilium* (Basel, Froben, 1530); text in *LB* 1. 1033–44. Cf. F. Bierlaire, 'Erasmus at school: the *De Civilitate*', in R. L. De Molen, *Essays in the Works of Erasmus* (New Haven, 1978).

10 Trans. from *CWE* 25, pp. 274–7.

11 Trans. from *CWE* 26, pp. 324–6.

12 Trans. from *CWE* 26, p. 320.

13 *Opus epistolarum* (Basel, Froben, 1529). Cf. Halkin, *Erasmus ex Erasmo*, p. 149.

14 Allen, *Ep.* 2203, VIII. 249–50, ll. 1–42.

15 M. P. Gilmore, 'Erasmus and Alberto Pio', in *Action and Conviction*, ed. T. Rabb and J. Seigel (Princeton, 1969), pp. 299–310; *ASD* IX. 1, pp. 313–425 (*Epistola ad fratres Inferioris Germaniae*), ed. C. Augustijn.

16 E. V. Telle, *Le Chevalier de Berquin. Déclamation des louenges de mariage* (Geneva, 1976); N. Henrard, 'Érasme entre Béda et Berquin', unpublished paper, University of Liège, 1974.

17 Allen, *Ep.* 2620, IX. 461, ll. 24–8, 7 Mar. 1532.

18 Allen, *Ep.* 2615, IX. 453, ll. 351–4, 2 Mar. 1532.

19 Allen, *Ep.* 2094, VIII. 46, ll. 47–52, Preface of 1529.

20 Allen, *Ep.* 2275, VIII. 364–5, ll. 21–46, to some Franciscans, 1530. The same year, Erasmus published the treatise of Alger de Liège, *De veritate corporis et sanguinis Domini in Eucharistia* (Freiburg, Emmeus). This treatise, written at the beginning of the twelfth century, did not use the word 'transubstantiation'.

CHAPTER 22: FREIBURG: THE FINAL HARVEST

1 *ASD* IX. 1, p. 292, ll. 238–40 (*Epistola contra pseudevangelicos*).

2 Allen, *Ep.* 2299, VIII. 403, ll. 68–90, 1530.

3 *ASD* IX. 1, pp. 284–86, ll. 22–35, 45–8, 72–5 (*Epistola contra quosdam qui se falso iactant evangelicos*, Freiburg, 1530), ed. C. Augustijn. 'Vulturius' was the sobriquet which Erasmus gave to Geldenhouwer.

4 *ASD* IX. 1, pp. 295–6, ll. 341–351.

5 Allen, *Ep.* 2615, IX. 456, ll. 458–60.

6 Charlier, *Érasme et l'amitié*, pp. 318–19.

7 Allen, *Ep.* 2159, VIII. 165, ll. 4–5.

8 Allen, *Ep.* 2534, IX. 340, ll. 19–37.

9 *Utilissima consultatio de bello Turcis inferendo* (Basel, Froben, 1530), ed. A. G. Weiler, in *ASD* V. 3, pp. 31–82. This little treatise was the commentary on Psalm 28 on the providential evidence of existence. See also Margolin, *Le Prix des mots et de l'homme*, pp. 3–38.

10 Cf. Bainton *Erasmus of Christendom*, pp. 258–9, LB V. 346–68.

11 Allen, *Ep.* 2492, IX. 265, ll. 37–8, 12 May 1531.

12 Allen, *Ep.* 2516, IX. 309, ll. 11–30, 5 Aug. 1531.

13 Allen, *Ep.* 2651, X. 23–24, ll. 10–13, 25–37, 19 May 1532.

14 Allen, *Ep.* 2443, IX. 157–68, 7 Mar. 1531. See V. Ghuysen, 'Érasme et Sadolet', unpublished paper, University of Liège, 1974.
15 Halkin, *Erasmus ex Erasmo*, p. 165.
16 Allen, *Ep.* 2394, IX. 61, l. 11, 1530.
17 Allen, *Ep.* 2518, IX. 314, ll. 39–46 (*Epistolarum floridarum liber unus antehac nunquam excusus*, Basel, Herwagen, September 1531).
18 Allen, *Ep.* 2700, X. 82, ll. 156–8.
19 *Epistolae palaeonaeoi* (Freiburg, Emmeus, September 1532).
20 Allen, *Ep.* 2620, IX. 461, ll. 24–8, 7 Mar. 1532; *Ep.* 2615, IX. 453, ll. 351–4, 2 Mar. 1532.
21 *LB* IX. 852C-D.
22 R. J. Schoek, 'Telling More from Erasmus', in *Moreana* 23 (1986), 11–20.
23 'Then he asketh me why I haue not contended with Erasmus whom he calleth my derlynge, of all this long whyle for translatynge of this word *ecclesia* in to thys worde *congregatio*. And then he cometh forth wyth hys fete proper taunte, that I fauour hym of lykelyhed for makynge of hys book of Moria in my howse. There had he hyt me lo saue for lakke of a lytell salte. I haue not contended wyth Erasmus my derlynge, because I found no suche malycyouse entent wyth Erasmus my derlynge, as I fynde with Tyndale. For had I fownde wyth Erasmus my derlyng the shrewde entent and purpose that I fynde in Tindale: Erasmus my derlynge sholde be no more my derlynge. But I fynde in Erasmus my derlynge that he detesteth and abhorreth the errours and heresyes that Tyndale playnely techeth and abydeth by/and therefore Erasmus my derlynge shall be my dere derlynge styll. And surely yf Tyndale had eyther neuer taughte them, or yet had the grace to reuoke them: then sholde Tyndale be my dere derlynge to. But whyle he holdeth such heresies stylle/I can not take for my derlyng hym that the deuyll taketh for hys derlynge' (*Complete Works of St. Thomas More*, New Haven Conn., 1973, Vol. 8, Pt. 1, p. 177); cf. Delcourt, *Érasme*, p. 85.
24 Allen, *Ep.* 2743, X. 129, 30 Nov. 1532. Cf. L. Thuasne, 'La lettre de Rabelais à Érasme', in the *Revue des bibliothèques*, 15 (Paris, 1905), 203–23; L. Febvre, *Le problème de l'incroyance au XVI' siècle. La religion de Rabelais*, 2nd edn (Paris, 1968), pp. 128, 441; M. A. Screech, 'Folie érasmienne et folie rabelaisienne. – Comment Rabelais a exploité les travaux d'Érasme', in *Colloquia Erasmiana Turonensia*, 1 (Paris, 1972), 441–52, 453–61.
25 Gerlo, *Érasme et ses portraitistes*, p. 56.
26 *Dilucida et pia explanatio Symboli quod Apostolorum dicitur* (Basel, Froben, March 1533), ed. J. N. Bakhuisen van den Brink, in *ASD* V. 1, pp. 205–320.
27 *LB* V. 1160 E-F.
28 *Liber de sarcienda Ecclesiae concordia deque sedandis opinionum dissidiis* (Basel, Froben, 1533), ed. R. Stupperich, in *ASD* V. 3, pp. 257–313; Eng. trans.: *On Mending the Peace of the Church*, in J. P. Dolan, *The Essential Erasmus* (New York, 1964), pp. 327–88. Cf. J. V. Pollet, 'Origine et structure du *De sarcienda Ecclesiae concordia*', in *Scrinium Erasmianum* 2. 183–95. See also R. Padberg, 'Erasmus und die Einheit der Kirche', in *Catholica* 2 (Munster, 1986), pp. 97–109.

29 *ASD* V. 3, 293, l. 224.
30 Trans. from *CWE* 49, p. 64; *LB* VII. 192E-F.
31 Trans. from Dolan, *The Essential Erasmus*, p. 380.
32 Dolan, *The Essential Erasmus*, p. 377.
33 Dolan, *The Essential Erasmus*, pp. 378–82.
34 Dolan, *The Essential Erasmus*, p. 386.
35 J. W. O'Malley, 'Erasmus and Luther. Continuity and discontinuity', in *Sixteenth Century Journal*, 5 (1974), 47–65.
36 Allen, *Ep.* 2853, X. 282, ll. 1–25 (1533).
37 Allen, *Ep.* 2846, X. 274, ll. 96–116 (1533).
38 Allen, *Ep.* 2874, X. 312, ll. 142–5, 1 Nov. 1533.
39 Allen, *Ep.* 2853, X. 283, ll. 38–42 (1533).
40 Allen, *Ep.* 2853, X. 283, ll. 42–6.
41 Allen, *Ep.* 2853, X. 283, ll. 46–9.
42 *Purgatio*, in *ASD* IX. 1, pp. 443–87, ed. C. Augustijn.
43 *De praeparatione*, in *ASD* V. 1, pp. 337–92, ed. A. Van Heck.
44 Allen, *Ep.* 2884 X. 327, l. 1.
45 *De praeparatione*, *ASD* V. 1, p. 344, ll. 110–14; pp. 358–9, ll. 457–61; p. 376, ll. 917–20.
46 *ASD*, V. 1, p. 362, ll. 538–44.
47 *ASD*, V. 1, p. 377, ll. 922–30.
48 Allen, *Ep.* 2136, VIII. 121, ll. 216–18.
49 *LB* V. 155E.

CHAPTER 23: RETURN TO BASEL: FAREWELLS

1 Allen, *Ep.* 2988 XI. 61, ll. 1–3.
2 Allen, *Ep.* 3049, XI. 219, ll. 75–101, to Tomicki, 1535.
3 *Ecclesiastes sive de ratione concionandi* (Basel, Froben, 1535) *LB* V. 765–1100. Cf. Béné, *Érasme et Saint Augustin*, pp. 372–424; Godin, *Érasme*, pp. 302–47; Chomarat, *Grammaire et rhétorique*, 2. 1059–71. A whole chapter is devoted to Ecclesiastes by R. G. Kleinhaus, in *Essays on the works of Erasmus*, ed. R. L. De Molen, pp. 253–66. See also. J. W. O'Malley, 'Erasmus and the history of sacred rhetoric', in *Erasmus of Rotterdam Society Yearbook Five* (Fort Washington 1985), pp. 1–29.
4 R. G. Villoslada, 'Erasmo y las missiones', in *Catolicismo* (Madrid, Nov. 1943). I know this article only through the analysis of it given in J. Cl. Margolin, *Quatorze années de bibliographie érasmienne*, No. 801.
5 Bainton, *Erasmus and Christendom*, p. 268, n. 63.
6 Allen, *Ep.* 3048, XI. 217, ll. 83–100, to Latomus.
7 Allen, *Ep.* 3048, XI. 217, ll. 102–4.
8 Allen, *Ep.* 3049, XI. 221, l. 163.
9 *Precationes aliquot novae* (Basel, Froben, 1535) *LB* V. 1197–1234. Cf. R. Padberg, *Erasmus von Rotterdam. Seine Spiritualität. Grundlage seines Reformprogramms* (Paderborn, 1979).

10 *LB* V. 1204F-1205A.
11 *LB* V. 1203B-D.
12 Allen, *Ep.* 2988, XI. 61, ll. 1-7, Freiburg, 23 Jan. 1535.
13 *De puritate tabernaculi sive Ecclesiae Christianae* (Basel, Froben, Feb. 1536), ed. Ch. Béné, in *ASD* V. 2, pp. 285-317. Cf. Halkin, *Erasmus ex Erasmo*, p. 195; Huizinga, *Erasmus*, p. 298.
14 Allen, *Ep.* 3048, XI. 217, ll. 83-100, 24 Aug. 1535. The Council which had been desired for so long was finally to come together at Trent in 1545.
15 J. Paquier, *Jérôme Aléandre et la principauté de Liège* (Paris, 1896), p. 305.
16 Allen, *Ep.* 3090, XI. 276, ll. 29-46, February 1536.
17 Allen, XI. 362-5. Cf. Reedijk, *Tandem bona causa triumphat*, pp. 22-5.
18 Allen, *Ep.* 3000, XI. 78, ll. 27-9, to Piotr Tomicki, Freiburg, 28 Feb. 1535. See M. Cytowska, 'Érasme et son petit corps', in *Eos*, 62. 135 (Wroclaw, 1974).
19 Erasmus was already saying this in 1517: Allen, *Ep.* 742, III. 171, l. 21, to Richard Pace, Louvain, 21 Dec. 1517; commentary of Chantraine, *Mystère et philosophie*, p. 276.
20 Allen, *Ep.* 3095, XI. 282, ll. 26-34.
21 Allen, *Ep.* 3130, XI. 337, ll. 28-9.
22 I have analysed these witnesses in 'Érasme et la mort', in the *Revue de l'histoire des religions*, 200 (Paris, 1983), 286-91. Cf. R. G. Villoslada, 'La morte di Erasmo', in *Rivista storica italiana* 63 (1951), 100-8; C. Reedijk, 'Das Lebensende des Erasmus', in *Basler Zeitschrift*, 57 (1958), 23-66; N. Van der Blom, 'Die letzten Worte des Erasmus', in *Basler Zeitschrift*, 65 (1965), 195-214; *idem*, 'Erasmus laatste woorden', in *Rotterdamse Jaarboek*, 7th series, 4 (1966), 164-76.
23 Huizinga, *Erasmus*, p. 300.
24 E. Major, 'Die Grabsträtte des Erasmus', in *Gedenkschrift zum 400 Todestage des Erasmus von Rotterdam* (Basel, 1936), pp. 299-315; B. R. Jenny, 'Tod, Begräbnis und Grabmal des Erasmus von Rotterdam', in *Basler Zeitschrift für Geschichte*, 86 (1986), 61-104; Br. Kaufmann, 'Das Grab des Erasmus', in *Erasmus von Rotterdam* (Basel, 1986), pp. 66-9, 247-50.

CHAPTER 24: ERASMUS'S PERSONALITY

1 This was a theme dear to Roland Bainton.
2 He was certainly not against philosophy or theology, having written 'Bonae literae reddunt homines, philosophia plus quam homines, theologia reddit divos': *ASD* IV. 2, p. 66, ll. 143-4 (*Querela*).
3 Trans. from *CWE* 7, 161, ll. 513-19; Allen, *Ep.* 1053.
4 Allen, *Ep.* 1891, VII. 208, ll. 183-91.
5 I have made a study of this point in 'La psychohistoire et le caractère d'Érasme', in *Storia della storiografia*, 8 (Milan, 1985), 73-90.
6 K. Popper, *The Poverty of Historicism* (London, 1957), pp. 151, 167.
7 Chomarat, *Grammaire et rhétorique*, 1. 36.
8 P. O. Kristeller, *Eight Philosophers of the Renaissance* (Stanford, 1964), p. 64.
9 Allen, *Ep.* 1342, V. 277, ll. 995-7, 1523.

CHAPTER 25: THE ASSESSMENT OF A LIFE'S WORK: LITERATURE, PEACE, THE PHILOSOPHY OF CHRIST

1 M. Cytowska, 'Érasme et les auteurs classiques', in *Eos* 72 (1984), 179–87. On the teaching of St Jerome in this area, we may note the enthusiasm of his disciple in the *Antibarbari: ASD* I. 1, p. 111, ll. 16–25. If Erasmus was so strict on the subject of the light literature of the ancients, he was no less severe on the French romances and even the mysteries performed in the Churches.

2 Allen, *Ep.* 373, II. 170, ll. 164–80, preface to the *Novum Instrumentum* of 1516.

3 J. H. Bentley, 'Erasmus. Jean Le Clerc and the principles of the harder reading', in *Renaissance Quarterly* 31 (1978), 309–21.

4 Trans. from *CWE* 24, p. 266, ll. 4–6.

5 On the poetry of Erasmus being inferior to his prose, see p. 34. Erasmus's enemies put in doubt the quality of his Latin and of his criticism of texts: Allen, *Ep.* 1479, V. 514–21. Erasmus was to reply vigorously in the *Ciceronian*. Cf. Chomarat, *Grammaire et rhétorique*, 2. 815.

6 Allen, *Ep.* 458, II. 332, ll. 1–4, 1516. In 1517, Erasmus wrote to Budé: 'I preferred the correct expression to the brilliant expression'. Cf. Allen, *Ep.* 531, II. 457, ll. 329–30.

7 M. Mann Phillips, 'Erasmus and the art of writing', in the *Scrinium Erasmianum*, 1 (Leyden, 1969), 335–50; A. Michjel, 'Érasme et les atticismes', in *Acta Conventus neo-latini Turonesis*, 2 (Paris, 1989), 1237–47; Chomarat, *Grammaire et rhétorique*, 2. 711ff.

8 M. Bataillon, 'Érasme conteur', in the *Mélanges de langue et de la littérature médiévales offerts à M. Le Gentil* (Paris, 1973), pp. 85–104; J. Cl. Margolin, 'L'art du récit et du conte chez Érasme', in *La Nouvelle française à la Renaissance* (Geneva/Paris, 1981), pp. 131–65.

9 Examples of obscure subtlety include: Allen, *Ep.* 551, II. 503, ll. 10–12, to Andreas Ammonius, 1517; *Ep.* 980, III. 606, l. 52, 1519; *Ep.* 1143, IV. 345, ll. 30–5, 1520.

10 Trans. from *CWE* 8. 220, ll. 105–6; Allen, *Ep.* 1206, IV. 501, ll. 96–8, 1521.

11 Allen, *Ep.* 421, II. 255, ll. 105–6, 1516.

12 On Erasmus's attitude to this problem, see L.-E. Halkin, 'Érasme, la guerre et la paix', in *Krieg und Frieden im Horizont des Renaissancehumanismus* (Weinheim, 1986), pp. 13–44; critical edition of the texts by O. Herding, *ASD* IV. 1 and IV. 2.

13 Allen, *Ep.* 928, III. 511, ll. 43–44; *Ep.* 2046, VII. 484, ll. 33–4. See also V. Beumer, *Erasmus der Europäer* (Frankfurt, 1969).

14 Trans. from *CWE* 9, p. 185, ll. 1–4; Allen, *Ep.* 1314, V. 129, ll. 2–3, to Ulrich Zwingli, 1523.

15 Allen, *Ep.* 1978, VII. 362, ll. 36–7, to Hermann von Wied, 1528.

16 *LB* IX. 1192F-1193A (*Responsio ad Albertum Pium*), 1529. In the *Symbolum* Erasmus recalls that war is not absolutely forbidden, but, he adds, 'it is better to be killed than to kill': *ASD* V. 1, p. 315, l. 286.

17 A good book could be made out of the pages in which Erasmus presents his spiritual programme.

18 Trans. from *Paraclesis*, in J. C Olin, *Christian Humanism and the Reformation*, p. 100; *LB* V. 141E.
19 J. Étienne, *Spiritualisme érasmien et théologiens louvanistes* (Louvain, 1956), p. 187.
20 Trans. from *Paraclesis*, in J. C Olin, *Christian Humanism*, p. 97.
21 *LB* IX. 1193B-C (*Apologia adversus Pium*), 1531.
22 Allen, *Ep.* 1202, IV. 492, ll. 235–7, 1521; *Ep.* 1342, V. 220, ll. 704–8, 1523; *Ep.* 1523, V. 598, l. 192, 1524; *ASD* IX. 1, p. 42, ll. 679–89; p. 46, ll. 820–1 (*De interdicto*).

CHAPTER 26: THE ERASMIAN MESSAGE: FROM THE CRITIQUE OF CHRISTIANITY TO CRITICAL CHRISTIANITY

1 In 1516, in the *Hieronymi opera*, vol. 3, folio 1 (Basel), Erasmus wrote: 'Alioque quo plus est dogmatum, hoc uberior haereseon materia. Et nunquam fuit sincerior castiorque christiana fides qua cum brevissimo illo symbolo contentus esset orbis.' 'Evangélisme sans dogmes' is in A. Renaudet, *Études érasmiennes* (Paris, 1939), p. 189.
2 O. Schottenloher, 'Érasme et la *Res publica christiana*', in *Colloquia Erasmiana Turonensia* 2 (1972), 667ff.
3 *LB* X. 1258A (*Hyperaspistes*). Cf. H. de Lubac, *Exegèse médiévale*, 4 (Paris, 1964), 469. We should recall that the *De sarcienda Ecclesiae concordia* (1533) was the synthesis of Erasmus's critical Christianity.
4 The expression is P. Mesnard's (*Érasme ou le christianisme critique*, Paris, 1969). Mesnard synthesized the work of Erasmus thus: 'It had regenerated man in purifying religion and baptizing culture.'
5 L.-E. Halkin, 'Érasme et la critique du christianisme', in *Revue de littérature comparée*, 52 (1978), 172–84.
6 Erasmus seems to have had little influence on the Catholic reformation, especially in Italy. Cf. G. Alberigo, *I vescovi italiani al Concilio di Trento* (Florence, 1959), p. 384, n. 1.
7 J. K. McConica, *English Humanists and the Reformation* (Oxford, 1965); Thomson and Porter, *Erasmus and Cambridge*, p. 97. In the Duchies of Cleves and Juliers, an attempt at an Erasmian reform was made without success. Cf. A. Franzen, 'Das Schicksal des Erasmianismus am Niederrhein', in *Historisches Jahrbuch* 83 (Freiburg, 1964), 84–112.
8 In 1557 Melanchthon read a magnificent eulogy of Erasmus in Wittenberg. Cf. L. Spitz, 'Humanism in the Reformation', in *Renaissance Studies in Honor of Hans Baron* (Florence, 1971), pp. 647ff.
9 Bruce Mansfield, *Phoenix of His Age. Interpretations of Erasmus c. 1550–1750* (Toronto, 1979). In this area a special place should be reserved for the Jansenist theologian Jean Richard. Cf. A. Stegmann, 'La réhabilitation de l'orthodoxie d'Érasme', in *Colloquia Erasmiana Turonensia*, 2. 867ff. See also J. Marsolier, *Apologie ou justification d'Érasme* (Paris, 1713).
10 R. J. Schoek, 'The place of Erasmus today', in *Erasmus of Rotterdam*, ed. R. L. De Molen (New York, 1971), pp. 77–92. On the profound agreement

between the ideas of Erasmus and the spirit of Vatican II, see G. Chantraine, 'Théologie et vie spirituelle chez Érasme', in the *Nouvelle revue théologique* 91 (Louvain, 1969), 808–10.

11 I shall cite only two examples from among the most amusing: the philosopher Bertrand Russell stated that Erasmus was the author of the *Manual of the Christian Soldier* 'which gave advice to illiterate soldiers' (*History of Western Philosophy*, London, 1946), p. 537, while the abbot L. Cristiani published a brochure under the title *Érasme, ennemi de la Chrétienté* (Liège, 1931).

Bibliographical Guide

INDEXES

Haeghen, F. Vander, *Bibliotheca Erasmiana. Répertoire des œuvres d'Érasme*, 3 vols, Gand, 1893 (photographic reprint 1961).

Margolin, J.-Cl., *Douze années de bibliographie érasmienne* (1950–61), Paris, 1963.

—— *Quatorze années de bibliographie érasmienne* (1936–49), Paris, 1969.

—— *Neuf années de bibliographie érasmienne* (1962–70), Paris, 1972.

Bietenholz, P. G., ed., *Contemporaries of Erasmus*, 3 vols, Toronto, 1985–7.

LATIN EDITIONS

Desiderii Erasmi Roterodami opera omnia, ed. J. Clericus, 10 vols in 11, Leiden, 1703–6.

Opera omnia Desiderii Erasmi Roterodami, Amsterdam 1969– .

Allen, P. S., ed., *Opus epistolarum Desiderii Erasmi Roterodami*, 12 vols, Oxford, 1906–58.

Holborn, H., *Desiderius Erasmus. Ausgewählte Werke*, Münich, 1933.

Ferguson, W. K., *Erasmi opuscula*, The Hague, 1933.

Reedijk, C., *The Poems of Desiderius Erasmus*, Leiden, 1956.

Reeve, A., *Erasmus' Annotations on the New Testament*, London, 1986.

Seidel Menchi, S., *Erasmo da Rotterdam, Adagia. Sei saggi politici*, Turin, 1980.

Telle, É.-V., *Érasme. Dilutio eorum quae J. Clichtoveus scripsit*, Paris, 1967.

ENGLISH TRANSLATIONS

Collected Works of Erasmus, Toronto, 1979– .

De Molen, R. L., *Erasmus* (Documents of Modern History), London, 1973.

Dolan, J. P., ed., *The Essential Erasmus*, New York, 1964.

Hillerbrand, H. J., ed., *Erasmus and His Age: Selected Letters of Desiderius Erasmus*, trans. M. A. Haworth, New York, 1970.

Levi, A. H., ed., *Praise of Folly* and *Letter to Martin Dorp 1515* , trans. B. Radice, Harmondsworth, 1971.

Miller, C. H., ed., *The Praise of Folly*, Toronto, 1979.
Olin, J. C., *Christian Humanism and the Reformation: Selected Writings of Erasmus with The Life of Erasmus by Beatus Rhenanus*, New York, 1965.
Phillips, M. M., ed., *The Adages of Erasmus: A Study with Translations*, London 1964.
Rupp, E. G., ed., *De Libero Arbitrio*, in *Luther and Erasmus on Free Will and Salvation*, London and Philadelphia, 1969.
Thompson, C. R., ed., *The Colloquies of Erasmus*, Chicago, 1965.

FRENCH TRANSLATIONS

Bujanda, J. M. De, *Érasme. Liberté et unité dans l'Église*, with texts translated by R. Galibois, Quebec, 1971.
Festugière, A.-M., *Érasme. Enchiridion militis christiani*, Paris, 1971.
Garaderie, M.-M. de la, *La Correspondance d'Érasme et de Guillaume Budé*, Paris, 1967.
Gerlo, A., ed., *La Correspondance d'Érasme*, 12 vols, Brussels, 1967–84.
Godin, A., *Érasme. Vies de Jean Vitrier et de John Colet*, Angers, 1982.
Marc'hadour, G., and Galibois, R., *Érasme de Rotterdam et Thomas More. Correspondance*. Sherbrooke, 1985.
Margolin, J.-Cl., *Guerre et paix dans la pensée d'Érasme*, Paris, 1973.
Mesnard, P., *Érasme. La philosophie chrétienne*, Paris, 1970.
Nolhac, P. de, and Rat, M., *L'Éloge de la Folie*, Paris, 1964.
Priel, Jarl, *Les Colloques d'Érasme*, 4 vols, Paris, 1912.
Sage, P., *Érasme, La Préparation à la mort*, Montreal, 1976.

SELECT SECONDARY WORKS

(Studies of Erasmus are so numerous that I mention here only a selection of books, and omit citing articles, reviews or collections of essays: the reader will find these among the notes.)
Actes du Congrès Érasme. ed. C. Reedijk, Amsterdam, 1971.
Aldridge, J. W., *The Hermeneutic of Erasmus*. Zürich, 1966.
Allen, P. S., *The Age of Erasmus*, Oxford, 1914.
—— *Erasmus' Lectures and Wayfaring Sketches*, Oxford, 1934.
Auer, A., *Die vollkommene Frömmigkeit des Christen nach dem Enchiridion des Erasmus*, Düsseldorf, 1954.
Augustijn, C., *Erasmus en de Reformatie*, Amsterdam, 1962.
—— *Erasmus: His Life, Works and Influence*, Toronto, 1991.
Bainton, R. H., *Erasmus of Christendom*, New York, 1969.
Bataillon, M., *Érasme et l'Espagne*, Paris, 1937.
—— *Erasmo y el erasmismo*, Barcelona, 1977.
Bédouelle, G., *Lefèvre d'Étaples et l'intelligence des Écritures*, Geneva, 1978.
Béné, Ch., *Érasme et saint Augustin*, Geneva, 1969.
Bentley, J. H., *Humanists and Holy Writ*, Princeton, 1983.

Bierlaire, F., *La Familia d'Érasme*, Paris, 1968.

—— *Érasme et ses Colloques: le livre d'une vie*, Geneva, 1977.

—— *Les Colloques d'Érasme: réforme d'études, réforme des mœurs et réforme de l'Église au XVIᵉ siècle*, Paris, 1978.

Bietenholz, P. G., *History and Biography in the Work of Erasmus*, Geneva, 1966.

Bijl, S. W., *Erasmus in het Nederlands tot 1617*, Nieuwkoop, 1978.

Blom, N. Van der, *Erasmus en Rotterdam*, Rotterdam–The Hague, 1969.

Boisset, J., *Érasme et Luther*, Paris, 1962.

Bolgar, R., *The Classical Heritage and its Beneficiaries*, Cambridge, 1954.

Bouyer, L., *Autour d'Érasme*, Paris, 1955.

Boyle, M. O'R., *Christianising Pagan Mysteries. Erasmus in Pursuit of Wisdom*, Toronto, 1981.

—— *Rhetoric and Reform. Erasmus' Civil Dispute with Luther*, Cambridge, Mass., 1983.

—— *Erasmus on Language and Method in Theology*, Toronto, 1977.

Brabant, H., *Érasme, humaniste dolent*, Brussels, 1971.

Buck, A., *Humanismus. Seine europäische Entwicklung*, Freiburg, 1987.

Cantimori, D., *Umanesimo e religione nel Rinascimento*, Turin 1973.

Chantraine, G., *Mystère et philosophie du Christ selon Érasme*, Namur, 1971.

—— *Érasme et Luther. Libre et serf arbitre*, Paris, 1981.

Charlier, Y., *Érasme et l'amitié*, Paris, 1987.

Chaunu, P., *Le Temps des réformes*, Paris, 1975.

Chomarat, J., *Grammaire et rhétorique chez Érasme*, 2 vols, Paris, 1981.

Christ von Wedel, C., *Das Nichtwissen bei Erasmus von Rotterdam*, Basel, 1981.

Colloque érasmien de Liège, ed. J.-P. Massaut, Paris, 1987.

Colloquia Erasmiana Turonensia, 2 vols, Paris, 1972.

Colloquium Erasmianum, Mons, 1968.

Commémoration nationale d' Érasme, ed. A. Gerlo, Brussels, 1970.

Crahay, R., *D'Érasme à Campanella*, Brussels, 1985.

De Molen, R. C., *Essays on the works of Erasmus*, ed. J.-P. Massaut, New Haven, 1978.

—— *The Spirituality of Erasmus*, Nieuwkoop, 1987.

Degroote, G., *Erasmus, pelgrim van de geest*, Brussels, 1955.

Delcourt, M., *Érasme*, 2nd edn, Brussels, 1986.

Delumeau, J., *Le Péché et la peur*, Paris, 1983.

Dix Conférences sur Érasme, ed. C. Blum, Paris, 1988.

Dolan, J. P., *The Influence of Erasmus, Witzel and Cassander in the Church Ordinances*, Münster, 1957.

Dresden, S., *L'Humanisme et la Réforme*, Paris, 1967.

Durand de Laur, H., *Érasme, précurseur et initiateur de l'esprit moderne*, Paris, 1872.

Érasme et la Belgique, ed. A. Gerlo, Brussels, 1969.

Erasmus, ed. T. A. Dorey, London, 1970.

Erasmus, De actualiteit van zijn denken, Amsterdam, 1986.

Erasmus von Rotterdam. Vorkämpfer für Frieden und Toleranz, Basel, 1986.

Étienne, J., *Spiritualisme érasmien et théologiens louvanistes*, Louvain 1956.

Febvre, L., *The Problem of Unbelief in the sixteenth century: The religion of Rabelais*, trans. B. Gottlieb, Cambridge, Mass., 1982.

—— *Au cœur religieux du XVIᵉ siècle*, Paris, 1957.

Flitner, A., *Erasmus in Urteil seiner Nachwelt. Das literarische Erasmus-Bild von Beatus Rhenanus bis zu Jean Le Clerc*, Tübingen, 1952.

Fokke, G. J., *Christus verae pacis auctor et unicus scopus. Erasmus und Origen*, Louvain, 1977.

Froude, J. A., *Life and Letters of Erasmus*, New York, 1986.

Garanderie, M. M. de la, *Christianisme et lettres profanes (1517–1535)*, 2 vols, Lille–Paris, 1976.

Garin, E., *L'Éducation de l'homme moderne (1400–1600)*, Paris, 1968.

—— *Erasmo*, Florence, 1988.

Geanakoplos, D., *Greek scholars in Venice*, Cambridge, Mass., 1962.

Gebhardt, G., *Die Stellung des Erasmus von Rotterdam zur römischen Kirche*, Marburg, 1966.

Gedenkschrift zum 400 Todestage des Erasmus von Rotterdam, Basel, 1936.

Gerlo, A., *Érasme et ses portraitistes*, 2nd. edn, Nieuwkoop, 1969.

Gibaud, H., *Un inédit d' Érasme: la premier version du Nouveau Testament, copiée par Pierre Meghen (1506–1509)*, Angers, 1982.

Gilmore, M. P., *Humanists and Jurists*, Cambridge, Mass., 1963.

—— *The World of Humanism*, New York, 1952.

Godin, A., *Érasme, lecteur d'Origène*, Geneva, 1982.

Gutmann, E., *Die Colloquia familiaria des Erasmus von Rotterdam*, Basel, 1958.

Halkin, L.-E., *Érasme et l'humanisme chrétien*, Paris, 1969.

—— *Erasmus ex Erasmo*, Aubel, 1983.

—— *Érasme. Sa pensée et son comportement*, London, 1988.

Heep, M., *Die Colloquia familiaria des Erasmus und Lucian*, Halle, 1927.

Heer, Fr., *Die dritte Kraft*, Frankfurt, 1959.

Hendricks, O., *Erasmus in Leuven*, Bussum, 1946.

Hentze, W., *Kirche und kirkliche Einheit bei Desiderius Erasmus von Rotterdam*, Paderborn, 1974.

Hoffmann, M., *Erkenntnis und Verwicklichung der wahren Theologie nach Erasmus von Rotterdam*, Tübingen, 1972.

Holeczek, H., *Erasmus Deutsch*, Stuttgart, 1983.

—— *Erasmus von Rotterdam. Novum Instrumentum*, Stuttgart, 1986.

—— *Humanistiche Bibelphilologie als Reformproblem*, Leiden, 1975.

Huizinga, J., *Erasmus*, London, 1952.

A. Hyma, *The Youth of Erasmus*, 2nd edn, Michigan, 1968.

Kohls, E. W., *Die Theologie des Erasmus*, 2 vols, Basel, 1966.

—— *Luther oder Erasmus*, Basel, 1972.

Kristeller, P. O., *Renaissance Thought*, 2 vols, New York, 1965.

Lecler, J., *Toleration and the Reformation*, 2 vols, London, 1960.

Lindeboom, J., *Erasmus. Onderzoek naar zijne theologie*, Leiden, 1909.

J. McConica, *English Humanists and Reformation Politics under Henry VIII and Edward VI*, Oxford, 1965.

—— *Erasmus*, Oxford, 1991.

Mangan, J. J., *Life, Character and Influence of Desiderius Erasmus Roterodamus*, 2 vols, New York, 1927.

Mann, M., *Érasme et les débuts de la Réforme française*, Paris, 1934.

Mansfield, B., *Phoenix of His Age. Interpretations of Erasmus c. 1450–1750*, Toronto, 1979.

Marc'hadour, G., *L'Univers de Thomas More*, Paris, 1963.

Margolin, J.-Cl., *Érasme par lui-même*, Paris, 1965.

—— *Recherches érasmiennes*, Geneva, 1969.

—— *Érasme: le prix des mots et de l'homme*, London, 1986.

—— *Érasme dans son miroir et dans son sillage*, London, 1987.

Markish, S., *Érasme et les juifs*, Lausanne, 1979.

Marlier, G., *Érasme et la peinture flamande de son temps*, Damme, 1954.

Massaut, J.-P., *Josse Clichtove, l'humanisme et la réforme de l'Église*, 2 vols, Paris, 1968.

—— *Critique et tradition*, Paris, 1974.

Mesnard, P., *Érasme ou le christianisme critique*, Paris, 1969.

—— *L'Essor de la philosophie politique au XVIe siècle*, 3rd edn, Paris, 1969.

Mestwerdt, P., *Die Anfänge des Erasmus*, Leipzig, 1917.

Meyers, J. J. M., *Authors edited, translated or annotated by Desiderius Erasmus . . . in the City Library of Rotterdam*, Rotterdam, 1982.

Nève, F., *Recherches sur le séjour et les études d'Erasme en Brabant*, Louvain, 1876.

Newald, R., *Erasmus Roterodamus*, Darmstadt, 1970.

Nolhac, P. De, *Érasme, sa vie, son œuvre*, Louvain, 1935.

Oelrich, K. H., *Der späte Erasmus und die Reformation*, Münster, 1961.

O'Malley, John W., *Rome and the Renaissance*, London 1981.

Olin, J. C., ed., *Luther, Erasmus and the Reformation*, New York, 1969.

Padberg, R., *Erasmus als Katechet*, Freiburg, 1959.

—— *Erasmus von Rotterdam. Seine Spiritualität. Grundlage seines Reformprogramms*, Paderborn, 1979.

Pavlovskis, Z., *The Praise of Folly. Structure and Irony*, Leiden, 1983.

Payne, J. B., *Erasmus: his theology of the sacraments*, Richmond, 1970.

Peremans, N., *Érasme et Bucer*, Paris, 1970.

Petruzellis, N., *Erasmo pensatore*, Naples, 1969.

Pfeiffer, R., *Humanitas Erasmiana*, Berlin, 1933.

Phillips, M. M., *Erasmus and the Northern Renaissance*, London, 1980.

Pineau, J.-B., *Érasme. Sa pensée religieuse*, Paris, 1923.

Pollet, J. V., *Julius Pflug. Correspondance*, 6 vols, Leiden, 1969–82.

Rabil, A., *Erasmus and the New Testament*, San Antonio, 1972.

Reedijk, C., *Erasmus en onze Dirk. Die vriendschap tussen correspondance en Dirk Martens*, Haarlem, 1974.

—— *Tandem bona causa triumphat*, Basel, 1980.

Renaudet, A., *Érasme, sa pensée religieuse d'après sa correspondance (1518–1521)*, Paris, 1926.

—— *Études érasmiennes (1521–1529)*, Paris, 1939.

—— *Érasme et l'Italie*, Geneva, 1954.

Reynolds, L. D., and Wilson, N. G., *D'Homère à Érasme*, Paris, 1984.

Rummel, E., *Erasmus and his Catholic Critics*, Nieuwkoop, 1989.

Schätti, K., *Erasmus von Rotterdam und die Römische Kurie*, Basel–Stuttgart, 1954.

Schneider, E., *Das Bild der Frau im Werk des Erasmus von Rotterdam*, Basel, 1955.

Schoek, R. J., *Erasmus grandescens*, Nieuwkoop, 1989.

Schottenloher, O., *Erasmus im Ringen um die humanistiche Bildungsform*, Berlin, 1933.

Screech, M. A., *Ecstasy and the Praise of Folly*, London, 1980.

Scrinium Erasmianum, ed. J. Coppens, 2 vols, Leiden, 1969.

Seidel Menchi, S., *Erasmo in Italia (1520–1580)*, Turin, 1987.

Smith, P., *Erasmus*, New York, 1962.

—— *Erasmus. A study of his life, ideals and place in history*, New York, 1923.

—— *A Key to the Colloquies of Erasmus*, Cambridge, Mass., 1927.

Sowards, J. K., *Desiderius Erasmus*, Boston, 1975.

Stange, C., *Erasmus und Julius II. Eine Legende*, Berlin, 1937.

Stupperich, R., *Erasmus von Rotterdam une seine Welt*, Berlin and New York, 1977.

Telle, É.-V., *Érasme et le septième sacrament*, Geneva, 1954.

Thomson, D. F. S., and Porter, H. C., *Erasmus and Cambridge*, Toronto, 1963.

Thompson, G., *Under Pretext of Praise. Satiric Mode in Erasmus' Fiction*, Toronto, 1975.

Tracy, J. D., *Erasmus. The Growth of a Mind*, Geneva, 1972.

—— *The Politics of Erasmus*, Toronto, 1978.

Treu, E., *Die Bildnisse des Erasmus von Rotterdam*, Basel, 1959.

Villoslada, G., *Loyola y Erasmo*, Madrid, 1965.

Vischer, W., *Erasmiana*, Basel, 1876.

Vocht, H. De, *Érasme, sa vie, son œuvre*, Louvain, 1935.

—— *History of the foundation and the rise of the Collegium trilingue Lovaniense*, 4 vols, Louvain, 1951–5.

Williams, G. H., *The Radical Reformation*, Kirksville, 1990.

Winkler, G. B., *Erasmus und die Einleitungsschriften zum Neuen Testament*, Münster, 1974.

Woodward, W. H., *Desiderius Erasmus concerning the aim and method of education*, 2nd edn, New York, 1964.

Index

Index of Works